SOFTWARE DESIGN

Concepts and methods

PRACTICAL SOFTWARE ENGINEERING SERIES

Volume 1 *Software Engineering: Concepts and Management*, Allen Macro
Volume 2 *Software Specification and Feasibility*, Allen Macro
Volume 3 *Software Design*, Wayne Stevens
Volume 4 *Software Implementation*, Michael Marcotty
Volume 5 *Software Estimating and Technical Quality*, Allen Macro

PRACTICAL SOFTWARE ENGINEERING SERIES

SOFTWARE DESIGN

Concepts and methods

WAYNE P. STEVENS

PRENTICE HALL
NEW YORK LONDON TORONTO SYDNEY TOKYO SINGAPORE

First published 1991 by
Prentice Hall International (UK) Ltd
66 Wood Lane End, Hemel Hempstead
Hertfordshire HP2 4RG
A division of
Simon & Schuster International Group

© Prentice Hall International (UK) Ltd, 1991

All rights reserved. No part of this publication may be reproduced, stored in a retrieval system, or transmitted, in any form, or by any means, electronic, mechanical, photocopying, recording or otherwise, without prior permission, in writing, from the publisher. For permission within the United States of America contact Prentice Hall Inc., Englewood Cliffs, NJ 07632.

Unix is a registered trademark of AT&T Bell Laboratories.

Typeset in 9½/12pt Times
by Keyset Composition, Colchester, Essex

Printed and bound in Great Britain
by Dotesios Printers Ltd, Trowbridge, Wiltshire.

Library of Congress Cataloging-in-Publication Data

Stevens, Wayne P., 1944–
    Software design : concepts and methods/Wayne P. Stevens.
      p. cm. — (Practical software engineering)
    Includes bibliographical references.
    ISBN 0-13-820242-7 : $40.95
    1. Computer software—Development. I. Title. II. Series.
QA76.76.D47S75   1990
005.1—dc20   89-39816
                                                                     CIP

British Library Cataloguing in Publication Data

Steven, Wayne P. (Wayne Paul), *1944–*
    Software design: concepts and methods. – (Prentice Hall International series in practical software engineering)
    1. Computer systems. Software. Design
    I. Title
    005.1′2

    ISBN 0-13-820242-7

---

1 2 3 4 5   95 94 93 92 91

CONTENTS

EDITOR'S PREFACE	vii
INTRODUCTION	xi
ACKNOWLEDGEMENTS	xiii
LIST OF FIGURES	xiv

CHAPTER 1   INTRODUCTION TO SOFTWARE DESIGN 1

1.1 What is software design? 1
1.2 Design objectives 5
1.3 Software design methods 6

CHAPTER 2   ARCHITECTURAL SOFTWARE DESIGN 12

2.1 Independent pieces reduce complexity 12
2.2 Structured Analysis 19
2.3 Essential Systems Analysis 30
2.4 Design of real-time systems 47
2.5 Structured Design 62
2.6 Box Structured Design 88
2.7 Petri nets 101

CHAPTER 3   INTEGRAND SPECIFICATIONS 120

3.1 Flowcharts 121
3.2 Structured Programming 125
3.3 Structured Natural Language 130
3.4 Action Diagrams 134
3.5 State transition diagrams 136
3.6 Jackson charts 143
3.7 Decision tables 146

CHAPTER 4 DATA BASE DESIGN CONCEPTS ... 153

    4.1 Entity-relationship data model ... 154
    4.2 The enterprise schema ... 158
    4.3 Normalization ... 164
    4.4 Data base description ... 166
    4.5 Physical data base design ... 170
    4.6 Data administration ... 172
    4.7 Comments on data base design ... 172

CHAPTER 5 OTHER DESIGN TOPICS ... 174

    5.1 Software design tools ... 175
    5.2 Design reviews ... 179
    5.3 Code reuse ... 179
    5.4 General systems principles ... 187
    5.5 Abstract Data Types ... 188
    5.6 Object-Oriented ... 189
    5.7 Portability ... 197
    5.8 Issues with time-dependencies ... 202
    5.9 Performance ... 204

CHAPTER 6 CONCLUDING REMARKS ... 206

    APPENDIX A: DATA FLOW DEVELOPMENT MANAGER ... 208
    APPENDIX B: AVOIDING DEADLOCKS WITH DATA FLOW ... 219
    APPENDIX C: PROBLEMS ... 226
    APPENDIX D: ANSWERS TO PROBLEMS ... 229
    APPENDIX E: GLOSSARY ... 236
    APPENDIX F: RECOMMENDED READING ... 240
    APPENDIX G: REFERENCES ... 241

    INDEX ... 245

EDITOR'S PREFACE

The 'PSE series', five volumes on practical software engineering topics, is intended for several purposes and their appropriate audiences.

First, as a whole, the series is intended as a basis for guidelines in software engineering practice, for people who engage directly in programming computers at a non-trivial level, as the whole or a part of their work. Typically, this list will include software engineers of greater or lesser experience, amateur programmers who are generally of little (or intermittent) experience, and computer scientists. They will, by and large, be involved in some or all of the activities that make up software development, such as system specification, software requirements definition and design, implementation, testing and quality assurance.

Second, the series is intended for the comprehension of others involved in software development. In this category are managers of software engineers and the managers of these managers (and so on), commercial staff who buy or sell software, or contract for services to provide it, quality assurance people, personnel officers, and operatives in associated disciplines – such as mechanical, electronic and production engineering – who may work with software development staff on composite systems.

Third, the series is intended as a text for courses in software engineering, both for academic-level and industrial/business courses in continuing education.

The breadth of this address may possibly invoke reaction, if not disfavor. For it is not immediately apparent that the third objective is compatible with the other two, certainly concerning the academic component of education as distinct from practical training courses.

A prevailing sentiment in business and industry, as we have found, seems to be that academic material is pretty irrelevant to real, everyday problems of software development. It teaches (the argument goes) computer science; it does not provide (the argument continues) for good practices in software engineering to be learned. On the other hand, academics might repost – with some justification – that software engineering in the big, wide world is in a state of such glorious shambles that the kindliest and most socially useful act that they can commit is to refrain from enabling it to be learned, and some may even opt for its prevention.

It is a lamentable state of affairs to summarize the problem as a gap between two

viii   EDITOR'S PREFACE

deficiencies, for that makes three problems of it. Yet, that is the case and, seen that way, it goes some way to justify the stated aims of this series. Whether they eventuate is another matter altogether.

We have set the series out as five, monograph-length volumes. Four of these correspond to the main activities in software development:

1. Specification and feasibility.
2. Design.
3. Implementation.
4. Software estimating and technical quality.

These are the Volumes 2–5 respectively, and their authors are Michael Marcotty (Volume 4 – *Software Implementation*), Wayne Stevens (Volume 3 – *Software Design*) and Allen Macro (Volumes 2 and 5). There is also a volume whose subjects cover matters intrinsic to all four other volumes; in that sense it is the 'orthogonal' title in the series, and is called Volume 1; it covers:

5. Software engineering; concepts and management.

The impetus to read books of this sort usually arises from some recognized need; the disincentives to do so, merits of the work apart, include a misjudgment by people of what they need to know, and what they may be likely to understand. For example it is commonplace to find software development staff, at the programming level, who think and say they have no need to interest themselves in management matters, no wish to, and no facility anyway. Nothing could be more unwise. Practitioners may prevent good management practice, by others, if they are unaware of the scope and modalities concerned in it. Equally, it is commonplace to find managers – and others not especially knowledgeable in the subject, but involved one way or another – for whom 'software' is an uncharted territory (of the 'here be dragons' sort) and to whom 'software engineering' is an arcane – perhaps profane – art, conducted in some hermetic ritual by its initiates. To some degree this attitude is understandable, if not justified. The terminology of software and its development may seem more alien to non-practitioners than that of any other subject, and apparently changes too rapidly for a start to be made in understanding it. In fact, this conclusion is only true up to a point. A basic method in cognition is that of classification and, once the basic classes are identified in this subject, as in any other, the problems of volatile terminology are lessened.

With this understanding, and in order to be helpful (with a modest reservation about the merits of books in this series, for it is the province of readers and critics to judge), we recommend that software *practitioners* and participants on sources offering software engineering modules, should read Volumes 1 and 5 as well as their rather narrow, subject-interest topics in Volumes 3 and 4. Chapter 1 of Volume 1, being elementary, may be read for passing interest only by these populations, and for an understanding of the basic problems in comprehension that many managers, and others, have. Volume 5 (*Quality*) should be read with especial care.

The *managers* and 'others' referred to should – in our view – start with Volume 1, progress to Volume 2, and then read Volume 5 with particular acuity. Anyone in these categories who also wishes to achieve some insight into the 'arcana' of software engineering should attempt Volume 3 (*Software Design*); Volume 4 requires some preliminary grasp of computer programming considerably beyond the level of Basic on a Personal Computer – which is about the limit for many people in this class.

Students (in, for example, computer science) may benefit from a close acquaintance with Volumes 3 and 4. An interesting question, of considerable topicality, is what should be read by students in schools of business management or by undergraduates in the cognate disciplines of software engineering such as electronic engineering. In the first case, we would recommend 'the management Volume' 1, and Volume 5; for the cognate disciplines such as electronic, production or mechanical engineering we would recommend the whole series, to be read in sequence, with the reservation that Volumes 3 and 4 may be beyond the detailed study of many in this class, and beyond their need to do so.

One other point of our policy might give rise to speculation or adverse comment, and an explanation is owed. The examples in each volume are not harmonized across volumes nor, necessarily, even within volumes. The reason is really quite simple. No one application of reasonable size would incorporate an example-set sufficient for all purposes; the priority is to demonstrate points in the text in the best way for that issue, not necessarily the most harmonized way. Also, obviously, a thematic example across volumes might be seen as counter to the modular approach of this series if, for example, one had to get Volume 2 in order to understand the examples in Volumes 3 and 4. One would not want to attract accusations of sharp commercial practice.

The present volume, to which these editorial remarks attach, is concerned with the design of software systems. In it, the author – quite correctly in my view – adopts the line that an exposition of underlying principles is required, rather than a compendium of so-called 'methods', of which there are many, certainly too many to treat adequately in one monograph length book. Some of the author's views may be contentious – I find some of them so. But this is a subject where perspectives differ, and alternative views of the same issues sound like different opinions when they are not really so far removed. Perspective is the essence of design, more so than in any other topic of software engineering, although it is true that perspective pervades all issues in this series.

Allen Macro
Rotterdam 1990

INTRODUCTION

This book is intended to improve the reader's understanding of how to design software. It does so primarily by describing what software design is and explaining the basic concepts of good software design methods. Practicing software designers too busy to keep informed about evolving design methods will find a summary of the more important modern ones here, with a description of each and how it is used. Then, as they have time or need to explore one or more in greater depth, a specific book is recommended for each which explains it fully and in a clear, understandable way. Thus practicing designers can expand their knowledge of software design step by step, as appropriate, and without having to do extensive research. Those readers who desire an understanding of important design concepts without having to read numerous books should also find this volume useful, especially Chapters 2 through 4. Those who manage software designers may benefit from a better understanding of the methods their designers use, and may identify additional ones that their designers *should* use. Those new to software design will find an explanation of important design concepts, and obtain a perspective on software design before exploring specific methods in detail. Those with in-depth knowledge of an included method will find little that is new in its presentation here. Those interested in the leading edge of each technology will find it in the latest periodicals, usually written with the assumption that the reader already has an understanding of the basics – which is what this book intends to impart.

The most important part of this book is Chapter 2, which describes architectural software design – ways to decompose whole systems into parts. The next most important chapters are 3 and 4. A complete software design includes specifications for components that make up the system; Chapter 3 describes various common ways to define individual components. Chapter 4 explains those concepts of data base design with which designers who concentrate primarily on functional decomposition should be aware. Recommendations and general design suggestions are given in Chapter 5 as well as some software design issues such as reuse and portability. Chapter 6 is a short conclusion and comments. Following Chapter 6 are two appendices on executing data flow diagrams. These are for those readers who are interested in the technical detail about concepts discussed in the section 'Code reuse' in Section 5.3. Appendix C consists of problems on the material in Chapters 1–6; the answers to these problems are given in Appendix D.

The techniques for defining the requirements for the system, and for choosing what will be automated, the hardware to be used, and the input and output media and layouts (e.g. screens, reports, displays, sensors, and controllers), and human factors are outside the scope of this book. An understanding of the meaning and use of diagrams unique to the Ada® environment requires an understanding of Ada® itself, which is beyond the scope of this book. Readers who need to understand Ada® are referred to *Software Engineering with ADA* by Grady Booch (1983). Readers interested in articles covering much of the latest about common methods are referred to IEEE (1986). Those readers interested in the basic concepts and background on the subject of CASE by some of the best authors in that field are referred to *Computer-Aided Software Engineering (CASE)*, by Elliot Chikofsky (1989). An overview of software design, seen in the context of the whole software development process, is in Volume 1 of this series (Macro 1990), and in *The Craft of Software Engineering* by Allen Macro and John Buxton (1987). It is not the intent here to describe all available design methods or graphical notations, of which there are many. Readers interested in books which describe a broad range of existing software design techniques are referred to *Software Design: Methods & techniques* by Lawrence J. Peters (1981), and *Structured Analysis & Design of Information Systems* by A. Ziya Aktas (1987). Readers interested in a survey of current software methods are referred to the survey by Teledyne (1989). Many of the design methods in this book can be used to enhance the design phase of Information Engineering, especially Essential Systems Analysis (Section 2.3) and Structured Design (Section 2.5). Information Engineering uses Action Diagrams (Section 3.4) for specifying individual software components.

ACKNOWLEDGEMENTS

There are a number of people who gave advice and guidance on this book. First and foremost are the authors of the texts for the software design methods and topics included here who took time to consult, reviewed the material that describes their methods, and gave their permission to extract diagrams and text from their material. These authors are Paul Ward, Stephen Mellor, Stephen McMenamin, John Palmer, Larry Constantine, Dr Harlan Mills, Richard Linger, Alan Hevner, James Peterson, Brad Cox, Tom De Marco, Larry Larson, John Gall, Walt Doherty, Dr. Frederick Lochovsky, and Dionysios Tsichritzis. I also appreciate the advice from Lloyd Williams, Larry Larson, and Jay McMahon.

Thanks are also due to IBM for the support in terms of incidental time, research resources, computer resources, and materials that were all of significant help in the preparation of the book. In addition, Index Technology whose design tool Exceleration was used to produce many of the diagrams. Thanks are due to Academic Press, Systemantics Press, IBM, and Prentice Hall for their permission to extract diagrams and text from their publications.

A special thanks goes to the reviewers who read early drafts and gave such valuable feedback: Elliot Chikofsky, Michael Marcotty, Bob Maegerlein, William Fry, Charles Bontempo, Helene Schiffman, Fred Benfer, three anonymous (to me) reviewers chosen by Prentice Hall, and, of course, our series editor, Allen Macro, who spent countless hours making suggestions for this book.

Thanks and appreciation also go to my friends and family, and especially my wife, Penny, who have borne with me through the substantial amounts of time and effort it took to produce this book.

Wayne P. Stevens

LIST OF FIGURES

FIGURE 1.1	'What' or 'how' can depend on the vantage point	3
FIGURE 1.2	A software life cycle model (from Macro, 1990)	4
FIGURE 1.3	The software design process	9
FIGURE 1.4	Method and notation strengths	10
FIGURE 2.1	Size can increase difficulty exponentially	13
FIGURE 2.2	Theoretical savings if totally independent	14
FIGURE 2.3	Organization chart	15
FIGURE 2.4	Indented list	15
FIGURE 2.5	A traditional systems flowchart is a data flow diagram	20
FIGURE 2.6	Data flow diagram symbols	21
FIGURE 2.7	A diagram for constructing a Kleeper boat	22
FIGURE 2.8	Sample data flow diagram	24
FIGURE 2.9	Sample flowchart	25
FIGURE 2.10	Leveled data flow diagrams	26
FIGURE 2.11	Balanced data flow diagrams	27
FIGURE 2.12	Unbalanced data flow diagrams	27
FIGURE 2.13	Balanced data flow diagrams	28
FIGURE 2.14	Local files in data flow diagrams	28
FIGURE 2.15	Fundamental activity of a payroll system	33
FIGURE 2.16	Custodial activities of a payroll system	33
FIGURE 2.17	Essential memory of a payroll system	34
FIGURE 2.18	Event-partitioned DFD for part of the Traffic Violations system	37
FIGURE 2.19	Poorly partitioned essential activity	38
FIGURE 2.20	Poorly partitioned essential activity: one response	39
FIGURE 2.21	Correctly partitioned essential activity	39
FIGURE 2.22	An event-partitioned DFD	40
FIGURE 2.23	Car Rental example of object partitioning	42
FIGURE 2.24	Object-partitioning of essential memory data stores	42
FIGURE 2.25	Explanation of symbols used in A-graphs	45
FIGURE 2.26	Store handling and distribution	46

LIST OF FIGURES   XV

FIGURE 2.27	Cruise Control	48
FIGURE 2.28	Context schema	49
FIGURE 2.29	Maintain Auto Speed	49
FIGURE 2.30	Maintain Active Status	51
FIGURE 2.31	Sequentially linked transformations	51
FIGURE 2.32	Parallel transformations	52
FIGURE 2.33	Flow convergence/divergence conventions	52
FIGURE 2.34	Combining time-continuous and time-discrete flows	53
FIGURE 2.35	A continuous flow as a time function	53
FIGURE 2.36	Time-continuous data flows	53
FIGURE 2.37	Event flows and control transformation	54
FIGURE 2.38	Airspace Status as a store	55
FIGURE 2.39	Use of an event store	55
FIGURE 2.40	Prompted data transformations	57
FIGURE 2.41	Combination of time-continuous and time-discrete behavior	58
FIGURE 2.42	Separation of time-continuous and time-discrete behavior	58
FIGURE 2.43	Relationship of essential and implementation models	60
FIGURE 2.44	Structure chart symbols	63
FIGURE 2.45	Sample structure chart	64
FIGURE 2.46	An initial structure chart	66
FIGURE 2.47	Types of binding	67
FIGURE 2.48	Communicational binding	68
FIGURE 2.49	Sequential binding	68
FIGURE 2.50	Functional binding	69
FIGURE 2.51	An improved structure	71
FIGURE 2.52	What is communicated	72
FIGURE 2.53	One function contained within another	73
FIGURE 2.54	Separating multiple functions	73
FIGURE 2.55	Control variable	74
FIGURE 2.56	A further improved design	75
FIGURE 2.57	Functional modules	76
FIGURE 2.58	Type of connection	77
FIGURE 2.59	Segmenting a global data area	80
FIGURE 2.60	Size of the connection	81
FIGURE 2.61	Final structure chart for Update Orders	83
FIGURE 2.62	Data flow diagram for Update Orders	84
FIGURE 2.63	Interdependent modules	85
FIGURE 2.64	Call versus data flow	86
FIGURE 2.65	A black box diagram	89
FIGURE 2.66	A state box diagram	91
FIGURE 2.67	The Master File Update state box	91
FIGURE 2.68	Clear box diagrams	92–3
FIGURE 2.69	Expansion and derivation	94

LIST OF FIGURES

FIGURE 2.70	Reorder Policy clear box	94
FIGURE 2.71	Reorder Policy state box	95
FIGURE 2.72	A hand-held device that accepts stimuli and produces responses	97
FIGURE 2.73	A stimulus–response table	97
FIGURE 2.74	A stimulus–response history	97
FIGURE 2.75	A Petri net graph	102
FIGURE 2.76	Machine shop pre- and post-conditions	103
FIGURE 2.77	A Petri net model of a simple machine shop	104
FIGURE 2.78	Bigger machine shop pre- and post-conditions	106
FIGURE 2.79	An example of a more complex machine shop, modeled by a Petri net	107
FIGURE 2.80	A marked Petri net	107
FIGURE 2.81	A different marking	108
FIGURE 2.82	A larger marking	108
FIGURE 2.83	A marked Petri net to illustrate the firing rules	109
FIGURE 2.84	The marking resulting from firing transition t_2 in Figure 2.83	110
FIGURE 2.85	The marking resulting from firing transition t_4 in Figure 2.84	110
FIGURE 2.86	The marking resulting from firing transition t_3 in Figure 2.85	110
FIGURE 2.87	A flowchart of a small program	112
FIGURE 2.88	Translating computation and decision nodes in a flowchart to transitions in Petri net	113
FIGURE 2.89	A Petri net representation of the flowchart in Figure 2.87	114
FIGURE 2.90	Modeling a non-primitive event	114
FIGURE 2.91	Representing one Pctri net within another	115
FIGURE 2.92	A Petri net graph	116
FIGURE 2.93	A Petri net structure represented as a 4-tuple	116
FIGURE 3.1	Flowchart symbols	122
FIGURE 3.2	Comparison of traditional code and structured code	123
FIGURE 3.3	Flowchart for the left-hand side of Figure 3.2	124
FIGURE 3.4	Basic Structured Programming control structures	126
FIGURE 3.5	Additional Structured Programming structures	128–9
FIGURE 3.6	General 'IF' construct	130
FIGURE 3.7	'IF' via sequence of two loops	131
FIGURE 3.8	Single sufficient structure	132
FIGURE 3.9	Syntax-checking algorithm	132
FIGURE 3.10	Depiction of syntax-checking algorithm	133
FIGURE 3.11	Example: Action Diagram	134
FIGURE 3.12	Action Diagram for the right-hand side of Figure 3.2	135
FIGURE 3.13	Other Action Diagram symbols	136
FIGURE 3.14	A state transition diagram	137
FIGURE 3.15	Garage door opener state transition diagram	138
FIGURE 3.16	Determine Mode of Operation	139
FIGURE 3.17	Manage Control Mode	140

FIGURE 3.18	Control Cruise Control Engagement	141
FIGURE 3.19	Alternative state transition diagram	142
FIGURE 3.20	Screen hierarchy diagram	142
FIGURE 3.21	Jackson chart constructs	144
FIGURE 3.22	A sample report	144
FIGURE 3.23	Jackson chart for report	145
FIGURE 3.24	Process report program	145
FIGURE 3.25	Decision table	147
FIGURE 3.26	Linked decision tables	148
FIGURE 3.27	Decision table with all sections	149
FIGURE 3.28	Triangular decision table	149
FIGURE 3.29	Decision tree	150
FIGURE 3.30	Jackson charts vs. decision tables	151
FIGURE 4.1	Data base design steps	153
FIGURE 4.2	Entity–relationship diagram for medical data base	156
FIGURE 4.3	Ternary relationship set	157
FIGURE 4.4	Two relationships sets between the same entity sets	157
FIGURE 4.5	Recursive relationship set	158
FIGURE 4.6	Entity types and attributes for insurance company example	159
FIGURE 4.7	Relationship types for insurance company example	160
FIGURE 4.8	Some constraints for insurance company example	161
FIGURE 4.9	Enterprise description for insurance company example	162
FIGURE 4.10	Some simple transactions for the insurance company	163
FIGURE 4.11	Hierarchical schema for insurance company example	168
FIGURE 4.12	DBTG-network schema for insurance company example	169
FIGURE 4.13	Relational schema for insurance company example	170
FIGURE 5.1	Design specifications	177
FIGURE 5.2	Calls rivet integrands	183
FIGURE 5.3	Read & Edit & Select & Sort & Print	186
FIGURE 5.4	Abstract Data Type	189
FIGURE 5.5	Reusable objects	196
FIGURE 5.6	Environment interfaces	198
FIGURE 5.7	Cumulative computer cycles	205
FIGURE A.1	Data flow diagram for A $\rightarrow$ B $\rightarrow$ C	209
FIGURE A.2	Multiple inputs and outputs	210
FIGURE A.3	ReadA & Increment & Increment.2 & WriteB	210
FIGURE A.4	ReadA & Increment & Increment & WriteB	210
FIGURE A.5	ReadA & Select.A & Select.B & Print, Select.B2 & WriteB	211
FIGURE A.6	P: A & B & C, B: $\rightarrow$ D & E & F, D2 & G & 2F $\rightarrow$.	211
FIGURE A.7	P: A & S & C, S2 & D. S: & H & I &, H2 & K & 2.	212
FIGURE B.1	Example: merge-deadlock	220
FIGURE B.2	Potential merge-deadlock	220
FIGURE B.3	Example: loop-deadlocks	220
FIGURE B.4	Potential loop-deadlocks	221

CHAPTER ONE
INTRODUCTION TO SOFTWARE DESIGN

Software design is a process of inventing and selecting programs that meet the objectives for a software system. Input includes an understanding of the following:

1. Requirements.
2. Environmental constraints.
3. Design criteria.

The output of the design effort is composed of the following:

1. An architecture design which shows how pieces are interrelated.
2. Specifications for any new pieces.
3. Definitions for any new data.

An architecture depicts the relationships among the pieces that will comprise the software system; diagrams are especially useful for depicting architectures. Software design can be a complicated task of meeting the requirements for the system while balancing various constraints and criteria. Software design methods can assist by providing ways to describe evolving designs as well as techniques and criteria for evaluating alternatives, all of which help to produce good designs. In order to design software, the designer must have an understanding of the requirements and the hardware and software environments. Only then should an appropriate software design method be selected. A useful order for design is not necessarily top down but, rather, from to independent dependent requirements.

1.1 WHAT IS SOFTWARE DESIGN?

Software design is a process of inventing, improving, and selecting among alternative solutions, and then describing computer programs that meet users' requirements within the constraints of the environment and based on relevant criteria. A software design is a usable and understandable description of the chosen alternative. A good software design is one that describes a system that will meet all its requirements. The 'best' software design is the alternative that most adequately meets and most appropriately balances the requirements, constraints, and criteria. For example, the 'best' design for a car is one that includes the combination of features most likely to sell it, is within the intended price range, has the best mileage consistent with the engine size, uses parts that last longest and are as strong as possible, etc., and does so for the lowest possible manufacturing cost consistent with delivering the new model by a specified date. Similarly, the 'best' software design may be the one that balances the most functions, the highest quality, the greatest ease of use, the most adaptability, the least use of computer resources, the fastest development, the easiest maintenance, and can be delivered by the desired date. Often objectives for software design are not, and cannot be, crisply defined and prioritized, though we do try to be as precise as possible with respect to the functions required of the software. However, the designer still needs to understand and balance the objectives appropriately.

Included in this book are methods for the activity called 'Detailed software design' in Figure 1.2. The central activities of software design are creating and evaluating alternative solutions, which demands a good understanding of the requirements, environmental constraints, and design criteria. The requirements for the software – as expressed by the functional specifications – and environmental constraints are covered in Volumes 1 and 2 of this series (Macro 1990; 1991). The environmental constraints are primarily the hardware, software and physical environment in which the designed software will run. As for design criteria, these are generally included as part of each design method. This book describes important methods, concepts, and notations for designing software. As defined in Volume 1 of this series (Macro 1990), software is 'the dynamic behavior of programs, designed and implemented for some defined purpose, on the equipment for which they are destined'.

Some definitions from *Webster's Ninth New Collegiate Dictionary* (1983) are as follows:

1. The verb design: to conceive and plan out in the mind, to devise for a specific function or end, to make a drawing, pattern, or sketch of, to draw the plans for.
2. The noun design: a mental project or scheme in which the means to an end are laid down, a preliminary sketch or outline showing the main features of something to be executed, the arrangement of elements that go into human productions.

The preceding definitions indicate three concepts that are important to the design process:

1. Design includes creative mental effort. Thus we should use techniques that help *people* with that creative mental effort.
2. Design shows how smaller pieces are combined to form the whole.
3. Design may be expressed with diagrams, especially architectural designs, which show how smaller pieces combine to form the whole. Software designers also draw design diagrams: data flow diagrams, call hierarchy charts, data model diagrams, flowcharts, and system flowcharts.

Sometimes the term 'analysis' is applied to what should more properly be called design: computer professionals sometimes state (incorrectly) that they are 'analyzing' a system, even though the result of their effort is a proposed new software solution. *Webster's*

WHAT IS SOFTWARE DESIGN? 3

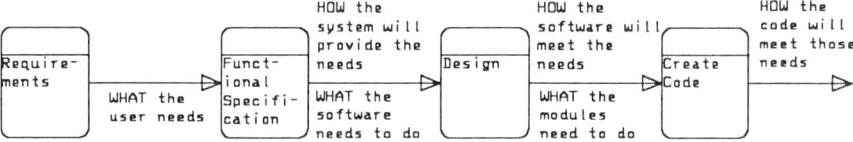

FIGURE 1.1 'What' or 'how' can depend on the vantage point

defines analysis as 'separation of a whole into its component parts'. One can analyze a current system to see what functions it performs; one can analyze requirements to see if they are consistent; and one can even analyze a particular design to see if it meets some set of criteria. However, the activity of creating a proposed new alternative is more properly called 'design'. Another common belief is that design can be identified as the step that *translates* the 'what' into the 'how'. A problem with using inputs and outputs to identify which is the design step is that most specifications can be viewed as a 'what' or a 'how', depending on one's perspective. An *input* to a development activity tends to be seen as a 'what', regardless of the phase of the development process (as shown in Figure 1.1). An *output* of a creative process is a 'how', but it also becomes the 'what' of the next development activity. This ability to see any form of specification as a 'what' or a 'how' applies whether one is looking at the functional specification, architectural design, specifications for the code, or even test cases.

The most important input to design is *understanding*. The designer should understand the inputs, outputs, and functions that the user requires. Note that not all software 'users' are people. Software may also be used by other software, or even hardware components (e.g. subroutines and interrupt handlers respectively). Design choices can be improved if the designer better understands: the objectives of the system; the user's job; changes likely for the software in the future; the execution environment(s); available components; subsystem capabilities; and the cost of alternatives in terms of time, money, and complexity for development, maintenance, execution, and ease of use. Design involves making choices between conflicting objectives, even in the best design, because the best design should include as much of any one objective as can be realized without sacrificing others. The hard choices are achieving the proper balance among the objectives. Since understanding the requirements for the software is so important, one crucial criterion for the functional specifications is to convey this understanding to the designer.

The output of the design effort is the input to the implementation of the software, and is composed of the following:

1. An architectural design showing the relationships among the components that will comprise the software, including the data in and out of each component.
2. The specifications for each component to be created.
3. A design for any new stored data to be used by the system.

Much of the literature calls pieces of programs 'modules'. However, since the term 'module' has been used for pieces at many architectural levels, this series has adopted the use of the term 'integrand' to describe the lowest level component of a program. A

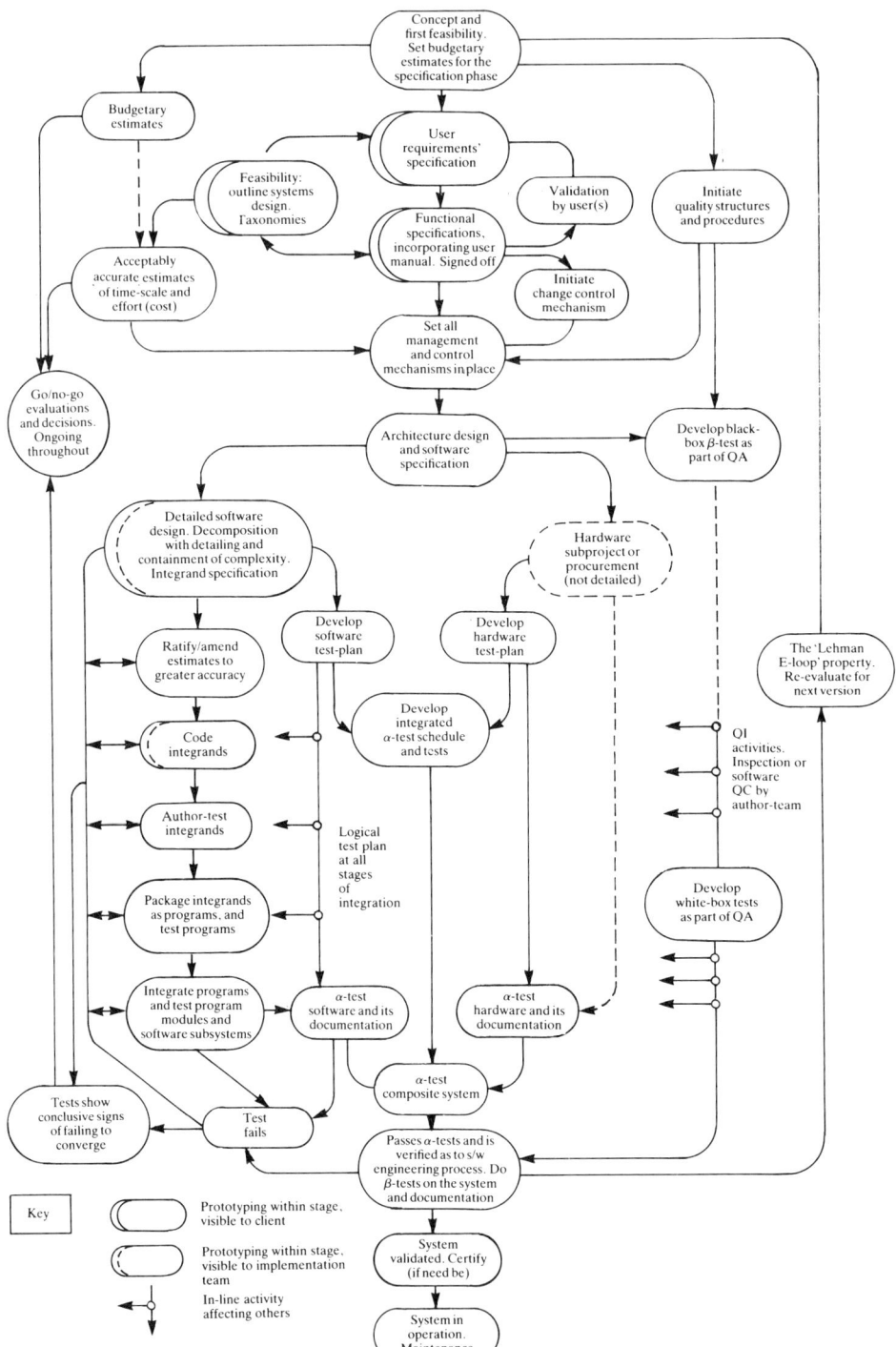

FIGURE 1.2 A software life cycle model (from Macro, 1990)

'design module' represents a component that will be executable when implemented and is comprised of one or more integrands, or for which the number of integrands that will eventually comprise it has not yet been decided. In this book, the term 'module' will mean 'design module' unless otherwise specified.

1.2 DESIGN OBJECTIVES

The purpose of *design* is to create a solution that best meets the criteria for the software. The purpose of a *method* is to help the designer to achieve a good design. A complete software design method includes criteria for choosing between various design alternatives; these criteria help designers to meet software design objectives, including making the software simple, flexible, and easy to change, read, and test. The methods help designers to achieve these design goals, which are somewhat abstract and not easily measured, by substituting goals that are more clearly defined and measurable. For example, Structured Design (see Section 2.5) includes measurements that evaluate alternative functional decompositions based on specific objectives such as binding, coupling, single implementation of any function, and eliminating control parameters. However, other methods have other criteria. Essential Systems Analysis (see Section 2.3) requires that 'fundamental processes' include everything necessary to allow the system to become idle after responding to an input. Only binary, enabling control signals go into data transformations in transformation graphs (see Section 2.4). Box Structured Design (Section 2.6) requires that state data be separated from the processes that access and update it in prescribed ways.

1.2.1 Quality

Designers should strive for designs that:

1. Meet the users' needs.
2. Contain no errors.
3. Are easy to understand, implement, and change.
4. Make use of appropriate and available components and subsystems.
5. Perform well.
6. Best balance the objectives within the constraints of the system and the environment.

The ability to create high-quality designs is increased by a good understanding of the requirements, environment, and design methods.

The objective of software development is to meet a realistic set of the users' needs. Preventing errors is important in all phases and is easier to achieve if the complexity of the design and development process can be reduced. Making software that is easy to understand, implement, and change is covered in 'Independent pieces reduce complexity' (Section 2.1) and 'Structured Design' (Section 2.5). Writing code that is easy to understand is the theme of Volume 3 of this series (Marcotty 1991). Reusing high-quality components is one of the best ways of achieving high-quality software. Making use of existing software components is the topic of 'Code reuse' in Section 5.3. Performance is also discussed in Section 5.9. Software quality in general will be covered later in this series. The difficulty of best balancing the objectives makes design a human activity, and one that improves with experience. That is why it is supported by design tools rather than performed automatically. Developers can learn from the experiences of earlier designers by using good design methods.

Throughout the development process, it is important to remember that the original objective is to meet the users' needs, as defined by the functional specifications. However, functional specifications are an abstraction of the users' real needs. (Some developers under contract may have to meet only the functional specifications rather than the needs of the user. However, it is proper to inform the customer whenever it is found that the functional specifications fail to meet the user's actual needs.) It is also important to validate the product *with* the users and not just against the functional specifications, the test data, or even what the users originally said their needs were. This validation can be even harder than meeting functional specifications and often takes all the validator's communication skill and perception.

1.3 SOFTWARE DESIGN METHODS

What is a design notation, and what is a method? A design *notation* is a language, which may be graphical, used to depict and describe design alternatives. *Webster's* defines *method* as 'a way, technique, or process of or for doing something'. A design method has a name, a procedure and a notation. The procedure of a design method is its explicit rules and guidelines. Data flow diagrams, called hierarchy diagrams, and entity relationship diagrams are examples of design notations. Structured Programming (see Section 3.2) is a method, but it lacks design criteria for evaluating and choosing among various alternative designs (even though it includes rules for how the code is to be structured). Essential Systems Analysis (Section 2.3) and Structured Design (Section 2.5) are methods which contain both design rules and ways to compare alternatives.

1.3.1 Design order

There are a number of possible orders in which to design software. It can be designed top down, bottom up, input to output, output to input, from the middle to the boundaries, or in many other possible orders. Which way is best and how does the designer decide? In the early 1970s 'top down' was often believed to be the right way for everything. This may have been inferred (though incorrectly) from Harlan Mills' popular recommendations for 'top down development' (e.g. IBM 1977). One example of top down development was building higher level subroutines before lower level ones. However, a better description of the point of top down development is to produce *independent* parts before developing parts that depend on those independent parts. For example, assume that file types are specified in the job control language, that update access is declared when 'opening' the file, and that data are accessed by a 'read' statement. Top down development recommends that the statements be developed in that same order, so that each statement can be validated based on preceding statements plus new information. If the job control language were written last, then the file type specified in the job control could make previously written 'open' or 'read' statements invalid.

Similarly, the answer to the order for design is to design the independent parts before the dependent ones, which yields various orders depending on the problem and is *not* always top down. One way to find the independent parts is to identify the essence of the system – why it is needed (see 'Essential Systems Analysis', Section 2.3, for concepts that can help to identify the essence of a system). This may be primarily outputs, such as for a system providing information about a city when a tourist points to topics of interest on the screen. If the essence is primarily outputs, design the output parts first and work backwards towards the inputs. If the essence of the system is its inputs, as might be true for a system which monitors the status of critical points in a nuclear power plant, design the input parts of the system first, and work towards the outputs. The essence of a system may be internal calculations, such as for a system which is to control the trajectory of an object in orbit. In this case, calculations dominate; inputs and outputs can be added as necessary to gather the data and send out commands. Naturally, any combination may occur, such as business applications that are input *and* output constrained (e.g. an application may map a pre-defined data base record to a specified screen layout). The approach, though, is the same: determine what the independent parts are, and design them first. Then determine which parts depend on the ones designed, design them next, and so on.

1.3.2 Designing software with time-dependencies

There are types of computer software called 'real-time' or 'event-driven', such as software for airplane control systems, radar systems, and systems which control independent machinery. Developers of real-time systems are concerned with many of the same things as developers of more traditional business applications, such as functional decomposition, data flow diagrams, life cycle development, integration, complexity, reuse, abstract data types, distributed processing, and concurrency. However, there are also differences. Developers of real-time systems are more likely to implement systems with distributed components (e.g. multiple processors within an airplane control system) and may thus be more interested than business developers have been in the past in issues with asynchronous execution and state transition diagrams. Real-time design technologies are changing even more rapidly than technologies for business applications. Because designers of real-time systems often have to pay explicit attention to control, events, and asynchronous execution, they need diagrams that allow depictions of these. Data flow diagrams can be used to depict relationships among asynchronously executing components but need to be augmented to show the real-time concepts of event and control flows.

There are a number of graphical notations and methods which can be applied successfully to the design of software with time-dependencies. Particularly recommended are data flow diagrams and the notation of 'transformation schema' (see Section 2.4.3), an extension to data flow diagrams to add control flow, developed by Ward and Mellor along with their method for designing real-time systems. Their method also uses state transition diagrams and state machines. Petri nets (discussed in Section 2.7) are a valuable tool used to describe and analyze systems requirements where timing and asynchrony have to be dealt with explicitly. State machines are used for real-time design – see 'State transition diagrams', Section 3.5, and 'Box Structured Design' in Section 2.6.

1.3.3 Getting started

How does one get started designing software? Do *not* come to the task already armed with a favorite method. First, the designer should be familiar with the execution environments, capabilities of languages, generators, subsystems, and available components. Next, the designer should understand the requirements for this particular software including inputs, outputs, and functional capabilities. These should be contained in the functional specifications (see Macro 1990, Section 5.3). Based on an understanding of the requirements and the environment, the most appropriate architectural design method is then chosen (as depicted in Figure 1.3).

There are two major reasons for using a software design method: to aid in the design process and to communicate the result to others. Choosing a method involves balancing both these objectives with some other practical ones. Since designs should be understandable by others, it is important to use a notation that the reader already knows, otherwise readers will have to cope with learning a new notation while at the same time trying to understand the design. In most cases, the use of one of the generally accepted design notations – so that the design can be easily understood – outweighs the possible advantages of a unique notation. The value of choosing standard methods along with their notations is that the reader is generally familiar with them, they are well integrated with the notation, and they have been used and refined so that earlier problems, inconsistencies, and difficulties have been eliminated. However, designers often improve on the *methods* as experience is gained in evaluating design alternatives and in making choices during design.

While generalities can be made regarding how to match a method with a particular type of problem, such generalities may not be of much practical value; few software systems are purely of one type or another. Also, the designer may be required by a company standard to use a specific design method, so the form of the design may be more familiar to the reader. However, as the computing environment evolves and the types of software change, the advantages of using a different design method may increase. Designers of traditional business applications may find themselves turning more to real-time methods to help with the design of distributed applications. The designer should try to identify the

SOFTWARE DESIGN METHODS 9

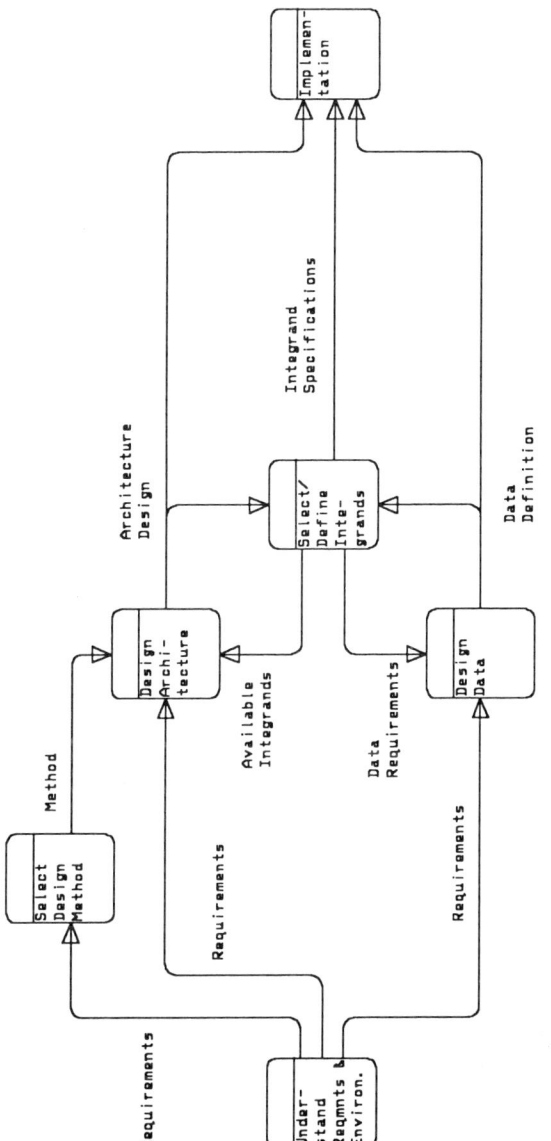

FIGURE 1.3 The software design process

10　INTRODUCTION TO SOFTWARE DESIGN

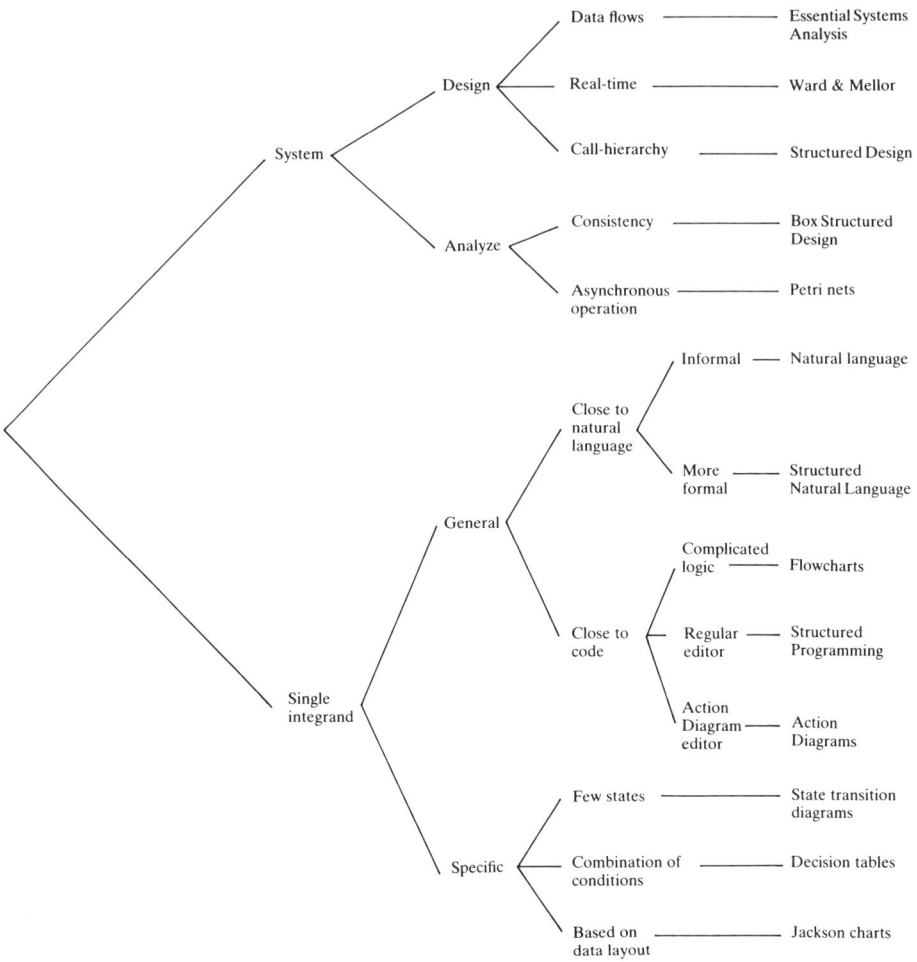

FIGURE 1.4 Method and notation strengths

most dominant and/or constraining feature of the problem at hand and attempt to match a design method that most clearly displays this feature so that it can be dealt with explicitly during design. The matching will be easier if the designer knows several good design methods and has a working understanding of the requirements. The strengths of the various software design methods and integrand specification syntaxes included in this book are shown in Figure 1.4. However, design methods are not mutually exclusive but, rather, are overlapping and complementary, so that the more methods the designer knows, the more ideas and approaches are available for use on each problem.

Some designers prefer to concentrate on designing functions and adding the data to the functions; others prefer the opposite. In either case, the design of the functions and data should proceed in parallel so that the designs stay consistent (since design efforts on each often affect requirements for the other). The choice of whether to view functions or data as the primary focus for design is just a matter of preference in many cases. However, those systems where the data are the dominant factors and the most likely to change are probably better designed by concentrating primarily on the data (e.g. those designing a new data base that will be accessed using existing generalized query software will find it advantageous to take a data view); and conversely where functions or processes are the most likely to change (e.g. those designing a generalized query program will find it advantageous to take a functional view). An advantage of designing based on the dominant factor in the requirements is that the resulting system may then be easier to modify as the requirements change. There are also situations where the functions already exist (e.g. users have query programs, report writers, etc., and need extracts of data for analysis) – in this case, data design is the proper choice since the functions do not have to be designed. Conversely, if the software to be developed will be working only with data which is already available in the files and data bases to be accessed, designing functions is appropriate, since there is no data to design.

After the architecture and data are designed, the integrands are specified (see Figure 1.3 and Chapter 3 below). The results are inputs to implementing the integrands (see Volume 3 of this series, Marcotty 1991), and are generally composed of textual and schematic representations of algorithms, and the data used by integrands. Chapter 2 covers architectural design methods, Chapter 3 includes ways to define integrands and Chapter 4 summarizes data base design.

CHAPTER TWO
ARCHITECTURAL SOFTWARE DESIGN

Methods and graphical notations for designing software architecture with which modern software designers should be familiar include the following:

1. **Structured Analysis** – characterized by using data flow diagrams to design systems.
2. **Essential Systems Analysis** – an improvement to Structured Analysis which suggests concentrating first on the 'essence' (the basic purpose) of the system.
3. **Ward–Mellor method** – a method for designing real-time applications, which is based on the concepts of Structured Analysis and Essential Systems Analysis and uses an adaptation of the data flow diagram that allows depicting control flows.
4. **Structured Design** – which includes concepts and measures for evaluating function decompositions to help reduce complexity and enhance the reuse of components, and which can be used with other architectural software design methods.
5. **Box Structured Design** – which uses the concepts of black boxes, state boxes, and clear boxes to analyze systems and assure that components combine to comprise the correct overall systems objectives. The concepts in Box Structured Design can also be used with other architectural software design methods to assure rigorous decompositions.
6. **Petri nets** – which are especially useful for modeling and analyzing the behavior of systems with asynchronous components.

2.1 INDEPENDENT PIECES REDUCE COMPLEXITY

2.1.1 Architecture

For any system that will require more than a few pages of source statements to implement, reduction of complexity, which makes all activities associated with design and development difficult, is crucial. The greater the complexity, the longer we take to solve

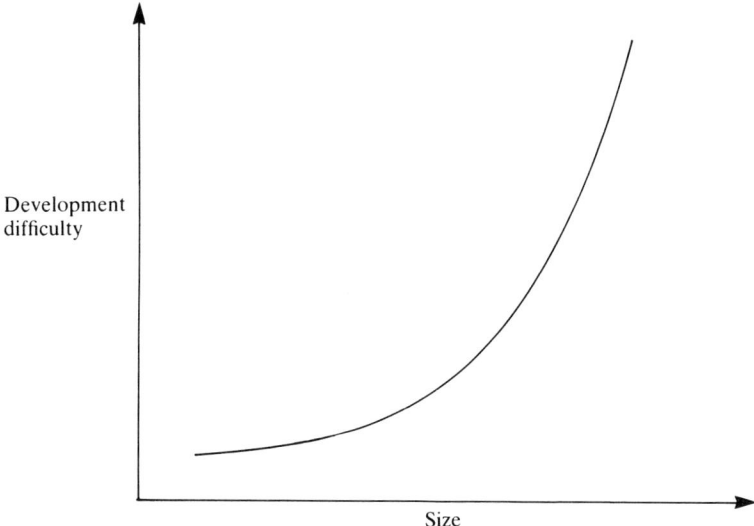

FIGURE 2.1 Size can increase difficulty exponentially

the problem, the fewer alternatives we can see and the more errors we tend to make during design and development. The larger the project is, the more complex it becomes and the more important it is to reduce that complexity. Problem solving can be made easier when each part of the problem can be solved relatively independently. The more independent the parts of the problem are, the more the complexity is reduced. Also, systems need to be corrected and enhanced. If two functions are dependent, it is difficult to make a change to one without affecting the other. If they are designed as independent parts, then they can be understood, tested, corrected, and replaced independently, making it simpler and faster to do each job, thereby increasing quality and productivity. Thus, when developing large systems, one important way to improve productivity is to design the system as combinations of independent, simpler pieces. The more independent the pieces, the more the slope of the curve in Figure 2.1 can be reduced (Stevens 1981). If the components were *entirely* independent, complexity would only increase linearly with size, as shown by the lower line in Figure 2.2; a 100-page program would then take only 100 times as long to develop as a one-page program. However, unless pieces share something, they will not be part of the same system. So, although it is unlikely that complexity can be reduced to a straight line, the more *independent* the pieces can be made, the more complexity can be reduced and productivity increased.

Webster's Ninth New Collegiate Dictionary (1983) defines *architecture* as 'the art or science of building; specifically: the art or practice of designing and building structures' – where a 'structure' is defined as 'the aggregate of elements of an entity in their relationships to each other'. Most manufacturing industries use diagrams to help design and communicate that combination of 'interdependent elements or parts' – i.e. the architecture. For example, industries that manufacture physical products often produce design 'blueprints'. The architectural design of a house can include several blueprints as

14   ARCHITECTURAL SOFTWARE DESIGN

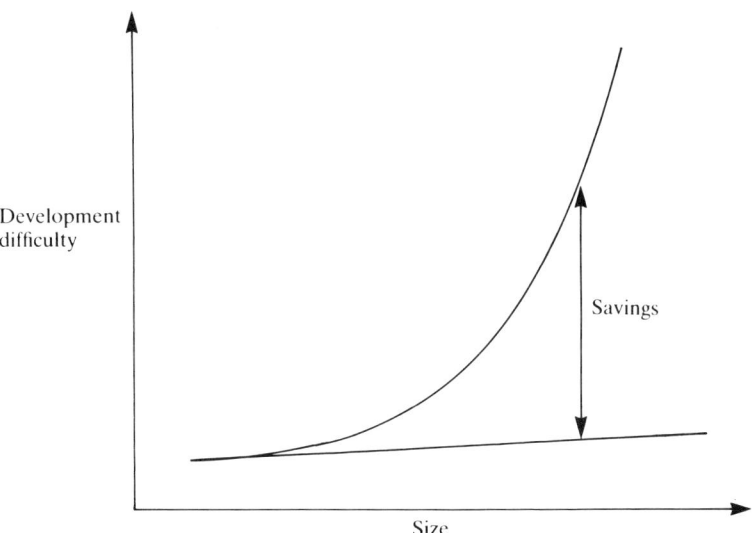

FIGURE 2.2 Theoretical savings if totally independent

well as other diagrams, including ones for structure, wiring, and plumbing. Designers of computer hardware use circuit diagrams, wiring diagrams, timing diagrams, and blueprints. Designers of computer software use diagrams too, including call hierarchy charts, data flow diagrams, data model diagrams, flowcharts, systems flowcharts, and screen and report layouts (which graphically illustrate the arrangement of words).

Diagrams are excellent for depicting the relationships among many components, allowing the designer to view and work with all this information in one image. Consider an organization chart, such as that shown in Figure 2.3: one can get an overall view of the structure more rapidly than from a paragraph containing the equivalent information in words. Even an indented listing of an organization, as shown in Figure 2.4, can be understood more easily than a paragraph of descriptive text because it depicts relationships graphically (i.e. through the indentation). With textual descriptions, relationships are expressed one by one – the reader has to assemble and remember the combination. Also the *lack* of a relationship can be discerned immediately in a diagram, but requires a complete search of equivalent text, with no good way to determine that its existence has not been overlooked. On the other hand, text is excellent for conveying abstract ideas, such as 'honesty', 'PC/DOS', and 'Validate Input', which would be difficult or impossible to convey graphically. Design diagrams are usually a combination of graphics and text: the graphics depicting objects and their relationships and the text describing or naming the abstract ideas represented by the data and functions.

Design can be divided into two types of activities:

1. Architectural design – how parts are related to make the whole.
2. Detailed design of any required new parts.

INDEPENDENT PIECES REDUCE COMPLEXITY   15

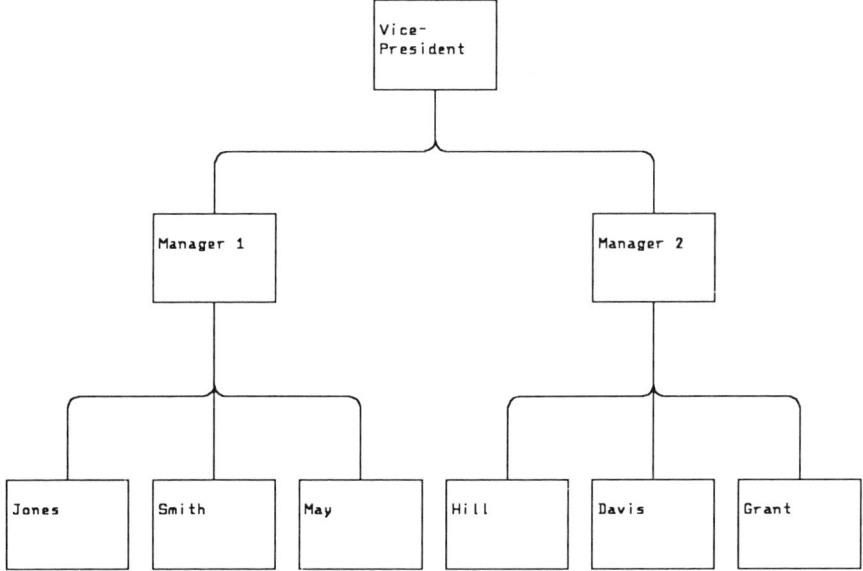

FIGURE 2.3 Organization chart

Vice president
  Manager 1
    Jones
    Smith
    May
  Manager 2
    Hill
    Davis
    Grant

FIGURE 2.4 Indented list

Architectural design creates a set of related components that satisfy the requirements. The architectural design process may be repeated through one or more levels, since a component at one level may be a combination of subcomponents at the next lower level. The techniques used for architectural design differ among industries, but often include drawings or diagrams to show the relationship of the parts. Typically, those architectural diagrams show the information needed to understand the interrelationship of the parts while deferring details of how to build each part. In a building complex, for example, the high level architectural design may show how the buildings are arranged on site to form the complex. Then, each building has an architectural drawing, such as a blueprint, showing how that building will be constructed. There may be other blueprints showing further details of each floor within a building. The architectural design at the various levels may repeat the design activities of the preceding level, or may require different skills and result in a different way of representing the design. For example, the building complex may be shown as a drawing of how it will finally look. The blueprints that describe various levels of building design may be quite similar to one another, but the interior design of the furnishings of each room may be shown as a picture or drawing.

One important aspect of dividing a system into independent pieces is *deferral*. One way in which division into independent parts helps to reduce complexity is that it allows concentration on one part of the problem and deferring decisions on other parts until later. But the idea of deferral is more global than just independent pieces. The idea is to be able to concentrate on part of the problem and defer consideration of other parts of the problem to a different time. Weinberg, in his book *An Introduction to General Systems Thinking* (1975), expresses this idea as the 'lump law':

> If we want to learn anything, we mustn't try to learn everything.

DeMarco, in *Structured Analysis and System Specification* (1978), expresses the same idea as a simple rule:

> Defer anything you can get away with.

Marcotty (1991) calls this idea 'constructive procrastination'.

Deferral is similar to decomposition in that it isolates parts of the problem so that each can be solved without having to consider the whole. Deferral is also one reason why design diagrams usually do not show *everything* necessary to construct the software. Showing only what is necessary to accomplish and validate the architectural design keeps architectural diagrams simple and easy to understand and use. There are many times and ways in which designers can choose to deal with 'more' or with 'less'. This concept of deferral – culled from the experiences of many designers and creators of design methods before us – recommends choosing the path of deferring whatever we can until later.

2.1.2 Hierarchies are crucial

When programs are divided into independent pieces in order to reduce complexity, each piece should be of a size such that it can be understood individually. It is difficult to understand a diagram containing more than ten or twenty objects because our short-term memory can handle only about seven plus or minus two interrelated 'chunks' accurately at any one time (see Miller 1956). As the number of chunks increases, our error-rate rises rapidly because we have to deal with, understand, and remember each chunk and remember its relationship to all the others. Since the designer should also divide diagrams into levels that can be understood one at a time, the number of objects recommended for each level of a diagram is about seven plus or minus two. In addition, diagrams with five to ten objects are usually small enough to be displayed on a single screen or printed on a single page. However, if integrands are about one page of specifications, then large systems will consist of many integrands. Thus a second key concept in reducing complexity is to use hierarchies. This allows the designer to work with both small integrands *and* small diagrams.

Methods use different kinds of diagram hierarchies. With one kind of hierarchy, each object in the hierarchy will have a physical existence of its own such as the organization chart shown in Figure 2.3 where each object is a person and the diagram indicates the hierarchical relationships among them. Such hierarchies usually show several hierarchical levels on one diagram, with the bottom level object from one chart repeated as the top object on the next level in order to illustrate the context. For example, Figure 2.3 could be the top levels of an organization. The organization under Jones can be shown on another hierarchical management chart, with Jones repeated at the top of that chart. Since only about three levels can be shown on one page, with the bottom level repeated as the top of the next chart, each page displays only two additional levels of the hierarchy.

In another type of hierarchy used by some methods, an object in one diagram is completely defined by a second diagram that depicts the relationship of the first object's parts. An object on the upper level diagram is a logical representation of the combination of the lower level parts. An example of such a hierarchy is a 'parts explosion' chart, which is often included in owner's manuals for a machine such as a lawn mower or a household appliance. Some of the parts shown on one chart may be subassemblies themselves, such as a motor, which has a lower level parts explosion diagram to describe it. The machine and its parts do not have separate existences (as do people depicted by a management chart), but, rather, the machine exists only as a combination of its parts. One advantage of this type of hierarchy is that the diagrams can display the interactions between the components on one level without also having to display the relationships between levels.

2.1.3 Architectural software design methods

Software design methods and notations can be separated into two categories: those useful for architectural design and those that help define parts. In general, modules can be connected in various ways, and the architectural methods include diagrams that show the connections while deferring details relevant to the construction of a module. Sequence, iteration, and choice constructs, however, are not ways to connect integrands, but, rather, are descriptions of the three sufficient control structures needed to build the code *within* a given integrand. Thus, methods that include depiction of sequence, iteration, and choice constructs are recommended for defining individual integrands.

The following methods and associated graphical notations are recommended for architectural software design and are described below in this chapter:

1. Structured Analysis – data flow diagrams.
2. Essential Systems Analysis – data flow diagrams.
3. Ward–Mellor – transformation graphs.
4. Structured Design – structure charts.

Each of these software design methods:

1. Includes a graphical design notation that depicts the interrelationship among the pieces in the architecture.
2. Supports hierarchical decomposition (for projects large enough to include parts made up of other parts).

3. Includes criteria for evaluating designs.
4. Defers depicting how to build a module (desirable, since that reduces the complexity of the design effort).

Often, the top levels of software architectures are represented as data flow diagrams (see 'Structured Analysis', Section 2.2) with structure charts used for lower architectural levels (see 'Structured Design', Section 2.5).

Two methods are recommended for analyzing current or proposed systems. These can also be used with the architectural design methods above:

1. Box Structured Design.
2. Petri nets.

These methods are also described below.

Given that a designer has a high level specification that is large enough to need expanding to lower levels in order to implement it more easily and accurately, how is that expansion done? That is, how does one decide which functions to group? The answer depends on the problem and the designer. The basic approach is to maximize *independence* among the parts. However, what causes parts to be dependent depends on the particular problem and its environment. Thus the decomposition may be based on the following:

1. Minimum communication (as with 'Structured Design' below).
2. Functions (as with 'Structured Design' below).
3. Business organization (so that each part of the company can control its part of the system).
4. Geographical organization (so that each location can control its part of the system).
5. Data organization (if the data are expected to change more often than functions).
6. Data layout (as with Jackson design).
7. The real-world problem (so that each part of the system is dependent on one part of the real-world problem only).
8. Screen or menu hierarchies (in business application generators which implement applications as hierarchies of user screens).
9. User commands (as with 'Object-Oriented' in Chapter 5).
10. Performance considerations (putting parts where appropriate computer power is available).
11. Hardware capabilities (putting parts where functions exist).
12. Security requirements (isolating parts based on levels of security access).
13. Timing (where timing is a constraining design criterion).
14. Event/response (as with 'Essential Systems Analysis' below).
15. Available components (to take advantage of what already exists).

Just as there are a large number of ways and reasons to choose a particular route between two places, there are a large number of reasons for, and ways to, decompose systems requirements. The basic approaches for decomposition for the architectural methods in this chapter are as follows:

1. Structured Analysis – based on data flows.
2. Essential Systems Analysis – based on event/responses.
3. Ward–Mellor – based on real-time event/responses.
4. Structured Design – based on functional components with minimum coupling.
5. Box Structured Design – based on stimulus/response and state variables.

2.1.4 Deliver the software in stages

Another way to help meet the objective of reducing complexity is to design and develop in such a way that parts of the system are delivered to the user as it is developed. This approach can yield smaller design tasks that are more manageable and of higher quality. Yourdon and Constantine (1979) explain that computer projects with a design phase of more than two years may not get out of design. The computer hardware and software changes so much in two years that the design is out of date and needs to be redone, which takes another two years, is then also out of date again, and so on. Moreover, the needs of the users, and even the individuals themselves, change in a two-year period. Advantages of delivering the software as it is developed include:

1. Delivered parts *must* be fairly independent of parts delivered later, thus helping to meet the objectives of functional decomposition in reducing the complexity of designing and implementing the software.
2. Delivered parts help in obtaining early feedback, which can improve the design of later parts.
3. The users begin to see benefits before the entire system is complete.

An example of the success of delivering software as it is developed is the effort to rewrite IBM's on-line ordering system, the Advanced Administrative System (AAS), which was first written before the existence of modern terminal support subsystems (such as CICS). IBM attempted to rewrite AAS four times with no success – it was just too big a project. The solution was to rewrite it in stages. A parallel CICS system was connected to the AAS machine and as each part was rewritten it was implemented on the CICS machine and removed from the AAS machine. Management can decide the order in which to migrate parts, and whether a change can be accommodated by migrating the part, or by modifying the old part without migrating it. This project was successful as soon as the first part was migrated.

2.2 STRUCTURED ANALYSIS

2.2.1 Data flow diagrams

Structured Analysis is characterized by the use of *data flow diagrams* to analyze and design systems. Structured Analysis also includes the concepts of Structured 'English', minispecifications, and keeping design information in a data dictionary. Two early books

20 ARCHITECTURAL SOFTWARE DESIGN

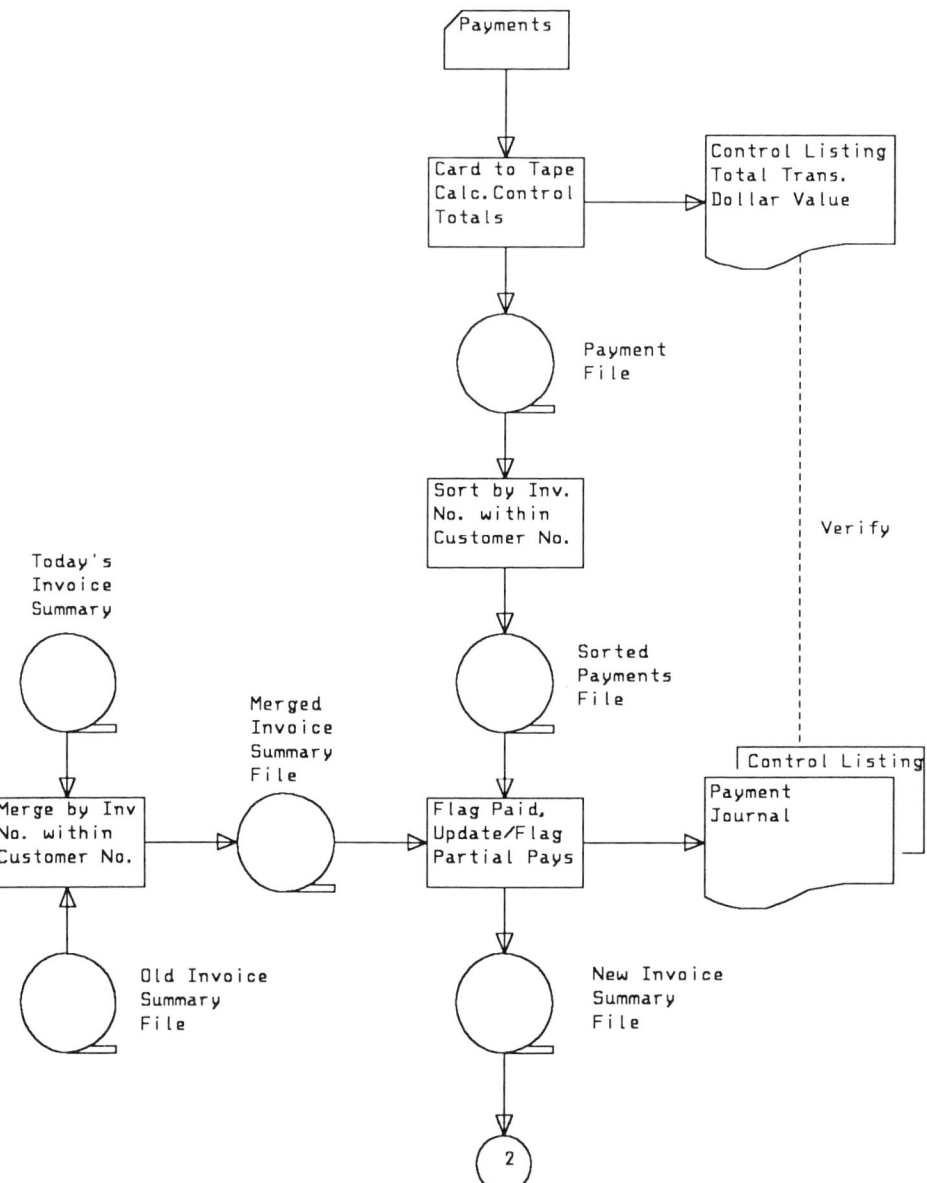

FIGURE 2.5 A traditional systems flowchart is a data flow diagram

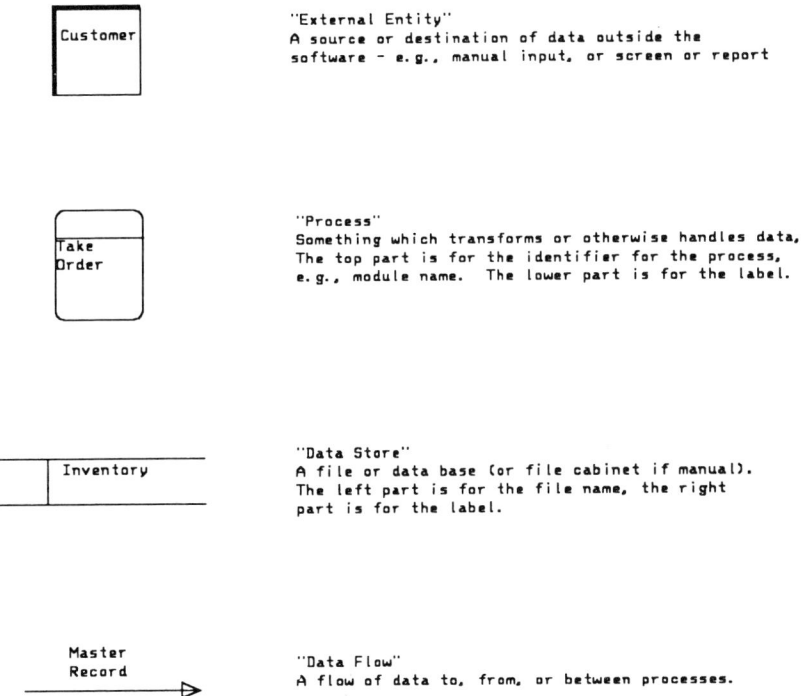

FIGURE 2.6 Data flow diagram symbols

on Structured Analysis are *Structured Analysis and System Specification* by Tom DeMarco (1978) and *Structured Systems Analysis: Tools and techniques* by Chris Gane and Trish Sarson (1979). Data flow diagrams were not new with the introduction of Structured Analysis. DeMarco (1978) points out that data flow diagrams have been used with software design since the 1940s. For example, a 'systems flowchart' (see Figure 2.5) is not really a flowchart at all, but, rather, a data flow diagram which shows the flow of data between steps in a job or jobs. Data flow diagrams also seem to arise naturally as people who have no special computer training draw pictures to describe flows of information – even if they have never seen or heard of a formal data flow diagram.

Gane and Sarson included a syntax for data flow diagrams which is commonly known as 'Gane and Sarson' syntax; the syntax in DeMarco's book is called the 'Yourdon syntax' (Yourdon being the publisher). While there are devotees of each of the common data flow diagram syntaxes, the Gane and Sarson notation (slightly modified) will be used in this book (see Figure 2.6). It provides for both the *identifier* of the object and a *label*, which is important for automating the design and development process (though some tools have added identifiers to the Yourdon syntax). In addition, the Gane and Sarson process symbols are rectangles, rather than circles, which allow designers to put more natural words in the symbol (with circles, designers tend to use a short–long–short combination of words to fit the circle). The original difficulty of drawing Gane and

22 ARCHITECTURAL SOFTWARE DESIGN

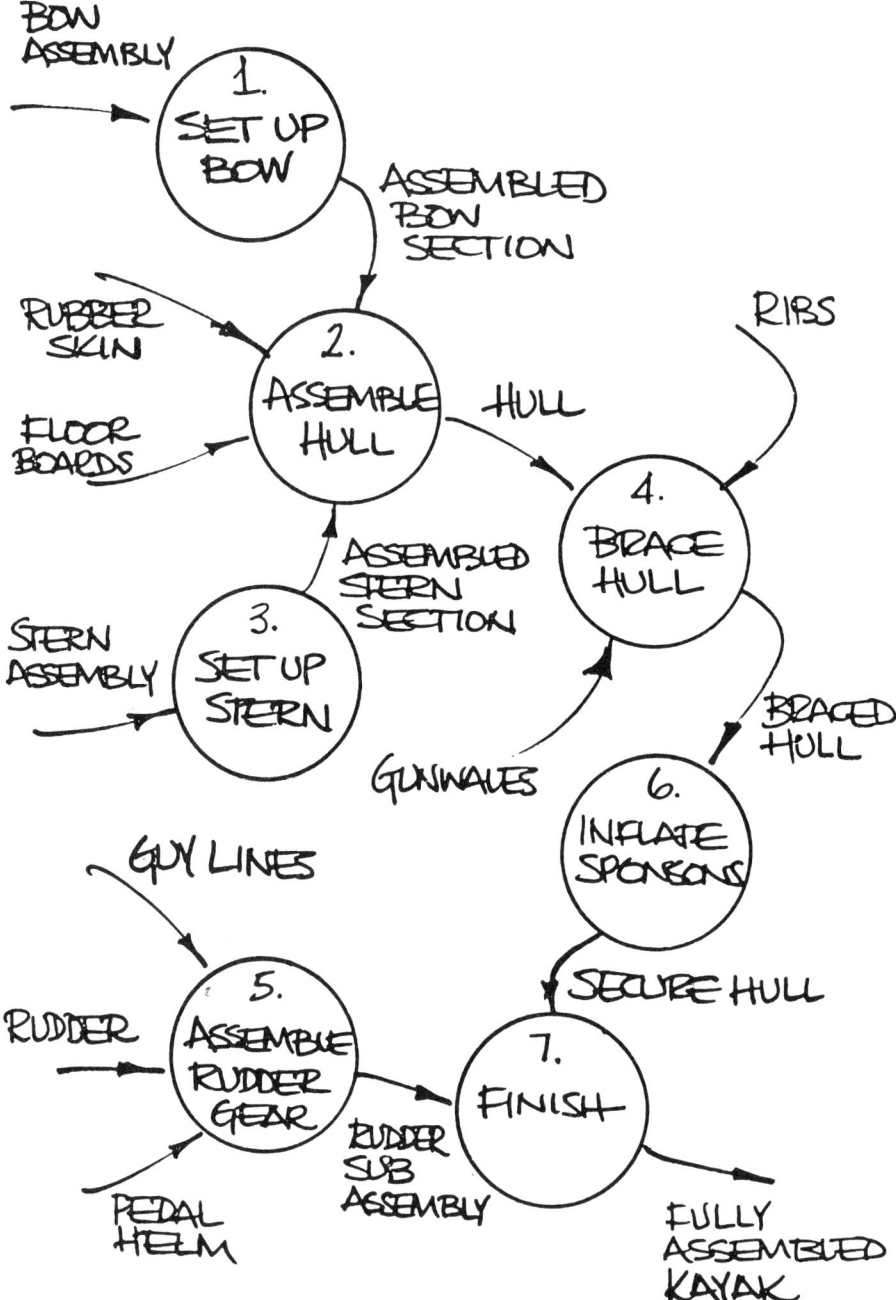

FIGURE 2.7 A diagram for constructing a Kleeper boat

Sarson's symbols (which have lines *within* a symbol and thus cannot be put on a template easily) is not a problem when using graphical tools. However, the differences between the Yourdon and the Gane and Sarson notations are so minor that the choice of which to use is largely a matter of individual preference. Information given below in this section and in Figures 2.6–2.14 are based on, or reprinted with permission from, *Structured Analysis and System Specification* (DeMarco 1978), which is also recommended for those readers who desire more detail than is included in the section below.

DeMarco illustrates the value of data flow diagrams versus the kind of system specifications and software design specifications that often result when attempting to use text to describe how multiple objects interrelate. The example includes instructions for assembling a folding boat and the diagram for this procedure is shown in Figure 2.7. A portion of the original text that prompted DeMarco to draw the diagram is included below.

Assembly Instructions for KLEEPER Folding Boats

1. Lay out hull in grass (or on carpet). Select a clean, level spot.
2. Take folded bow section (with red dot), lay it in grass, unfold 4 hinged gunwale boards. Kneel down, spread structure lightly with left hand near bow, place right hand on pullplate at *bottom* of hinged rib, and set up rib gently by pulling towards center of boat. Deckbar has a tongue-like fitting underneath which will connect with fitting on top of rib if you lift deckbar lightly, guide tongue to rib, press down on deckbar near bow to lock securely. Now lift whole bowsection using both arms wraparound style (to keep gunwales from flopping down) and slide into front of hull. Center seam of blue deck should rest on top of deckbar.
3. Take folded stern section (blue dot, 4 'horseshoes' attached), unfold 4 gunwales, set up rib by pulling on pullplate at *bottom* of rib. Deckbar locks to top of rib *from the side* by slipping a snaplock over a tongue attached to top of rib. . . .

The relationship of the steps is much easier to see using the diagram in Figure 2.7 than the preceding text. Not only does the reader of the text need to imagine the overall relationships of the steps to one another, those relationships are buried among a number of details that are generally unfamiliar to the reader. This mixing of relationship of the pieces with the details, especially unfamiliar details, makes understanding of both the relationships and the details difficult. A diagram allows the overall organization to be understood before attempting to understand the details. The diagram also allows the details to be grasped one group at a time while viewing the relationship that the group has to the whole. Another advantage of the diagram is that it can show several dimensions, while the text is necessarily one-dimensional – and the reader has to determine the other dimensions while trying to understand the details. Note that the diagram alone does not contain a description that is sufficiently complete for the boat to be assembled; details about each step are also necessary.

Arrows on a data flow diagram (as in Figure 2.8) show possible *flows of data*, rather than the *flow of control* that arrows represent on flowcharts (see Figure 2.9). For example, a chart that showed the possible flow of paperwork in an office would show data

24 ARCHITECTURAL SOFTWARE DESIGN

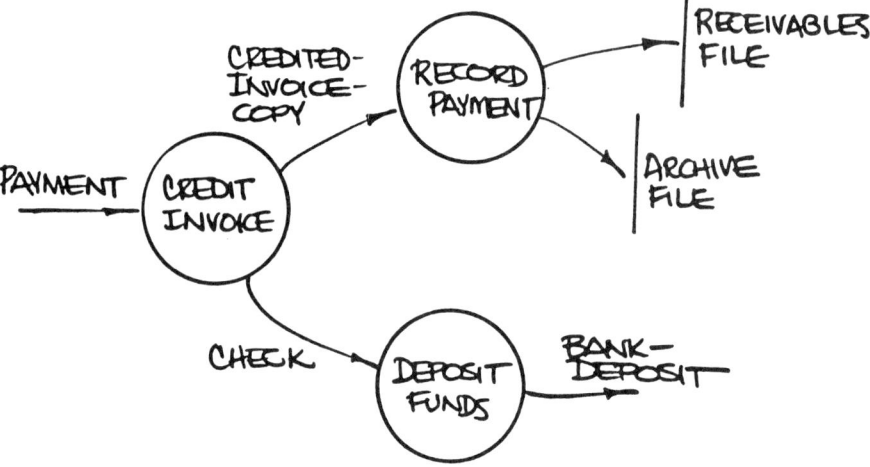

FIGURE 2.8 Sample data flow diagram

flows, not who worked for who or in what order people did the work. In general, one cannot tell by looking at a data flow diagram what is going to be executed or in which sequence, because that depends on which data are passed (as in an office). Any and all flows of data may leave a node in a data flow diagram before it has completed executing, whereas in a flowchart the arrow leaving means the process *has* completed its execution. Because flowcharts show flow of control, they include decisions and loops. Data flow diagrams, however, do not show loops of control – they are implicit. Each group of data tends to go through the diagram once, but nodes are still able to process the next group of data. The connections in a data flow diagram show the possible paths for the data but do not show whether or not data will be passed. When first drawing data flow diagrams, there may be a tendency to include the *control flow arrows* that are in flowcharts and that are inappropriate in data flow diagrams. Arrows connecting nodes in data flow diagrams should depict possible conduits for information flows and never a transfer of execution to the next node. A data flow diagram can represent manual or automated processes in the same diagram as well as relationships between manual and automated processes. Another value of a data flow diagram is its ability to show manual processes that can be automated later without having to change the diagrams. In addition, data flow diagrams can be understood easily by end-users and management.

There is an important distinction between data flow and global shared data. Although in both cases many integrands access the same data, with data flow only one integrand can access it at any one time. The 'flow' of data from one integrand to another is fundamentally a flow of 'ownership' (the data may or may not actually move – see Appendix A). With data flow, one integrand must give up access to the data in order to pass that data to the next integrand. This restriction makes it much easier to design with data flow than with integrands that share global data since it eliminates many of the concurrence issues inherent in asynchronous execution of integrands that can all access global common data simultaneously.

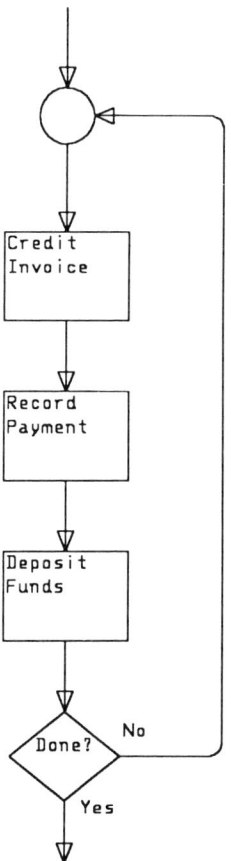

FIGURE 2.9 Sample flowchart

2.2.2 Leveling data flow diagrams

Figure 2.10 shows part of a leveled DFD set. The top of a leveled set of DFDs is called the *Context diagram*, and is the 'parent' of the next level of diagrams. There can be as many diagrams at the next level as there are nodes in the parent DFD (although there may be fewer if any of the nodes in the parent represent primitive processes). Each diagram on the second level describes the node that it represents in its parent diagram and can itself be a parent for third level diagrams that represent its nodes. There is no need for off-page connectors because each page is a complete diagram. Data flows that simply end on a diagram represent the flows shown connecting to the node on its parent diagram. Nodes are expanded as lower level diagrams until each node is a primitive process – one not described by a further data flow diagram.

26   ARCHITECTURAL SOFTWARE DESIGN

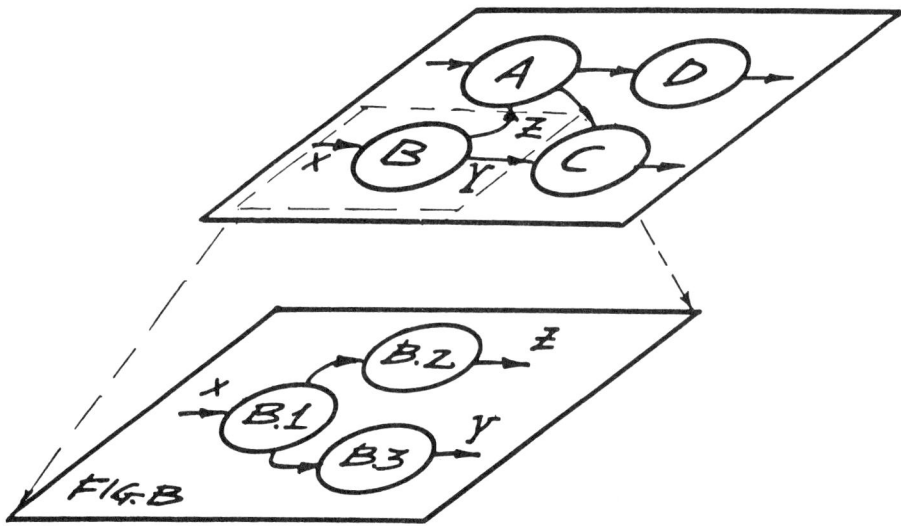

FIGURE 2.10 Leveled data flow diagrams

A node that has a lower level diagram expansion has no existence of its own, and is completely represented by its lower level diagram. The concept of *balancing* is that the lower level diagram has the same data coming into and going out of its boundaries (though not necessarily in the same flows) and has the same function as that depicted for the node at the higher level. DeMarco's rules for balancing are that all data entering a child diagram must also enter the associated node on the parent diagram. Outputs from the child diagram must also exist as outputs from the associated node on the parent, with one exception: trivial rejects (reject paths that require no revision of state information) need not be balanced between parent and child.

The diagrams in Figure 2.11 are balanced because the flows in and out of diagram 4 are the same as for node 4 in the parent diagram. They would still be in balance if diagram 4 had a trivial reject data flow. However, the diagrams in Figure 2.12 are not balanced because the child diagram, which is the expansion of node 2, does not have an input data flow called M, shown entering node 2 of the parent diagram, and has a flow S, not shown leaving node 2 of the parent diagram. The diagrams in Figure 2.13 are balanced *if* the flow 'Order' into node 6 of the parent diagram is a combination of only the flows into the child diagram, which are labeled 'Authorization', 'Order-Coupon', and 'Payment'.

DeMarco's rule for showing data stores in hierarchies of data flow diagrams is to show a data store at the first level that it is used by two or more modules. Figure 2.14 shows two diagrams that are balanced. The file ALPHA is referenced by processes on the child diagram and thus shows up there. ALPHA is not referenced by other processes on the parent diagram and thus is extraneous to showing the connections between those processes. The same is true of flow XXX, which shows up on the child diagram but is not relevant to the parent diagram.

STRUCTURED ANALYSIS 27

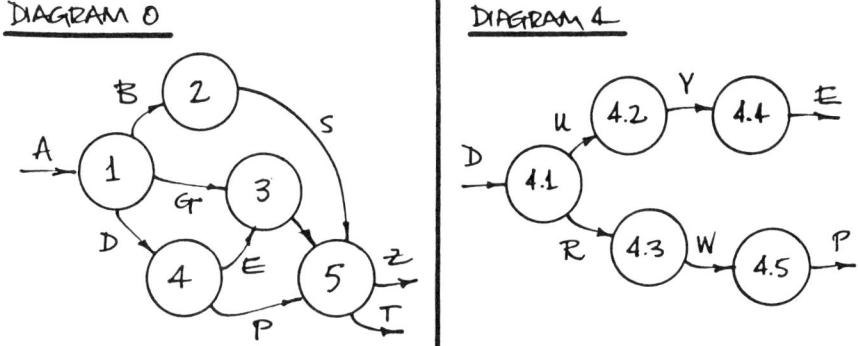

FIGURE 2.11 Balanced data flow diagrams

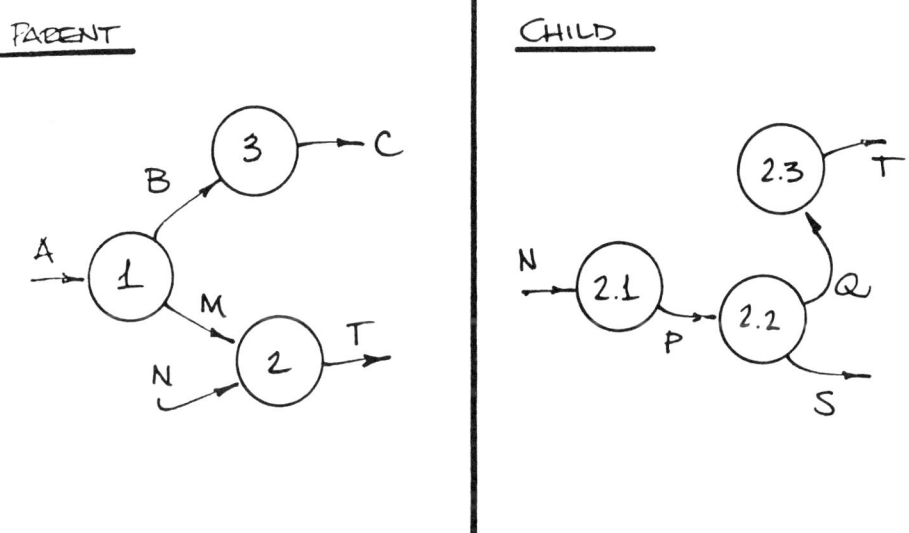

FIGURE 2.12 Unbalanced data flow diagrams

Leveling data flow diagrams is important for diagrams with more than a few nodes. Leveling allows each of the diagrams to be captured on a page and allows the entire set of diagrams to be understood one page at a time. There is no need to view another page in order to get the whole description; it is all there together. Managers can get an overview of the system by looking only at the top levels of the diagram, and developers can focus only on those parts of current interest.

28   ARCHITECTURAL SOFTWARE DESIGN

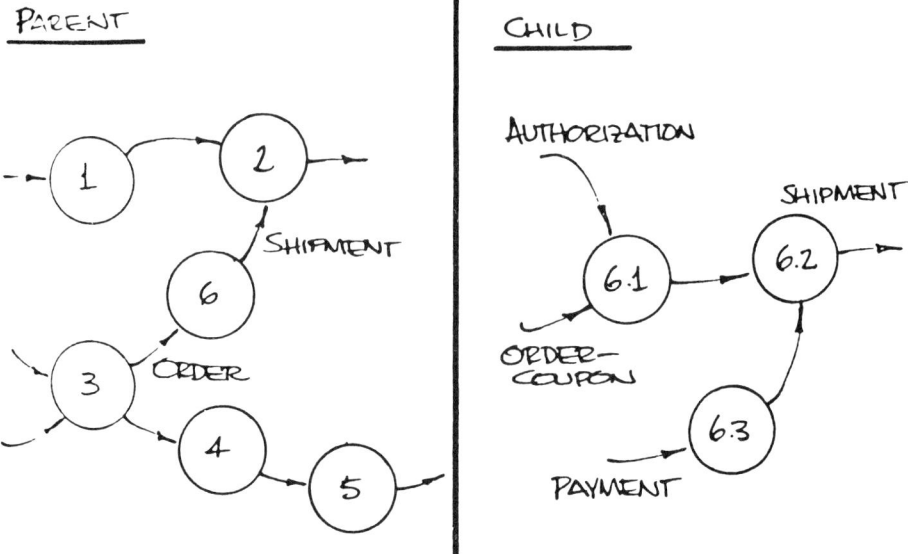

FIGURE 2.13 Balanced data flow diagrams

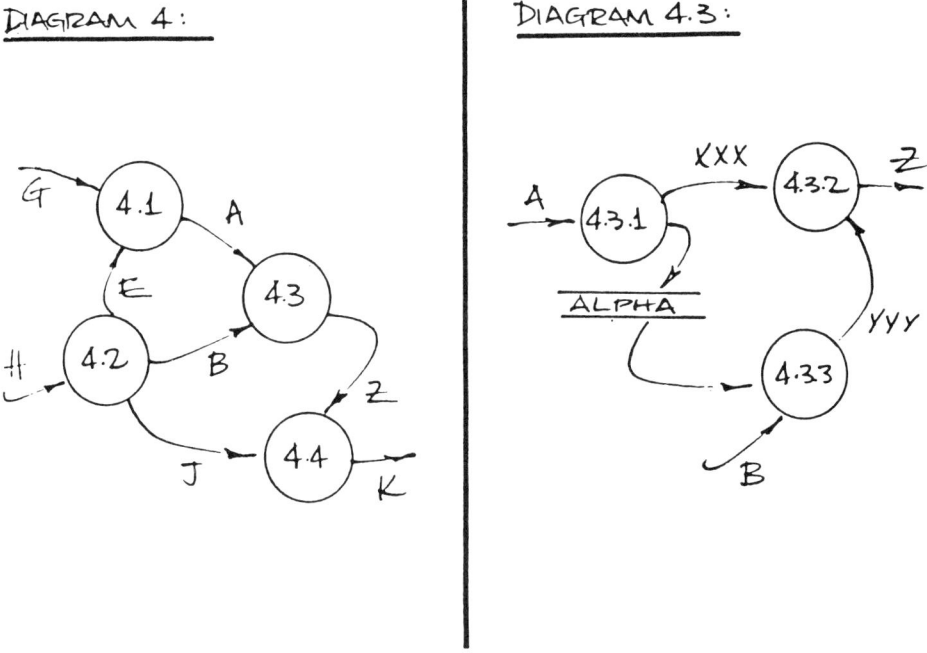

FIGURE 2.14 Local files in data flow diagrams

2.2.3 Comments on structured analysis

DeMarco's book (along with Gane and Sarson's) popularized the concept of using data flow diagrams for requirements analysis and then, later, software design. Structured Analysis has been the basis for a number of other methods that include data flow diagrams, such as Essential Systems Analysis and the Ward–Mellor method (discussed in this chapter below). Those methods rely on the descriptions of data flow diagrams in both books. Data flow diagrams will become even more important as businesses build distributed applications, since data flow diagrams can depict the various parts of the application running asynchronously and sending messages. Connecting integrands with data flows rather than with calls or global data can greatly improve the ability to reuse code (see 'Code Reuse', Section 5.3). The concepts of designing objects connected by data flows can also be used to help design systems of objects that pass messages, as with Object-Oriented programming (see 'Object-Oriented', Section 5.6). Thus it is advantageous to know and understand data flow diagrams and how to design with them (see 'Essential Systems Analysis', next in this chapter). *Modern Structured Analysis* by Ed Yourdon (1988) contains information on using data flow diagrams with other techniques in the life cycle.

DeMarco labels nodes with a numeric schema that denotes their position in the hierarchy (see Figure 2.11 for an example), and other texts have recommended the same. This recommendation is a step backwards; the computer software industry moved from machine language to assembler partly so that meaningful textual names could replace numeric labels for instructions and data. Using numeric names to denote a position in the (current) hierarchy would also mean that changes to the hierarchy would require changes to names of modules and thus to call statements in their callers. In addition, since good functional designs usually result in a number of modules being reused more than once within that same hierarchy, numeric names will either require different names for the same module or will prevent any single name from reflecting the places it occupies in the hierarchy. Giving modules numeric names also loses a chance to help describe a component's function as a textual name could.

Since the nodes in data flow diagrams represent functions, they should be labeled with a verb and, when possible, the object of that verb. For example, good names for functional nodes include: 'Read Order Record', 'Validate Change Transaction', and 'Write Updated Master Record'. Generic nouns such as 'Record', are clearer if they are qualified; 'Update Sales Record' is clearer than 'Update Record' (which is clearer than 'Update'). The present imperative form of the verb is more dynamic and easier to grasp quickly, e.g. 'Edit Input Data' is easier to work with than 'Data Editing' or 'Data Edit'. The arrows in data flow diagrams represent a flow of data. Thus they should be labeled with modified nouns such as 'Transaction Record', 'Updated Master', and 'New Order'. Check that the data that is output from a node is consistent with the function of that node (e.g. a 'Valid Order' may be created by a node named 'Validate Order', but is unlikely to be produced by a node named 'Print Histogram').

Another of DeMarco's suggestions, which has seldom been used and which has been intentionally avoided here, is his suggestion to annotate the diagrams with the conditions for receiving data streams (e.g. AND, OR, EXCLUSIVE OR conditions). Since such conditions will be implemented *inside* each module, putting them on the diagram duplicates this information. Such conditions are also details that are easier to decide when defining or designing the individual modules.

2.3 ESSENTIAL SYSTEMS ANALYSIS

Stephen McMenamin and John Palmer, in their book *Essential Systems Analysis* (1984), improve on the approaches expressed earlier by DeMarco (who also wrote the introduction to it) and Gane and Sarson. With Essential Systems Analysis, the designer first describes the *essence* of a system (the reason for its existence) and then an *incarnation* (specific implementation) of it. The distinction between the essence and the incarnation of the system is described in more detail below. McMenamin and Palmer also include a method for partitioning the system, called 'event-partitioning', and show how to use data flow diagrams to document the system during design activities. (McMenamin and Palmer assume that designers understand the basic concepts of Structured Analysis and data flow diagrams – see Section 2.2.) The information given below and all quotes in this section, as well as Figures 2.15–2.24, are based on, or reprinted with permission from, *Essential Systems Analysis* (but using the Gane and Sarson notation for the diagrams). *Essential Systems Analysis* is recommended for those who desire an in-depth understanding of how to design systems using data flow diagrams.

2.3.1 Essence

One way to identify the *essence* of a system is to first ask the question: 'What would the system need to have even if it were implemented with perfect technology?' The technology used to implement a software system can be viewed as consisting of two parts: the processor, which executes the instructions, and a container, which stores data and supplies that data to the processor. A perfect system would have both a perfect processor and a perfect container. The processor would be infinitely fast, cost nothing, and never fail. The container could hold an infinite amount of data, be able to access anything within it instantly and in any order, and would also cost nothing, and never make a mistake.

> *Essential activities* are all the tasks that the system would have to perform even if you could implement it using perfect technology.

A payroll system will pay employees even if implemented on a perfect computer, but would not have to keep an audit trail because it could not make, or be caused to make, errors in performing its tasks.

> *Essential memory* consists of the data that the system would have to remember if all it did was carry out the essential activities.

For example, information about total year-to-date pay must be kept on any payroll system that has to report such data to the employee or governmental authorities.

> 'The *essence* of the system consists of the essential activities and the essential memory.'

The essence of the system corresponds to the requirements for the system's implementation – those things that the system must accomplish regardless of how it is implemented. The essence of the system will not include *all* the requirements for a system, since some of those requirements would not be necessary if the implementation technology were perfect and could not be corrupted (such as an audit trail). Also, when identifying the essence, the concepts of a perfect system are applied only to the implementation of the system being designed, not to the world at large or to other systems with which this system has to interface. Essential activities may be required in order to compensate for imperfections in the real world. For example, in an order-processing system, updating available quantities when goods spoil or are lost are valid essential activities.

2.3.2 Incarnation

The implementation of a specific design in the real world, using real technology, is the *incarnation* of the system. The incarnation is something one can see, feel and touch, while the essence is a set of ideas. The incarnation includes implementation of the essential activities and essential memory plus additional activities and memory needed because the implementation systems are not perfect. It includes the software, hardware, people, communication equipment, printers, paper, etc. People working, computers executing programs, job control language, terminals dispensing money and auditors checking the audit trails are all part of the incarnation of the system. The incarnation is implemented with real computers and people who execute the activities. The incarnation of the system's memory is all the information needed by the activities in the implemented system whether stored in people's memories, on paper or in magnetic form in the computer system. Conversely, the essence of the system will not contain elements that exist only because of a specific implementation or are included in an implementation to compensate for having to implement the system on imperfect technology. Such considerations have to do with cost, finite capacity, performance and the various benefits of alternative implementation technologies.

2.3.3 Essential activities

Essential activities are initiated by an event (e.g. the arrival of a transaction or the time of day), consist of a set of planned responses to that event and usually access essential memory. Two kinds of essential activities can be distinguished – fundamental activities and custodial activities:

32 ARCHITECTURAL SOFTWARE DESIGN

1. Fundamental activities help to justify the existence of the system.
2. Custodial activities acquire and store (in the system's essential memory) information needed by the fundamental activities; they also update the stored information so that it remains correct.

In an order-processing system, fundamental activities include checking for quantities in stock, pricing orders and printing invoices. In a payroll system, such as the one shown in Figure 2.15, one purpose of the system is to pay the employees; thus producing checks is a fundamental activity. The activities that keep track of employees' time, salary, and deductions are performed in order to be able to pay the employees, not because the organization needs that information independently of its use for paying employees; they are thus not fundamental activities. In a real-time system such as an automobile speed control, fundamental activities include changing the position of the throttle and releasing the throttle if the driver disengages the control.

Custodial activities are essential activities and are therefore necessary even if the system were implemented with perfect technology. As with all essential activities, they are initiated by an event and consist of planned responses to that event. However, unlike fundamental activities, their responses update essential memory rather than respond to the world beyond the system. For an order-processing system, custodial activities include changing the recorded stock quantity as goods are received and shipped, updating prices, and recording information about new products. For a payroll system, custodial activities include keeping track of employees' salary, time, and deductions (as indicated above and shown in Figure 2.16).

In practice, activities are seldom either purely fundamental or custodial, but, rather, are *compound activities*, which include both fundamental and custodial actions. This is especially true at the higher levels of abstraction. As the essential activities are expanded to lower and lower levels of detail, the distinction between fundamental and custodial activities often becomes more visible. However, at any level, the characteristics that define either the fundamental or custodial types of essential activities help to identify the essential activities of the system.

2.3.4 Essential memory

A fundamental activity can seldom produce its planned responses using only the information contained in the event which initiates that activity (such as the arrival of an order or a time card). All external information gathered by essential activities at the time of the initiating event are, by definition, part of the stimulus to an essential activity. However, fundamental activities usually need information that has been made available to the system earlier, and then stored, in order to accomplish their tasks. *Essential memory* is the set of all data elements which are required by the system's fundamental activities and which must be remembered by the system.

In the payroll example, in order to write a paycheck, the system needs information about an employee's rate of pay, total pay this year, total deductions this year, withholding status and address. This information is put into essential memory and kept

ESSENTIAL SYSTEMS ANALYSIS   33

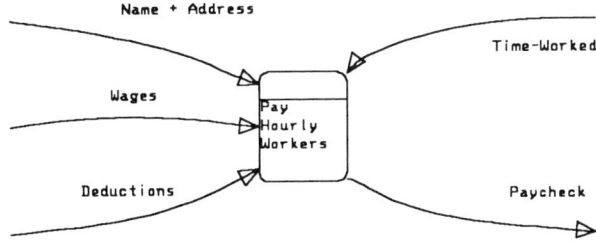

FIGURE 2.15 Fundamental activity of a payroll system

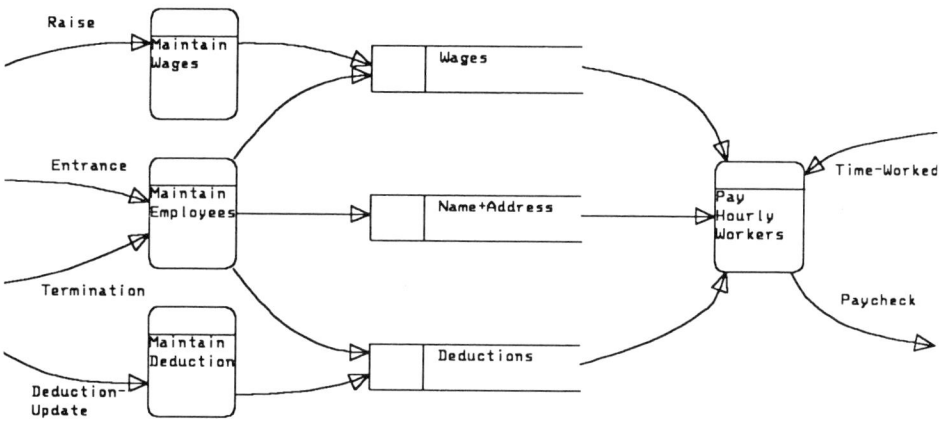

FIGURE 2.16 Custodial activities of a payroll system

up to date by custodial (or compound) activities so that it is available when needed by fundamental activities. Essential memory for the 'produce paycheck' activity does not include the employee's name and hours worked since they are part of the stimulus for writing weekly payroll checks. (The activity that writes pay checks may update essential memory with name and hours worked, however.) Data in the essential memory includes data from outside, or produced by, the system that must be stored for use by the essential activities. The essential memory also contains information that supports how the essential activities need to access data. For example, mailings may have to be printed in zip code order to satisfy postal regulations; reports to the government may have to be in social security number order; and internal summary reports for departmental budgeting purposes may have to be grouped by department. Essential memory is depicted as one or more normal data stores on data flow diagrams, as shown in Figure 2.17, which shows the essential memory for a 'Pay Hourly Workers' system. Each data store represents a subset of the essential memory.

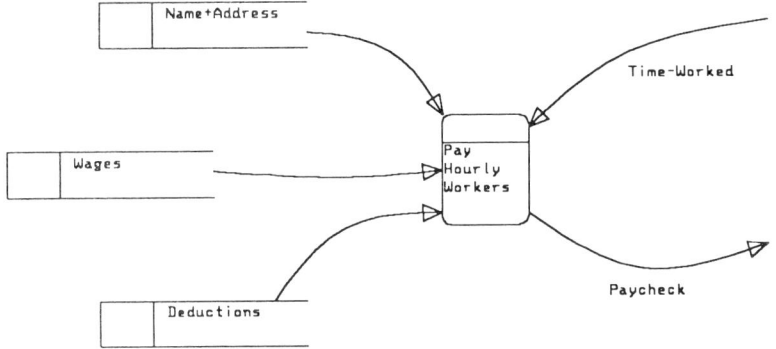

FIGURE 2.17 Essential memory of a payroll system

2.3.5 Finding the essence

Often the essence of a new system is based on the capabilities of an existing system, which may be manual, automated, or a combination of both. In any case, there are six characteristics that make finding the essence of an existing system difficult:

1. Fragmentation.
2. Conglomeration.
3. Extraneousness.
4. Redundancy.
5. Convolution.
6. Vastness.

Systems are almost always *fragmented* because it is difficult for all parts of the system to exist in exactly the same place – in fact, this is impossible if those activities are manual. Different activities may take place at different locations, even in a system that contains only one fundamental activity, such as 'Produce Cars'. Activities in a system may be in close proximity, such as on the same shop floor, or widely distributed in various geographical locations. Conveyor belts are often needed to move products from one activity to the next. Activities may take place in several computers in the same room or in remote locations connected by communication lines. The choice of a particular fragmentation is often due to the imperfections of the technology rather than being related to the essence of the system. Fragmentation hides the essence of a system in the same way that separating a jigsaw puzzle into its pieces hides the puzzle's original picture. The challenge for the designer is to gain sufficient understanding of the fragmented system so that a picture of the essence of the entire system emerges. Identification of nonessential activities that exist because of fragmentation or because of other characteristics described below can help to reduce the complexity of understanding the system and clarify the system's essence.

Conglomeration is the opposite of fragmentation. A conglomerate is formed when two or more disparate elements are merged, as happens when several previously unrelated companies organize into a 'conglomerate'. Conglomeration can occur with software systems when activities from unrelated systems are combined on the same processor, or unrelated pieces of essential memory are stored in the same file or segment of a data base. For example, order processing and production control may be executed on the same processor, and that processor may execute other systems as well. A back-order data base could contain the sales representative's name (to facilitate communication with the customer in case of further delays).

Data and activities that exist to compensate for the limitations of imperfect technology are *extraneous* and are not part of the system's essence. Two common types of extraneous activities and data are:

1. Transportation-related activities and data.
2. Administrative activities and data.

If the system were perfect and implemented on a single processor that executed all the essential activities, then there would be no need for the clerks who are part of the system to enter data into the computer, send data from one clerk to another or from one processor to another, or change the form or the medium on which the data are stored. Nor would it be necessary to edit data entered by clerks for errors or produce those administrative reports that assure that the system is performing correctly, because if the system were perfect, then all its parts, including the clerks, would be perfect. Conversely, identifying data entry, editing, data movement and administrative activities can also help to point to the essence of a system because the essence is the answer to the questions: 'Why are these activities being performed?' 'Where is the entered data going?' and 'What is it that administrative reports assure is being performed correctly?' Note that receiving data from outside the system and checking that data for correctness are essential activities, and are often done by people. However, those processes are distinct from both entry of data into the computer by clerks and checking for their data entry errors.

Systems often contain *redundant* components, e.g. backup computers, more than one clerk in a store, the same data stored in multiple files or data bases and the same report going to more than one person. The difficulty is in distinguishing those redundancies due to imperfect technology from those that carry out essential activities. Essential activities that appear redundant may, in fact, actually accomplish different tasks using the same functional capability. For example, the same on-line text-editor may be used as a tool to help with three different essential activities: creating letters, creating documentation, and creating source code. Activities can still be essential activities even though they make redundant use of the same functional capabilities. Redundancies that are due to imperfect technology, however, are not part of the essence of the system.

The objective in many puzzles, video games, and road rallies is to reach a goal using intentionally cryptic, convoluted clues. While the procedures of a software system should ideally be clear, even essential procedures may need to be more *convoluted* than would be necessary on a perfect system. Examples of essential activities that are convoluted to compensate for imperfect systems include scanning all or part of a file to determine a total, maximum, or minimum amount; sorting data; and updating indices used to access data in various orders. Convolution of activities tends to hide the essence of a system, which is to obtain and use the information.

One of the more difficult characteristics that can hide the essence of a system is *vastness* – the basic size of the system. There are systems, such as cities, that are so large that it is practically impossible for one person ever to understand all of the city in detail. The vastness can be geographic, in that the system is distributed in many locations, even spanning the globe; or it can be vast in terms of the number of lines of code, which can be hundreds of thousands or even millions. Though the essence may be small, the size of the incarnation can discourage attempts to discover it.

Ward and Mellor (1985) in *Structured Development for Real-Time Systems* point out the following four additional things that can be ignored when looking for the essence in an existing system:

1. Changes in the form of data – if the system changes the format of data, but the data keeps the same values, those translations are not part of the system's essence.
2. Implementation technology verification – because of the possibility of errors or failures, the system may validate data, especially when it is received from another node. This checking may be important, but it is part of the incarnation.
3. Internally imposed time delays – essential memory is necessary to store data needed by the system in order to handle a later external stimulus. However, storage or buffering used simply to coordinate processing by various components within the system from the *same* external stimulus is not part of the system's essence but is due to the implementation technology.
4. Implementation organizations of data – organizations other than that of the essential model are part of the incarnation.

2.3.6 Modeling the system

The recommended approach to modeling the system is to model the essence of the proposed system first. The model of the essence is partitioned in order to be more easily understood – partitioning both essential activities and essential memory (see below). Once a particular incarnation of the system's essence is chosen, custodial activities are added to the essential model. The model should show the important characteristics while allowing unimportant details to be ignored and deferred to later activities. The model should show:

1. Events from outside the system that require response, such as the entering of a time card.
2. Essential activities that respond to those specific events, such as the printing of the weekly paycheck.
3. The essential memory that the system needs to support these activities, such as the record of the yearly totals of pay and deductions.
4. Interactions within essential activities, and between essential activities and essential memory, such as how the activity that calculates deductions also adds to the year-to-date total of deductions.

ESSENTIAL SYSTEMS ANALYSIS 37

Data flow diagrams are used to depict activities (nodes), essential memory (data stores), and interactions among activities and between the system and its environment (arrows). Entity–relationship diagrams (see Chapter 4) can depict essential memory, and data dictionary definitions can specify the details of interactions and of essential memory. Primitive activities can be described with Structured English (see 'Structured Natural Language', Section 3.3) or with other integrand specification approaches, such as those in Chapter 3. For more on building the essential and incarnation models, see the topic 'Build both essential and implementation models' in Section 2.4.5.

2.3.7 Event-partitioning

Event-partitioning segments the diagrams based on events. Each diagram contains essential activities only, and each activity contains the system's *entire* planned response to a single event. To be properly event-partitioned, two criteria must be satisfied, as follows:

1. Each essential activity must contain all the actions that would result from a single event if the system were perfect.
2. The system *must become idle* after the actions are performed (until the same or another event occurs).

An example of a properly event-partitioned system is given in Figure 2.18, which shows

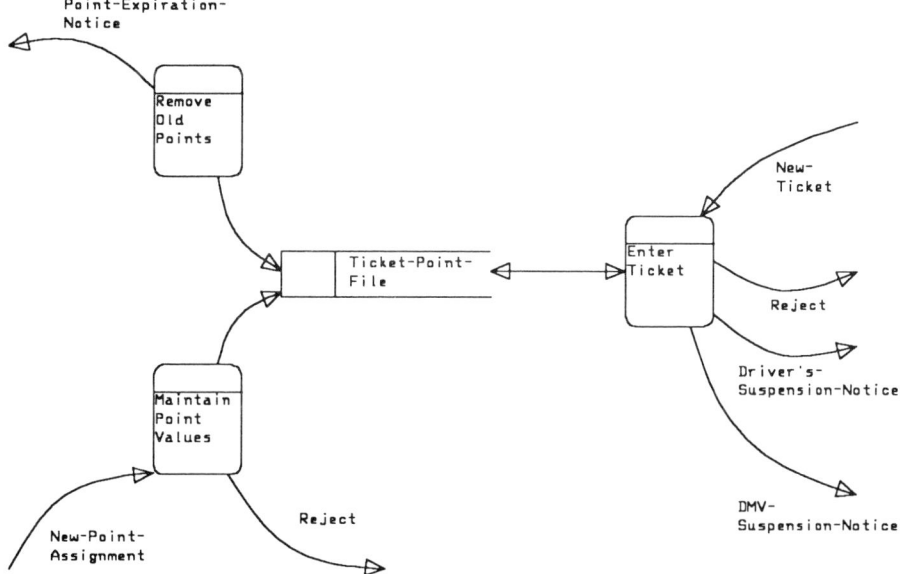

FIGURE 2.18 Event-partitioned DFD for part of the Traffic Violations system

38   ARCHITECTURAL SOFTWARE DESIGN

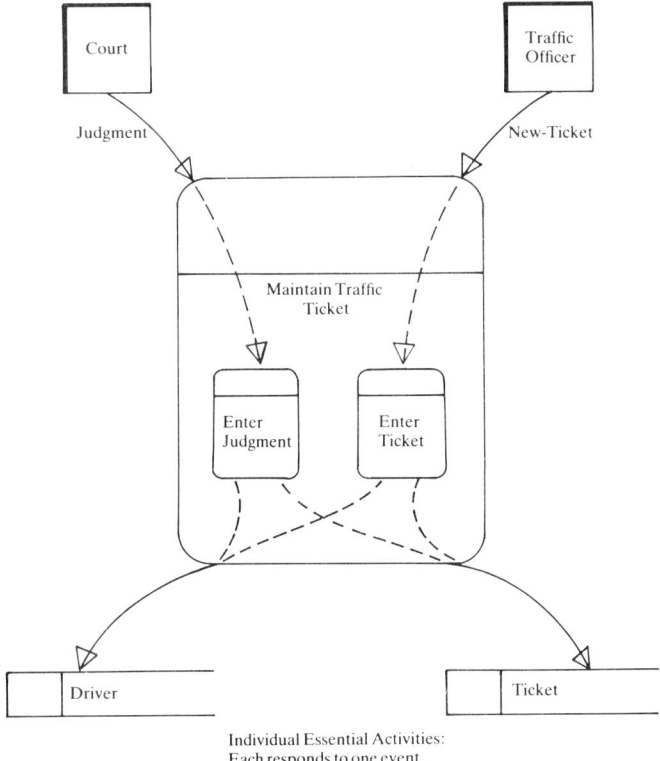

FIGURE 2.19 Poorly partitioned essential activity

part of the essence of a Traffic Violations system. To see that each process represents the system's entire planned response to a single event, compare it with the following list of events:

1. A traffic offer submits a new ticket for a traffic violation.
2. The Motor Vehicle Department establishes new point values for violations.
3. It is time to remove old points.

However, the diagram in Figure 2.19 is not properly partitioned because it contains the system's responses to two events from outside the system being modeled: 'Traffic Officer Submits Traffic Ticket' and 'Court Issues Judgment.' The diagram in Figure 2.20 has also been improperly partitioned. Since the 'Re-order Stock' activity has no input event, it would appear to respond to a temporal event. However, re-ordering of stock occurs when the inventory drops below the re-order point, which is not time-related, but, rather, results from some 'Material-Request' event. The response of a system to a 'Material-Request' may be to order more stock, i.e. the system does not always become idle with just a 'Material-Shipment'. Thus 'Re-order Stock' must be part of the same activity as

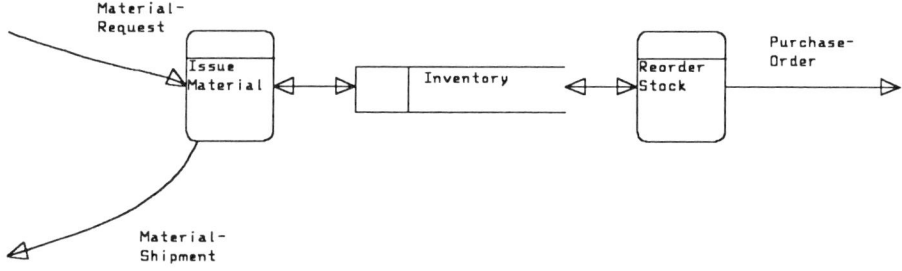

FIGURE 2.20 Poorly partitioned essential activity: one response

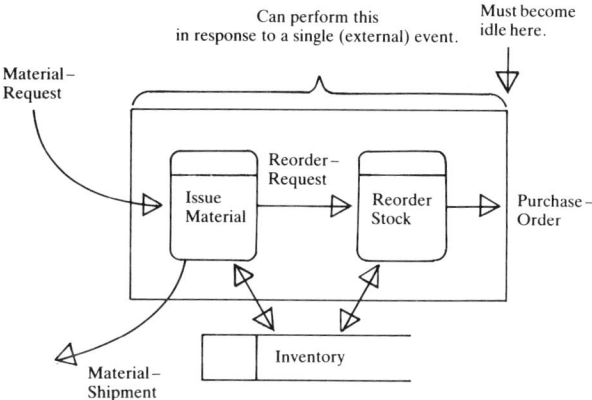

FIGURE 2.21 Correctly partitioned essential activity

'Material-Shipment' in order for the system to be properly event-partitioned. Figure 2.21 shows a properly partitioned essential activity because it contains all the actions that can result from a 'Material-Request' (on a perfect system).

While a properly event-partitioned system has essential activities only, these include both fundamental and custodial activities. Since each process in a properly event-partitioned system contains all the essential actions that can arise from a given event, the outputs of such processes are merely system responses and updates to essential memory. Thus the only connections or flows between the event-partitioned processes are via essential memory, as depicted in Figure 2.22. Immediate communications between subactivities must occur within the activity. Otherwise, another process could be triggered by an event, which would mean that the system was not properly partitioned. Conversely, the data that are to be communicated between essential processes are stored in essential memory. That storing allows for a time delay until the next activity uses the

40 ARCHITECTURAL SOFTWARE DESIGN

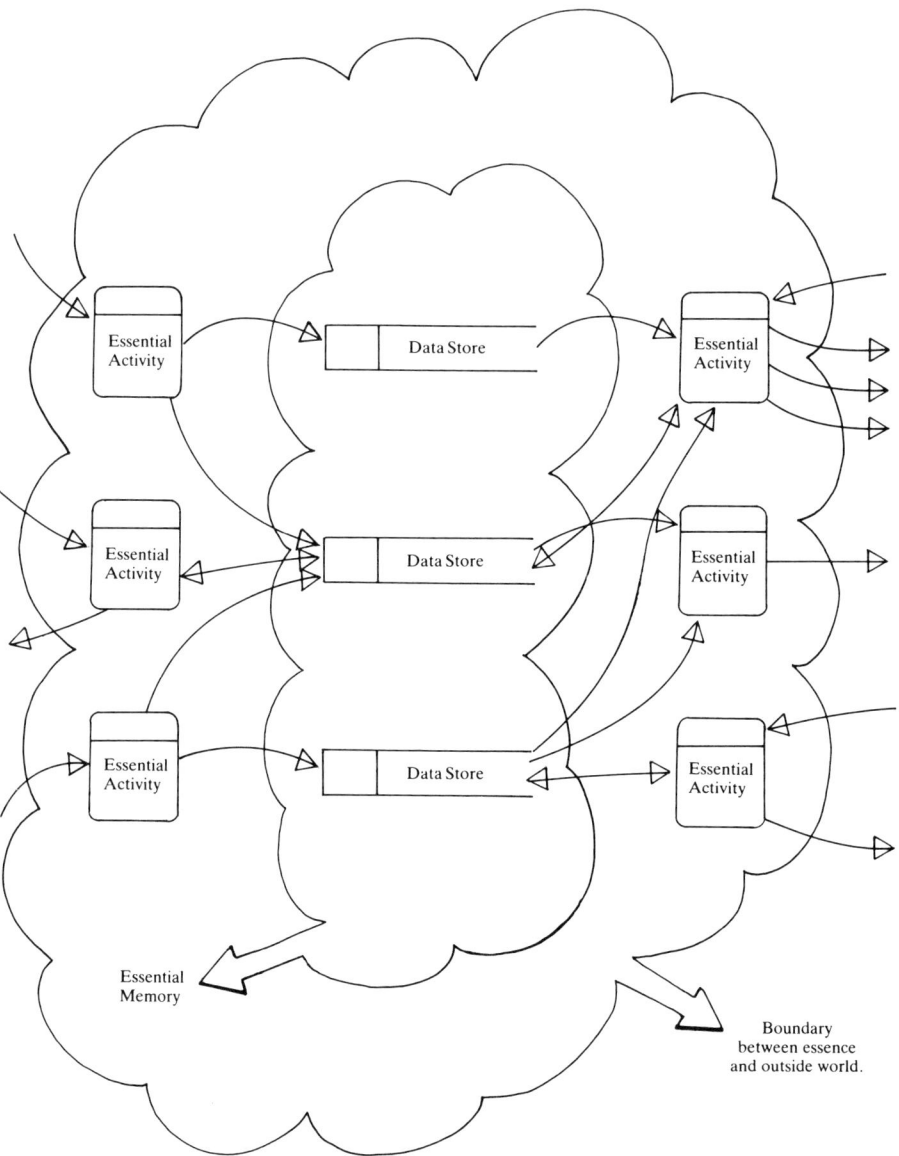

FIGURE 2.22 An event-partitioned DFD

information left in essential memory (when the proper event triggers that activity). Once the system has been properly event-partitioned at the high levels, the individual processes are expanded to lower levels of data flow diagrams that show the interactions among the subactivities. The result is properly partitioned if, at the top levels, all actions resulting from an event are in the same essential activity.

Event-partitioning is a way to view parts of a process that must be grouped in any design in order for the system to perform correctly. In the example in Figure 2.20, until the 'Re-order Stock' activity is part of the same activity as 'Material-Shipment' (i.e. 'Re-order Stock' can be executed by 'Material-Shipment' without a further external stimulus to the system), any design of the system will contain an error. Designs could combine essential activities without causing an error, but would not achieve the reduction of complexity that could be achieved through further decomposition into single essential activities. For systems that go idle after processing external stimuli, there is always a way to event-partition the design. Event-partitioning can also be applied to systems that do not go idle after each transaction, such as an airline traffic control system, if there are additional actions the system performs as the result of external stimuli. If so, a single activity would contain all the *additional* actions that the system must perform in response to each external stimulus.

2.3.8 Object-partitioning

Essential memory should also be partitioned. Such partitioning schemes lie in the field of data modeling and data base design (see Chapter 4). However, McMenamin and Palmer recommend a way to partition the essential memory with a technique which they call *object-partitioning*, which consists of the following four steps:

1. List the essential memory data elements. For a car rental agency, possible essential memory elements are shown in the 'preliminary step' box of Figure 2.23.
2. Identify objects outside the system that the elements describe, as shown in 'Step 1' of Figure 2.23 for the car rental agency.
3. Group the elements with the object they describe, as with 'Step 2' of Figure 2.23.
4. Assign to each group of elements the name of the object they describe, see 'Step 3' in Figure 2.23.

Figure 2.24 shows a result of another object-partitioning, this time for a student registration system – elements in that diagram are associated with their real-world objects and are shared among various essential activities. Object-partitioning does not result in elements each being stored in a different file or segment of a data base, nor does object-partitioning occur as a result of event-partitioning (because essential memory is used for communication among separate essential activities). Singular names are recommended for data stores as in Figure 2.24 (while those stores, of course, hold many different records). Readers interested in more detail about object-partitioning are referred to McMenamin and Palmer (1984).

Preliminary step *Essential Memory Data Elements:* Mileage Make-Of-Car Renter-Name Renter-Address Automobile-ID Driver's-License-Number Credit-Card-Number Model-Year	**Step 1** *Objects:* Automobile Renter
Step 2 *Groups:* Automobile-ID, Mileage, Model-Year, Make-Of-Car Renter-Name, Driver's-License- Number, Credit-Card-Number, Renter-Address	**Step 3** *Automobile:* Automobile-ID, Mileage, Model-Year, Make-Of-Car *Renter:* Renter-Name, Driver's-License- Number, Credit-Card-Number, Renter-Address

FIGURE 2.23 Car Rental example of object-partitioning

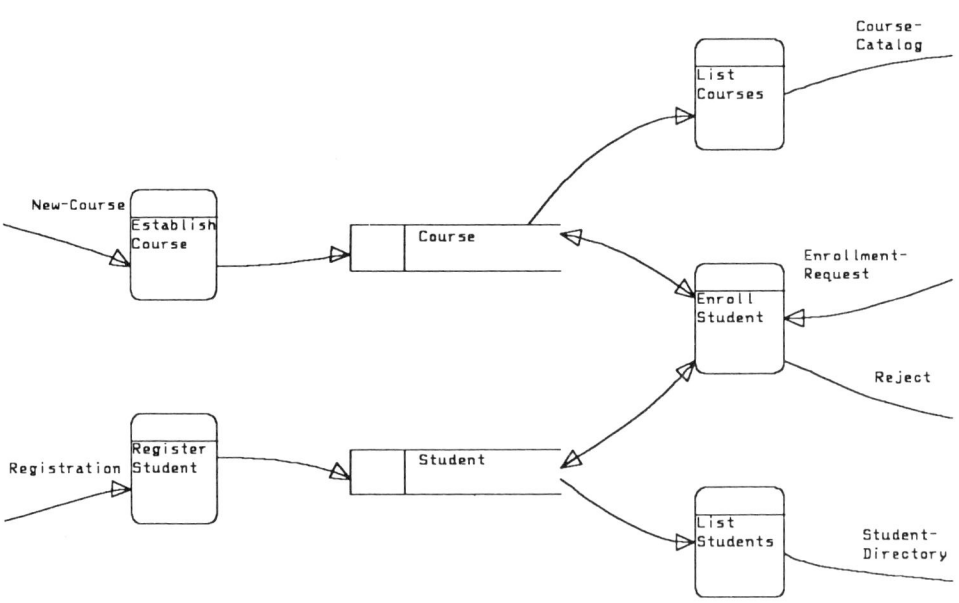

FIGURE 2.24 Object-partitioning of essential memory data stores

2.3.9 Designing the incarnation

The objective is not just to understand the system that would run if we had perfect technology, but to design a real system that runs on existing technology with its speed, storage, cost, and other real constraints. The purpose of identifying the essential activities first is to allow the essence to be understood independently of a particular implementation. Then, the constraints of the intended system implementation are considered and design choices made. To design the incarnation of a system that works even though the technology is necessarily imperfect, several additional factors are considered that are intentionally excluded during the study of the essence of the system. Four categories of such factors are as follows:

1. Cost.
2. Capacity.
3. Capabilities.
4. Fallibility.

The hardware, software, training, human activities, maintenance, etc., of the system being developed are not free – the benefits of any system should be weighed against cost. First, the *cost* of these resources is a valid and important criterion to be considered and properly balanced against other criteria, such as the functional content of the system, in order to produce the best design. Second, all real systems have a finite *capacity* – a limit on how much work the system can perform and how much data it can store. More important, work takes time, which can reduce productivity for the user of the software. Thus performance is also a valid consideration to be balanced against other objectives. Third, the *capabilities* of any technology are limited. As desirable as it might seem to have systems that are equally good at everything, this choice is not available to designers. In addition, capabilities usually vary with the cost of an implementation, which then affects the incarnation chosen. Fourth, incarnations are *fallible* – they break down, make mistakes, and commit crimes (or are used to commit crimes). Thus systems need override and correction features as well as security capabilities. For example, one payroll system was designed to produce checks automatically on the fifteenth and last days of the month. The first time the computer was down on payday, it was discovered that the system would *not* produce checks on any other day. Such capabilities can make up as much as half or even more of the incarnation of a system.

2.3.10 Comments on Essential Systems Analysis

The concepts in Essential Systems Analysis are good improvements to the base of Structured Analysis laid earlier by DeMarco and by Gane and Sarson. The concept of 'essence' replaces the earlier recommendations of Gane and Sarson (1979) for describing the 'current physical', 'current logical', 'future logical', and 'future physical', which never worked well. Many people wasted time creating diagrams that turned out to be unnecessary, and argued about what was 'logical' and what was 'physical', since neither was well defined or distinguished. Modeling just the essence of the system reduces the details that have to be considered during this stage because it eliminates those that exist just because of a specific system implementation. Thus, the essence is a smaller model than any of the 'current physical', 'current logical', 'future physical', or 'future logical' models would have to be. (The essential model most closely matches the 'future logical' and the incarnation is like the 'future physical'.) A clear distinction is made between the essence and incarnation models, and the work is easier than creating four models. The concepts of Essential Systems Analysis can also be applied to building current logical or physical models if desired. Developing the current physical is not usually necessary but it can help to identify problems in the existing system, if desired.

Event-partitioning is valid for most, if not all, system partitioning. Independent on-line transactions, batch job steps, executable programs and commands, and systems that execute on asynchronous processors should satisfy the criteria of event-partitioning. Event-partitioning describes explicitly how designers may already be partitioning, but does so in a way that can be explained, understood, and consistently applied. Event-partitioning achieves a high degree of *independence* among transactions, which makes the systems easy to understand, develop, and maintain (see 'Structured Design' below in this chapter).

Data flow diagrams can be used to depict asynchronous modules that interact by passing data. The fact that data flow diagrams depict flows of data allows the nodes to be executed at the same time or at different times, and on the same processor or on different processors – as long as the data are moved among modules as indicated in the diagram. Each node in a data flow diagram can be allowed to execute simultaneously, limited only by the precedence implied by the flow of data, i.e. data must be created before it can be consumed. However, the first node in sequence can be working on the Nth unit of data while the next node is working on the $(N - 1)$st, the subsequent one on the $(N - 2)$nd, etc. (like a line of people standing still but passing pails of water along the line). Data flow diagrams also have an important characteristic that makes them particularly useful for designing asynchronous systems: data passed among modules are available to only one module at a time. Passing data among the modules does not lead to the problems of synchronization, coordination and locking that result when systems allow simultaneous access to data. (It is possible for data flow diagrams to deadlock, but only in restricted situations that are unlikely to represent a real-time system – see Appendix B.) It is possible to execute modules connected only by flows of data rather than by call statements (see Appendix A). The ability to use data flow diagrams for designing asynchronous systems makes Essential Systems Analysis an important method for software designers to know.

Other software design methods also include versions of data flow diagrams, including 'A-graphs' from Sweden, which are especially popular in the Nordic countries. A-graphs show similar concepts as data flow diagrams except with different symbols – they use a junction of arrows for a function and a box to represent a form. However, they can also show material flow. Figure 2.25 shows the symbols for A-graphs. Figure 2.26 is an example of an A-graph with both information and material flow. These diagrams are reproduced with permission from *Information Systems Development – A Systematic*

Symbols in A-graphs	Correspondence in described activity
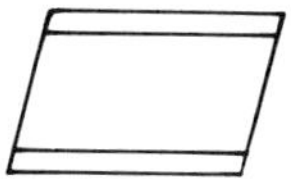 ▱	*Real set* Set of persons and/or material
▱	*Message set* Set of messages, e.g., documents or information by telephone
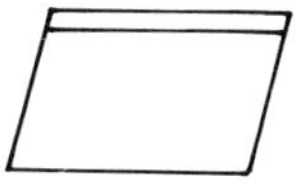 ▱	*Composite set* Set comprising persons/material as well as messages
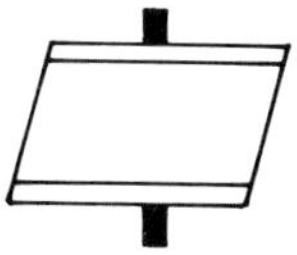 ▱ (with thick bars)	*Real flow* Flow of persons/material only
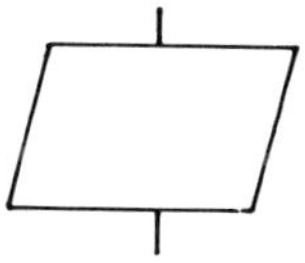 ▱ (with thin lines)	*Message flow* Flow of messages
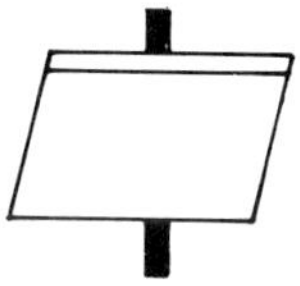 ▱ (with mixed lines)	*Composite flow* Flow of persons/material as well as messages
●	*Activity* People and other resources take part in the activity

All flows are assumed to go from top to bottom on the graphs, arrows are needed on upward and (possibly) horizontal flows only

FIGURE 2.25 Explanation of symbols used in A-graphs

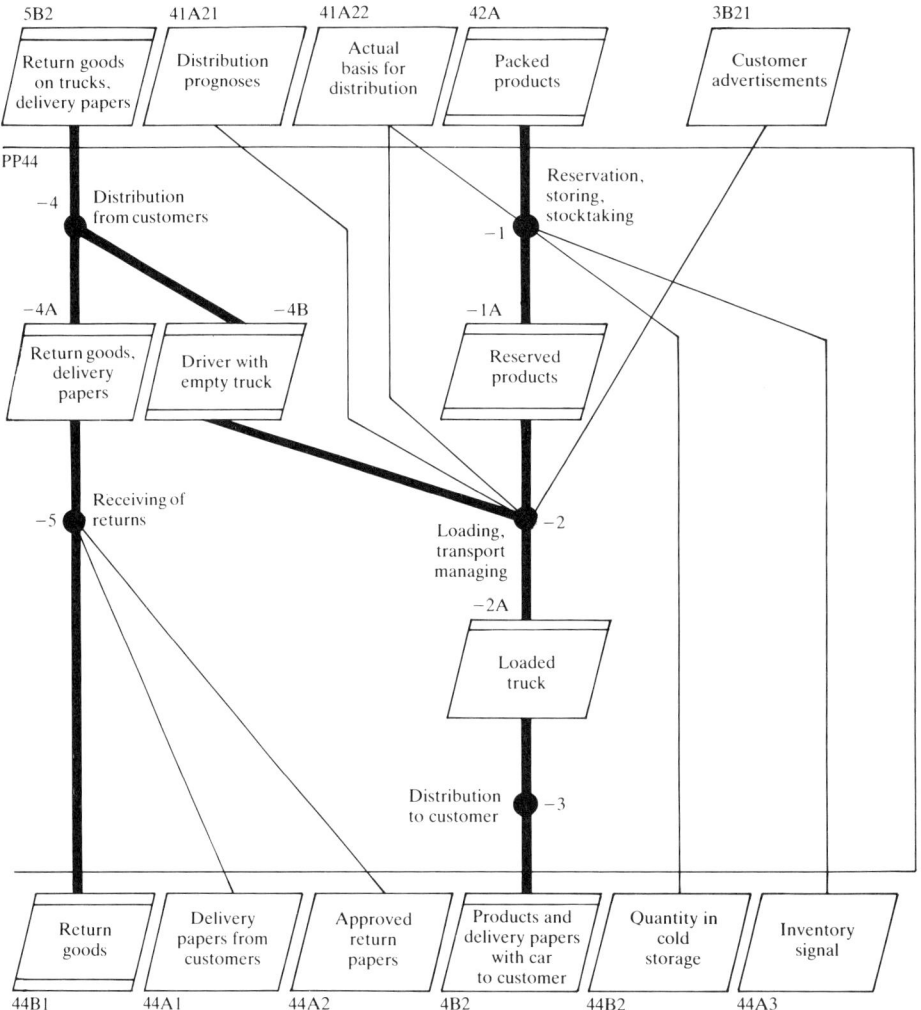

FIGURE 2.26 Store handling and distribution

Approach by Mats Lundeberg, Göran Goldkuhl, and Anders Nilsson (1981). Readers interested in understanding more about A-graphs and an associated design method using them are referred to that book.

2.4 DESIGN OF REAL-TIME SYSTEMS

2.4.1 Real-time systems

Some types of computer software are termed 'real-time' or 'event-driven'. However, it can be difficult to identify clearly what constitutes real-time or event-driven software. Paul Ward and Stephen Mellor in their book *Structured Development for Real-Time Systems* (1985) distinguish between real-time and other software such as on-line interactive systems by whether the *developers* must deal with the time dependencies. While on-line and other software must run in real-time and fast enough to satisfy requirements, the developers do not deal directly with timing considerations within the software. 'Real-time' software is software whose development requires the developer to deal with timing considerations such as asynchronous arrivals of control and data signals. Some examples of real-time software systems are operating systems, microcode for disk controllers, a cruise control, and an airplane control system.

Ward and Mellor describe a notation and a method for designing systems with real-time requirements, commonly called the Ward–Mellor method. Their notation adds graphic objects to represent real-time phenomena, such as flow and storage of events and control signals to the data flow diagram as used for Structured Analysis. The resulting diagram is called a transformation schema. Ward and Mellor use the term 'transformation' for a process symbol in the diagrams. Their term is used in this section for consistency with their treatment of the subject. Transformation schema diagrams are designed with concepts based, in part, on Essential Systems Analysis (see 'Essential Systems Analysis' above). The information in this section and Figures 2.27–2.43 are based on, or reprinted with permission from, *Structured Development for Real-Time Systems* (but using Gane and Sarson notation for the diagrams). *Structured Development for Real-Time Systems*, in three volumes, by Paul Ward and Stephen Mellor (1985), is recommended for those who desire an in-depth understanding of how to design systems with real-time requirements.

2.4.2 Example: cruise control

An 'add-on' cruise control for an automobile can illustrate the concepts and use of transformation schema to model real-time systems. When it is turned on, the cruise control maintains and displays the current speed of the car. The control maintains speed by monitoring both the throttle position and the rate at which the wheels turn, and then

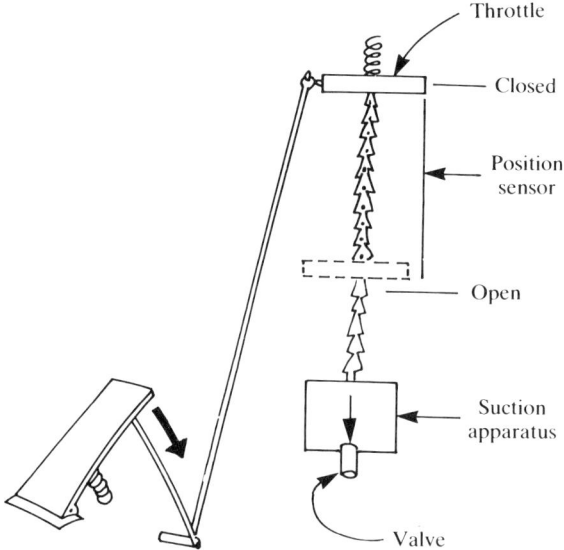

FIGURE 2.27 Cruise Control

controlling the throttle, as depicted in Figure 2.27. A sensor produces a signal proportional to the throttle's position. By adjusting a valve, the control causes a vacuum device to pull on a chain attached to the throttle; relaxing the chain allows the throttle to close again. The cruise control operates only when the engine is running and re-sets to its 'off' status when the engine is started. When it is on, the driver may tell it to 'start increasing speed', and it increases speed at a fixed rate until the driver tells it to 'stop increasing speed'. After that, it maintains the increased speed.

Naturally, the system can be turned off at any time, or the driver can override the system. To speed up, the driver can press the accelerator pedal – which simply allows the controlling chain shown in Figure 2.27 to go slack. The system continues trying to maintain the pre-set speed and thus automatically takes over when the driver releases the pedal. To slow down, the driver can step on the brake. If the cruise control senses that the brake is on, it stops trying to maintain the speed (but stays on). The driver may then tell it to 'resume speed', which again causes it to maintain the same speed to which it was set when the brake was pressed (if the control has not been turned off in the interim). Since speedometers are often inaccurate, the cruise control monitors the rotation speed of the wheels, and must therefore be calibrated when it is installed. In order to know the distance traveled for each tire rotation, the system accepts signals to 'start measured mile' and 'stop measured mile'. It then calculates and stores the factors needed to determine speed from the number of wheel rotations per time period. This calibration can be performed only if the cruise control is in 'off' status.

A top level transformation schema for the cruise control is shown in Figure 2.28. The cruise control is represented by the transformation called 'Maintain Auto Speed' and the

DESIGN OF REAL-TIME SYSTEMS   49

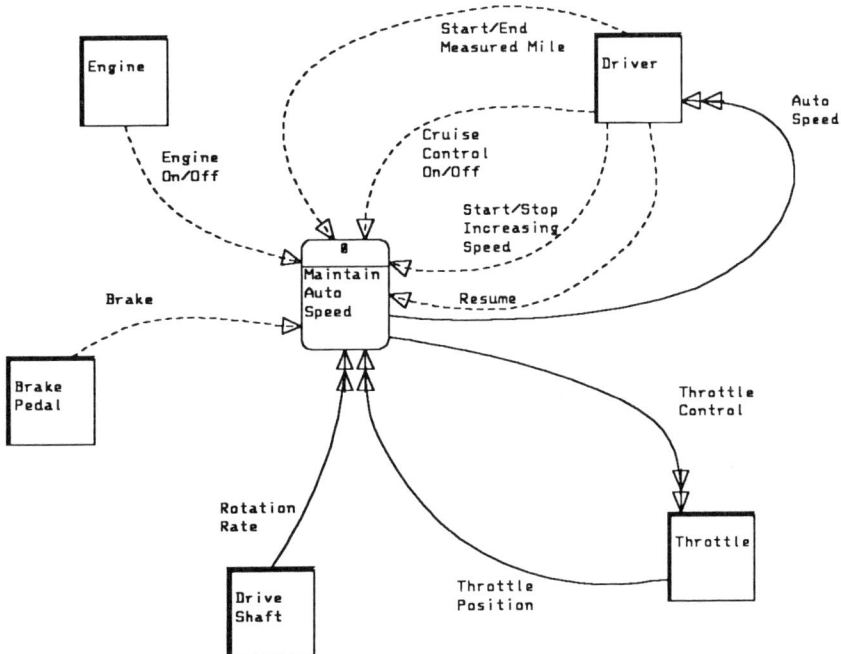

FIGURE 2.28 Context schema

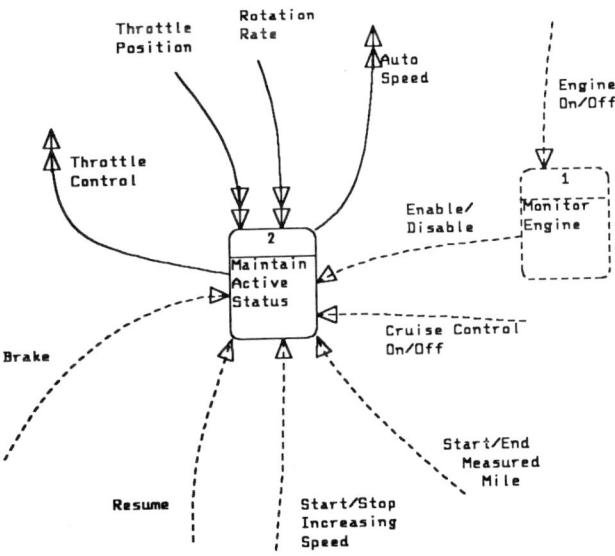

FIGURE 2.29 Maintain Auto Speed

inputs and outputs for the cruise control are shown entering and leaving that transformation. Figure 2.29 shows a first level expansion of the node 'Maintain Auto Speed' in Figure 2.28. Figure 2.30 shows an expansion of the transformation 'Maintain Active Status' in Figure 2.29.

2.4.3 Transformation schema

The basic transformation schema is like a data flow diagram. The transformations can be connected sequentially (as in Figures 2.29 and 2.31), which indicates a precedence – 'Prepare Message for Transmission' cannot use the 'Encoded Message' until it has been produced by 'Encode Message'. Transformations can also be parallel, as with 'Report Current Speed' and 'Manage Learning Mode' in Figure 2.30 and as with 'Produce Terrain Map' and 'Produce Weather Summary' in Figure 2.32. Parallel transformations are not dependent on each other and can execute in any sequence or simultaneously. Flows between transformations may be shown diverging or converging, as shown in Figure 2.33. The data are considered to be replicated on the diverged flows unless different names are shown on the diverged arrows, in which case the information on the single part of the arrow is the combination of the diverged flows.

Flows that connect transformations can be:

1. Time-discrete flows: shown with a single arrowhead.
2. Time-continuous flows: shown with a double arrowhead.
3. Flows of data: shown as solid arrows.
4. Flows of control: shown as dashed arrows.

Connections in data flow diagrams typically indicate discrete data entities or sets that flow between transformations. These are called time-discrete flows and are shown with a single arrowhead such as the 'Aircraft Identification Report' flow shown in Figure 2.34. A *time-discrete* flow is one that 'exists or has values only at individual points in time and is considered to have an undefined or null value at other times'. Time-discrete flows are similar to flows of records processed by business applications and the single-headed arrows are consistent with business-application data flow diagrams. Each point in time that the time-discrete flow has value(s) represents an occurrence or instance of the record to be processed. However, additional concepts are needed in order to represent real-time systems. One such concept is a *time-continuous* flow of data, such as the changing temperature shown in Figure 2.35. Time-continuous flows are those that exist at all points in time. Time-continuous flows (see Figure 2.36) are useful for representing continuously varying inputs of the environment that the system may use to control some technology, and are shown with a double arrowhead as in Figures 2.29 and 2.36. The transformation in Figure 2.36 senses the temperature in order to maintain it properly. Time-discrete flows may contain fields that have a continuous range of values – the distinction is whether the flow exists as a continuous-time function or has values only at discrete points in time.

Time-discrete flows (such as the 'Aircraft Identification Report' in Figure 2.34) are like data flows in normal data flow diagrams and can be viewed as a combination of the *data*

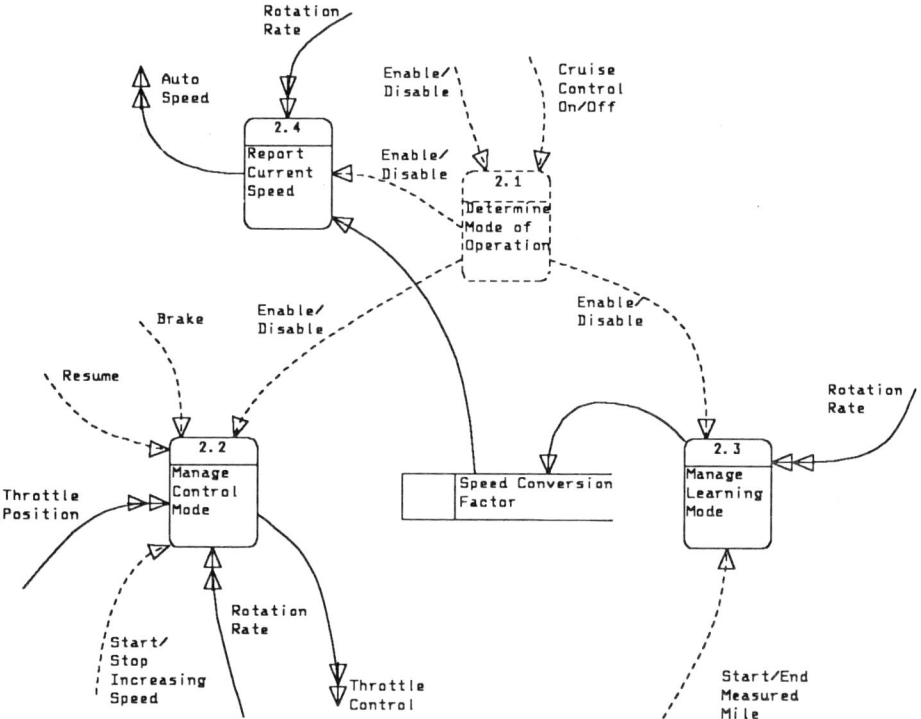

FIGURE 2.30 Maintain Active Status

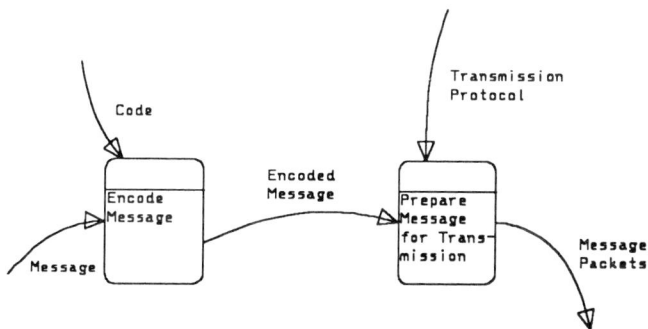

FIGURE 2.31 Sequentially linked transformations

52   ARCHITECTURAL SOFTWARE DESIGN

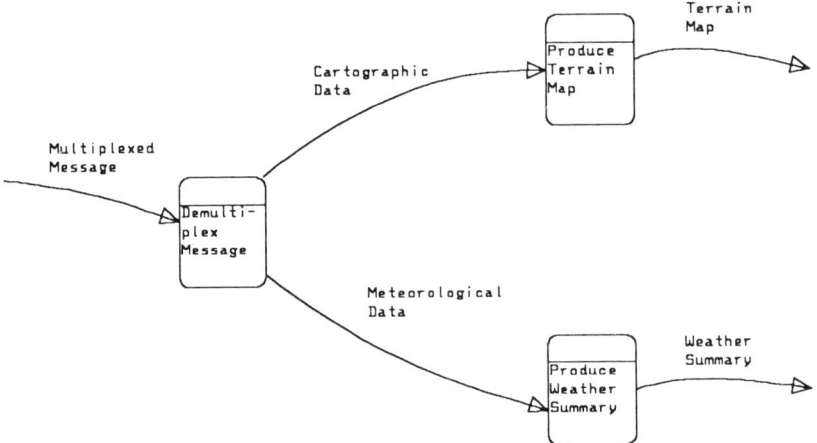

FIGURE 2.32 Parallel transformations

Convention	Interpretation
 Z — X, Y (crossing)	Two subsets of Z are used by two different successor transformations
 Z — (split)	All of Z is used by two different successor transformations
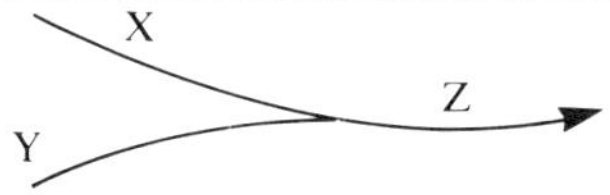 X, Y → Z	Z is composed of two subsets provided by two predecessor transformations
 (merge) → Z	All of Z may be provided by either of two predecessor transformations

FIGURE 2.33 Flow convergence/divergence conventions

DESIGN OF REAL-TIME SYSTEMS   53

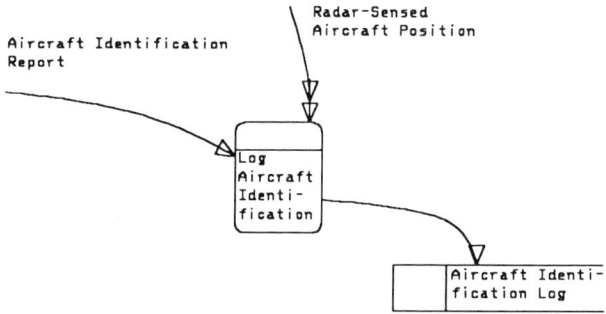

FIGURE 2.34 Combining time-continuous and time-discrete flows

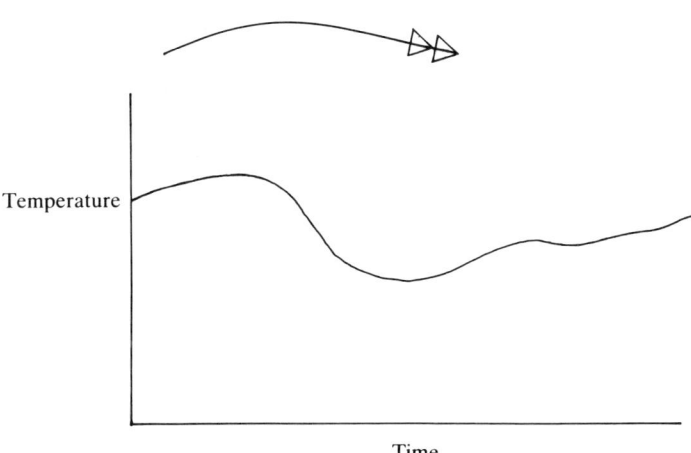

FIGURE 2.35 A continuous flow as a time function

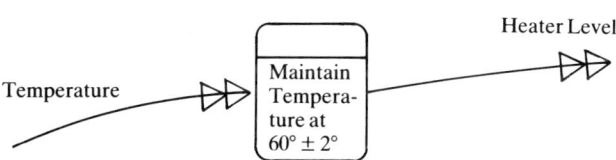

FIGURE 2.36 Time-continuous data flows

54 ARCHITECTURAL SOFTWARE DESIGN

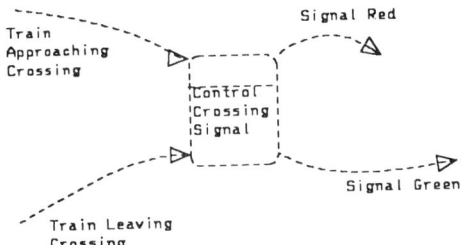

FIGURE 2.37 Event flows and control transformation

they contain and the *event* of the arrival of that data. Transformations can use the arrival of the data as a trigger to indicate that it is time to process the data that has arrived. (Naturally, transformations could also use only the data, or the event trigger, or neither.) Real-time systems, on the other hand, often have signals or triggers such as 'on', 'off' and 'reset' to indicate that something has happened or to give a command with no data content. Signals that have no associated data are called *event flows* and are shown as dotted arrows (see Figures 2.28 and 2.37).

A transformation schema distinguishes the two types of transformations, as in Figure 2.29, by showing a dotted line for the border of *control transformations* and a solid line for the border of *data transformations*. A control transformation, such as 'Monitor Engine' in Figure 2.29, is one that accepts only event flows as inputs and produces only event flows as outputs. Control transformations contain logic for processing event flows much as data transformations can contain logic for processing data. For example, the 'Control Crossing Signal' transformation in Figure 2.37 does not simply pass signals through. If a second train approaches the crossing before an earlier train has left, the light must not be turned green in response to the 'Train Leaving Crossing' signal.

Figure 2.30 shows a set of transformations operating on a *store* (see also Figure 2.38). The store notation is used to represent an item or set of data. An arrow pointing to a transformation from the store (such as the one into 'Report Current Speed' in Figure 2.30) means that the transformation may use something from the store. If the arrow is unlabeled, anything in the store may be used (see Figure 2.30); a label indicates what is used from the store. An arrow pointing from a transformation into a store (such as that from 'Manage Learning Mode' in Figure 2.30), indicates that transformation can add to, or change data in, the store. A double-headed arrow is a shorthand for an arrow-from, and an arrow-to, the store. Flows can enter or leave a store only via a transformation. Flows may not connect two stores directly or enter or leave a store from outside the diagram. Stores contain time-related data. The value, and even existence, of data in the store depends on when actions are performed by the various transformations. For example, 'Extract Aircraft Status' in Figure 2.38 can get different results based on when it looks at the data, and can even get a null value if it extracts the status of an aircraft that has been deleted by 'Delete Aircraft'. Connections between transformations and stores are shown as single-headed arrows.

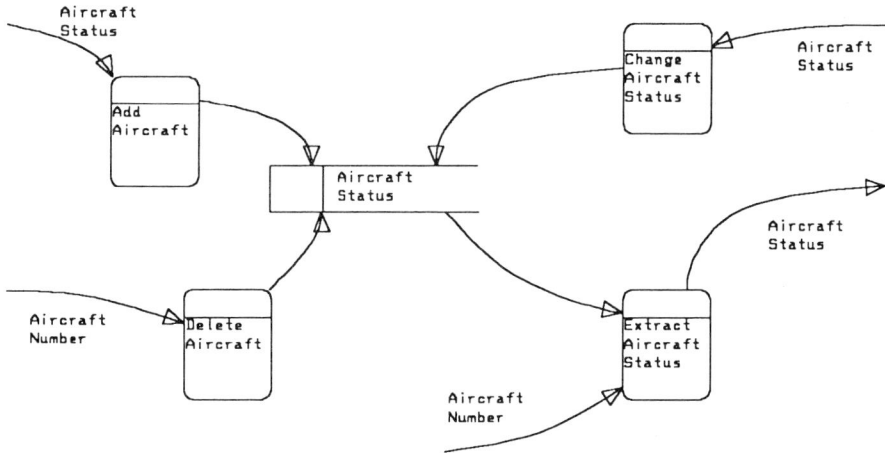

FIGURE 2.38 Airspace Status as a store

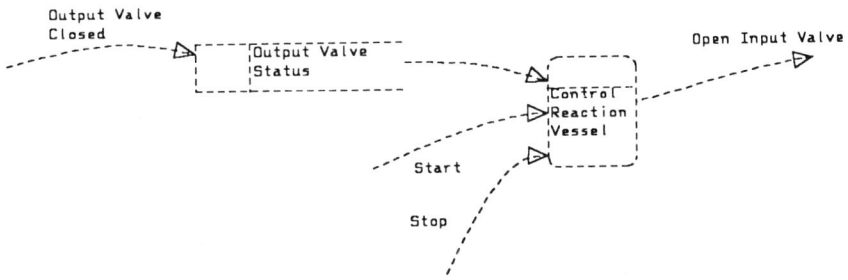

FIGURE 2.39 Use of an event store

Another type of store used in a transformation schema is called an *event store* (see Figure 2.39). Event stores are indicated by parallel dotted lines and can record occurrences of event flows. The 'Open Input Valve' signal in Figure 2.39 is issued only in response to 'Start' if the 'Output Valve Closed' signal has occurred in the interval since the last 'Stop' signal. Event flows can be connected directly to an event store rather than necessarily through a transformation (which is different than for a data store).

2.4.4 Hierarchies

The *rules* for expanding a transformation schema into lower level diagrams are similar to the rules for Structured Analysis expressed by DeMarco (1978) (see 'Structured Analysis' in Section 2.2). The *method* recommended for designing hierarchies is that of event-partitioning of 'Essential Systems Analysis' (Section 2.3). Nodes in a transformation schema can be expanded to a diagram that logically replaces the node using the following rules:

1. A data transformation can be expanded into a lower level diagram containing data transformations only or both control and data transformations. For example, Figure 2.30 is an expansion of the 'Maintain Active Status' transformation in Figure 2.29.
2. A control transformation may not be expanded into a lower level diagram.
3. A discrete data flow, continuous data flow, or event flow can be shown on the next lower level diagram only as a flow, or a set of flows, of the same type.
4. A data store or event store can be shown on the next lower level diagram only as a store, or set of stores, of the same type.

The highest level diagram in a set of transformation schema diagrams is called the *context schema* (e.g. Figure 2.28); it shows the interfaces between the system and its environment as well as the sources and destinations of flows that enter and leave the system. The sources and destinations outside the system are called *terminators* and are shown as boxes (similar to 'external entities' in data flow diagrams). In Figure 2.28, 'Engine', 'Driver', and 'Throttle' are all terminators. Terminators may represent people, hardware devices (e.g. switches, valves, and sensors), or other systems and are outside the scope of the system being described.

Lower level diagrams should have the same name as the transformation they represent in the next higher level diagram (as in Figures 2.28 and 2.29). Lower levels of the hierarchy do not show terminators – the flows entering and leaving their boundaries represent the flows in and out of the transformation they represent on the next higher level diagram. The lowest levels of the transformation schema diagrams are specifications for the transformations, such as state transition diagrams (see 'State transition diagrams', Section 3.5 and Figure 3.18, for example). The leveling process is continued until each transformation can be described in about one page or less of specifications or as a one-page diagram. Thus the number of levels depends on the overall complexity of the system being modeled. The use of a data store by transformations is shown at the highest level where that store is used by two or more transformations (as in Figure 2.30), and at any level below that where the store is used. Thus each store may appear several times within a set of transformation schema. Transformations have several forms: as a node within a diagram and also as a diagram that shows an expansion of that node or a transformation specification such as a state transition diagram. However, unlike data stores, each form of a given transformation should appear once only within a set of transformation schema. For example, 'Maintain Active Status' appears once (only) as a node in Figure 2.29 and once (only) as a diagram itself (Figure 2.30) and not as a state transition diagram (because it is described by a transformation schema diagram instead).

Ward and Mellor explicitly chose to make control transformations primitive (e.g. 'Monitor Engine' in Figure 2.29); they cannot be expanded into other control transformations (despite those rules given in their book that may imply otherwise). Rather, the leveling is based on data transformations, with control transformations decomposed from data transformations as they are relevant to the next lower level. For example, the diagram in Figure 2.30 includes the control transformation 'Determine

DESIGN OF REAL-TIME SYSTEMS   57

Mode of Operation', which is part of 'Maintain Active Status' in Figure 2.29. Allowing control transformations to be expanded would have meant that lower level diagrams would not show the connections to the data transformations which are being controlled. Were 'Determine Mode of Operation' expanded as part of 'Monitor Engine' in Figure 2.29, it would have been on a different diagram rather than in Figure 2.30. By having control transformations expand from data transformations, a leveled set of transformation schema can always show the relationships between control and data transformations, which is preferable to separate control flows and data flows since it keeps two closely related things together on the same chart.

A transformation schema should be built so that the control aspects of the system are shown as control transformations. Data transformations are used to modify time-continuous or time-discrete flows. Systems are modeled in such a way that event flows *into* a data transformation are not its primary input, but, rather, only *prompts* or controls on how the transformation's input data flows are processed. Those prompt signals always come from control transformations. For example, in Figure 2.40, the 'Maintain Temperature' transformation sends 'Heater Control' values only after receiving an 'Enable' and before receiving the next 'Disable'. The 'Change Aircraft Status' transformation in Figure 2.40 has as input a time-discrete flow (rather than a time-continuous one), again based on 'Enable' and 'Disable' prompts. 'Record Temperature Value' accepts time-continuous values for temperature but stores the time-discrete values that exist when the input prompt 'Trigger' occurs. It is also valid to use data transformations with no prompts – they simply behave in the same way all the time (e.g. as with processes in normal data flow diagrams). The control aspects of a data transformation are separated at a level where they can be shown controlling other transformations on that same diagram. Data transformations can produce control flows only if they control something *external* to that schema diagram. Data transformations may not send prompt signals to control other transformations *within* the same diagram.

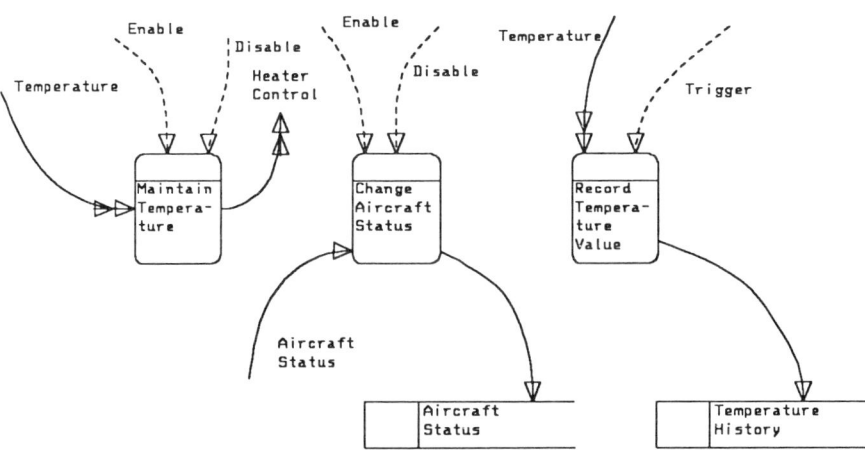

FIGURE 2.40 Prompted data transformations

58   ARCHITECTURAL SOFTWARE DESIGN

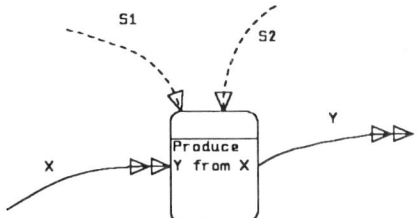

FIGURE 2.41 Combination of time-continuous and time-discrete behavior

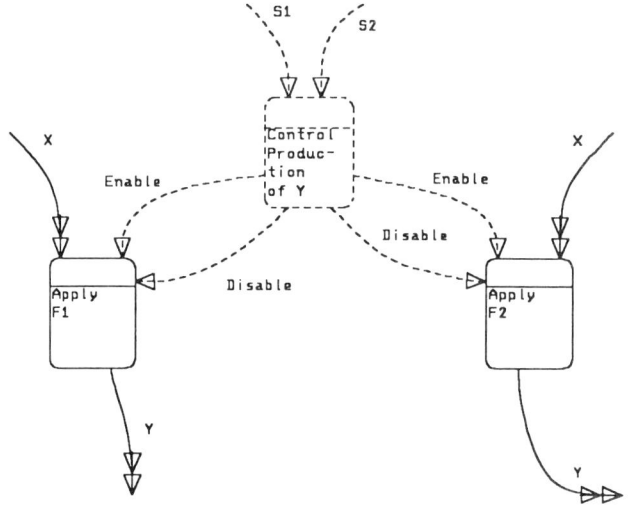

FIGURE 2.42 Separation of time-continuous and time-discrete behavior

As an example of the clarity that results from designing control signals as prompts, consider a system that performs either of two transformations on its input data: X as depicted by Figure 2.41. The signal $S1$ tells the system to produce a Y that is equal to $F1(X)$, after which additional signals $S1$ have no effect until an $S2$ signal occurs. The signal $S2$ tells the system to produce a Y that is equal to $F2(X)$, and additional $S2$ signals have no effect until after another $S1$. If this system were depicted as a single data transformation (as in Figure 2.41), it would hide the effect of the control. Figure 2.42 shows more clearly the effects of the control aspects of this system. All control signals into data transformations in Figure 2.42 (shown as dotted arrows) are in the form of prompts that enable and disable the performance of functions, rather than as signals that require logic in order to be interpreted, as in Figure 2.41.

The types of inputs and outputs of a transformation determine some of the execution characteristics of the implemented transformation. Transformations with only discrete-time inputs and outputs could be implemented to execute only at discrete instances. Transformations with time-continuous outputs must usually execute continuously in order to maintain that output (though not forever because there is usually at least an 'Off' state). Transformations with time-continuous inputs also probably execute continuously (but may use the input only at discrete points of time). It is possible for a single transformation to have both discrete and continuous inputs. For example, in Figure 2.34 the transformation 'Log Aircraft Identification' stores the continuous input of 'Radar-Sensed Aircraft Position' only when the time-discrete input 'Aircraft Identification Report' is received.

2.4.5 Build both essential and implementation models

Ward and Mellor recommend building a model based on the concepts of *essence* as described by McMenamin and Palmer (see 'Essential Systems Analysis', Section 2.3). The essential model represents requirements and the implementation model (or 'incarnation') represents the designed solution. The differences between the essential and implementation models can be illustrated by considering a system to control the filling of a reaction vessel with a liquid. Essential activities include the following:

1. Responding to a stimulus from the environment that it is time to fill the vessel by opening a valve.
2. Responding to the level in the vessel by closing a valve when it reaches a desired height.
3. Responding to a stimulus from the environment that the reaction is complete by opening an output valve.
4. Responding to an empty tank by closing the output valve.

These activities are required of any system regardless of whether it is implemented with analog components, a digital computer, or is even manual. A particular implementation could have specifications that include the following:

1. The sensing of conditions and operation of the valves will be performed by a microprocessor.
2. The level in the tank will be indicated by an analog voltage between -6 and $+6$ volts, with the high voltage indicating an overflow and the low voltage indicating empty.
3. The position of the input and output valves is controlled by setting 16-bit words in the digital-to-analog registers with all 1s indicating open and all 0s indicating closed. The analog output voltage will control the actual valves.

The builder of the system needs both the essential and implementation models in order to implement a working system. Neither model alone provides sufficient information to understand the complete incarnation. Figure 2.43 shows the relationship of the essential and implementation models. The content of either model increases in detail as lower levels of the hierarchical model are developed. Notice that the requirements (the 'whats') are not just at higher levels with the implementation information (the 'hows'), only at lower levels – both exist at each level of the design. For example, the requirements may include that the vessel mentioned above be filled to a depth of 0.685 ± 0.002 centimeters.

60   ARCHITECTURAL SOFTWARE DESIGN

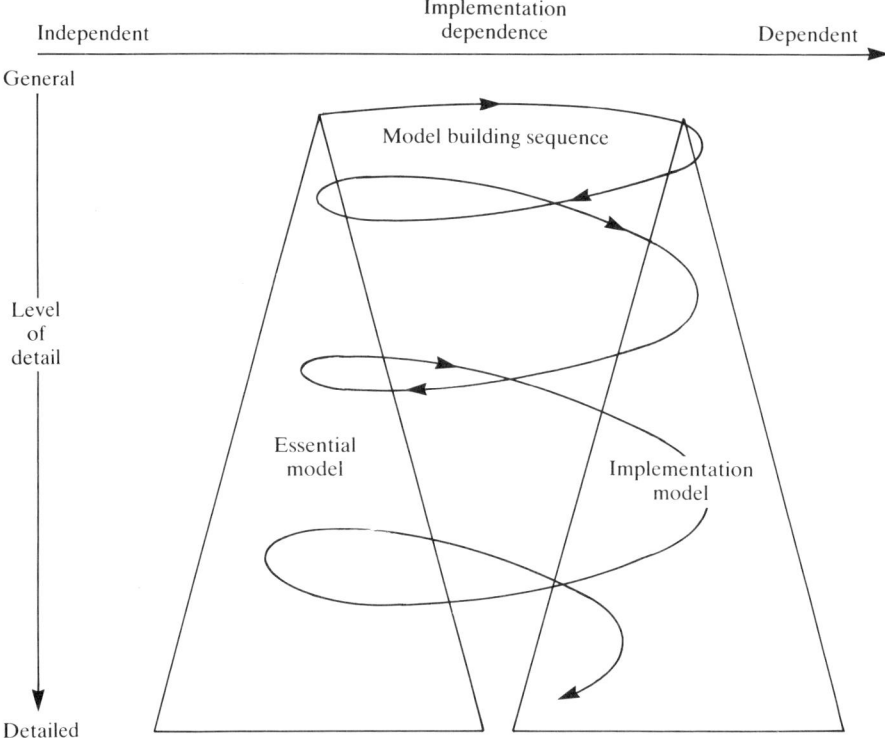

FIGURE 2.43 Relationship of essential and implementation models

While this depth information is certainly a detail (since the requirements can be understood to a great depth without understanding this piece of information), it is a detail of the *requirements* that is unrelated to any particular implementation. Conversely, the decision to use a microprocessor to control the filling is high level information, but is still part of the implementation model.

It is possible to complete the essential model first and then design the complete implementation model. The reverse order would not work, however, because the implementation model is dependent on the essential model. An advantage of defining the complete essential model first is to allow the user to validate the system earlier. The essential model captures the kinds of concepts in which the user is more interested and in language that is more natural to the user. The essential model is also smaller than if it were combined with the implementation information. Decreasing the size of the model can reduce the complexity for the users who review it. An alternative design approach is to build the two models as indicated by the spiral line in Figure 2.43, completing one level in the essential model and then a related level in the implementation model before defining the next level in the essential model. An advantage of designing the implementation model at the same time as the essential model is that ambiguities in higher levels of the essential model may be identified while building the implementation model. In this way the ambiguities may be resolved prior to work on lower levels. The choice of whether to define the essential model first or to build the two models in parallel depends on the firmness of the specification, availability of the user, and timing considerations of the system development in each particular situation.

2.4.6 Comments on the Ward–Mellor method

The transformation schema and the associated method for designing real-time systems are valuable contributions made by Ward and Mellor both for real-time systems and distributed business applications. They incorporate and build on the earlier methods of Structured Analysis, Essential Systems Analysis, and Structured Design. Thus, the comments regarding the advantages of Essential Systems Analysis over Structured Analysis also apply here (see the 'Comments on Essential Systems Analysis' in Section 2.3.10). The availability of Ward and Mellor's books, which describe how to design real-time systems using their diagrams, makes their notation easier to use than notations that lack an associated design method, such as Mascot (below). The transformation schema notation is also preferable to notations that show the data and control flows into a given transform only on separate diagrams. Consideration of a single transformation involves both its control and data flows and is easier when both can be shown on the same diagram.

Mascot-ACP

Mascot is a system produced by the Royal Signals Research Establishment in the United Kingdom. Its diagramming notation, known as ACP (activity-channel-pool) depicts similar information as transformation schema. Mascot-ACP is treated further in Volume 1 of this series (Macro 1990), with examples of its use. While those readers who are already committed to using Mascot will probably find it advantageous to continue to use Mascot for compatibility, readers who can choose a notation for depicting real-time systems may wish to use the transformation schema notation because of its use with the real-time design method in Ward and Mellor (1985).

SADT™

Structured Analysis and Design Technique (SADT™) is a proprietary concept developed by SofTech, Inc. (see IEEE 1977). Like transformation schema, SADT™ includes control signals. However, it graphically differentiates them from data signals by always having control signals attached to the top of processes and data signals to the sides. A slightly modified version, called IDEF0, is being adopted as a standard by some parts of the US Department of Defense and is popular for designing computer integrated manufacturing software. Readers interested in SADT™ are referred to Volumes 1 and 2 of this series (Macro 1990, 1991) and to *SADT: Structured Analysis and Design Technique* by David Marca and Clement McGowan (1988) (with a foreword by Douglas T. Ross).

2.5 STRUCTURED DESIGN

Structured Design is a method for separating a program into independent modules in order to make the program easier to design, implement, and maintain. It was developed by Larry Constantine (as in Yourdon and Constantine 1979), based on his research into the effects on maintenance costs of various characteristics of programs. Programs that were found to be less costly to develop and maintain, he observed, generally exhibited modular structures – and, in particular, certain kinds of modular structures. From those observations, Constantine developed a set of measures for evaluating alternative modular structures, incorporating them into a method called Structured Design. These measures can be used with all kinds of software modules, from design modules to integrands, including subroutines, macros, nodes in data flow diagrams, and Object-Oriented 'objects' (see Chapter 5).

Constantine observed that the independence of modules is a crucial factor in reducing the effort required to build and maintain software. Difficult problems in general – and software design problems in particular – can be made easier if they can be divided into independent pieces, which can be solved independently. The more independent the pieces are, the more the complexity is reduced (see Section 2.1.1). Two characteristics are useful to help to identify and enhance the independence of modules: *binding*, and *coupling*. Binding compares the strength of relationships *within* a module – modules with high binding can be more independent of other modules. Coupling compares the strength of relationships *between* modules – those with low coupling are more independent and thus produce systems that are simpler to develop and maintain. Binding and coupling are actually opposite measures of the same thing. In any software there are pieces of code that are highly related; the idea is to divide the system into modules so that highly related code is in the same module (giving high binding). The resulting modules can then have a low amount of coupling among them – because they do not contain code that is highly related to code in other modules. Binding and coupling are complementary measures. Changes that improve (increase) binding also improve (decrease) coupling and vice-versa – though often the change can be viewed more easily from one of the measures than from the other. The binding and coupling resulting from a specific interconnection of design modules can be identified from a diagram that shows the modules and their interconnections. If the modules call each other, they can be depicted on a diagram known as a 'structure chart'. Figures 2.44–2.64 are reprinted by permission of IBM Corp., where they have been used by the author for numerous classes in Structured Design.

2.5.1 Structure charts

A structure chart, also called a 'call hierarchy' chart, shows the calls among modules in a program. Figure 2.44 contains the symbols in a structure chart and Figure 2.45 shows an example of a structure chart. Diamonds and loop annotations on structure charts are optional and cannot be entirely rigorous, but are useful because they indicate placement of function (e.g. whether the caller or the called module tests the condition for

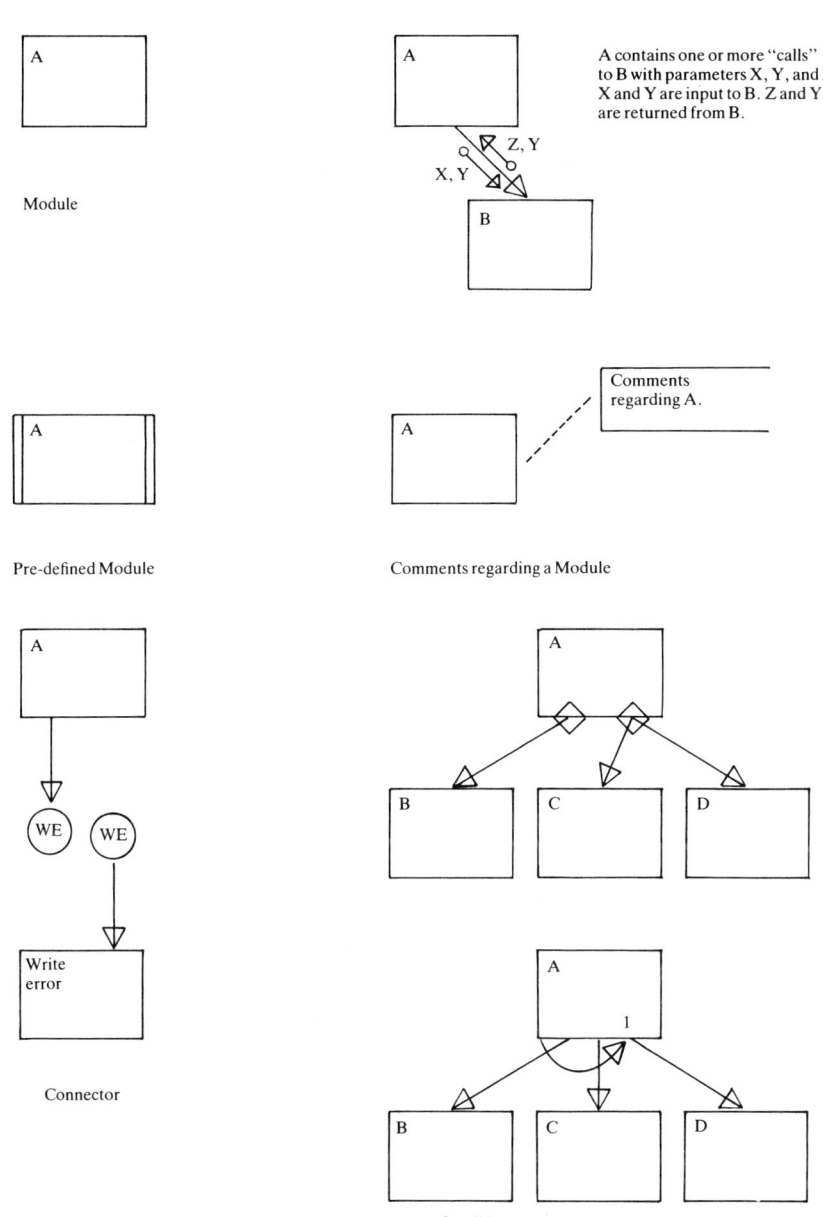

FIGURE 2.44 Structure chart symbols

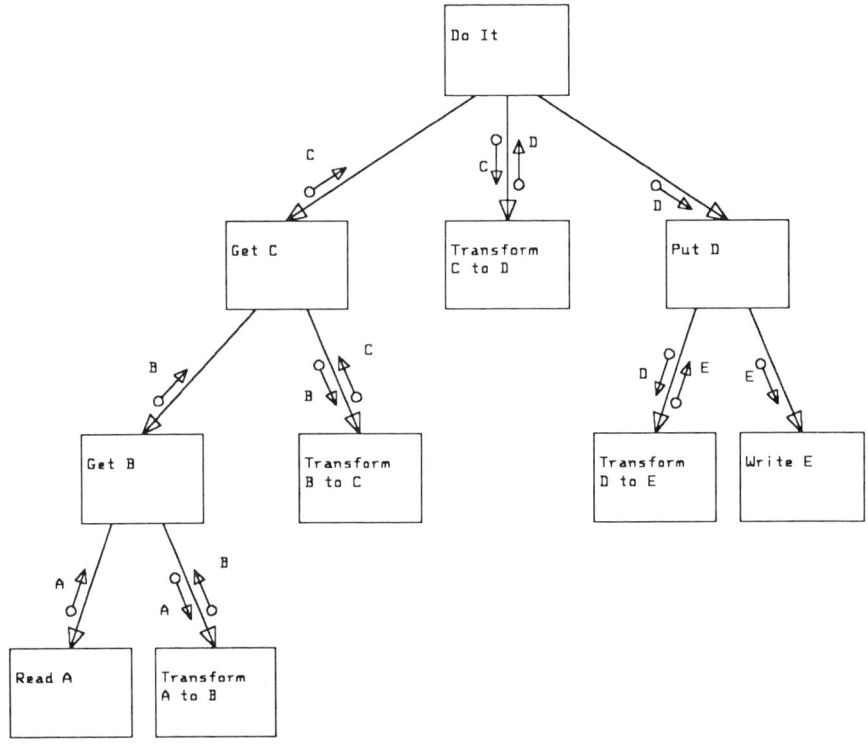

FIGURE 2.45 Sample structure chart

execution). There are additional symbols that depict other kinds of possible relationships between modules (see Yourdon and Constantine 1979). A module should be shown in one place on a structure chart only, even though it may be called from multiple modules, because showing a module in more than one place could result in designing two or more conflicting interfaces for the same module. Connectors can be used to avoid many crossed lines when modules are called from many places (see Figure 2.44). It is helpful to place modules so as to reduce the number of crossed lines, and, within that, in likely order of execution from left to right. Calling down or up across levels in a hierarchy is encouraged whenever a module is useful. However, when calling a module at a higher level, watch out for recursion (a module calling itself or another module that eventually calls the first one again), unless the intended language supports it.

2.5.2 Example: Update Orders

The following sample problem can illustrate some of the concepts of Structured Design. Designing systems as combinations of modules is more valuable for large systems: there is seldom value in separating one page of code into smaller pieces. Thus any example that

STRUCTURED DESIGN 65

can be included here can only illustrate the results (but will not really be too convincing due to its simplicity). The following are the specifications for a program to price orders for individual items (one item type per order):

1. Order-records contain Branch_Office_No, Customer_No, Item_No, Quantity
2. Check Branch_Office_No against the Branch Office data base.
3. Update the orders with the name and address from the Customer data base (with Customer_No as the key). Also add a flag indicating foreign customers (which can be found in the Customer record).
4. Update the order with Unit_Price, Price, Discount, and Tax; where Unit_Price = Price − Discount + Tax. Price, Discount, and Tax are found in the Item data base (with Item_No as the key). Foreign customers do not have to pay the tax.
5. Create an Updated Order file.
6. Print a report with one line per input order line which contains: Customer_No, Item_No, Quantity, Total Amount, Total Discount. Print a summary line with: Number of Customers, Grand Total Amount, Grand Total Discount, and Total Tax
7. Write an error message if Customer_No is not in the Customer data base, or Item_No is not in the Item data base.
8. Write all incorrect orders to an Order Error file for later corrections. Orders are incorrect if the Branch_Office_No, the Customer_No, or an Item_No is invalid.

An initial structure chart for the above program is shown in Figure 2.46. The following discussion shows that this chart is not a very well-designed solution, although it does meet the functional objectives of the problem specifications. The chart also meets its intent of being a fertile ground for illustrating binding and coupling problems.

2.5.3 Binding

The strength of relationships between pieces of code *within* a module varies from weak to strong (see Figure 2.47). The types of binding may be easiest to understand from the viewpoint of Constantine's original research. He asked various developers why they put pieces of code in the same module, and then grouped their answers into categories. The answers ranged from the weakest answer: 'Well, I had to put them *somewhere*' (which Constantine labeled 'coincidental' binding), to the strongest 'These pieces were both necessary as part of getting this one thing accomplished' (which he called 'functional' binding). Functional binding is the strongest type of binding; designing so that all modules have functional binding is one of the primary recommendations of Structured Design. Design requires identifying only functional binding, which can be determined from the test for functional binding described below. However, understanding the characteristics of types of binding lower than functional binding can help to identify modules that are *not* functionally bound (as well as to evaluate results of other design methods).

Coincidental binding is at the low end of the scale of binding. It describes the situation where the strongest reason for two pieces of code to be in the same module is that the

66   ARCHITECTURAL SOFTWARE DESIGN

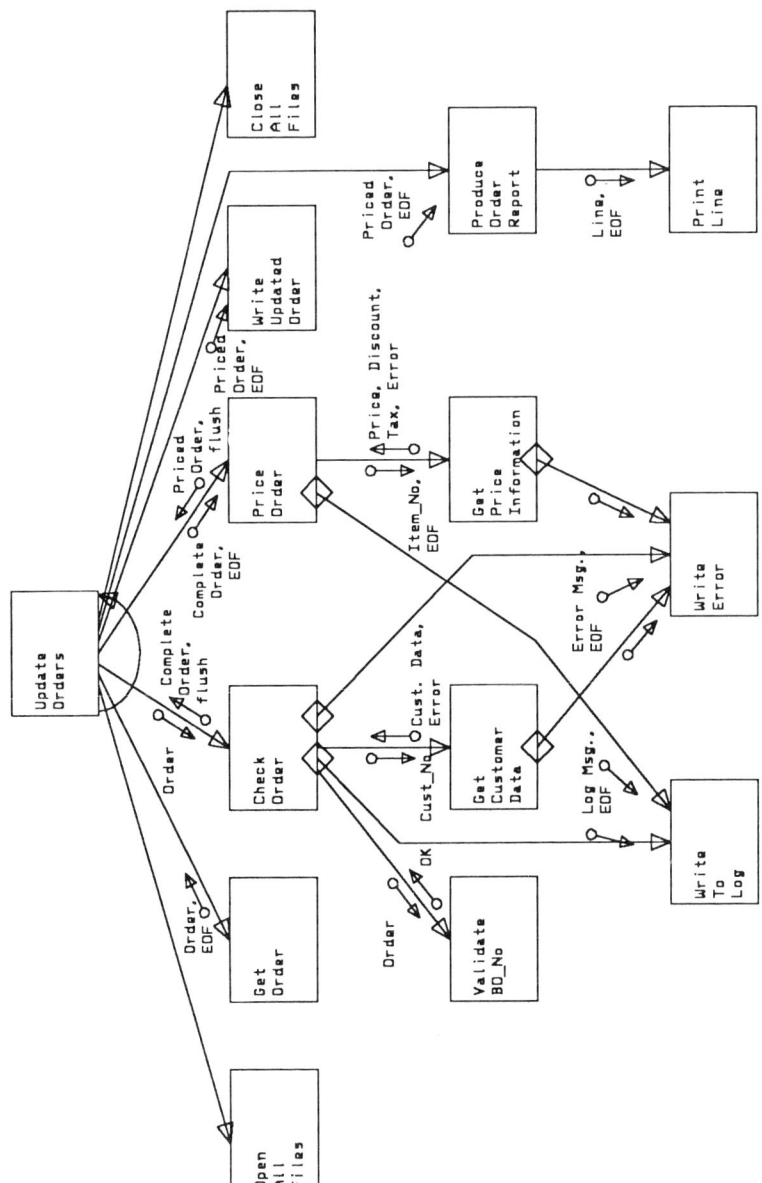

FIGURE 2.46 An initial structure chart

STRUCTURED DESIGN 67

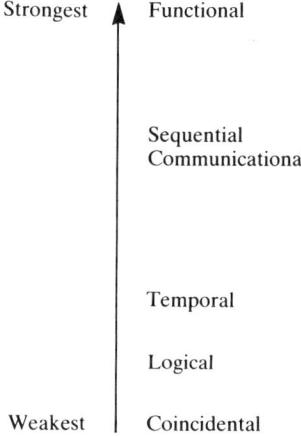

FIGURE 2.47 Types of binding

designer had to put them somewhere. Combining 'Get Orders' in Figure 2.46 with code to 'Write Error' (messages) would result in coincidental binding, since the two functions do not share data, execute at different times and, in general, have nothing that relates them. It is difficult to give modules containing coincidental binding good simple descriptive names because the parts do not combine to perform any one function.

Logical binding exists when the strongest reason for the pieces of code to be together is that they perform logically similar functions – often with the same verb – but with different data. Combining 'Get Customer Data' and 'Get Price Information' would result in logical binding. Modules such as 'Edit Any Data' and 'Do Any Trigonometry Function' (e.g. sine, cosine, tangent) would also be logically bound. The parts of a logically bound module are very loosely related – they do not share data or even execute during the same invocation of the module. Modules with logical binding often require a control parameter from their callers to indicate which function is to be performed and then branch based on that parameter to the function to be executed.

Temporal binding (relating to 'time') exists when the strongest reason for having the pieces of code in the same module is that they are executed during the same execution of the module. 'Open All Files' and 'Close All Files' in Figure 2.46 are examples of modules with temporal binding. So are modules such as 'Initialize the Program', 'Get All the Program's Data Now', 'Clean-up', and 'Terminate'. Temporally bound pieces of code do not share data, but only the time when they are to execute. Temporal binding is slightly stronger than logical binding because the temporally bound parts execute at the same time. However, pieces of code that are logically or temporally bound are still weaker than the types of binding discussed next because they do not share data.

Communicational binding exists when the strongest relationship between two pieces of code is the sharing of the same input and/or output data, as illustrated by Figure 2.48. If the data that one piece of code creates are used by the next, this is called *sequential*

68   ARCHITECTURAL SOFTWARE DESIGN

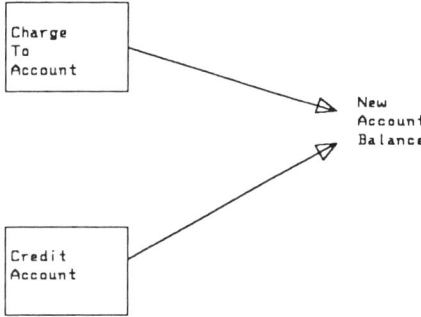

FIGURE 2.48 Communicational binding

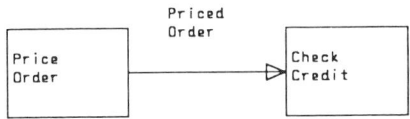

FIGURE 2.49 Sequential binding

binding (see Figure 2.49). Combining 'Price Orders' and 'Write Updated Orders' in Figure 2.46 would result in sequential binding because 'Price Orders' produces the priced order that 'Write Updated Orders' uses as input. Communicational and sequential binding differ little in their strengths. However, sequential binding is slightly stronger because the processes are more dependent and related since the process producing the data has to execute first. With communicational binding the processes could execute in either order. However, both types of binding are significantly stronger than the preceding types because the pieces of code share data, which was not true of coincidental, logical, or temporal binding.

Functional binding is the strongest type. It says 'These parts are necessary to get this one thing accomplished.' A type of binding that applies to two related pieces of code is the *strongest* reason that relates them. Since types of binding often contain characteristics of types that are lower on the scale, it is not the presence of given characteristics, but the inability to find any stronger reason that determines how strong the relationship is between two pieces of code. The binding assigned to each module is the *weakest* binding that exists between any two pieces of code within them. A functionally bound module has everything it needs (and only what it needs) to accomplish a single specific objective. If a module is functionally bound, its *function can be described with a simple phrase*, such as 'Square Root', 'Sine', 'Edit Name Field', and 'Read File A'.

Mechanical examples – where the pieces are almost always functional (and reusable) – illustrate functional binding. The engine of a car and its parts are functional (see Figure 2.50). The motor contains pieces, which include a water pump, a fuel injector, and a fuel

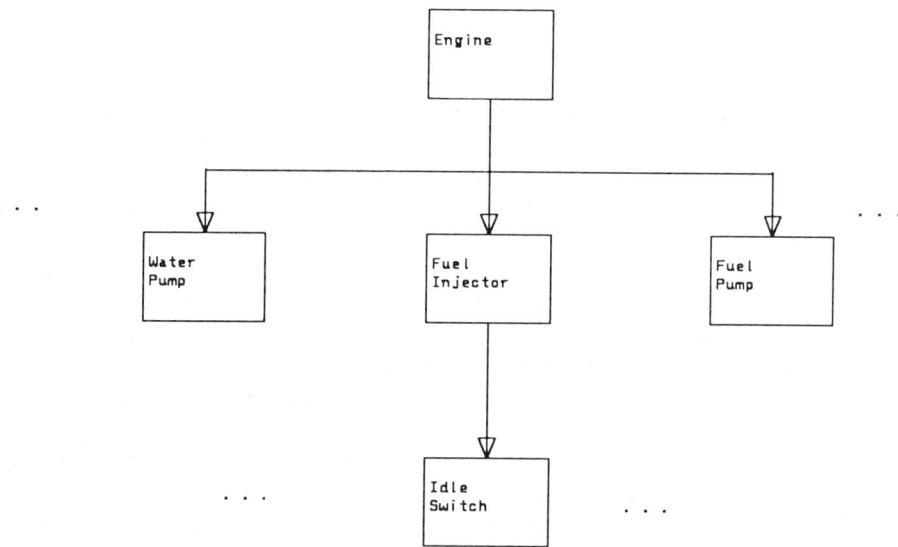

FIGURE 2.50 Functional binding

pump. The fuel injector is made up of pieces, including an idling switch. The functions of each of these pieces can be described with a simple phrase – the motor provides power for the car, the water pump pumps water, the fuel injector delivers mixed fuel and air to the cylinders, the idling switch adjusts the fuel mixture (to reduce pollution when the car idles), and the fuel pump pumps fuel. However, half of a fuel injector is not functional because it does not have all that it needs to perform a task (although if enough parts are eliminated, one can eventually be left with an idling switch – which is functional). Neither is a combination of a water pump and a fuel pump functional – any description of what this combination accomplishes must either include several parts (e.g. pumps water *and* pumps fuel) or leave one of the functions unmentioned. The combination is not functional because it includes more than is necessary to perform a single complete function. Modules with multiple functions are harder to develop and maintain than if the functions were in separate, independent modules.

Functional binding applies to modules at any level of a hierarchy – not just the bottom ones. Examples of functional modules in Figure 2.46 include 'Get Order', 'Get Price Information', 'Write Updated Order', and 'Write Error'. Examples of functional modules that might be in a payroll system include 'Produce Hourly Payroll', 'Calculate Deductions', 'Calculate State Tax Deduction', 'Print Check', and 'Calculate Overtime'. Like functional mechanical pieces, functional modules tend to have simple interfaces – they are easily replaced and are reusable. A fuel pump in a car can be replaced by any other fuel pump that performs the same function and meets the interface and environment constraints. A module that calculates the sine of an angle can be replaced by any other that also performs the same calculation correctly and meets the interface and environment constraints.

To test for functional binding, describe the module's function. The description should include all the actions of its parts, just as the function of an engine includes the combined effect of all its pieces. For a called module, the function should be what is accomplished for its caller between when it is called and when it returns, independent of whether there is a hierarchy of modules below it or not. For example, 'Price Orders' in Figure 2.46 includes all the functions below it, including 'Get Price Information'. Analysis of the phrase that describes the function can indicate whether the module is functional. A module is not functionally bound if its description *must* include several verbs, clauses, or phrases in order to describe what it does. It also may not be functionally bound if phrases including verbs that are not specific, such as 'Handle', or that indicate multiple functions, are combined in the same module. For example, the name of the module 'Check Order' in Figure 2.46 is not an accurate description of the function it accomplishes for its caller because it returns a complete order. A more descriptive name would be 'Check Order and Get Customer Data', which then exposes the fact that its binding is not functional. It would be more functional if its function was 'Get Complete Order', which it could be if it called 'Get Order' as in Figure 2.51. In Figure 2.51, the functions of opening and closing each file have also been combined into the modules which read or write to the respective file (instead of being grouped into the temporally bound modules 'Open All Files' and 'Close All Files', as in Figure 2.46). Phrases that indicate time, such as 'Initialize' or 'Terminate', describe modules that are probably temporally bound. Verb phrases without a specific object, such as 'Edit *All* Data' are indicative of logical binding. If there just is no simple phrase that adequately describes the combination of things in the module, it may be coincidentally bound.

2.5.4 Coupling

Coupling indicates how independent modules are. It can be used to compare alternative structures to determine which would be simpler to implement. The more independent the modules, the more complexity is reduced and the easier it is to design, write, understand, debug and change the resulting software. Coupling is increased by anything that increases the need to consider one module in order to design, write, understand, debug, or change another. There are four aspects of coupling, as follows, any of which can increase coupling.

1. What is communicated.
2. Type of connection.
3. Size of connections.
4. Clarity.

Coupling can be used to evaluate the relationships between macros, paragraphs within a program, or even segments of code within the same module. Coupling is lower when the modules can define private local variables (which in some systems may require that they be separately compiled).

STRUCTURED DESIGN 71

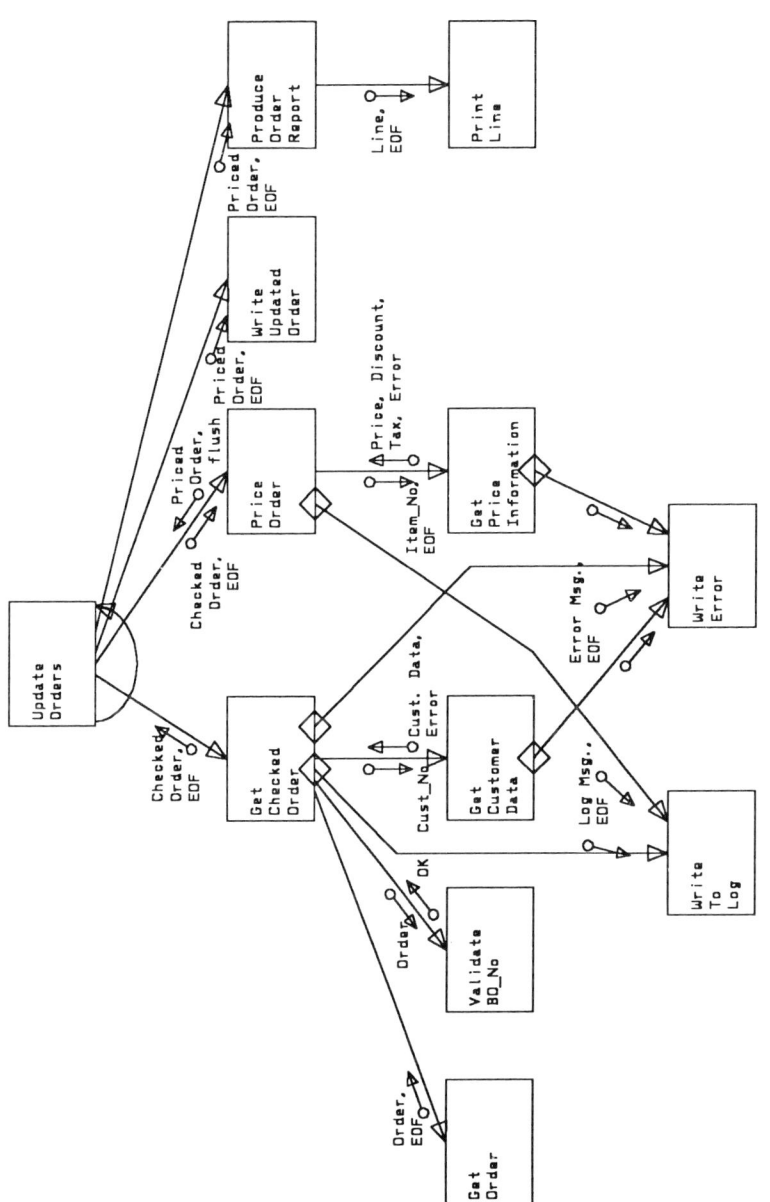

FIGURE 2.51 An improved structure

72 ARCHITECTURAL SOFTWARE DESIGN

WHAT IS COMMUNICATED

Two things can be shared between modules: control and data. Sharing control results in higher coupling than sharing data. There are various ways in which control and data can be shared to affect the coupling. Having one module modify the internal code of another module causes the highest coupling relative to what is communicated (see Figure 2.52). An example of modifying code could be an assembler module called 'Get Date' which has an internal branch instruction that must be modified by each caller to control which format of the current date is to be returned (Julian, month/day/year, or day/month/year). The modified code is treated as data by the module that modifies it, but the code is control to the module which contains it. Modifying code in another module makes it more difficult to develop, understand, or debug the resulting software than any other way of sharing control.

A simpler, though still complex, way in which modules can share control is for one module to branch directly to an unlabeled instruction or location inside another module based on, for example, an offset from the entry point (possible in assembler). A module that calculates the tangent (which equals sine divided by cosine) and contains code to calculate the sine and cosine could be invaded this way. Modifications to a module during maintenance may change the offsets and may result in unpredictable results if its entry is based on offsets. The interface is slightly clearer (and thus lower coupling) if the branch is to a labeled instruction, but such a branch is still difficult to observe, trace, and understand. However, it is not necessary even to check for such complex connections in most high level languages because they do not support branching directly to an instruction, labeled or not, and support call statements only to defined entry points.

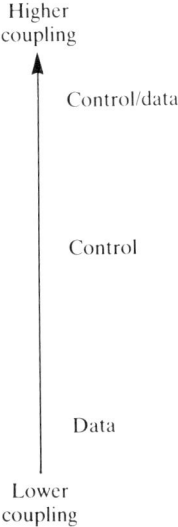

FIGURE 2.52 What is communicated

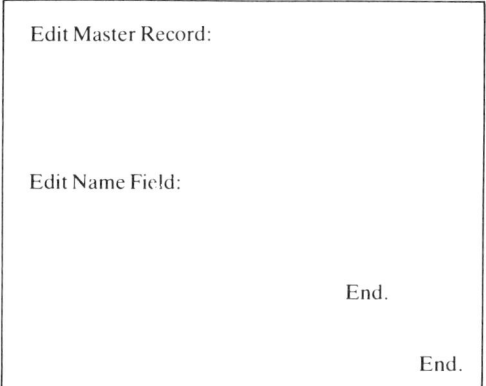

FIGURE 2.53 One function contained within another

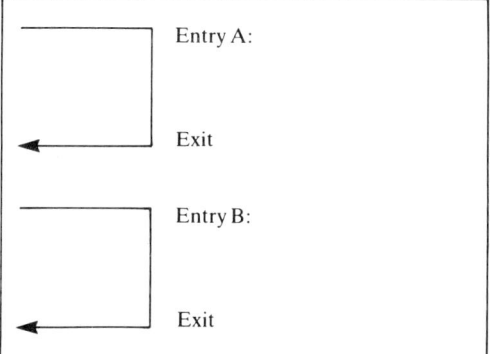

FIGURE 2.54 Separating multiple functions

The next weakest type of coupling – and less complex – occurs when the instructions that comprise one function are contained within another function, as in Figure 2.53. If the functions must share local variables, the coupling at least can be reduced by separating the code, as illustrated in Figure 2.54. Whenever a module must contain more than one function, coupling is lower when the entry and exit points for each of the functions are entirely separate, than when common entry or exit points are used (see Figure 2.54). Multiple entry points can be useful when a module *must* be initialized by some other module. In this case, a second entry point for initializing reduces the complexity and number of parameters for the main entry point, thus reducing coupling for the main entry point.

If control is shared, the simplest way to share it is by passing control variables (e.g. control flags). For example, consider the trigonometry routine in Figure 2.55: the caller sets one control switch to indicate which function is desired, and another control switch to

74   ARCHITECTURAL SOFTWARE DESIGN

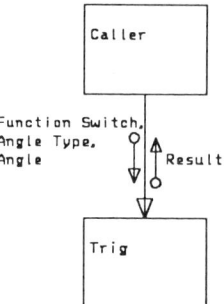

FIGURE 2.55 Control variable

indicate whether the angle is in degrees or radians. In Figure 2.51, the module 'Price Order' returns 'flush' in order to tell 'Update Orders' to bypass those orders with invalid item numbers. If multiple independent control switches are passed, it is clearer to pass each element of control in a separate parameter than to combine the control information into a single parameter. For example, two parameters named 'Flush Switch' and 'Print Switch' are easier to understand than a single parameter named 'Return Code', or some other equally general name. Combining various *independent* control flags into a single control flag with multiple values decreases the clarity – there is no way of giving the combination a descriptive name – and often restricts future flexibility by eliminating some useful combinations of the various flags. If the various conditions are mutually exclusive, i.e. only one of them can be true, then it may be clearer and simpler to pass the conditions as values of one control flag.

It can be proven that anything that can be executed on a computer can be created with modules that pass only data. Therefore, unless there are arbitrary restrictions, there is always an alternative where control does not have to be passed between modules. For example, if 'Price Order' in Figure 2.51 returned the priced order to 'Update Orders', as in Figure 2.56, the 'flush' can be eliminated. However, since it now returns a 'Priced Order' to its caller, the name 'Get Priced Order' better describes the new function. Similarly, Figure 2.57 is an alternative decomposition of the 'Trig' function in Figure 2.55 that does not require passing control parameters. Notice that the solution in Figure 2.57 avoids duplicating the code in 'Cosine'.

In order to determine whether a particular piece of data is control or not, determine whether it is used *to control another module*. A variable is used for control if its sender intends to tell the receiver what to do, e.g. the sender's function will not complete correctly if the receiver fails to respond to the field as intended. The callers of 'Trig' in Figure 2.55 care very much whether 'Trig' properly interprets the function switch and returns the answer to the desired function. If the sender's function is not affected by what the receiver does in response to the field, then it is not control. The 'Validate BO_No' module in Figure 2.56 passes back an OK flag; but its function is not affected by the caller's response to that information (e.g., prints the bad data, or throws it away and keeps only the good). If the most descriptive name for a *parameter* is a verb or a verb plus

STRUCTURED DESIGN   75

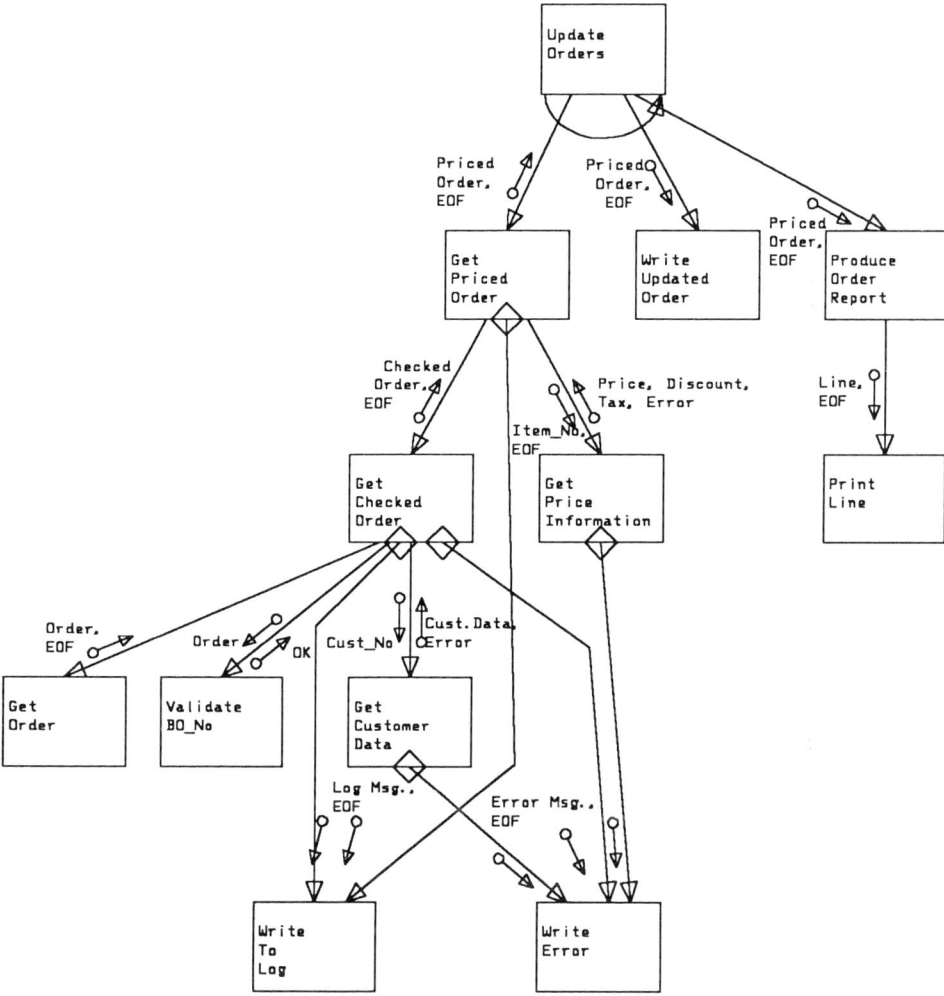

FIGURE 2.56 A further improved design

object, such as 'Get Next Record' or 'Send Error Message 3', then it is probably control. Data parameters should be able to be best described as a noun or an adjective plus noun, such as 'Master Record', 'Angle', 'Invalid Data' or 'Error'. Another way to spot control being passed is to ask, 'Can the receiver do more than one thing?' If so (as with the 'Trig' function in Figure 2.55), a flag is usually required to tell it which function is desired. Testing the intent of the communication between modules is more effective in determining what is control than looking at the format of the parameter. Control flags are not always binary, and some binary fields are not control flags. For example, the function switch passed to 'Trig' in Figure 2.55 has several possible values, but is still a control

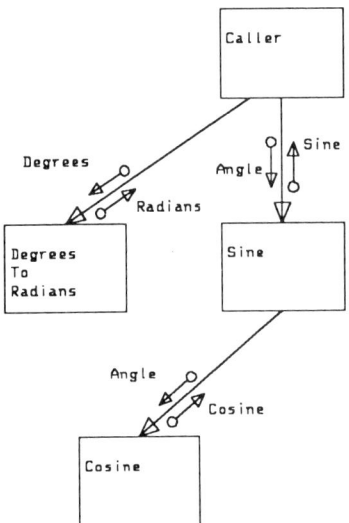

FIGURE 2.57 Functional modules

parameter. Conversely, a field that denotes male or female is binary, but is probably not control.

Coupling can be made even lower if self-defining data are passed. This reduces still further the need to understand the internals of the module that sends the data in order to understand the passed data. Accepting self-defining data can also broaden the range of data that a module can handle, which increases the chance that the module will be reused. Unfortunately, there is no generally accepted standard for self-defining data at this time. An even lower level of coupling would result from passing an 'Abstract Data Type' (see 'Abstract Data Types', Section 5.3). Then the modules would not even depend on the format of the data they share, self-defining or not.

TYPE OF CONNECTION

There are various types of connections between pieces of code. They can share global data, data internal to the module, parameters passed with a call statement, or data passed *without* the transfer of control of a call statement (see Figure 2.58). The highest coupling (which is least desirable) occurs when pieces of code have direct access to the same global data area – especially if those pieces of code can execute asynchronously. One way in which a global data area can be established is via 'external' variables (i.e. declaring variables within a module to be externally accessible by other modules). Examples of shared data areas are Fortran common, shared control blocks in an operating system, and shared variable areas in on-line systems. Shared global variables are a complex and restrictive way to share data between independent modules. All modules typically have access to each variable in the global data area and can change it at any time (whether by design or by error). Thus when it is discovered that some element of data is bad, it can be

STRUCTURED DESIGN   77

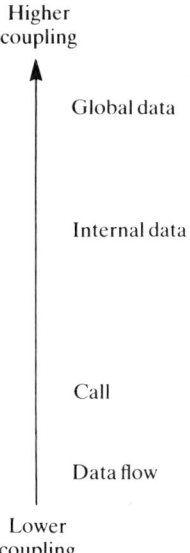

FIGURE 2.58 Type of connection

almost impossible to determine which module contains the error, since all modules are potential culprits. The larger the system, the more code has to be searched to find the error. If the global data area is accessed directly, then there is almost no way to trace which code uses which data. This can make problem determination very difficult. Since a global variable is shared by all modules, it must be used serially by the modules that update it. If there are multiple callers for a module, each of which passes data to the module via the global variable, then that module cannot be used asynchronously by its callers or they would overlay each other's parameters. Making sure that callers use a module serially in an on-line or other asynchronous environment can be very complex, involving the use of resource locks or other methods of synchronizing asynchronous actions. Errors made with such serialization mechanisms tend to be intermittent and timing-dependent, making them among the hardest of errors to debug. Shared global data areas often contain many variables and include both data and control variables. (See Stevens 1981, pages 49–53, for a more detailed explanation of shared data areas and how to reduce their coupling.)

While it may seem that data in files and data bases would cause the same problem as a shared global data area, there are significant differences. The biggest difference is that data on an external device are usually accessed via a single piece of code (the file or data base access method). Thus the users do not have direct access to the shared data. If multiple simultaneous updates to files or data bases are required, then the data base management system or file access method usually has a facility to assure data integrity across the multiple updates. Such locking mechanisms are seldom available for global data areas in memory. Another difference is that sometimes data on external devices are accessed by only one program at a time, so that problems inherent in asynchronous updates to shared data are not encountered. A third difference between files and global data areas is that the latter are often used for sharing data between modules when the same data could have been passed as parameters on calls or via data flow.

The next weaker type of coupling results from functions within the same module having the ability to access all internal data. The ability to share the internal variables makes the connections between the functions more difficult to understand. For example, even to determine if a variable is actually used by both functions requires searching both pieces of code – and there will still be the possibility that the reference has been missed or has been accomplished via a compiler statement that equates two variables. With invocation mechanisms that do not limit data sharing, such as a 'perform' statement in COBOL, it is possible for coding errors in one piece of code to change variables used only by another. Thus if it is difficult to find an error (as it often is), there is always the possibility that other pieces of code may have caused the error. When such sharing of local variables is prevented by the invocation mechanism, such as with a 'call' instruction, the problem is localized to the module that has access to the local variables in error.

Passing data as call parameters results in lower coupling than previous types of connections because it is clearer and allows the modules to be treated more independently in several ways. The language processor limits data sharing to variables defined in the call interface. The call statement eases debugging by eliminating the need to check other modules as to why local variables are in error. The ability to trace data passed by the call can also assist in debugging. A call interface can support multiple asynchronous callers without having to serialize their use.

Modules are even more independent – lower coupled – if data are passed between them *without* the transfer of control inherent in a call statement, as is depicted in data flow diagrams (see 'Structured Analysis', Section 2.2). The call statement (used, for example, by the modules in Figure 2.56) requires that the caller determine when the called module is to start, make sure that all the necessary data are passed to it and respond properly to any errors. In addition, a call statement forces synchronization between the modules because the caller's next instruction must be assumed to be invalid until the called module has completed execution. Thus a call may restrict the caller to be on the same computer, at the same time, and be in the same language. Although each of these requirements of a call can be eliminated by the right support system, the definition of the call statement restricts the two modules to run synchronously even if their functions could have been run asynchronously.

There is a substantial difference betwen directly sharing global data and passing data – so much difference in fact that they are at opposite ends of this dimension of coupling. With a shared data area, all modules can access it at any time (if not literally simultaneously, at least alternately and in various orders). Thus, designing, understanding, checking, debugging, etc., may require simultaneous understanding of many modules. When data are passed, only one module has access to them at a time. Thus, if data are found to be incorrect, the cause can be traced to the single module that had access to the data between the time at which it was good and that at which it became bad. However, sometimes the use of global data is unavoidable because that is the only communication vehicle available in an on-line system or other execution environment.

STRUCTURED DESIGN 79

Note, however, that the use of a global data area will make it very difficult to distribute the system's pieces in the future.

There are at least two ways in which the complex effects of sharing a global data area can be reduced, as follows:

1. Limiting the number of modules that can *change* each data element and document clearly which modules they are. If the number of modules that change a given data element can be reduced to one, then much of the complexity of sharing global data can be avoided (because then there is no multiple simultaneous update of the same data).
2. Segmenting the area so that a minimum number of modules contain the definition of each segment of the data (see Figure 2.59). Then include within each module only the labels for those elements used by that module. Such segmentation can reduce the number of potential connections through the global data area drastically since modules seldom require access to every field in the global data area.

SIZE OF CONNECTIONS

The less data are shared, the lower the coupling – as depicted in Figure 2.60 – but there are some subtleties that warrant further discussion. One is that coupling is affected by the quantity of data passed each time the interface is used. Coupling is not affected by how many callers a module has or by how many times an interface is executed. If the interface between two modules were a pipe carrying water, then it would be the *size* of the pipe that affected coupling, not how much water ended up going through the pipe. For example, the interface to the module 'Trig' in Figure 2.55 is larger than the interface to the module 'Sine' in Figure 2.57. To reduce coupling caused by the size of a module's interface, reduce the amount of data needed in the interface, even if only by one variable (usually coupling improvements are made one parameter at a time anyway).

Another subtlety of size is related to the number of parameters. The objective is to reduce the number of *fields* that have to be understood rather than the number of *names* that are declared in the interface. A call interface is clearer (and thus has lower coupling) if each independent element of data is passed as a separate variable. If some fields are logically related, such as the number of hours worked each day of the month, then it is simpler to pass them as a structure. Combining unrelated data into a single structure would make coupling stronger because the same *amount* of data would still have to be understood, but the form would make it more difficult to understand those data. For example, the module 'Validate BO_No' in Figure 2.56 is passed the complete order. However, all that is needed for its validation is the 'BO_No'. Passing only the 'BO_No' reduces the coupling, even though the number of parameters is not reduced, because it is now dependent on less data. That change also increases the chances that 'Validate BO_No' is reused, since modules with only the 'BO_No' can call it (without being required to have an order).

CLARITY

The easier it is to understand the interface between modules, the simpler it is to design, check, implement, test, debug, or change the software. Implicit or obscure interfaces make it more difficult to comprehend the effects of existing code or the effects of possible

80 ARCHITECTURAL SOFTWARE DESIGN

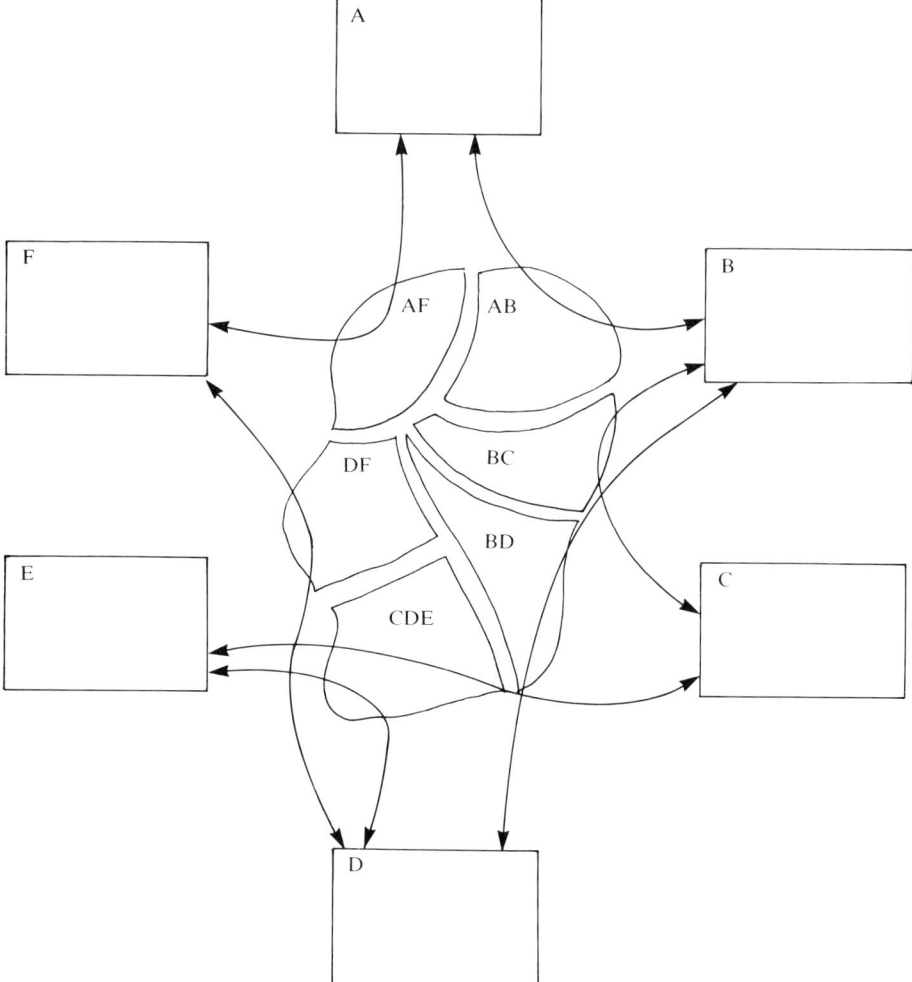

FIGURE 2.59 Segmenting a global data area

changes because it is harder to understand how a module might affect, or be affected by, another module. A clear, explicit interface helps reduce how much has to be considered in order to understand the action of, or proposed change for, a given module because it makes it less likely that the internals of one module have to be understood in order to understand or change the other. Anything that helps make the interface clearer reduces coupling. There are several ways to make interfaces clear, as follows:

1. Define sharing and interfaces explicitly (rather than sharing data or control implicitly or in undefined ways, as illustrated with control coupling above).

FIGURE 2.60 Size of the connection

2. Give a well-defined, understandable name to each element or array in the interface. For example, 'Quantity' is clearer than 'Field_1'.
3. Give a well-defined, understandable name to the module that indicates its function. For example, if 'Get Price Information' were called 'Get Necessary Information', it would be harder to discern when and how to use it. Names are clearer if modules are functional (see 'Binding' in section 2.5.3). Clarity is obscured by the use of numeric names (e.g. '1.2') or prefix letters in names of modules, such as those assigned to prevent name clashes.
4. Supply text that describes the module's function and how to use it.

Another way to achieve clarity is to consider each module as a 'black box', which is something that can be used without having to understand its internal construction, much as we use radios. A clear interface should be so easy to understand that other people can use it without ever having to look at the code inside the module.

In summary, to achieve the least coupling, choose the lowest alternative on each aspect of coupling, i.e.:

1. Share data only (and not control).
2. Pass the data by data flow if possible (and use a call statement otherwise).
3. Pass as few data fields as possible.
4. Make the interface as clear as possible.

By making choices 1 and 2 before design commences, the only aspects that need to be concentrated on during design are numbers 3 and 4. Note that reducing coupling, which reduces complexity, is not the only objective to be satisfied when designing software. Proper designs involve balancing reduced coupling with other objectives, such as performance. Naturally, it is desirable to trade the least increase in coupling for the biggest increase in the other objectives. Knowledge of how to reduce coupling can help the designer to choose the most appropriate balance.

2.5.5 Example with structure charts

Structured Design has usually been presented in the literature as recommending the use of call hierarchies. This is because calls are the best connection mechanism available in many environments. A good call hierarchy that results from applying Structured Design principles to the 'Price Order Records' problem is shown in Figure 2.61. This structure is an improvement over that in Figure 2.56. The module 'Get Valid Order' has been extracted from 'Get Checked Order' to reduce the complexity of the latter module and to make the 'Get Valid Order' function available for possible reuse in another program. The call from 'Get Price Information' to 'Write Error' has been moved to 'Get Priced Order', which eliminates having to pass 'EOF' to 'Get Price Information' (as in Figure 2.56). The call to 'Write Error' from 'Get Customer Data' in Figure 2.56 has also been moved to 'Get Checked Order' ('Get Checked Order' gets the error passed to it from 'Get Customer Data' regardless). 'Get Customer Data' can then be used in programs that do not require the same error message, or who require it to be sent to a different place.

2.5.6 Example: using Structured Design with data flow diagrams

The measures of Structured Design can also be used to evaluate other types of structural decomposition, including data flow diagrams, call hierarchies, source segments, macros, Abstract Data Types, Object-Oriented concepts, and Jackson design. The coupling concepts of Structured Design show that modules connected only by data flows are more independent than those connected by data *plus* the transfer of control of a call statement. In addition, the call statement embeds the name of a specific module into the internals of the calling module, which also makes called modules more dependent. Thus systems with modules connected only by flows of data are simpler than systems with call hierarchies.

Designing for data flows is like designing system flowcharts (as shown in Figure 2.2), and thus anyone who can design a system flowchart already knows how to design for data flows. Designing for data flows can be made easier by relating it to how people interact in an office or similar working arrangement. People in an office work simultaneously and asynchronously and may share data by sending forms to one another. Data flow diagrams depict processes that can execute independently of one another and communicate by passing data. Flowcharts and notations that depict sequence, iteration, and choice constructs describe how one individual performs a task and similarly can be used to describe the logic *within* an integrand. Data flow connections are a natural way to connect integrands or modules produced by other people, because they model a way of interacting that comes naturally to people. A good data flow diagram that results from

STRUCTURED DESIGN 83

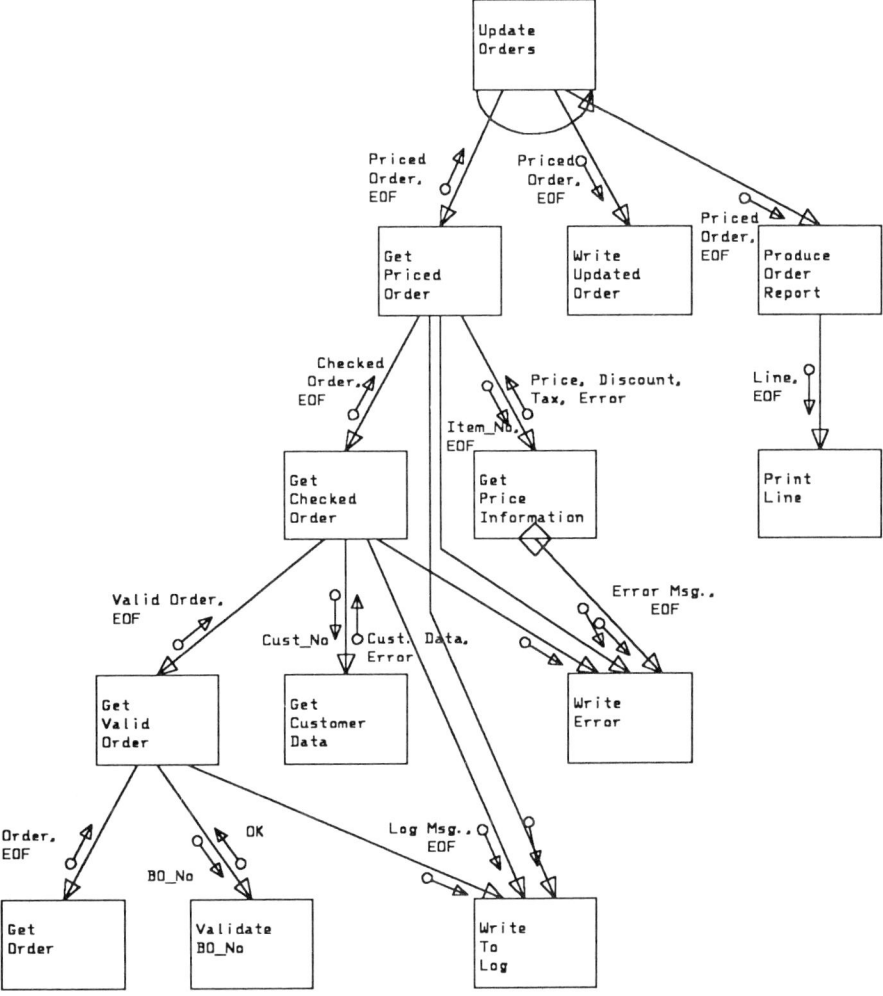

FIGURE 2.61 Final structure chart for Update Orders

applying Structured Design principles to the sample problem for updating orders is shown in Figure 2.62.

Many of the concepts useful for designing for data flows are given in Structured Analysis and Essential Systems Analysis (see Sections 2.2 and 2.3 above). Most of the concepts of Structured Design apply equally to data flows as to call hierarchies, including the concepts of functionality and independence. However, a couple of areas warrant discussion:

1. Passing minimum data elements.
2. When to use a call even with a data flow alternative.

84 ARCHITECTURAL SOFTWARE DESIGN

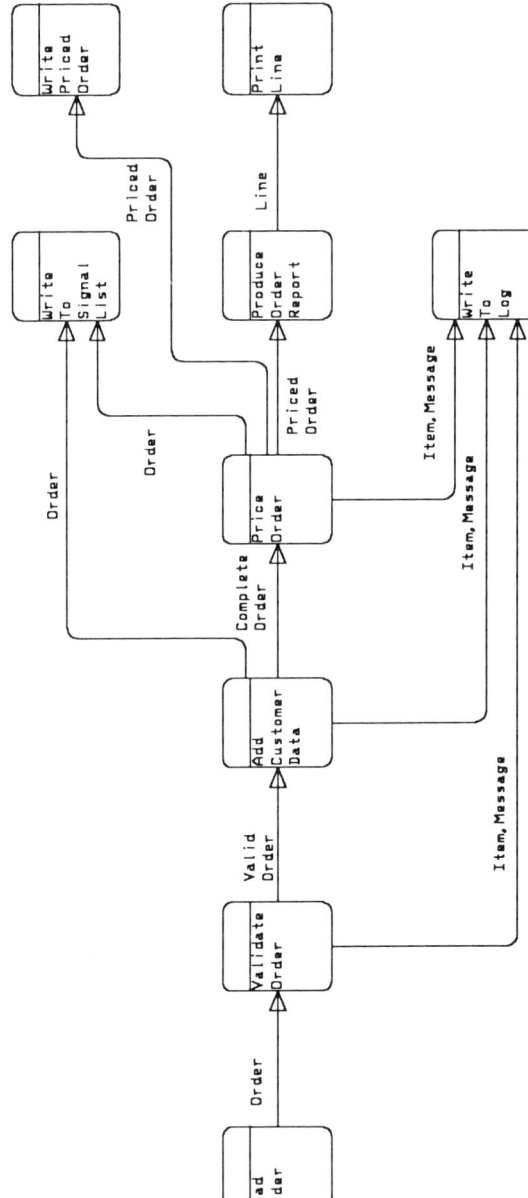

FIGURE 2.62 Data flow diagram for Update Orders

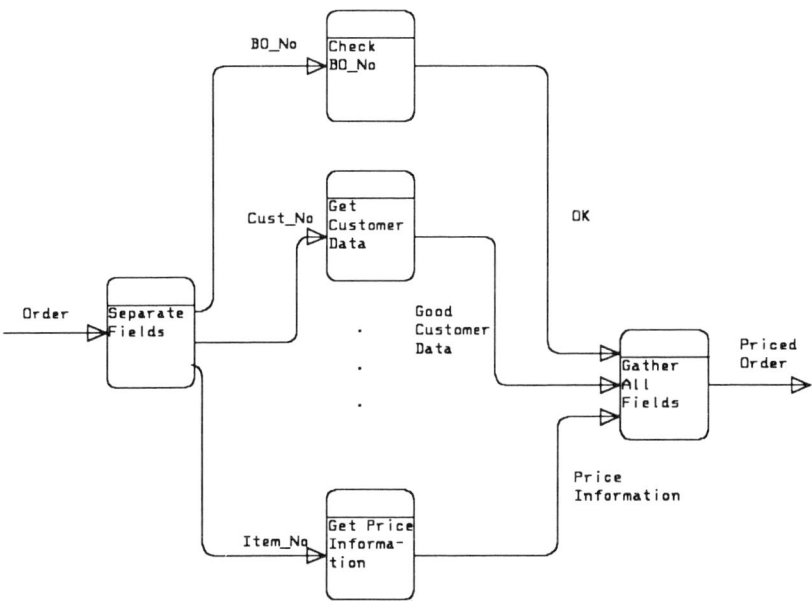

FIGURE 2.63 Interdependent modules

With call hierarchies, Structured Design recommends reducing to a minimum the number of data elements (i.e. parameters) passed to a called subroutine, thus achieving the maximum independence. However, attempting to minimize data into each module with data flows can lead to such structures as the one illustrated in Figure 2.63, which, while it may look functional, can handle processing for independent fields only. If the processing of one field requires knowledge of some other field, a new flow of data will have to be added or the structure changed to accommodate that need for data. Thus, as the processing of each field changes, the structure and grouping of processing for the fields may have to be changed. In addition, in Figure 2.63 there are activities, separating the fields and gathering them again, which lack analogs in the real world and are therefore not in the alternative design in Figure 2.62 (and thus are extra effort to design and implement). In order to assure that all fields from a given form are gathered properly, a key would have to be assigned to each field to associate it with a particular set of data. In addition, the modules that process fields have to send some information forward to the gathering function even if they decide to leave a field empty. With the design in Figure 2.62, each function has access to the entire order. It can access the information it needs and update fields as appropriate. The modules are more independent of one another because the structure has not assumed a particular independence among the individual fields.

With a well-designed structure chart, such as that illustrated in Figure 2.61, the transformation of data takes place primarily in lower level modules such as 'Read Order' and 'Check BO_No'. There also are modules which primarily contain the control of

86 ARCHITECTURAL SOFTWARE DESIGN

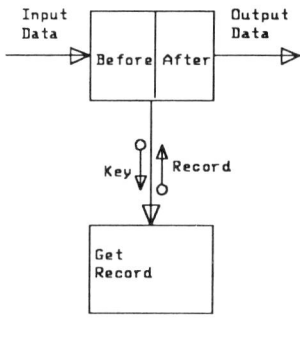

Call

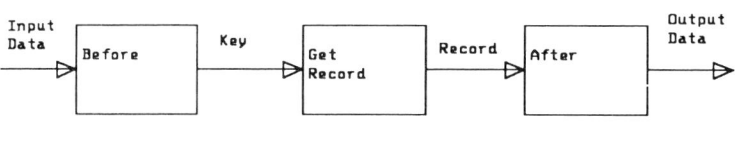

Data flow

FIGURE 2.64 Call versus data flow

which lower level module to call next and which handle errors, such as 'Get Valid Order' and 'Get Checked Order' in Figure 2.61. In simple cases, the relationship between the structure chart and the data flow diagram is that the lower level modules are connected in the data flow diagram which has no need for the data-routing type modules from the structure chart (compare Figures 2.61 and 2.62). However, the transformation is seldom so simple and, even in this case, some of the data manipulation is within 'Get Checked Order' and 'Get Priced Order' (adding the data to the order). In this case, a way to relate designing for data flow to designing for call hierarchies is depicted in Figure 2.64. The 'Before' code executes before the call to get the record and the 'After' code executes after the call. (This is easier if there are no loops or branches that connect the 'Before' and 'After' codes.) With a call interface, the 'Before' and 'After' codes may be in the same module as shown on the left in Figure 2.64. With data flow connections, it is possible to separate the 'Before' and 'After' codes – if they are independent functions – into different modules that can be independent of each other. For example, 'Get Checked Order' in Figure 2.61 first calls 'Get Valid Order' (the 'Before' code), then calls 'Get Customer Data' (the call), and afterwards calls the error routines and returns a checked order to

'Get Priced Order' (all the 'After' code). In Figure 2.62, 'Add Customer Data' gets the record, with modules to the left performing the 'Before' functions and those to the right the 'After' functions.

When is it advisable to use a call interface even when a data flow interface is available? If data flow connections are available, use them for most connections among modules. However, use a call whenever the returned data are essential for the completion of a single function, i.e. the 'Before' and 'After' are functionally bound. For example, if some module needs a system service such as a date or a resource lock, a call is probably more appropriate than a data flow connection.

When designing for data flows, an office can be a useful model to answer questions about alternative designs that might otherwise seem equally functional. For each design alternative, assume that each module is a person. Then see if the data flow connections would result in an efficient office where everyone has enough information and independence to allow them to work on their assigned tasks. If a proposed design divides a function across several people so that they start to become dependent on each other in order to perform their own tasks, then try to group the dependent parts of the functions into single modules.

2.5.7 Comments on Structured Design

Structured Design contains concepts and measures for functional decomposition which are relied upon by many other methods which then do not have to repeat a definition of similar concepts. Structured Programming recommended limiting control flows – to understand the interactions between various 'segments' more easily (see 'Structured Programming', Section 3.2). Structured Design recommends reducing the coupling even further by also minimizing the data references between modules. The concepts and measures of Structured Design can be used with any software design to help reduce the complexity and the need for developers to communicate with each other in order to develop their portion of the system. Structured Design and Structured Analysis (including the concepts of Essential Systems Analysis) are very compatible. Typically, Structured Analysis is used to develop a hierarchy of data flow diagrams until the nodes on the lowest level diagrams are single batch programs or on-line transactions. Then those nodes can be further decomposed as call hierarchies (unless there is a data flow mechanism for connecting integrands, as illustrated in Appendix A, in which case the data flow diagram hierarchy can be extended all the way to the integrands). I do not recommend converting data flow diagrams to call hierarchies. If the end result will be a call hierarchy, design it that way. While some simple data flow diagrams can be converted, there are those that cannot be converted (e.g. one with a module that makes multiple copies of its inputs with the number of copies being controlled by the input data). For more detail on how to use Structured Design, readers are referred to *Using Structured Design* (Stevens 1981). For a description of the complete theory of Structured Design see *Structured Design* by Yourdon and Constantine (1979).

88   ARCHITECTURAL SOFTWARE DESIGN

2.6 BOX STRUCTURED DESIGN

The concepts of *black boxes* and *state machines* can be combined into a method that can be applied during the analysis and design of computer software. These concepts and their specific application to the analysis of information systems have been formulated and described by Harlan Mills, Richard Linger, and Alan Hevner in their book *Principles of Information Systems Analysis and Design* (1986). The information in this section and Figures 2.65–2.74 are based on, or reprinted from, their book with the permission of Academic Press, Inc. (and the term 'state machine' in their text has been replaced with their more recent choice of 'state box'). Of significant importance in 'Box Structured Design' are the abilities to expand a system into parts and to recombine (synthesize) defined parts to recreate the top level system definition (as will be described below). Both are performed in such a way that the integrity of the analysis and synthesis is maintained and provable for the data *and* the functional definitions.

Box structures are a way of describing systems, with three basic structures called:

1. Black box (where only the stimulus and resulting response are visible).
2. State box (which makes the internal state visible).
3. Clear box (four ways to combine yet lower level black boxes) that can be nested again and again in a hierarchical structure.

The first step when using box structures is to model the current or future system as a black box. The black box can then be represented as a state box and the state box by a clear box. The clear box includes various combinations of black boxes arranged in sequence, iteration, choice, and concurrent structures. Then each of the black boxes in the clear box can again be described as a state box, clear box, and lower level black boxes. These expansions can continue as necessary to describe the system being modeled.

2.6.1 Black box

A black box can be used to describe any mechanism or system that one cannot look inside to see *how* it works, i.e. like a box that is *black* on the outside so that the observer cannot see inside. However, the black box can still be analyzed by giving it various inputs and observing its responses. Examples include radios and televisions (people can get the station by turning the knobs without ever having to understand the internal circuits), pumps, motors and a module that calculates the sine of an angle. Many mechanisms can be analyzed so well by this method that no additional understanding of the internals is required in order to use the mechanism productively. A black box is defined as:

> 'a mechanism that accepts stimuli and for each stimulus produces a response before accepting another stimulus; furthermore, each response is uniquely determined by the history of stimuli accepted by the black box.'

A black box, as shown in Figure 2.65, accepts stimuli, and for each stimulus (S), produces a response (R) before accepting the next stimulus. It produces the same external

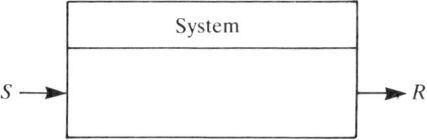

FIGURE 2.65 A black box diagram

responses to the same stimuli as the system it is modeling, with no claim to having the same internal implementation. The black box is independent of the way the system being modeled is constructed. Instead, it deals only with the behavior visible to a user in terms of stimuli and responses and is uniquely determined by the system's stimulus history. The system being modeled will, presumably, be the current or future software system. However, this black box approach can be applied to any system, including manual procedures, that accepts inputs from the environment and produces responses one at a time.

Mills *et al.* exclude initial states as a part of general black box modeling. Box Structured Design works with systems that depend only on stimulus histories and that can be presumed to have some ability to re-set or initialize the state variables to some power-on value, or initial null value, at the start of any stimulus history – as is usually assumed with computers anyway. This limitation on general black box modeling significantly reduces the complexity of general black box analysis while still leaving a tool able to model most, if not all, software systems of interest (because there is usually a way to set software systems to some initial state).

2.6.2 State box

Some systems are more difficult than others to analyze from the outside, especially if the system maintains an internal state. In this case, the output does not necessarily result directly from the current input, but can depend on the entire history of inputs to the system. Examples of such systems include a calculator, an encryption device, and the central processing unit of a computer with its main memory. The existence of internal states does not necessarily make the system difficult to analyze as a black box, especially when the internal states can be viewed. For example, radios may remember and display the stations that the user can assign to buttons; motors have a visible inertia even after the power is removed; and calculators maintain and show their running total as a series of numbers is added. In each case the internal state is visible, making the analysis of the black box significantly easier. Similarly, a symbolic debugging facility that can display the values of variables of a program (its internal state) during execution can help discover why the program is failing.

A state box is an abstraction of a system in which the internal state is visible. A state box (see Figure 2.66) is defined as a:

> *state*, which incorporates the stimulus history, and a *machine*, another (usually simpler) black box that carries out the transitions, of the state box.

The state of the state box in Figure 2.66 can be viewed, and even implemented, as a master file. The machine part of the state box would then be the equivalent of a file-update program which accepts transactions, updates the state based on the transactions, and produces an output report (as in Figure 2.67). Since this concept of a master file update system is a familiar one to many software designers, it can serve as a useful comparison for understanding the concept of a state box. Outputs of the state box are dependent on the values of the current inputs and the state variables, which are data fields containing information that represent the box's internal state. A state box is a natural abstraction to use for analyzing a system: no historical information is needed, only current values of the input and of the state variables are needed to determine the outputs.

2.6.3 Clear box

A state box can be expanded into one of four types of clear boxes (see Figure 2.68), as follows:

1. Sequence.
2. Alternation.
3. Iteration.
4. Concurrent.

In the clear boxes in Figure 2.68, machine parts M1 and M2 are black boxes, each accepting as input stimuli the stimulus of the clear box and the current state, and producing as its response both the update to the internal state and the response of the clear box. In the alternation structure, machine part C accepts the stimulus and the current state and sends the stimulus to M1 or M2 without affecting the state. Whichever machine receives the stimulus also has the current state as input, updates the state of the clear box and produces its output response. In the iteration structure, C either transmits the stimulus to M1 or passes it through as the clear box's response.

Not only is it possible to expand the hierarchy from the top down, but it is also possible to derive higher levels from the lower level components (see Figure 2.69), which is an important and valuable contribution made by Mills, Linger, and Hevner. This example of the use of box structure design to derive the response characteristics of an overall system illustrates the concepts of black boxes, state boxes, clear boxes, and their use in the description of systems. Box Structured Design can be used to describe the design of a new software system or, as in this example, to describe an existing system.

2.6.4 Example: US Navy Supply System Reorder Policy

Box Structured Design concepts were used to analyze the US Navy supply system in the mid-1950s and that analysis led to a major change and improvement in the Navy's inventory control. Up to that time, their 'K months of supply' policy, as it was called, had

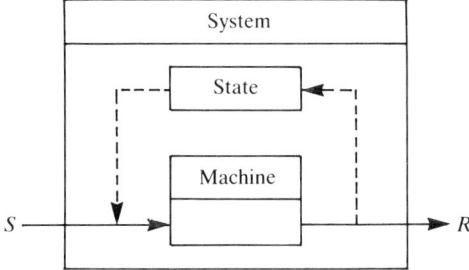

FIGURE 2.66 A state box diagram

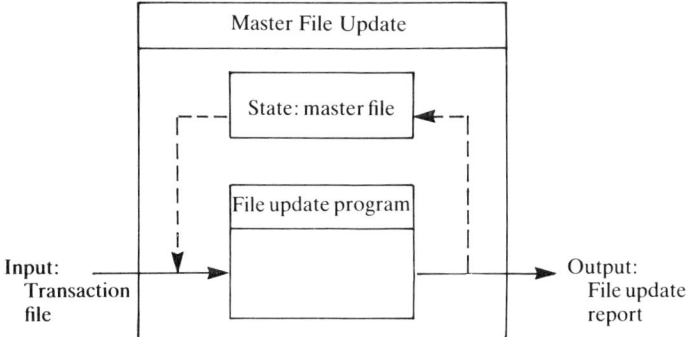

FIGURE 2.67 The Master File Update state box

seemed quite sensible. Its objective was to maintain K months of average demand of each item either on order or in inventory. The value of K varied from item to item and was chosen by the inventory manager based on the variability of demand, length of time to obtain more, and the consequences if the item were out of stock. Once K was chosen for an item, each month's order could be determined by a simple calculation. The average demand was calculated by taking a twelve-month running average so the effects of unusual months would seem to average out. For example, if the time taken to obtain a certain size anchor is nine months, some months' demand was three times other months', and the importance of not having an outage warranted another four months' safety factor, then K would be $9 + 3 + 4 = 16$.

FORMULATING THE SUPPLY SYSTEM CLEAR BOX

The business policy thus includes determining the twelve-month running average demand, A:

$$A = (D + D1 + D2 + \ldots + D11)/12$$

where D (the current stimulus) equals the current month's demand, $D1$ equals the

92   ARCHITECTURAL SOFTWARE DESIGN

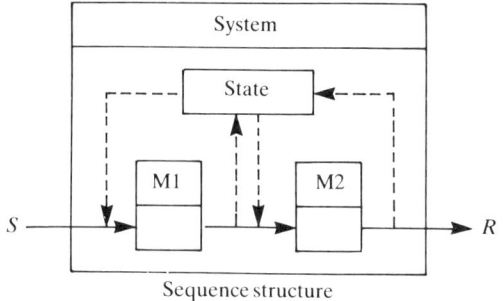

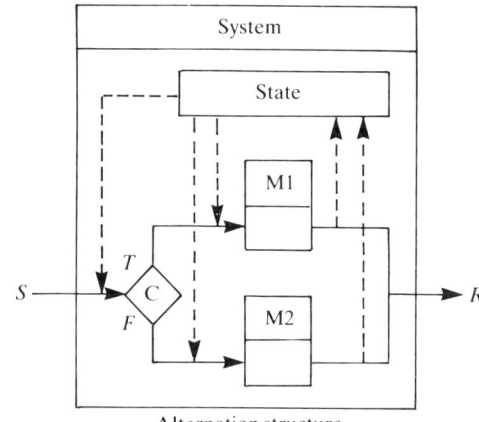

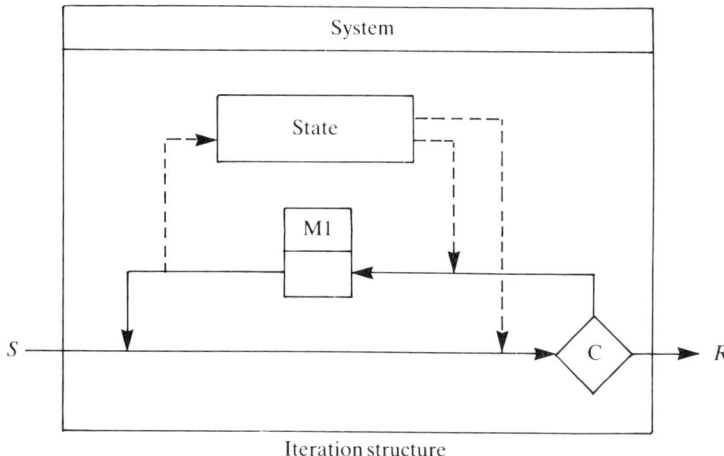

FIGURE 2.68 Clear box diagrams

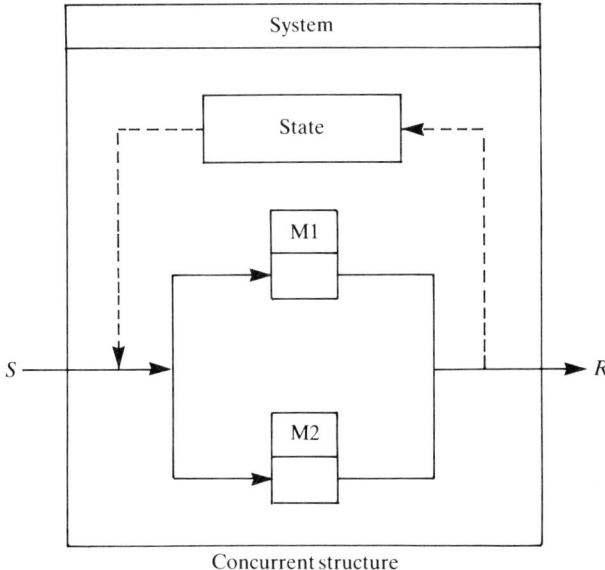

Concurrent structure

FIGURE 2.68—contd.

demand one month ago . . ., and $D11$ equals the demand eleven months ago. Filling the current month's demand reduces the inventory, I, of parts in stock and on order:

$$I = I - D$$

The desired inventory is K times the twelve-month average demand, i.e. KA. The amount to re-order, R, is the desired inventory (KA) less the new updated inventory of parts in stock and on order:

$$R = KA - I = K(D + D1 + \ldots + D11)/12 - I$$

Placing the order for R parts increases the current number of parts in stock or on order by the number just ordered:

$$I = I + R$$

Since the only stimulus each month for this clear box is D, the state variables that are kept from the preceding month in order to perform the above calculations are:

$$K, I, D1, D2, \ldots, D11$$

Next month, the current month's demand becomes $D1$, $D1$ becomes $D2$, etc., so there is a custodial activity necessary in order to be ready for the next month's calculations. That activity sets $D11 = D10$, $D10 = D9$, . . . , and $D1 = D$. A clear box that describes the K months of supply policy is shown in Figure 2.70. This can now be rigorously converted into a state box which contains no sequence.

94   ARCHITECTURAL SOFTWARE DESIGN

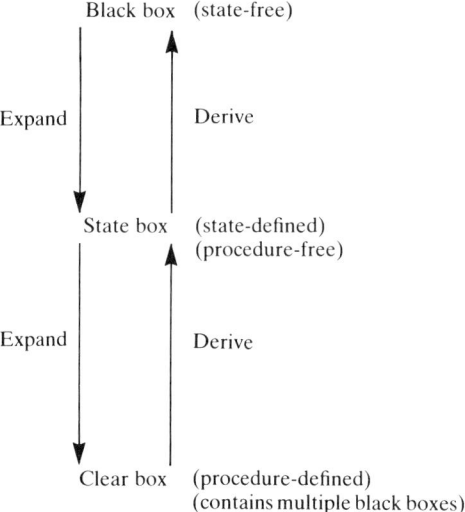

FIGURE 2.69 Expansion and derivation

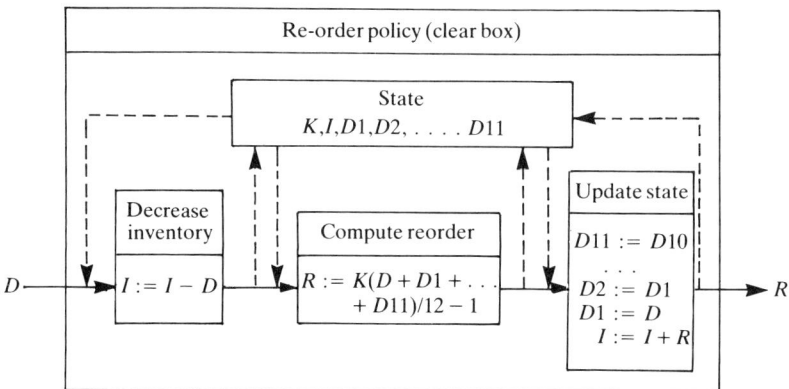

FIGURE 2.70 Reorder Policy clear box

THE SUPPLY SYSTEM STATE BOX

To *deduce* a state box from its clear box, one combines the effect of the lower level black boxes into a single set of expressions which depend only on the stimulus of the clear box and the values of the state variables when the stimulus arrives (i.e. none of the computations may use the results of other computations in the set). There is only one such state box for each clear box (though there may be more than one equivalent way to describe it), and that state box is a procedure-free description of that clear box.

To deduce the state box from the clear box in Figure 2.70, expressions are deduced that calculate the response, R, and the new state variables in terms only of the stimulus, D,

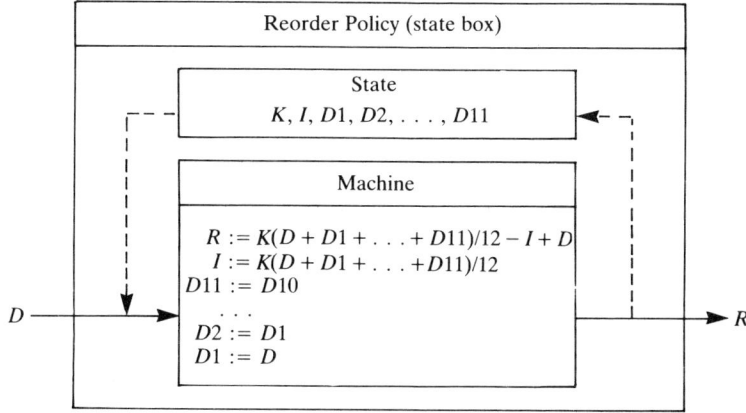

FIGURE 2.71 Reorder Policy state box

and the existing values of the state variables when the stimulus D arrives. This is called a procedure-free description, i.e. the instructions in the machine part of the state box are independent of each other for values used in their calculations (and thus can be executed in any sequence or in parallel). Eliminating dependencies in the calculations can be accomplished by identifying uses of values calculated in earlier sequential processes in the clear box and substituting equivalent expressions in terms of the stimulus and state variables. For example, the calculation for R in the middle box in Figure 2.70 uses a value of I which is modified in the first box. By substituting $(I - D)$ for I, the calculation for R depends only on D and the values the state variables had when D arrived. The resulting expression is:

$$R = K(D + D1 + \ldots + D11)/12 - (I - D)$$

Similarly, the complete expression for I becomes:

$$I = (I - D) + R = (I - D) + K(D + D1 + \ldots + D11)/12 - (I - D)$$
$$= K(D + D1 + \ldots + D11)/12$$

and the expressions $D11 = D10$, $D10 = D9 \ldots$, $D1 = D$ can remain unchanged. Thus the clear box in Figure 2.70 has the state box shown in Figure 2.71.

THE SUPPLY SYSTEM BLACK BOX

To *deduce* the black box from a state box expansion of it, one captures the effect of the stored state and computations of the state box in a single set of computational statements, or in some other way of specifying what the state box's response is to its stimuli. There is only one such black box for a given state box, i.e. the one that has the state box's stimulus response relationship (although there may be more than one way to describe its relationship of stimuli and responses), and its description is state-free.

In order to deduce the black box for the clear box in Figure 2.71, it is necessary to eliminate the state variables and calculate the response, R, in terms of the stimulus history only. Let $D[m]$ represent the current month's demand stimulus, $D[m-1]$ represent the stimulus one month ago, ..., and $D[m-12]$ indicate the stimulus twelve months ago. When a demand, $D[m]$, arrives, $D1$ will equal $D[m-1]$, $D2$ will equal $D[m-2]$, ..., and $D11$ will equal $D[m-11]$. Thus when $D[m]$ arrives, the value of the state variable I (which was calculated the month before) is:

$$I = K(D[m-1] + D[m-2] + \ldots + D[m-12])/12$$

Thus the expression for R becomes:

$$R = K(D + D1 + \ldots + D11)/12 - (I - D)$$
$$= K(D[m] + \ldots + D[m-11])/12 - K(D[m-1] + \ldots + D[m-12])/12 + D[m]$$
$$= K(D[m] - D[m-12])/12 + D[m]$$

Since the middle terms of the demand history cancel out, the re-order quantity, R, ends up depending on only two demands – the current month's and the demand twelve months ago, which is the same month last year. Rather than smooth seasonal demands, this system ends up accentuating them. Moreover, this re-order policy had been used by many organizations for decades without even a suspicion that this pattern existed. Despite constant observation of the system, its black box behavior became clear only after being derived from the definition of its components.

2.6.5 Modeling with Box Structures

DISCOVERING BLACK BOX BEHAVIOR

Black box analysis provides a way to understand and *predict* the behavior of existing and proposed systems. Conversely, black box analysis – and Box Structured Design – are useful only on systems that produce predictable outputs, i.e. outputs that depend only on the stimulus history. Thus calculators, cars, radios, and computers can be modeled as black boxes. A roulette wheel cannot be represented adequately by a black box, even though it has stimuli (spins) and responses (a number), since the numbers are independent of its stimulus history. A mechanism whose *only* stimulus is a push of a button and which delivers a reading of the current temperature when the button is pushed is also not a black box, since the same stimulus history produces different responses. However, that part of the mechanism that receives both the measurement of the current temperature and the button push as stimuli can be a black box. Black box analysis can only be applied when the responses can be uniquely determined by the stimulus history of the black box. Conversely, once it is determined that a system can be modeled by a black box, the stimulus history of a black box is sufficient to guarantee unique responses.

Most of the systems we use as black boxes, such as radios, televisions, cars and calculators, have instruction books that explain what stimulus (pushing keys, turning knobs) produces what output. However, not all systems have such instruction books (e.g. procedures of current manual systems may not be documented). A way is needed to

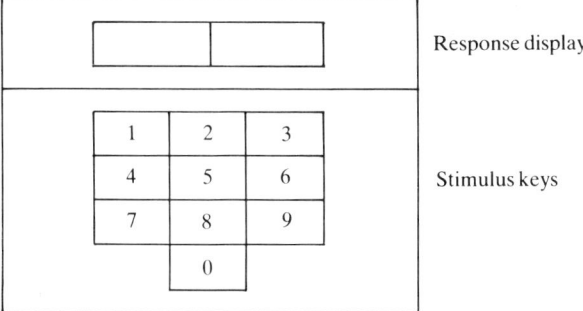

FIGURE 2.72 A hand-held device that accepts stimuli and produces responses

Stimulus	Response
3	3
6	9
1	7
9	10
6	15

FIGURE 2.73 A stimulus–response table

Stimulus history	Response
3	3
3 6	9
3 6 1	7
3 6 1 9	10
3 6 1 9 6	15

FIGURE 2.74 A stimulus–response history

determine and record black box behavior regardless of the availability, or correctness, of instruction books. A *stimulus–response* table is one way to record black box behavior (though only for finite sequences). Figure 2.73 shows the stimuli and resulting responses for the device shown in Figure 2.72 (which is not a calculator). Each row of the table depicts what is called a *black box transition* which is the system's response to each stimulus. The transitions depicted in Figure 2.73 are 3 → 3, 6 → 9, 1 → 7, 9 → 10, and 6 → 15 (where arrows represent transitions). By recording the stimulus and the system's response to it, the black box behavior of the device can be studied. However, in general the response from a black box depends not only on the most recent stimulus but on the entire history of stimuli. For example, Figure 2.73 shows that the device's response to a stimulus of 6 is a 9 once and a 15 the next time. Thus its response must be based on more than the most recent input. Since the output depends on the stimulus history, it may be more useful to depict the entire history beside each response, as in Figure 2.74 (where the most recent stimulus is at the right-hand end of each stimulus history line).

The table showing the system's response to the entire *stimulus history* can now be analyzed for relationships between the response and the preceding history. Inspection of Figure 2.74 yields the observation that each response except the first one is the sum of the two preceding stimuli (and the first one could be taken to be the sum of 3 and 0 for consistency). This observation, if correct, makes the system's responses predictable. Naturally, if future observations show this observation to be incorrect, then a new relationship can be postulated based on the additional stimulus–response information. The transitions as shown in the stimulus history table are the only information about the system that must be tracked in order to analyze its black box behavior.

Naturally, more sophisticated systems than the device depicted in Figure 2.72 can include more complex stimuli and responses – these need not be single numbers. A computer may read an entire file as a stimulus, and produce a large report as its response. An aircraft control system may take inputs from many sources and produce a variety of control responses. An encryption machine may accept an encoding key and a string of text and produce encrypted output text. Note that one way to view the very purpose of an encryption machine is to produce a result that *cannot* be analyzed by observing the black box stimuli and responses (though it *is* predictable by someone who knows the hidden stimulus of the encoding key).

DESCRIBING BLACK BOXES AS STATE BOXES

While a stimulus history table is a useful tool for determining the relationship between the response of a black box and its stimulus history, stimulus histories can become arbitrarily long. Thus stimulus histories are not practical ways to depict the inner workings of the black box. However, because we have specifically avoided having to probe inside the real object modeled by the black box, we cannot represent a black box by its actual working. We need a way to represent the internals of *any* black box regardless of the actual internal implementation of the mechanism or system it models. Such a representation need only produce the same responses as the actual system to the same stimulus history in order to allow further adequate analysis. The *state box* provides just such a generic representation of the equivalent inner workings of the black box.

A black box that converts a stimulus history into a response can be simulated by a state box that converts the stimulus and its current internal state into a response and a new internal state. This new state then becomes the current state for processing the next stimulus. A black box may be represented as many different state boxes, as long as the stimulus response characteristics of each state box are identical to those of the black box. To *expand* a black box into a state box, one induces some set of state variables and computational statements so that the state box produces the same responses for each stimulus history as does the black box. Many such state boxes are possible for a given black box, and each includes a state-defined description. The state box starts to open up the black box by separating the stored state data. The machine part of the state box is the part that takes the stimulus and the current state data and produces both the response and an updated state. Mills *et al.* show that every black box has a state box description. To see that this is true, first consider that a black box is defined by a stimulus–response history, i.e. a stimulus and stimulus history are sufficient to produce a unique response and new stimulus history.

(stimulus, stimulus history) → (response, new stimulus history)

For a state box, a stimulus and a state are sufficient to produce the response and the new state, i.e.

(stimulus, state) → (response, new state)

Since the state is just a representation of the stimulus history, the term 'state' in the above expression for the state box can be replaced by the stimulus history, which yields the same description as the preceding one for the black box. Thus *every black box can be described by a state box.*

EXPANDING STATE BOXES INTO CLEAR BOXES

To *expand* a state box into a clear box, one induces a combination of black boxes in sequence, iteration, choice, and concurrent structures that calculates the same response and updated state variables from the state box's stimulus as does the state box. There can be many such expansions, and each is a procedure-defined description of that state box. Mills *et al.* state that:

> it is a consequence of the Structure Theorem of Structured Programming that every system described by a state box has a clear box description.

See 'Structured Programming', Section 3.2, for a description of the structure theorem and Marcotty (1991) for a proof of the Structure Theorem from an earlier paper by Mills (1972). Naturally, it would be possible to have other types of clear boxes than the four chosen by Mills *et al.* However, the four types of clear boxes above are sufficient to model software systems.

2.6.6 Comments on Box Structured Design

Box Structured Design is primarily an analysis technique since it is used more to model the behavior of a system than to display or choose its actual architecture. The choices for clear boxes may be sufficient to model systems of interest. However, there is nothing in the decomposition of state boxes to clear boxes to make them relate to modules that will, or should, be in the actual implemented system – as a design notation should. The concepts of how to choose one set of modules versus another when decomposing come from design methods such as Structured Analysis and Structured Design (Sections 2.3 and 2.5). Many technical papers use the technique of black box analysis either implicitly or explicitly and *Principles of Information Systems Analysis and Design* (Mills *et al.*, 1986) is an excellent description of black boxes applied to software. Components produced by other software design methods can be treated as clear boxes, state boxes, or black boxes and the results combined into higher level clear boxes, state boxes, or black boxes. Thus,

Box Structured Design is valuable not only as a method of analysis, but also because the concepts contained within it can be used with other methods to strengthen those methods. Properly leveled data flow diagrams should have the data that flow in and out of the boundaries of a lower level expansion the same as the data going in and out of the higher level box that it represents. In addition, the composite of the functions of the lower level diagram should constitute a complete and correct version of the node represented by the diagram. However, methods of Structured Analysis usually state these constraints without indicating how to analyze (or synthesize) the functions or prove that the data and functions are consistent in the hierarchy. Nodes in a data flow diagram are black boxes since they function in the network based simply on their stimulus–response histories. Diagrams of interconnected clear box structures are data flow diagrams or transformation schema diagrams. Thus, concepts of Box Structured Design can also be used for real-time systems. The concepts of Box Structured Design formulated by Mills, Linger, and Hevner are valuable additions to Structured Analysis, Essential Systems Analysis, Structured Design, and any approach that embodies functional hierarchical decomposition.

Black box modeling can add a significant advantage to any modeling approach – it reduces the need to concentrate on many details of a system and allows concentration on the analysis of a relevant subset of the available details. The *synthesis* of box structures back into higher level descriptions is a particularly valuable technique for the design, development, and verification of software (and other systems). Although we tend to view the system as something being designed from a high level specification downwards, once components of a system exist, they take on a life of their own. The designer also has little or no control over components that already exist. Even newly designed components can undergo further design as well as maintenance changes – both of which can alter their function and output data. Many experienced designers can remember how changes as the result of design errors, user requests, management dictates, or budget cuts have resulted in components not meeting the original design specifications. The result can be that the overall system fails to meet *its* high level objectives – even though each component is functioning correctly, including those with the modified objectives. For example, a people-mover system was designed for a large airport to provide adequate movement of passengers changing airplanes and going to and from the parking lots. Design simulations were based on a given speed for the cars and derived the number of cars and routes for tracks necessary to meet the volume and transfer-time objectives. After the tracks were built, and presumably for valid reasons, the speed of the cars was decreased. As a result, the system fails to provide adequate volume and transfer speed. At the current speed, the tracks would have to be totally re-routed to provide the intended transfer speed. So, as in the example of the Navy Ordering Policy above, even changes that appear entirely proper when evaluated for each component can result in an overall system operation that fails to meet the original objectives.

As the design and implementation progress, it is important to reconstruct the definition of the overall system from the *current* component definitions in order to identify what the real overall system actually accomplishes, because if the overall system fails to meet the objectives of its users, it does not matter how well each of the components meets its objectives. Nor does it matter how good the original design was if that is not what is implemented. While many software design methods include hierarchical structures, few if any include procedures to ensure that lower levels of the structure accurately reflect both the data and functions implied by the higher level component. For example, Structured Analysis uses hierarchies of data flow diagrams where lower level diagrams are supposed to reflect the expansion of a node at the higher level (see 'Structured Analysis', Section 2.2). However, Structured Analysis does not recommend techniques for assuring that lower level functions combine to produce the function indicated at the higher level (though it does state that the data in and out of the lower level diagram should match the data in and out of the higher level component it represents). Unlike Box Structured Design, Structured Analysis does not recommend any way to verify that the current lower level diagrams still reflect the same data and function.

The state box is conceptually similar to an Abstract Data Type (see 'Abstract Data Types', Section 5.5). A state box is encapsulated within a system that includes a black box to describe all possible uses of that state. Abstract Data Types have been used in technical literature on computer software to provide a more formal means of describing software specifications. However, no one describes the application of Abstract Data Types to software and integrates that concept with black box theory as well as do Mills, Linger, and Hevner. While their book was written for the developers of information systems, the concepts apply equally well to the design of any computer software. As the authors point out: 'With its wide applicability, the state box is a general model of computer science and engineering.'

2.7 PETRI NETS

2.7.1 General description

Petri nets were designed for *modeling systems*, especially those with independent, asynchronous components. Much of the analysis of concurrency, deadlock, and other problems of such systems is accomplished via Petri net descriptions of these systems. For example, Petri nets can model business systems, hardware systems, software systems, and even social systems. Petri nets are especially useful for analyzing systems by building a mathematical representation of the system and then using Petri net theory to study the structure and dynamic behavior of the model. Petri nets were developed from a doctoral dissertation by Carl Adam Petri (1962) entitled *Kommunikation mit Automaten*, which was the basis for a theory of computer systems with communication between asynchronous components. Conferences on Petri nets in both the United States and Europe and literature by researchers and Carl Petri have advanced the theory and use of Petri nets significantly. Software designers do not all have to be experts in Petri net theory but they should be aware of those kinds of problems with asynchronous systems that fall within the domain of Petri nets. Then, if such problems are encountered they can be pursued in the

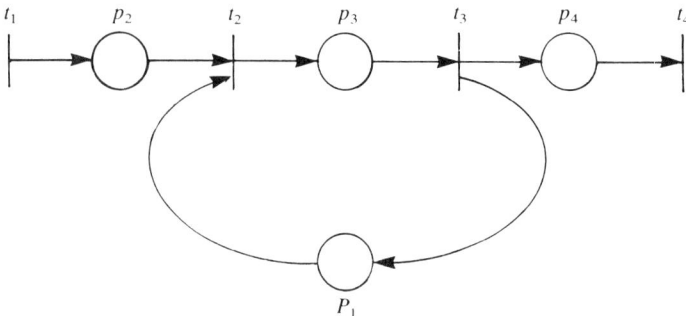

FIGURE 2.75 A Petri net graph

context of current analysis techniques. James Peterson's book, *Petri Net Theory and the Modeling of Systems* (1981), is recommended for those who desire an in-depth understanding of Petri nets. The information in this section and Figures 2.75–2.93 are based on, or reprinted with permission from, Peterson 1981.

Petri nets model two basic concepts as follows:

1. *Conditions*, which are logical descriptions of the state of the system which may either *hold* (be true), or *not hold* (be false).
2. *Events*, which are actions that take place based on the state of the system. The state of the system consists of the set of conditions.

Petri nets can be represented in terms of graphs or by set-theory notation. While the set-theory notation is common and especially useful for analysis and providing conclusions about Petri nets, graphs, such as that in Figure 2.75, can help to illustrate the concepts of Petri net theory. (The Petri net in Figure 2.75 will be derived below.) A Petri net contains *places* and *transitions* – in Petri net graphs, a place is represented by a circle, and a transition by a bar. Generally, events are modeled by the transitions in a Petri net. Arrows connect places to transitions and transitions to places. The places with arrows pointing to a transition are known as *input places* of that transition. Input places can be viewed as the necessary conditions for that event to occur and are called *pre-conditions*. Places that are pointed to by an arrow from a transition are known as *output places* of that transition. The output places can be seen to represent the conditions resulting from that event, and are called *post-conditions*. A place can have more than one arrow pointing to or from a given transition and can be an input and an output place for the same transition.

2.7.2 Example: simulating a machine shop

As an example of modeling a system with a Petri net, consider a simple machine shop with one machine (which was the origin of the Petri net in Figure 2.75). There are four occurrences of 'events' that are significant for such a machine shop:

E1. An order arrives.
E2. Processing starts (on an order).
E3. Processing (of an order) is complete.
E4. An order is sent for delivery.

There are two conditions for the machine:

1. The machine is idle, waiting for work.
2. An order is being processed.

There are three conditions for an order:

3. An order is waiting (for processing).
4. An order is being processed.
5. An order is complete.

However condition 2 for a machine is the same as condition 4 for an order. Thus there are four significant conditions for the machine shop:

C1. The machine is idle, waiting for work.
C2. An order is waiting (for processing).
C3. An order is being processed.
C4. An order is complete.

The pre-conditions and post-conditions for the machine shop are as follows (and are summarized in Figure 2.76):

1. Event E1 (an order arrives) has no pre-conditions, but results in the post-condition of C2 (an order is waiting).
2. Event E2 (processing starts on an order) requires that an order be waiting and the machine shop be idle (i.e. conditions C1 and C2 are pre-conditions for Event 2). The result of Event 2 is C3 (an order is being processed).
3. Event E3 (processing is complete) requires a pre-condition of C3 (an order is being processed) and results in post-conditions of C4 (an order is complete) and C1 (the machine is idle, waiting for work).
4. Event E4 (an order is sent for delivery) requires a complete order (C4) and has no post-conditions.

A Petri net, as shown in Figure 2.77, can be constructed from the events, conditions, and pre- and post-conditions in Figure 2.76 by using a transition to model each event and a place to model each condition. There are four transitions in the Petri net, t_1–t_4, for

Event	Pre-conditions	Post-conditions
E1	None	C2
E2	C1, C2	C3
E3	C3	C4, C1
E4	C4	None

FIGURE 2.76 Machine shop pre- and post-conditions

104   ARCHITECTURAL SOFTWARE DESIGN

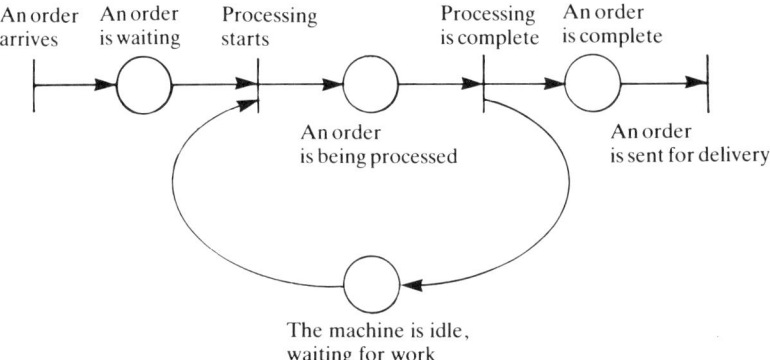

FIGURE 2.77 A Petri net model of a simple machine shop

each of the events E1–E4, respectively, and places p_1–p_4 for each of the conditions C1–C4, respectively. Arrows are drawn from places to the transitions based on Figure 2.76, with an arrow to a transition from each of its pre-conditions and an arrow from a transition to each of its post-conditions. For example, the transition 'Processing starts' has two pre-conditions: 'The machine is idle waiting for work' and 'An order is waiting'. The Petri net has an arrow from both those places to the transition 'Processing starts'. Similarly, the transition 'Processing starts' has one post-condition, 'Processing is complete', which is represented in the Petri net by the arrow from that transition to the place 'Processing is complete'.

2.7.3 Example: a more complicated machine shop

As an example of a more complicated system, consider a machine shop with three different machines and two operators. Assume that orders require two steps: processing by machine M1 and then by either machine M2 or M3. Employee E1 can operate machines M1 and M2 and employee E2 can operate machines M1 and M3. This time consider the conditions first. There seem to be six conditions for an order:

1. An order has arrived and is waiting for machining by M1.
2. An order is being processed on M1.
3. An order has been processed by M1 and is waiting to be processed by M2 or M3.
4. An order is being processed on M2.
5. An order is being processed on M3.
6. An order is complete.

However, considering the operators (which this system must also model), there are two ways in which an order might be processed on machine M1, and, although fixed, it can be helpful to add which operator is operating M2 and M3. This yields:

1. An order has arrived and is waiting for machining by M1.
2. An order is being processed on M1 by operator E1.

3. An order is being processed on M1 by operator E2.
4. An order has been processed on M1 and is waiting to be processed on M2 or M3.
5. An order is being processed on M2 by operator E1.
6. An other is being processed on M3 by operator E2.
7. An order is complete.

There are three more conditions for machines – each idle – and two more for operators – when they are idle:

8. Machine M1 is idle.
9. Machine M2 is idle.
10. Machine M3 is idle.
11. Operator E1 is idle.
12. Operator E2 is idle.

Combining these last two lists (and, for convenience, grouping by similar types) yields the following list of conditions:

(a) An order has arrived and is waiting for machining on M1.
(b) An order has been processed on M1 and is waiting to be processed on M2 or M3.
(c) An order is complete.
(d) Machine M1 is idle.
(e) Machine M2 is idle.
(f) Machine M3 is idle.
(g) Operator E1 is idle.
(h) Operator E2 is idle.
(i) An order is being processed on M1 by operator E1.
(j) An order is being processed on M1 by operator E2.
(k) An order is being processed on M2 by operator E1.
(l) An order is being processed on M3 by operator E2.

Next, we consider events in this system; first the ones necessary to cause each of the conditions above:

(i) An order arrives (causes a).
(ii) Operator E1 finishes an order on machine M1 (can cause b).
(iii) Operator E2 finishes an order on machine M1 (can also cause b).
(iv) Operator E1 finishes an order on machine M2 (can cause c).
(v) Operator E2 finishes an order on machine M3 (can also cause c).
(vi) (d is caused by the same conditions as the ones causing b).
(vii) (e is caused by E1 finishing on M2 – already included above).
(viii) (f is caused by E2 finishing on M3 – already included above).
(ix) (g can be caused by E1 finishing on M1 – already included above).
(x) (g can be caused by E1 finishing on M2 – already included above).
(xi) (h can be caused by E2 finishing on M1 – already included above).
(xii) (h can be caused by E2 finishing on M3 – already included above).
(xiii) Operator E1 starts an order on machine M1 (causes i).
(xiv) Operator E2 starts an order on machine M1 (causes j).

106 ARCHITECTURAL SOFTWARE DESIGN

(xv) Operator E1 starts an order on machine M2 (causes k).
(xvi) Operator E2 starts an order on machine M3 (causes l).

The preceding list covers each condition of starting and stopping jobs by operators on machines. However, there is as yet no 'An order' sent for delivery to balance 'An order' arriving. Adding that, and sorting into a more logical sequence, yields the following list of events:

1. An order arrives.
2. Operator E1 starts an order on machine M1.
3. Operator E1 finishes an order on machine M1.
4. Operator E2 starts an order on machine M1.
5. Operator E2 finishes an order on machine M1.
6. Operator E1 starts an order on machine M2.
7. Operator E1 finishes an order on machine M2.
8. Operator E2 starts an order on machine M3.
9. Operator E2 finishes an order on machine M3.
10. An order is sent for delivery.

The pre-conditions and post-conditions for each event are shown in Figure 2.78. As with the simple machine shop, a Petri net can be constructed from the events, conditions and the table in Figure 2.78. Figure 2.79 shows a Petri net that models this machine shop.

2.7.4 Executing Petri nets

Placing a small dot in the circle that represents a place in the Petri net indicates that a given condition that a place represents is true. The dots are known as *tokens*, and can be thought to reside in the places in a Petri net. A specific distribution of tokens across places in a Petri net is called a *marking*, such as are shown in Figures 2.80–2.82. The marking in Figure 2.80 can be represented as (0,3,1,2), with each position representing the places p_1–p_4, respectively. Similarly, the marking in Figure 2.82 can be represented as (0,30,1,17). A place can contain more than one token – indicating, for example, that

Event	Pre-conditions	Post-conditions
1.	None	a
2.	a, g, d	i
3.	i	g, d, b
4.	a, h, d	j
5.	j	b, h, d
6.	b, g, e	k
7.	k	c, g, e
8.	b, f, h	l
9.	l	c, f, h
10.	c	None

FIGURE 2.78 Bigger machine shop pre- and post-conditions

PETRI NETS 107

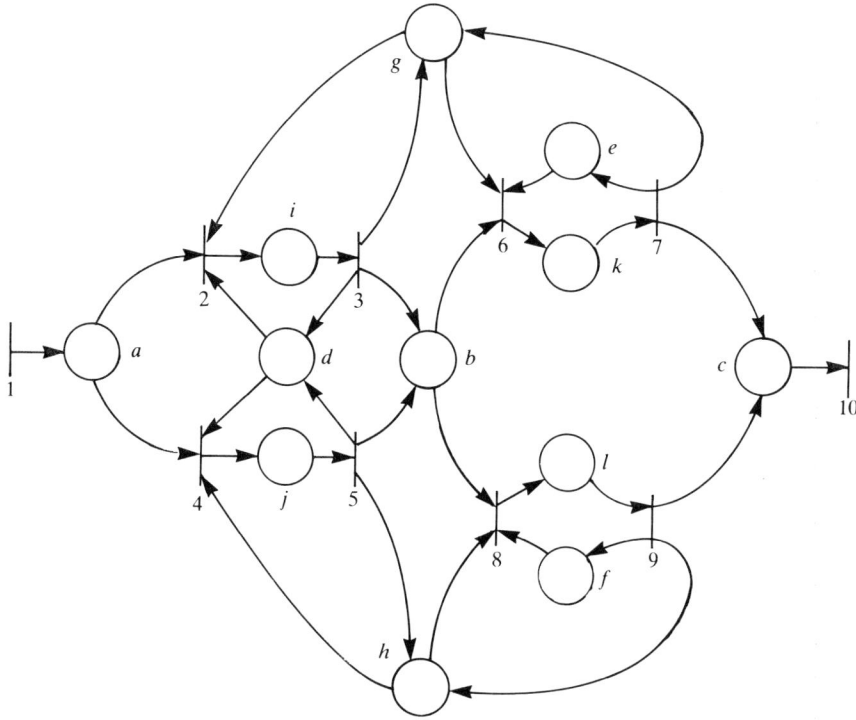

FIGURE 2.79 An example of a more complex machine shop, modeled by a Petri net

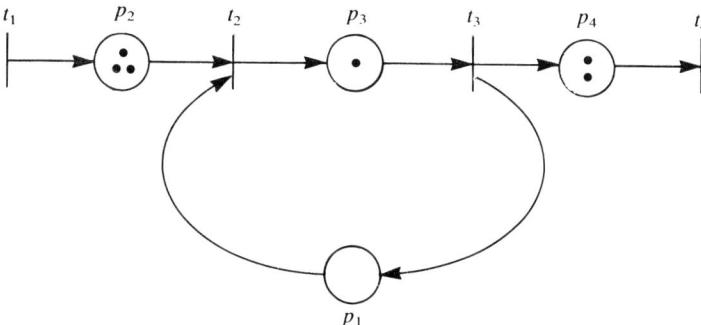

FIGURE 2.80 A marked Petri net

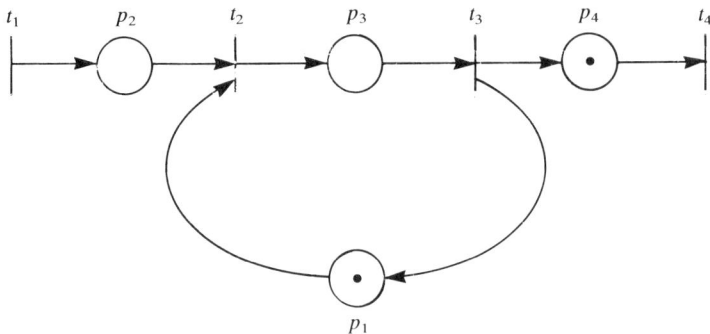

FIGURE 2.81 A different marking

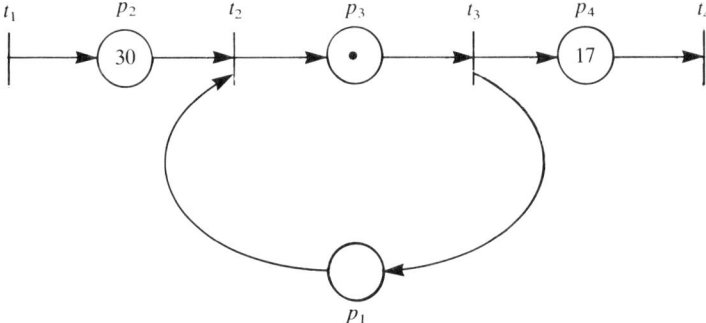

FIGURE 2.82 A larger marking

more than one order is waiting. Although the number of tokens is usually small, it is possible to have any number of tokens in a place. When the number of tokens in a place is large, the convention is to write the number in the place, as illustrated by Figure 2.82. Since the number of tokens that may be in a place is unlimited, there are an infinite number of markings for a Petri net.

Given a marking for a Petri net, it is possible to *execute* the net, whence the number and position of tokens may be changed. The rules for executing a Petri net are as follows:

1. A transition is *enabled* if each of its input places has at least one token for each arrow connecting that input place to the transition.
2. Any enabled transition may *fire*.
3. When a transition fires, one token is removed from each input place for each arrow connecting that input place to the transition, and a token is put into each output place for each arrow connecting the transition to that output place.
4. When there are no longer any transitions enabled, execution *halts*.

Firing a transition will (usually) change the marking. The number of tokens in the net changes when a transition fires unless there is an equal number of arrows into and leaving

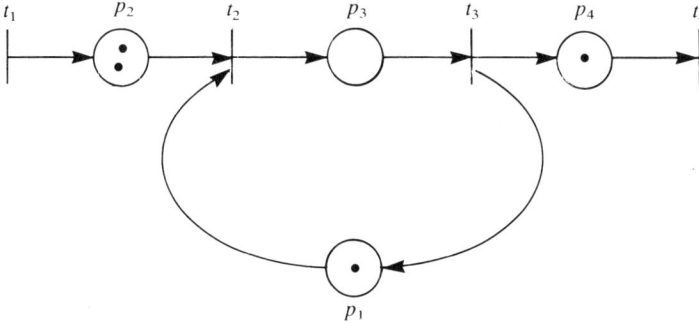

FIGURE 2.83 A marked Petri net to illustrate the firing rules

a transition. This is because the firing of a transition removes one token for each arrow coming in and deposits a token for each arrow leaving. The tokens are not necessarily objects that flow through a system (though a system *can* be modeled that way), but, rather, are a convenient way to view the current state of a Petri net. It is desirable that the number of tokens can change because the number of pre-conditions do not, in general, have to match the number of post-conditions. Thus Petri nets may not conserve tokens – conservation of tokens is, in fact, one of the questions that can be asked of a given Petri net (see below in this section). However, the firing of a transition can never make the number of tokens in any of its input places negative, because a transition is enabled to fire only if there are sufficient tokens available in each of its input places. If there are several transitions that can fire, which one fires is indeterminate. The various possible firing orders and the results are also characteristics of Petri nets, which can be analyzed to draw conclusions about the systems they model. Note that in a data flow diagram, *any* available data can enter a process; in a Petri net, *each* place must have a token in order for a transition to fire. Petri nets may look a little like data flow diagrams, but they are significantly different.

As an example of executing a Petri net, consider the marked net in Figure 2.83 (which is the simple machine shop in Figure 2.77). There are two enabled transitions: t_2 and t_4. (In order for t_3 to be enabled there would have to be at least one token in place p_3.) It is possible for either one of the enabled transitions to fire. If transition t_2 is the first to fire, the following tokens will change:

1. One token is removed from t_2's input place, p_1 (leaving p_1 empty; the machine is no longer idle).
2. One token is removed from t_2's input place, p_2 (leaving p_2 with one, in this case one more job).

The resulting marking is as shown in Figure 2.84. Now transition t_3 is enabled and thus may fire. However, transition t_2 is no longer enabled (since p_1 is empty).

110 ARCHITECTURAL SOFTWARE DESIGN

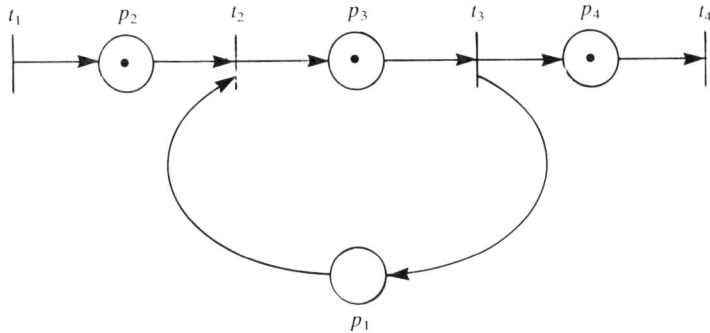

FIGURE 2.84 The marking resulting from firing transition t_2 in Figure 2.83

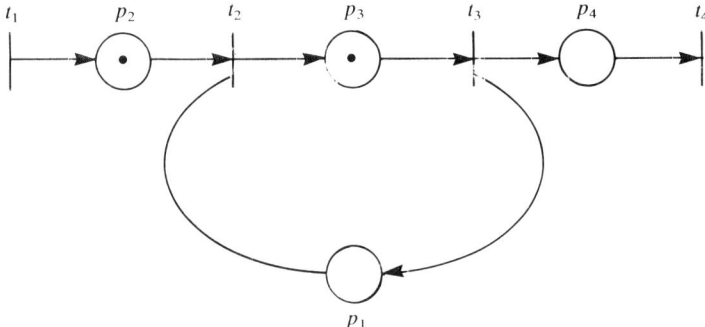

FIGURE 2.85 The marking resulting from firing transition t_4 in Figure 2.84

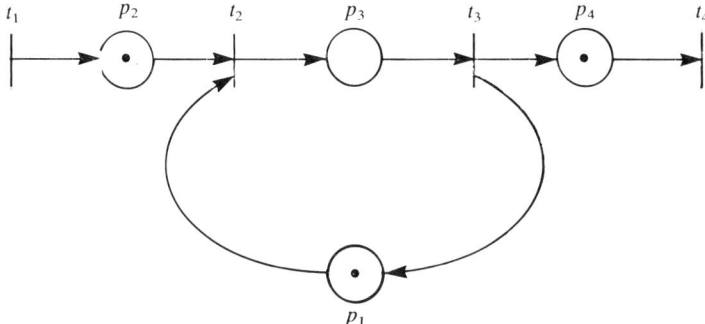

FIGURE 2.86 The marking resulting from firing transition t_3 in Figure 2.85

If transition t_4 is the next to fire, then:

1. One token is removed from p_4.

The result is shown in Figure 2.85. Assume t_3 fires next. This will:

1. Remove one token from p_3.
2. Add one token to p_1.
3. Add one token to p_4.

This is shown in Figure 2.86. A different sequence of transition firings will produce a different sequence of markings.

The rule for Petri nets is that any enabled transition may fire. This leads to an apparent *non-determinism* in Petri nets. While the choice of which transition fires is made randomly, the analysis of Petri net executions considers all possible sequences of those firings. For example, when transitions t_3 and t_4 are both enabled, either a finished order may be sent for delivery or the order being processed may finish first. Since both sequences can occur at various times, the Petri net analysis allows both possibilities. Thus Petri nets can be used to study situations in real-life systems where several things are happening concurrently and where the order of events is not unique, but where any sequence of events is possible.

2.7.5 Petri net simulation of computer programs

Petri nets have often been used to model computer hardware and they can also model computer software. If Petri nets are developed for each program in a system of programs, then the combined Petri net can model the concurrent execution of the various programs in the system. In fact, hardware pieces can easily be included since there is no distinction in a Petri net as to what the places and transitions have to represent. Petri nets can best represent control structure; and the control structure of programs is often represented by a flowchart, such as that shown in Figure 2.87. Since the flowchart has nodes connected by arrows, it might seem that one would map the nodes in a flowchart to the places in a Petri net, and the arrows in the flowchart to transitions. However, the meanings of the symbols in the two charting notations are more similar if opposite mapping is applied, as in Figure 2.88: nodes in a flowchart represented by transitions in the Petri net and each arrow in the flowchart represented as a unique place. This mapping is a better representation because, in a flowchart, the nodes indicate actions while, in a Petri net, the actions are modeled by transitions. The arrows in a flowchart are places where the current instruction counter can 'rest', a concept modeled by places in the Petri net. Figure 2.89 is the result of applying the mapping in Figure 2.88 to the flowchart in Figure 2.87. Execution of the flowchart can proceed by putting a single token in the place representing the arrow entering the flowchart. As that token moves from place to place through the net, it can be viewed as the program counter ready to execute the next function. Each place has a single output transition except for the places that represent decisions. These have two output

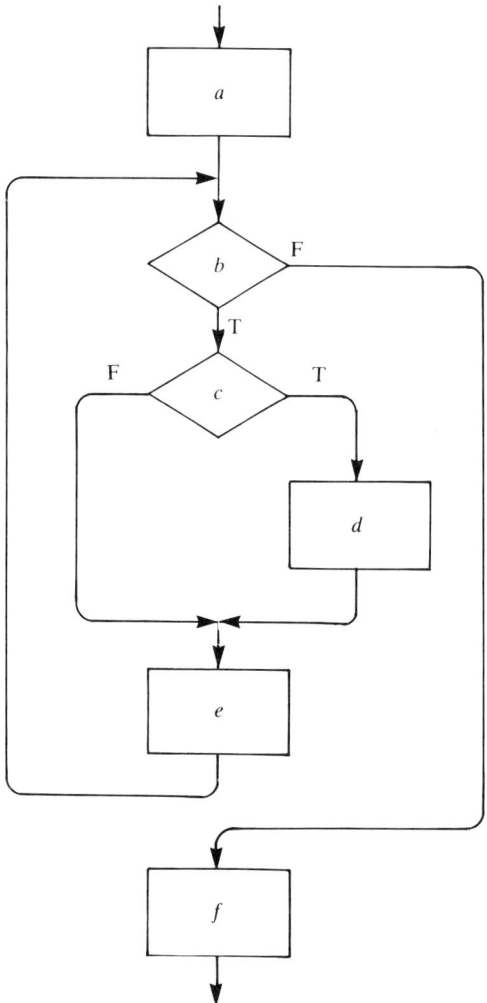

FIGURE 2.87 A flowchart of a small program

transitions, one for each outcome of the decision. The Petri net does not constrain which choice is made at a decision – thus allowing it to model the effects of either choice.

Petri nets can model parallel and concurrent processes. The processes may or may not have dependencies – both situations can be modeled by a Petri net. Since any transition which is enabled may fire, the sequence in which they actually fire is not determined in a Petri net. Thus, Petri nets do not depict the flow of time, but, rather, the occurrence of events. The execution of a Petri net represents a partial ordering of the sequence of these events. Since, in real life, events take variable amounts of time, Petri nets often concentrate on the *transitions* between real-life events, such as the *start* of processing or

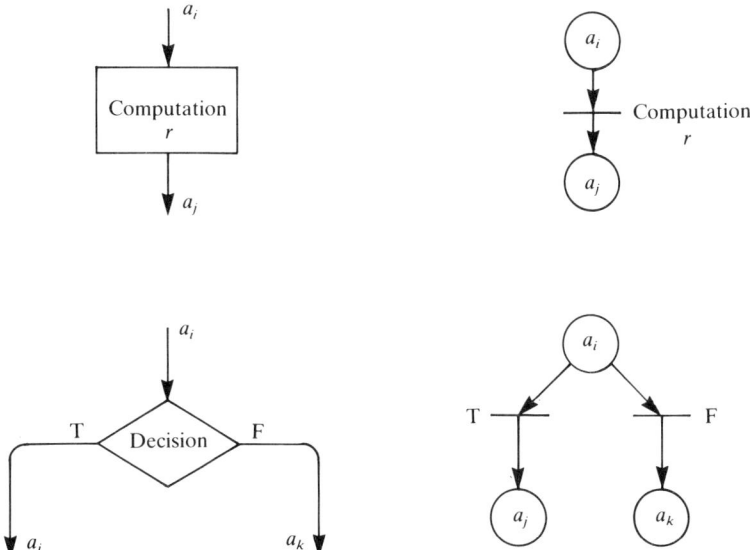

FIGURE 2.88 Translating computation and decision nodes in a flowchart to transitions in a Petri net

the *end* of processing, which can be thought of as an *instantaneous* event (see Figure 2.77). What is significant in Petri net theory is that, for instance, 'processing is complete' must follow the corresponding 'processing starts' event. The fact that Petri nets have no restriction on how long after the start of a job it can end allows the Petri net representation to study the possible effects of jobs of any length. However, as Peterson (1981) points out: 'One limitation in the modeling of systems by Petri nets is generally accepted. The firing of a transition (and the associated event) is considered to be an *instantaneous* event, taking zero time, and the occurrences of two events cannot happen simultaneously.'

Events modeled in a Petri net are called *primitive* events and are instantaneous and non-simultaneous. Petri nets can also model events that take a finite time to execute, which are called *non-primitive* events. A non-primitive event can be modeled by two primitive events plus a condition (the non-primitive event is occurring), as shown in Figure 2.90. Such a construct does not put restrictions on how long the event lasts, thus allowing study of the most general situation. However, it is always possible to be more specific about any event by adding more constraints to the net in the form of places and transitions. Sometimes a box is used to depict non-primitive events. The box notation in Figure 2.91 can serve a purpose that is important for any technique applied to large systems such as the ability to depict various parts of the system in a hierarchy (see 'Independent pieces reduce complexity', Section 2.1). That is, parts of a Petri net can be encapsulated and represented as a box on the next higher level chart.

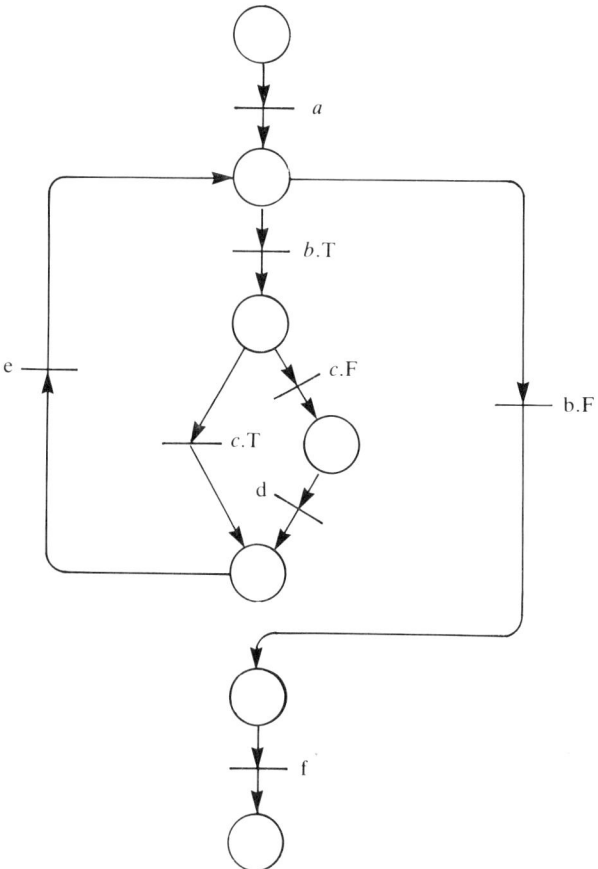

FIGURE 2.89 A Petri net representation of the flowchart in Figure 2.87

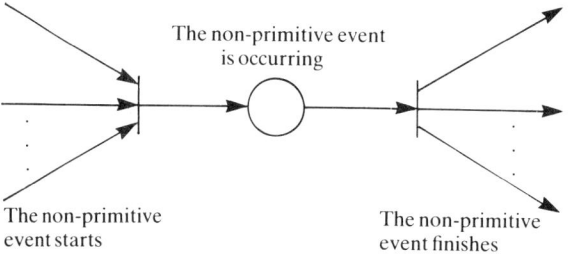

FIGURE 2.90 Modeling a non-primitive event

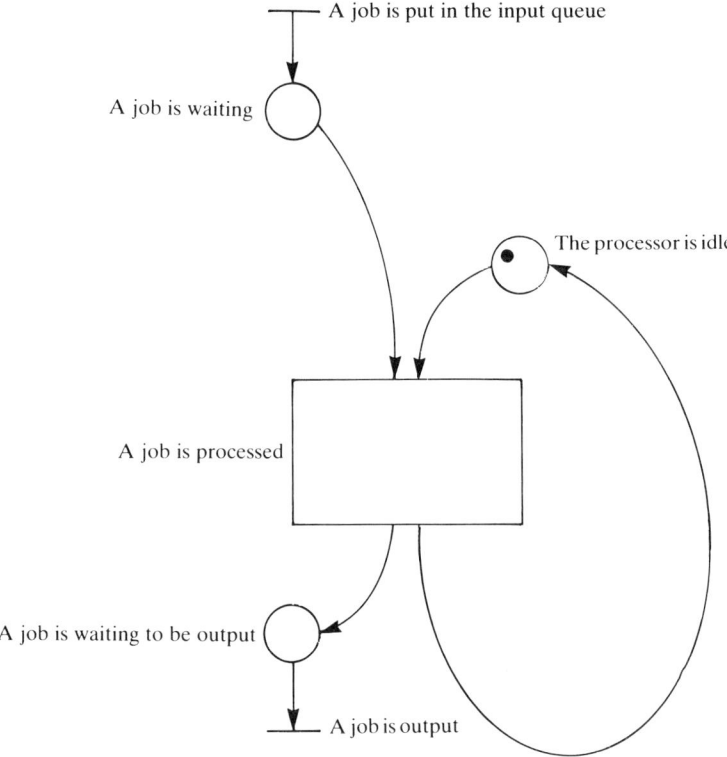

FIGURE 2.91 Representing one Petri net within another

2.7.6 Analysis of Petri nets

Much of the theoretical work with Petri nets is formulated in set-theory notation. A Petri net can be completely described by the set of places, P, which it contains; the set of transitions, T, which it contains; an input function, I, which maps each transition to its set of input places (those places having arrows pointing into the transition); and an output function, O, which maps each transition to its set of output places (those places pointed to by arrows from the transition). The structure of a Petri net is defined by its places, transitions, input function, and output function, and these can be gathered into a 'tuple' (or, since there are four components of this tuple, a 'four-tuple'). Thus a Petri net structure, C, can be represented as $C = (P,T,I,O)$. Figure 2.93 is an example of a Petri net structure described as tuples and is equivalent to the Petri net graph illustrated in Figure 2.92.

Independent, asynchronously executing processes can be modeled easily by separate Petri nets that are considered to execute at the same time. (In fact, any modeling

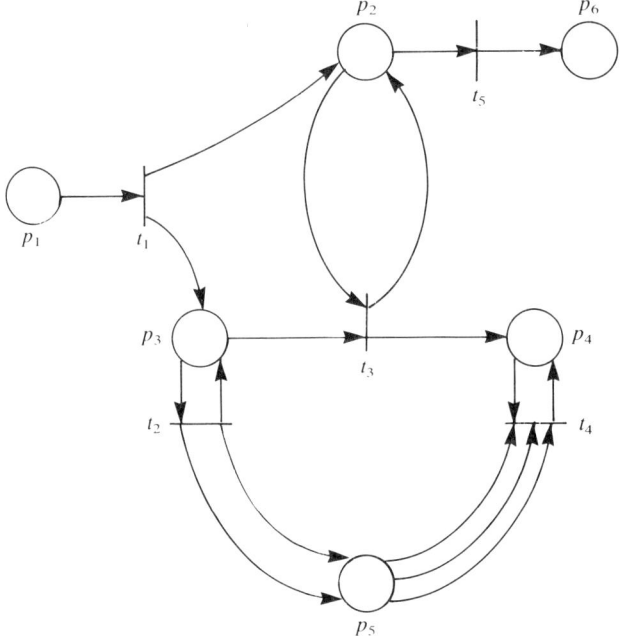

FIGURE 2.92 A Petri net graph

$$C = (P, T, I, O)$$
$$P = \{p_1, p_2, p_3, p_4, p_5, p_6\}$$
$$T = \{t_1, t_2, t_3, t_5\}$$

$I(t_1) = \{p_1\}$	$O(t_1) = \{p_2, p_3\}$
$I(t_2) = \{p_3\}$	$O(t_2) = \{p_3, p_5, p_5\}$
$I(t_3) = \{p_2, p_3\}$	$O(t_3) = \{p_2, p_4\}$
$I(t_4) = \{p_4, p_5, p_5, p_5\}$	$O(t_4) = \{p_4\}$
$I(t_5) = \{p_2\}$	$O(t_5) = \{p_6\}$

FIGURE 2.93 A Petri net structure represented as a 4-tuple

technique, even flowcharts, can be used the same way for *independent* processes.) However, it is its ability to support design of an *interdependent* set of asynchronous processes that makes Petri nets useful. They can be used to model interdependent asynchronous processes because transitions can fire asynchronously (especially if there are multiple tokens in the net). Refer to Peterson (1981) for descriptions of standard synchronization problems and Petri net solutions to them. However, the major strength of Petri nets lies in the ability to *analyze* the system being modeled. There are a number of questions about concurrent systems that can be analyzed using Petri nets. The most common problems mentioned in the literature include:

1. Safeness: can the number of tokens in a place ever exceed 1?
2. Boundedness: will the number of tokens in a place always stay finite?
3. Conservation: are tokens destroyed or created?
4. Liveness: can the system ever deadlock?
5. Reachability: can a given marking be reached from another marking?
6. Coverability: can any superset of a given marking be reached?
7. Firing sequences: are given sequences of transition firings possible?
8. Equivalence: are two nets equivalent?

Safeness can be applied to places as well as to the entire net. A place is safe if the number of tokens in the place will always be either 0 or 1. Can place p_3 in the net in Figure 2.81 ever have two tokens in it? (It had better not, since it represents a machine that can only process one order at a time – see Figure 2.77.) One use for safeness is to determine if a place can be implemented by a single binary storage device (e.g. a hardware 'flip–flop' or single binary bit). A Petri net is safe if all the places in the net are safe.

Boundedness is similar to safeness, but focuses on whether places can be implemented by finite storage. A place is bounded if the number of tokens in it can never exceed some finite integer K. For example, is there a limit to the number of tokens that can be in place p_4 in Figure 2.81? (In this case there should be no limit, since jobs may stack up forever if, for some reason, the jobs are not sent for delivery – see Figure 2.77.) As with safeness, a Petri net is bounded if all the places in the net are bounded.

If the Petri net is used to model systems that allocate resources, then the token may represent resources – such as cars to be rented. The renting of a car can be represented by the firing of a transition which moves a token to a place representing rental status. *Conservation* is an important property for such systems in that it guarantees that the system neither creates nor destroys tokens. Strict conservation is a very strong requirement and requires that every transition have the same number of input and output places (otherwise, when the transition fired, it would create more or fewer token than its firing would remove from the net). The net in Figure 2.81 does not have strict conservation: both t_2 and t_3 change the number of tokens in the net when they fire. However, tokens in the Petri net in Figure 2.81 do not just represent jobs, they can also represent the condition of the machine being idle when there is a token in place p_1.

A Petri net is *live* if every transition can be enabled. The transition might not be enabled currently, but there must be a way that the system could act that would result in the transition being enabled (i.e. have sufficient tokens in each of its input places). The Petri net in Figure 2.92 has a transition (t_1) that cannot be enabled once all the tokens have been removed from place p_1 (as there is no way ever to replace tokens into p_1). A Petri net that contains one or more places that cannot be enabled is considered deadlocked.

Related to liveness is the problem of *reachability*: given an initial marking, is there a way to reach some other desired marking? Alternatively, is there any way that some undesirable marking can ever be reached? For example, given an initial marking for the net in Figure 2.81 of (1,0,0,0), is it possible ever to reach the marking (0,1,0,0)? If so, the shop would have accepted a job it could never process; however, since that would represent a machine that was neither busy nor idle, this will not happen in that net. (If the possibility of a broken machine were also modeled by the net, then the condition might happen, but then it would be a different net.) Reachability is a basic property that can be used in pursuing many of the other issues with Petri nets.

More generally, *coverability* is the problem of determining whether, given an initial state, there is a reachable marking that includes some marking of interest as a subset. For example, in Figure 2.81, is it ever possible for both p_1 and p_3 to contain tokens simultaneously? (It should not be since then the machine would be both busy and idle at the same time.) Some questions can be posed in terms of whether a given sequence of transition firings can ever happen. Thus it becomes important to determine whether for a given net there is a way to fire a given transition, a given sequence of transitions, or even just a given set of transitions.

For optimization purposes, it is desirable to be able to show that two Petri nets are equivalent in some sense, i.e. can the Petri net be optimized without affecting its ability to meet the system's objectives? Unfortunately, it is somewhat difficult to show that two Petri nets are exactly equivalent since any change in the number of places, transitions, or connections between them creates a different net. Of course, what is of interest is whether the new net results in the same behavior. However, this requires demonstration that all possible behaviors of each of the nets are equivalent, which requires solutions to the problems above such as firing sequences, reachability, and coverability. Subsets of the general problem of equivalence include whether a net with a different number of places will generate the same sequence of transition firings or whether a net with the same number of places will generate the same sets of markings. In addition, it can be useful to show that one Petri net is a subset of another one.

There are limitations on what can be modeled by Petri nets. It is not possible to test an unbounded place for a given number of tokens – such as zero – and take action based on the result of that test. While it is possible to make extensions to Petri nets that allow such a test, doing so would damage the analytical power of the Petri nets because almost all of the analysis questions put to them would be rendered undecidable.

Peterson describes two major Petri net analysis techniques:

1. Reachability trees.
2. Matrix equations.

Reachability trees are like decision trees (see 'Decision tables', Section 3.7) in that they show each possible marking reachable from an initial marking, the markings reachable from each of those, etc. Peterson describes reachability trees and applies this analysis technique to deduce how the analysis problems discussed above can be related to characteristics within the reachability trees.

With matrix equations, a Petri net is represented as a matrix with a row for each transition and a column for each place. Each position in the matrix contains the count of the number of arrows from a place to a transition (in the input matrix) or from a transition to a place (in the output matrix). Transition firings and analysis can then be represented by operations in matrix algebra. Peterson relates the analysis problems above to characteristics of the matrices and matrix equations. Readers interested in details of these analysis techniques are referred to Peterson (1981).

2.7.7 Comments on Petri nets

When Peterson's book was published, objection to his treatment of Petri nets was voiced. Some people preferred, and were already developing, a more theoretical approach of viewing Petri nets more as a way of thinking about systems, and classifying various types of nets based on various situations or rules allowed for each class of nets. This approach was even given a different name, 'general net theory', to distinguish it from the type of use described by Peterson. Those interested in more detail about general net theory are referred to *Petri Nets, An Introduction* by Wolfgang Reisig (1982), although it contains a lot of technical notation, as is typical in Petri net publications. The book also contains an extensive bibliography, including references to books on Petri nets in other languages. (In fact it was written in German and translated into English.) Peterson's treatment of Petri nets seems more compatible with what designers need to understand in order to improve their ability to analyze and design software.

Many software designers may find the literature on Petri nets difficult to read because of its heavy use of technical notation. However, this notation has enabled various problems associated with asynchronous systems to be analyzed successfully. Software designers should at least be aware of the kinds of problems that can be analyzed with Petri nets so that they can take advantage of the substantial progress that has been made in the analysis of asynchronous systems using Petri nets.

CHAPTER THREE
INTEGRAND SPECIFICATIONS

Once the software architecture has been designed, the integrands shown in that architecture can be specified. Several notations are useful for specifying integrands. The first, historically, were *flowcharts*, followed by a coding refinement called *Structured Programming*, which makes the code easy enough to read (if integrands are small) that the code can document its own logic. *Structured 'English'* (or Structured 'Natural Language') applies Structured Programming concepts to natural language and *Action Diagrams* improve the readability of code even more by adding brackets to the graphical indentation of Structured Programming. *State transition diagrams* are useful for describing integrands in real-time systems and for describing application menus. Other useful graphical notations for depicting sequence, iteration, and choice include *Jackson charts* and *decision tables*.

Once a software architecture that most adequately meets the requirements, constraints, and criteria has been designed, the integrands shown in the architecture can be defined. These integrands, when combined as specified by the architecture, comprise the programs that constitute the automated parts of the system. The architectural design does not specify how the integrands are to be constructed, but does define the data passed to and from each integrand and the function, as implied by the name given to the integrand. The architectural design should have divided the system into integrands that are independent and have clearly defined interfaces so that integrands can be designed and developed relatively independently. Ideally, the integrand specifications can be written in about one page. There are a number of ways to specify the logic of an integrand. If an architectural design method uses a particular type of integrand specification, that specification is a natural choice unless the recipients of the design could understand an alternative better. Otherwise, choose the form of integrand specification that most naturally describes the type of integrand being specified and best communicates it to the recipient of the specification. Integrands are often specified with natural language text, or in a more structured form of natural language such as Structured English (or Structured 'Natural Language'). Narrative specifications can be preserved as prologue comments within the integrand itself. (This prologue narrative does not count as part of the one-page objective for integrands.) In order to keep integrands as independent of each other as possible, integrands should not contain lists of which other integrands call them (which would complicate maintenance), but may include lists of the integrands they call (because those lists can be changed as the integrand is modified). Once the integrand specifications are developed, they are combined with the architectural design as input to the implementation phase (see Volume 3 of this series (Marcotty 1991)).

3.1 FLOWCHARTS

3.1.1 Description

The sequence, iteration, and choice constructs of procedural languages describe how people step through jobs manually: what we do first, what next, what decisions we make, how we decide, and what actions are repeated. Each of these steps can be described with a flowchart, which is one way to visualize procedures within an integrand. The basic flowchart is made up of four symbols as shown in Figure 3.1, which can be used to describe the internal logic of an integrand. Flowcharts do not depict the ways to connect integrands, such as 'calls', 'forks', 'joins', 'on-conditions', interrupts, or other ways to branch to another integrand, with or without return.

Flowcharts can document any logic, even including that which folds and curls in on itself so much that it looks like a 'bowl of spaghetti'. An example of a ten-page bowl of spaghetti program, which was collapsed so that the branching could be seen on a single page, is shown on the left of Figure 3.2 (IBM 1977). Before proceeding, the reader is encouraged to see how hard it is to determine from the code on the left the conditions under which the function 'J' executes (*without* drawing a flowchart). A flowchart for the code on the left in Figure 3.2 is shown in Figure 3.3. Note that it is easier to determine the logic flow from the flowchart than from the code, which was even more difficult to understand when it spanned many pages.

3.1.2 Comments on flowcharts

Flowcharts have been used to describe computer programs for years. However, one major problem has discouraged their use. Flowcharts are so detailed that they reflect the code almost exactly, but in the main they were used to design code. As maintenance is performed, only the code is changed (there never seems to be sufficient time available to change the flowchart). As the flowchart becomes out of date, it rapidly becomes less than useless (i.e. harmful) because the developer can no longer depend on it to represent the code correctly. Also, functional decomposition techniques, such as Structured Design (see Section 2.5) and, originally, Structured Programming (Section 3.2), have led to

122 INTEGRAND SPECIFICATIONS

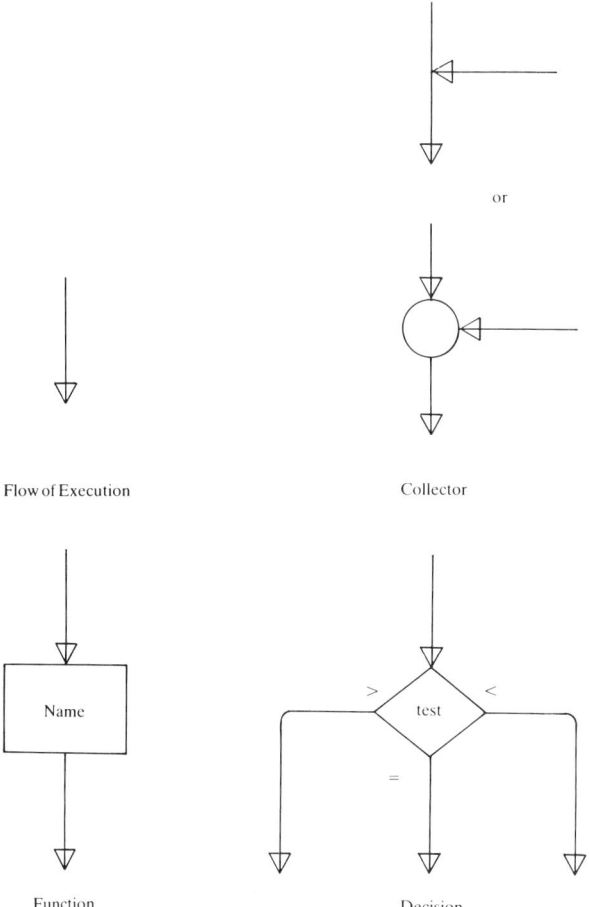

FIGURE 3.1 Flowchart symbols

developing integrands that require about one page of source code. Since the indentation of Structured Programming and Action Diagrams (see Sections 3.2 and 3.4) helps to represent the logic and makes single pages of source code fairly readable, it is desirable to write readable code and let that be its own documentation (for the code *within* an integrand), rather than trying to keep two forms of the same logic – flowcharts and code – in synchrony. Flowcharts can still be used to help depict logic that is too complicated to understand otherwise, but are not recommended as a way of documenting logic.

3.1.3 CCITT–SDL

CCITT–SDL is a more recent notation that combines, with the sequence, iteration, and choice depicted by flowcharts, specific formal symbols, such as the sending, saving, and

	'BOWL OF SPAGHETTI'	STRUCTURED CODE
	IF p GOTO label q	IF p THEN
	IF w GOTO label m	A function
	L function	B function
	GOTO label k	IF q THEN
label m	M function	IF t THEN
	GOTO label k	G function
label q	IF q GOTO label t	DOWHILE u
	A function	H function
	B function	ENDDO
	C function	I function
label r	IF NOT r GOTO label s	(ELSE)
	D function	ENDIF
	GOTO label r	ELSE
label s	IF s GOTO label f	C function
	E function	DOWHILE r
label v	IF NOT v GOTO label k	D function
	J function	ENDDO
label k	K function	IF s THEN
	END function	F function
label f	F function	ELSE
	GOTO label v	E function
label t	IF t GOTO label a	ENDIF
	A function	ENDIF
	B function	IF v THEN
	GOTO label w	J function
label a	A function	(ELSE)
	B function	ENDIF
	G function	ELSE
label u	IF NOT u GOTO label w	IF w THEN
	H function	M function
	GOTO label u	ELSE
label w	IF NOT t GOTO label y	L function
	I function	ENDIF
label y	IF NOT v GOTO label k	ENDIF
	J function	K function
	GOTO label k	END function

FIGURE 3.2 Comparison of traditional code and structured code

receiving of signals and the resulting states and actions of the parts of the system. CCITT–SDL was created when, in 1988, CCITT (International Telegraph and Telephone Consultative Committee) decided that a new language was needed to support telecommunications. The result is a graphical notation called the Specification and Description Language (SDL), based on the concepts of finite state machines and the sending and receiving of signals (as occurs in the design of electromechanical exchanges). Those interested in more information on CCITT–SDL are referred to CNETDP, 1987, which contains papers on CCITT–SDL.

124 INTEGRAND SPECIFICATIONS

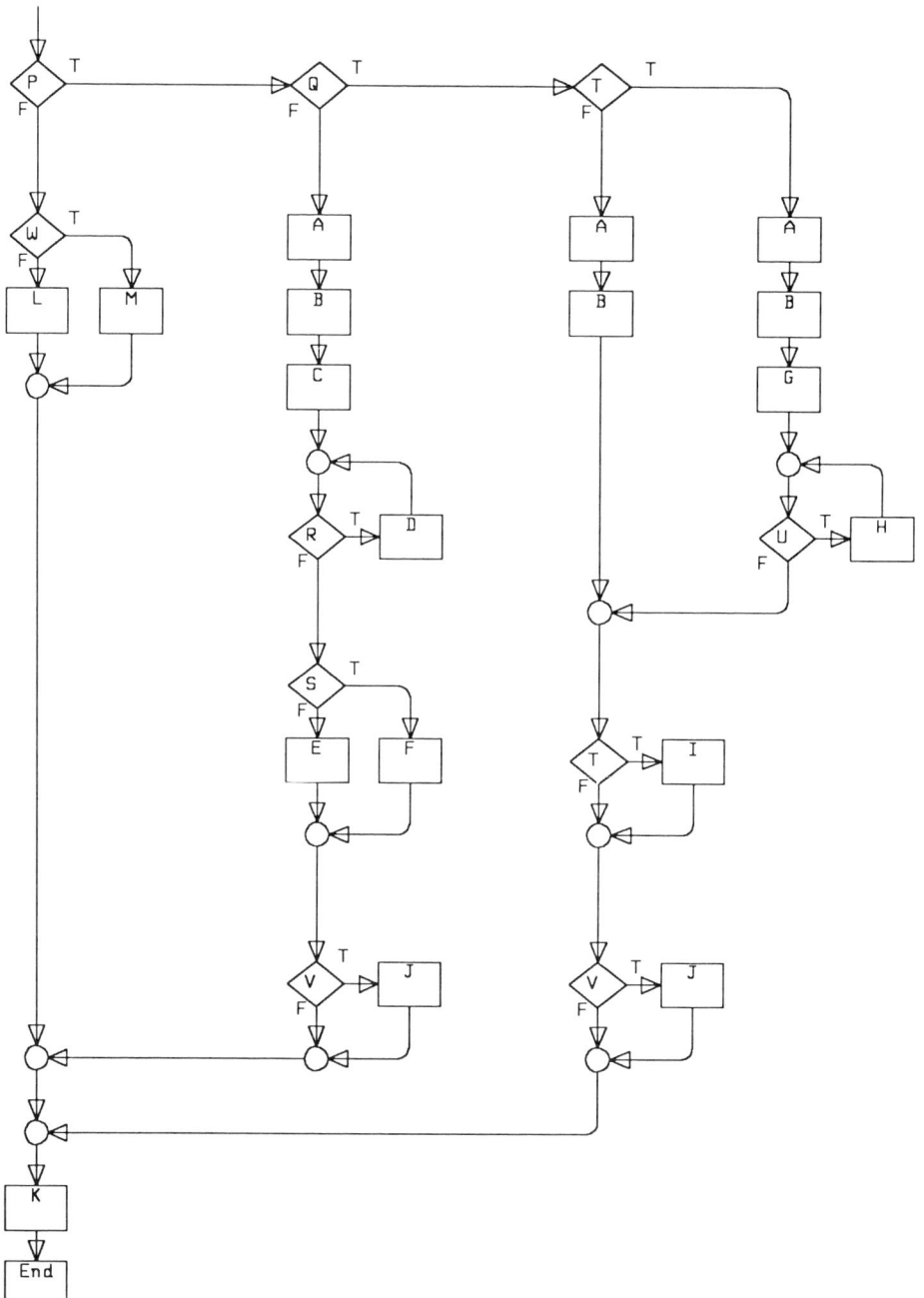

FIGURE 3.3 Flowchart for the left-hand side of Figure 3.2

3.1.4 BS 6224

Another graphical notation that adds specific formal symbols (such as events, time-outs, task activation, and synchronized and unsynchronized tranmissions), to sequence, iteration, and choice is BS 6224, which was developed by the British Standards Institution. Readers interested in a description of BS 6224 are referred to an extended synopsis given in Volume 1 of this series (Macro 1991), to BSI (1987), or to the British Standards Institution which can supply a copy of the latest standard.

3.2 STRUCTURED PROGRAMMING

3.2.1 Description

Structured Programming is a set of rules that specify how to structure code (especially branching code) within an integrand in order to make the code easier to understand, debug, and change. Structured code contains only *standard control structures*, which have just one control path in the top and one out the bottom – 'one-in/one-out'. For example, the code on the right-hand side of Figure 3.2 is structured. The basic Structured Programming control structures include sequence, iteration (DOUNTIL), and choice (IF), as shown in Figure 3.4. The one-in/one-out control structures of DOWHILE and CASE, as shown in Figure 3.5, are often included with the basic set to provide additional flexibility. Note that Structured Programming excludes the use of the GOTO instruction (except as necessary to implement the standard Structured Programming structures in languages that still do not support them). Any block within a control structure of Structured Programming can be another control structure – and thus also any sequence of control structures. The result is that the control structures are strictly nested within one another. Structured code is separated into *segments*, which are each one-in/one-out and approximately one page long. The one-page limit on the size of a segment helps to prevent the indentation pushing code off the right-hand side of the page. The nesting rules allow segments to be limited, even if arbitrarily, to one page. A one-in/one-out single-page segment can always be made by choosing a sufficiently small IF, DO, OR sequence, since each of these constructs has one path in the top, and one out the bottom and thus satisfies the requirements of a segment.

Structured code is *indented* to indicate the nesting of control structures. Each time another control structure is encountered, it is indented (usually by two columns), and the parts of each control structure are aligned. Indenting the code helps to depict the flow of control so that it is easier to see how the code branches than with code which is not indented. Structured code can always be depicted by simple indenting (because the control structures can only be embedded and not overlapped), while the branching logic of unstructured code cannot, in general, be depicted by a simple indenting scheme. The code on the right-hand side of Figure 3.2 is an 'equivalent' and structured form of the

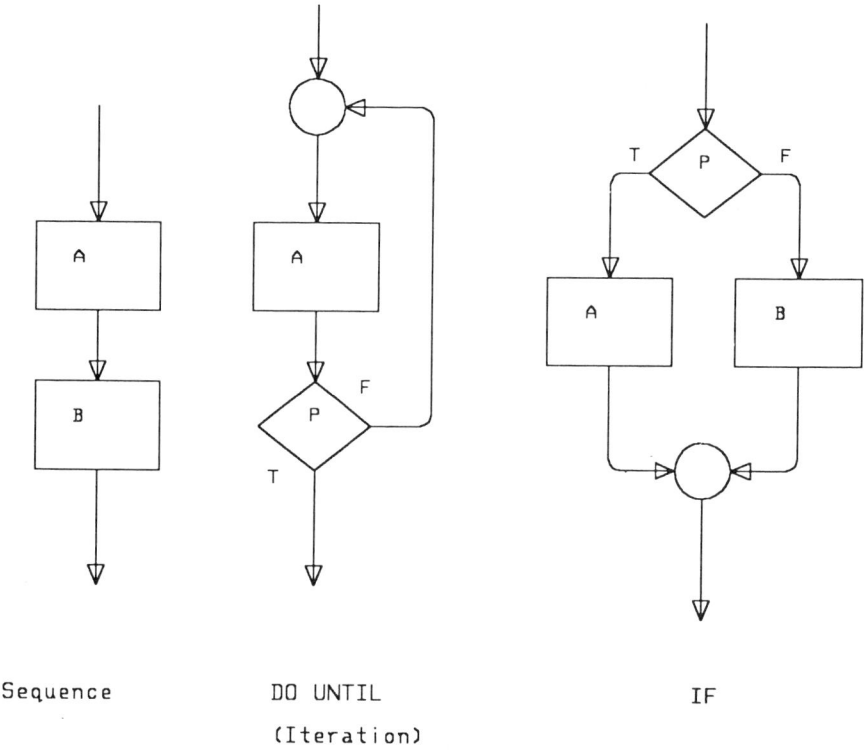

FIGURE 3.4 Basic Structured Programming control structures

program to its left. An 'equivalent' program is one that executes the same functions in the same order. Note how much easier it is to determine from the code on the right the conditions under which the function 'J' executes (even without drawing a flowchart) than it is with the code on the left.

The basic Structured Programming control structures of sequence, iteration, and choice, shown in Figure 3.4, are sufficient to write an equivalent program for any 'proper' program. A proper program is one with one starting point, one exit, no 'dead' code (code that cannot be reached for execution), and no necessarily-infinite loops. Any useful program can be converted into a proper program. To turn a program into an equivalent proper program, make sure it has only one starting point and one ending point and eliminate infinite loops and dead code. Multiple starting points can be replaced by a single starting point with a branch to each of the original starting points based on an added variable that is set to indicate which starting point was originally used. Similarly, a program with multiple exits can be made to have one exit by setting at each of the original exits a variable that indicates the exit and then branching to a common exit. Dead code can simply be eliminated because, by definition, it can never be executed. If necessarily infinite loops execute, they constitute an error that must be eliminated in order to have a correctly working program or, if they can never be executed, they can be eliminated as dead code. Given a flowchart for any proper program – no matter how complicated that flowchart is – it is always possible to construct an equivalent program that is structured. Any one-in/one-out portion of the flowchart can also be structured. One technique for constructing an equivalent structured program is contained in the Structure Theorem developed by Harlan Mills (1972). Readers interested in Mills' constructive proof are referred to Volume 4 of this series (Marcotty 1991).

Structured Programming does not include rules for segmenting code or for evaluating various choices for segments. One early Structured Programming class ended in failure because the instructor argued with the class for three days about the 'right' way to segment the first problem – when there were no rules by which to judge alternatives. Segments can be invoked by any available language mechanism such as an 'include', 'perform', or 'call' and still satisfy the rules of Structured Programming.

3.2.2 Comments on Structured Programming

Structured Programming is widely accepted and used. Writing procedural code in any other form will leave it much less readable and harder to maintain and will leave the author open to criticism for not using what has become standard programming practice.

Despite the concentration on coding rules, the division into single-page one-in/one-out segments was the biggest advantage of Structured Programming. The segmentation prevents control flows into or out of the middle of a segment – it all has to go in the top and out the bottom. Thus segments can be checked one at a time because they are connected in a simple and easily understandable way (although segments are easier to check one at a time if they perform some identifiable function – see 'Structured Design', Section 2.5). Structured Design takes the concept one more step and recommends that *data references* also occur only at the segment's boundaries (e.g. with the parameters on a call statement). Software designed with Structured Design principles seldom needs to be segmented because the integrands will already contain about one page of source code.

The structured code within an integrand can be much easier to read than unstructured code. The flow of the code is basically downward because there are no constructs that branch upward, except for the loop, which only repeats code already executed. Thus an integrand can be checked with basically one downward pass through the code. Because of this downward flow, errors tend to be found successively lower in the code when debugging (because once an error has been eliminated, the program should execute further and this generally means physically lower in the code).

For computer hardware design, there is a proof similar to the Structured Programming proof that any Boolean (binary) expression can be implemented from just OR, AND, and NOT components. However, the latter two are sufficient elements alone, since an OR can be constructed from an AND and a NOT. Since a NAND ('NOT AND') can be used to construct either a NOT or an AND, then the NAND alone is a sufficient element to implement any Boolean logic. Similarly for programming, the three Structured Programming constructs are not all necessary. The IF statement in Figure 3.6 can be

128   INTEGRAND SPECIFICATIONS

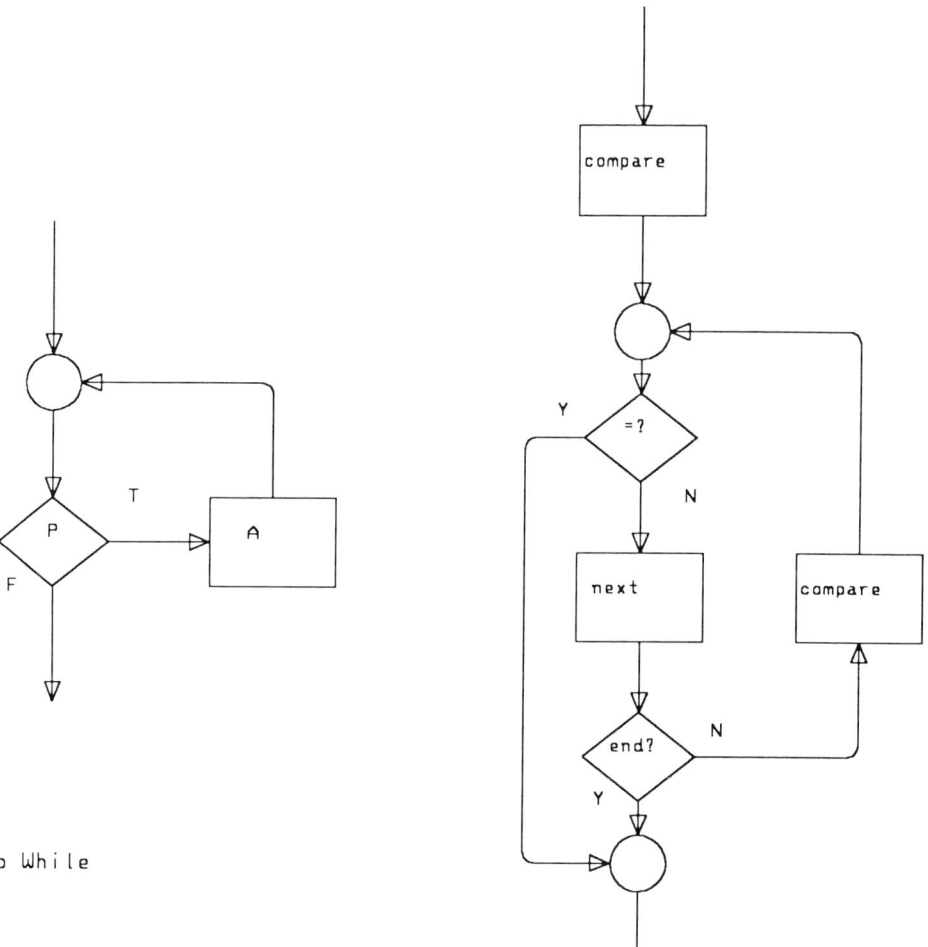

FIGURE 3.5 Additional Structured Programming structures

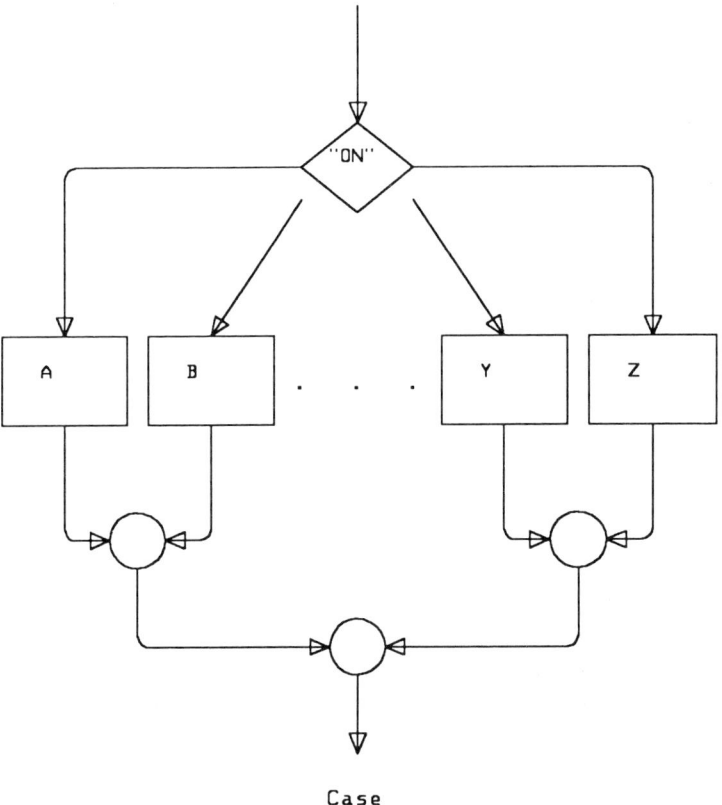

Case

FIGURE 3.5 – *contd.*

constructed from a sequence of two loops as in Figure 3.7. (Figure 3.7 is equivalent to Figure 3.6 even if A and B change P, R, or Q.) Thus, only two extra variables (e.g. R and Q) are required per program, regardless of the repeated or indented use of the same construct. Similarly, one general construct is sufficient for building any proper program. Figure 3.8 is a loop, and it is possible to nest it within itself to construct a sequence, including one equivalent to Figure 3.7. Thus the IF construct in Figure 3.7 can be made from nesting the construct in Figure 3.8. Since the construct in Figure 3.8 can build sequence, IFs, and loops, it is sufficient for building any proper program. Reducing the number of types of elements can be an advantage for hardware components because it reduces the cost of fabrication. However, the cost of duplicating software is nearly zero and reducing the number of Structured Programming constructs would make coding harder for people rather than easier. Thus the single construct shown in Figure 3.8 may be helpful for proofs and automatic generators, but it is unlikely to make manual coding easier.

130   INTEGRAND SPECIFICATIONS

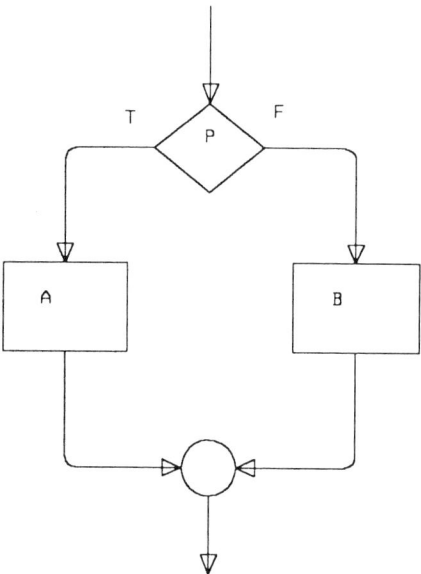

FIGURE 3.6 General 'IF' construct

Readers interested in more information about Structured Programming are referred to *A Structured Approach to Programming* by Joan K. Hughes, Glen C. Michtom, and Jay I. Michtom (1987).

3.3 STRUCTURED NATURAL LANGUAGE

3.3.1 Description

The concepts and indentation rules of Structured Programming can be used profitably with natural language. A sample of 'Structured English' is shown in Figure 3.9. Figures 3.9 and 3.10 are reprinted, with permission, from DeMarco (1978). The sample in Figure 3.9 is also useful in its own right, since it is an algorithm that can be used to check whether language or code is correctly structured. The algorithm turns verbal constructs (of sequence, repetition, and decision) into 'flowgraphs' (flowcharts). Figure 3.10 illustrates the algorithm in Figure 3.9. 'Structured English', as defined by DeMarco, is a way to write in a natural language narrative that is restricted to a limited syntax and a limited vocabulary. The syntax is limited to:

1. Simple declarative sentences, such as 'Draw a flowgraph for the description'.
2. Closed-end repetition constructs, such as 'Repeat the following replacement process until no further replacements are possible'.
3. Closed-end decision constructs, such as 'If there is a complete decision construct'.

STRUCTURED NATURAL LANGUAGE 131

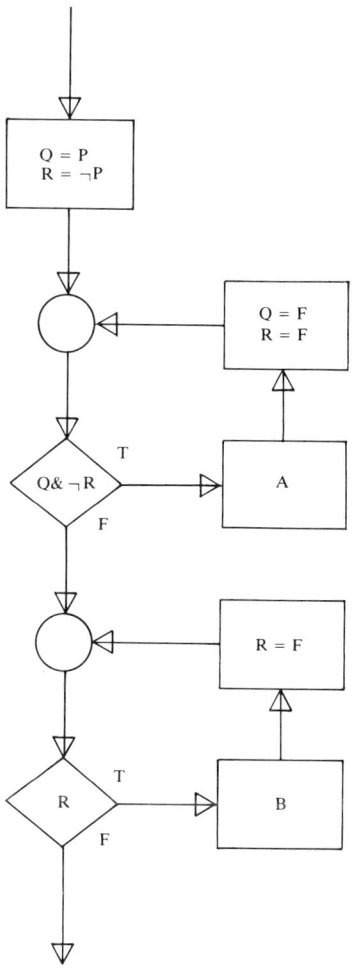

FIGURE 3.7 'IF' via sequence of two loops

The above may also be nested completely within one another. Imbedded constructs are indented to allow their structure to be determined easily. These rules for Structured Natural Language are the same as those for Structured Programming (see Section 3.2). DeMarco also allows the CASE construct, the DOWHILE (both shown in Figure 3.5), and compound conditions such as 'IF A & B & C & not D'. The vocabulary of Structured Natural Language is limited to:

1. Imperative language verbs, such as 'Replace' and 'Calculate'.
2. Nouns defined in the data dictionary, such as 'Employee' and 'Paycheck'.
3. Certain reserved words for logic formulation, such as 'if' and 'repeat'.

The rules for Structured Natural Language are chosen to encourage readability. For

132   INTEGRAND SPECIFICATIONS

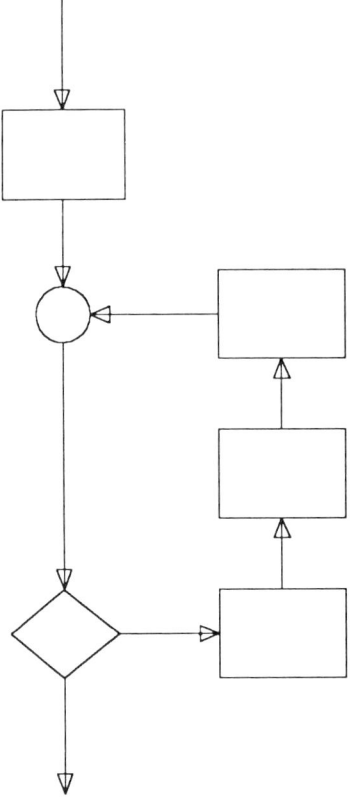

FIGURE 3.8 Single sufficient structure

1. Draw a flowgraph for the description.
2. Repeat the following replacement process until no further
   replacements are possible:
   2.1 If there is a complete Decision construct,
       Replace it with a Sequence construct.
   2.2 If there is a complete Repetition construct,
       Replace it with a Sequence construct.
   2.3 If there are two adjacent Sequence constructs,
       Replace them with a single Sequence construct.
3. If the entire flowgraph has now been replaced with a single
   Sequence construct,
   The description does conform to the limited syntax.

FIGURE 3.9 Syntax-checking algorithm

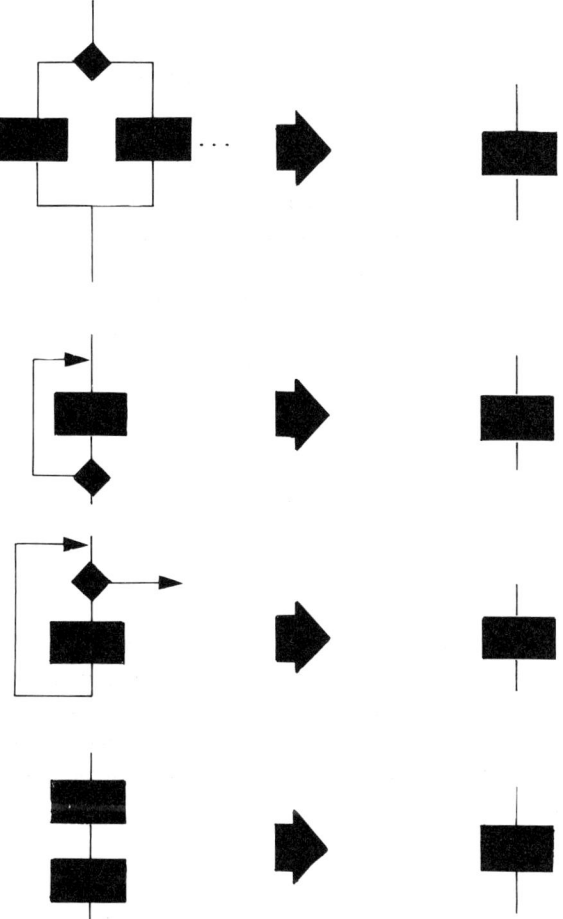

FIGURE 3.10 Depiction of syntax-checking algorithm

example, indentation is used to indicate the end of the closed constructs, rather than using the verbs such as ENDIF and ENDDO as defined by some computer languages. Those writing Structured Natural Language are encouraged to deviate from the standard vocabulary if deviating clearly improves readability. However, one of the advantages of the structured form is to simplify the possible interrelations among the decisions and repetitions, so this structure should be maintained. Sentences should be written so that they are readable by those people for whom Structured Natural Language is intended. An advantage of Structured Natural Language is the *absence* of a requirement that the result meets the syntax requirements of some computer language.

134   INTEGRAND SPECIFICATIONS

3.3.2 Comments on Structured Natural Language

Structuring Natural Language helps to bridge the gap between the unstructured nature of some verbal software specifications and the more formal syntaxes currently required for the computer. It should be possible to describe in Structured Natural Language integrands that will be implemented with procedural languages. Structuring the text can help to simplify and depict relationships between conditional statements within the text, while the process of structuring can help to identify situations or conditions not yet specified. While Structured Natural Language may be used for the initial software specifications, it is probably more frequently used for specifying individual integrands. Though several methods suggest 'Structured English' for specifying integrands, other techniques, such as those in this chapter, are more formal and may be preferable.

3.4 ACTION DIAGRAMS

3.4.1 Description

Action Diagrams are described by James Martin and Carma McClure (1985a; 1985b). Action Diagrams are an annotated form of structured, indented code. The annotations are brackets that connect the parts of each Structured Programming construct, as illustrated in Figure 3.11. Figure 3.12 shows an example of an Action Diagram for the right-hand side of Figure 3.2. Structuring the code ensures that the brackets do not have to overlap, and the indentation allows room for the brackets. Other symbols defined by Martin and McClure are shown in Figure 3.13.

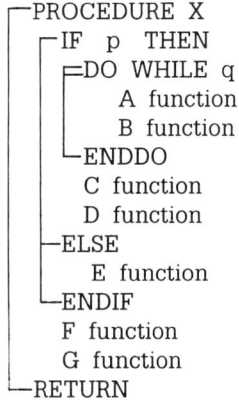

FIGURE 3.11 Example: Action Diagram

3.4.2 Comments on Action Diagrams

Action Diagrams are a helpful addition to structured code. They add graphics to indented code, and while the meaning of the added graphics is the same as the indentation, the brackets are a very helpful aid to the eye. The brackets are particularly helpful when trying to match the parts of a particular Structured Programming figure – especially on paper or video screens where the columns are not marked. Brackets can be added manually or automatically to any indented structured code, although Action Diagrams

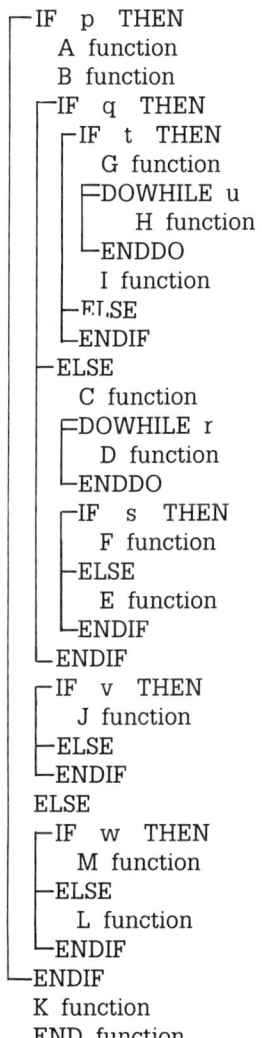

```
┌IF  p  THEN
│   A function
│   B function
│  ┌IF  q  THEN
│  │  ┌IF  t  THEN
│  │  │   G function
│  │  │  ═DOWHILE u
│  │  │      H function
│  │  │  └ENDDO
│  │  │   I function
│  │  ├ELSE
│  │  └ENDIF
│  ├ELSE
│  │   C function
│  │  ═DOWHILE r
│  │     D function
│  │  └ENDDO
│  │  ┌IF  s  THEN
│  │  │   F function
│  │  ├ELSE
│  │  │   E function
│  │  └ENDIF
│  └ENDIF
│  ┌IF  v  THEN
│  │   J function
│  ├ELSE
│  └ENDIF
│  ELSE
│  ┌IF  w  THEN
│  │   M function
│  ├ELSE
│  │   L function
│  └ENDIF
└ENDIF
  K function
  END function
```

FIGURE 3.12 Action Diagram for the right-hand side of Figure 3.2

136   INTEGRAND SPECIFICATIONS

Escapes

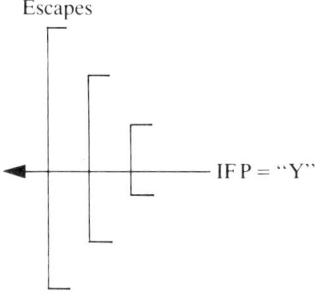

If it is necessary to escape through several levels of nested structures, this 'escape' is shown as a horizontal arrow breaking through one or more brackets with the escape condition shown to its right. When the escape condition is true, control is transferred to the exit of the outermost bracket through which the arrow is drawn.

NEXT iteration

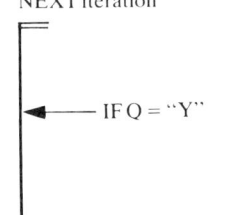

A 'next' instruction that skips to the end of the current loop, is shown by an arrow which does not break through the bracket. When the condition is true, control is transferred to the next iteration of the loop.

FIGURE 3.13 Other Action Diagram symbols

are not as practical with a normal text editor as with an editor that is specially constructed to add, modify, and delete the brackets.

While it is possible to add the Action Diagram brackets automatically as a developer enters code or chooses a Structured Programming figure, it is *not* possible to generate code from the Action Diagram graphics (i.e. from the brackets). The Structured Programming constructs could be partially generated, but not the calculations, input, output, or even the conditions for the loops and IFs. There is just not enough information depicted by the brackets to determine the code, i.e. the diagrams can come from the code, but the *code cannot come from the diagrams*. Thus, Action Diagrams do not constitute a base for generating code from diagrams. However, they are a way to show structured code that is easier to read than it is with just indentation.

3.5 STATE TRANSITION DIAGRAMS

3.5.1 Description

A system that responds to its inputs in the same way every time does not have to maintain internal states. However, some software systems or components react differently to the

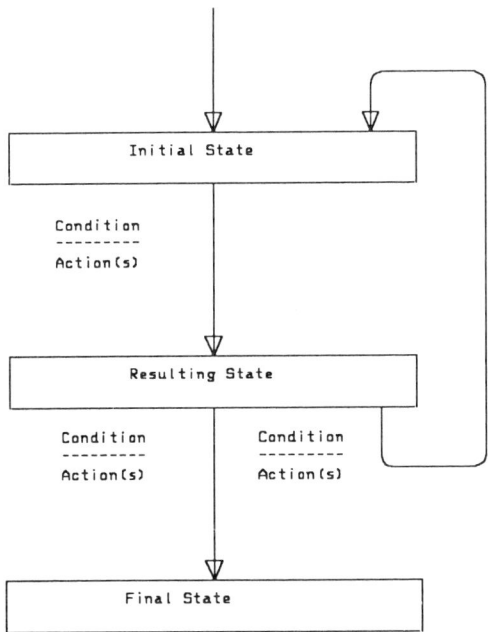

FIGURE 3.14 A state transition diagram

same input, depending on what 'state' they are in. Most of these can be described as a black box whose output responses depend on the input stimuli and the internal state maintained in the black box (see 'Box Structured Design', Section 2.6). If the number of internal states is small (which is more likely for components at lower levels) it may be helpful to visualize the system or integrand as having a set of distinct 'states' – it is considered to be 'in' one, and only one, of the states at any time. As the system moves to another state, or 'changes states', a 'transition' is said to occur. A *state transition diagram* is a diagram that has a box for each state and arrows that point to another state. The arrows indicate possible transitions (between states) and are annotated with the condition that will cause the transition (above the line) and the actions that are performed by the system if that transition occurs (below the line, see Figure 3.14). State transition diagrams are used by Ward and Mellor with their method for designing real-time systems (Section 2.4).

The 'initial state' is the state of the system when it starts, is turned on, or is re-set. It is represented in a state transition diagram by the state with no arrow from another state. Final states, if any, are the ones with no transitions leaving them. It is possible for multiple transitions to leave any given state and for a single transition to connect any two states. However, a given transition can move the system to one other state only (since the system is allowed to be in only one state at any time).

138   INTEGRAND SPECIFICATIONS

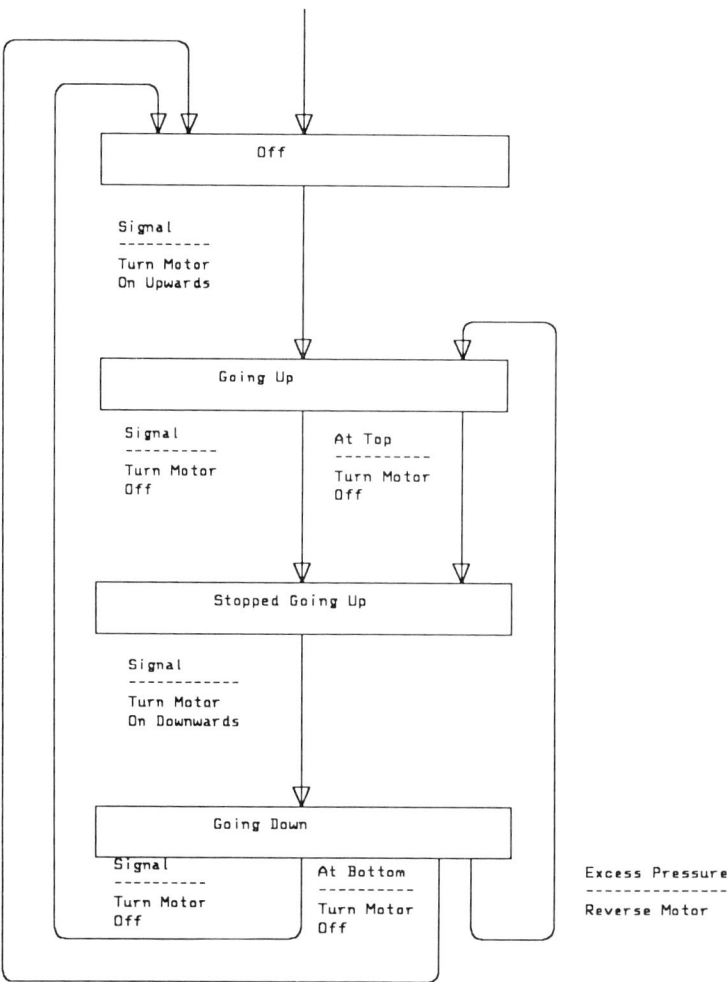

FIGURE 3.15 Garage door opener state transition diagram

3.5.2 Example: a garage door opener

An example of a state transition diagram for a garage door opener is shown in Figure 3.15. There is one input signal to the garage door opener, which can come from any of the radio units, the push button inside the garage, or from an outside key-lock. The opener cycles through its states each time there is a signal: from 'stopped', to 'going up', to 'stopped going up', to 'going down', to 'stopped going down'. When the door reaches the top or the bottom it stops and goes into the next state without a signal. If the door encounters an obstacle when going down, it reverses direction. Note that there is a

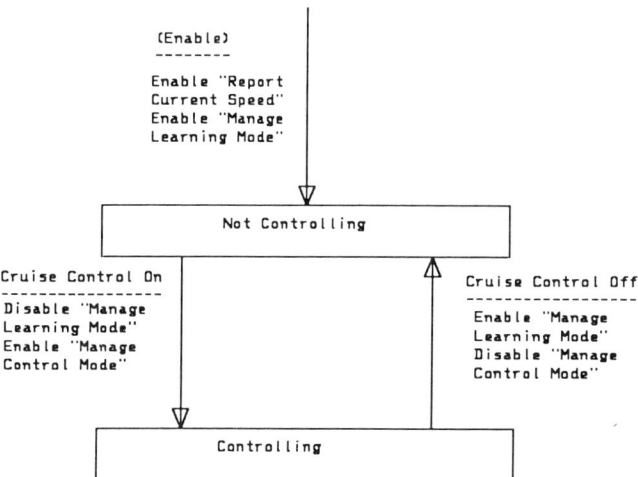

FIGURE 3.16 Determine Mode of Operation

difference between the states 'stopped going up' and 'off'. ('Off' is equivalent to 'stopped going down'.) While the door stops moving in each case, there is a different response from each of these states to the next signal. In fact, it is the different reaction to the same signal that requires internal states to be maintained and that makes the state transition diagram a useful tool.

3.5.3 Example: Cruise Control

State transition diagrams for the cruise control example in Section 2.4.2 are shown in Figures 3.16–3.18 and are reprinted by permission from Ward and Mellor (1985). Figure 3.16 shows the state transition diagram for the 'Determine Mode of Operation' control transformation shown in Figure 2.30. Figure 3.18 shows a state transition diagram for the 'Control Cruise Control Engagement' transformation in Figure 3.17 (Figure 3.17 is the decomposition of the 'Manage Control Mode' transformation in Figure 2.30 – see 'Transformation schema' in Section 2.4.3 for a description of this type of diagram). Each signal entering the 'Control Cruise Control Engagement' transformation in Figure 3.17 can be seen as a condition that causes one or more state transitions in Figure 3.18 (except for 'Disable', which disables all operations, regardless of the state). Notice that a single input signal, such as 'Brake', can show up on several transitions. Actions beside the arrows in Figure 3.18 show the signals that the 'Control Cruise Control Engagement' transformation sends to the data transformations in Figure 3.17.

State transition diagrams can be drawn with the states depicted as vertical or horizontal lines, as in Figure 3.19. Designers of business applications sometimes draw screen-hierarchy diagrams to represent the navigation among screens in an interactive dialog (see Figure 3.20). These screen-hierarchy diagrams are an example of state transition

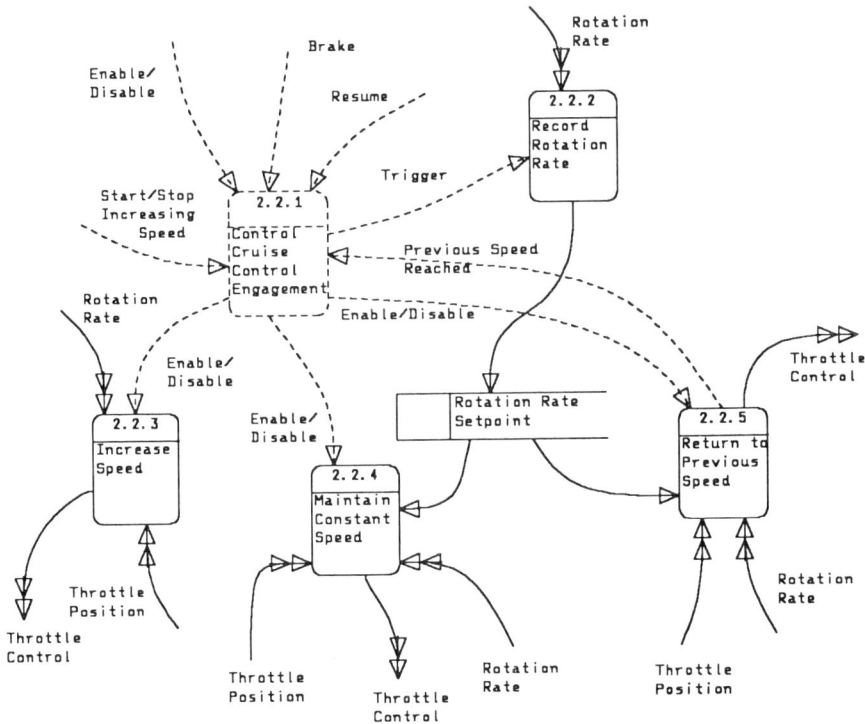

FIGURE 3.17 Manage Control Mode

diagrams – where the screen being displayed is equivalent to the state of the system and actions that the user can perform (such as pressing a function key) are the transitions which determine the next screen (i.e. the next state).

3.5.4 Comments on state transition diagrams

State transition diagrams are particularly helpful in describing the specifications for integrands with few states (e.g. two to ten), such as is often true with control transformations in transformation schema. If the integrand has only one state, a state transition diagram would be useless; as the number of states gets larger than ten, it becomes increasingly difficult to depict the states with a state transition diagram. If the state transition diagram can be divided into pieces, then it can accommodate more states, such as with the screen hierarchy in Figure 3.20. Since the interactions are hierarchical, a screen-hierarchy diagram can also be decomposed hierarchically. However, if transitions can occur between any of a large number of states, then a state transition diagram can become unwieldy.

STATE TRANSITION DIAGRAMS 141

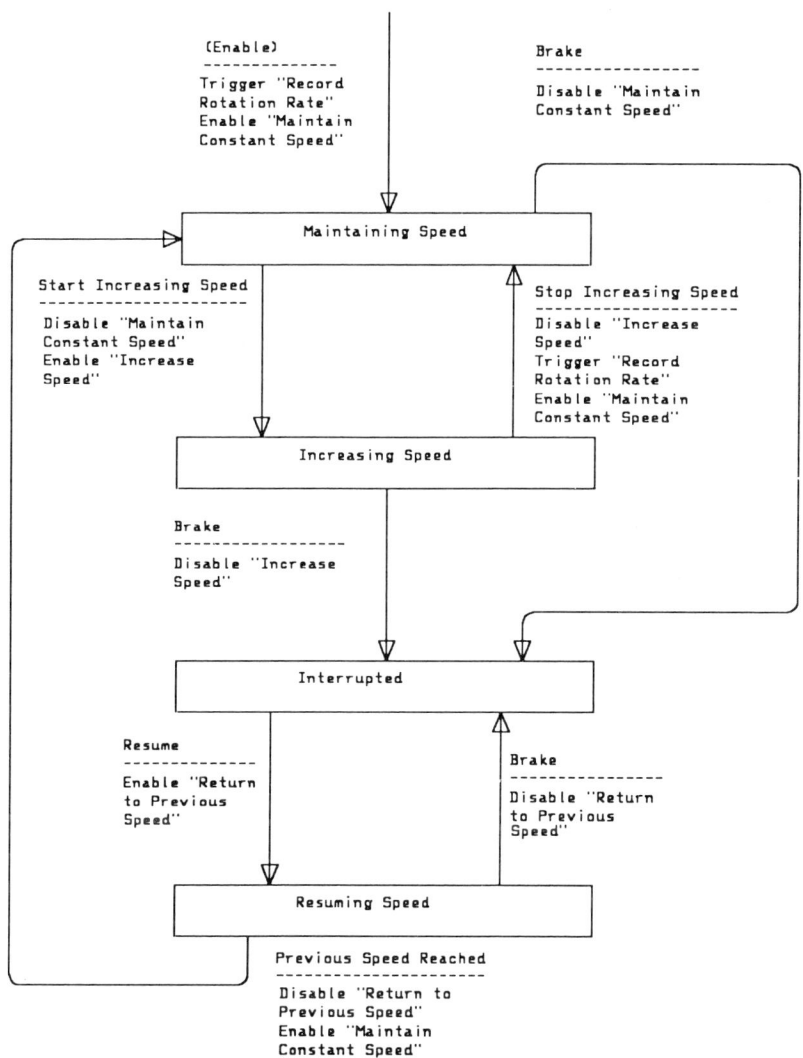

FIGURE 3.18 Control Cruise Control Engagement

142 INTEGRAND SPECIFICATIONS

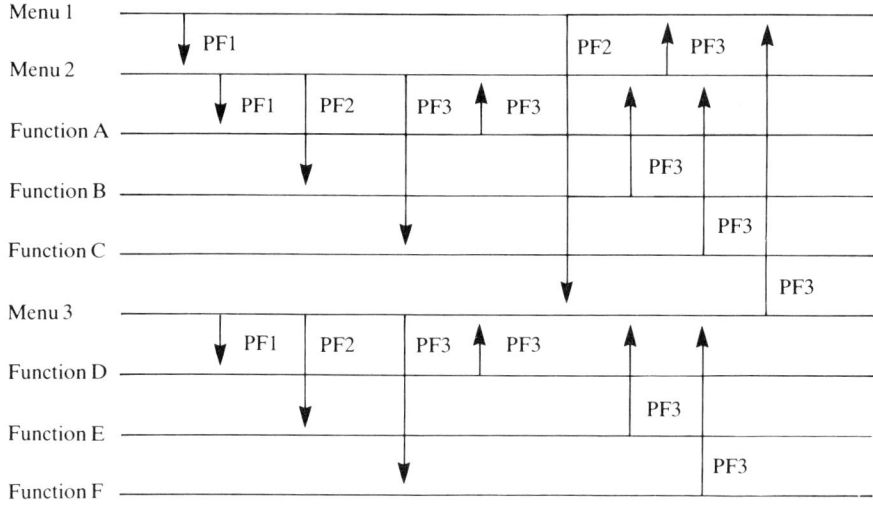

FIGURE 3.19 Alternative state transition diagram

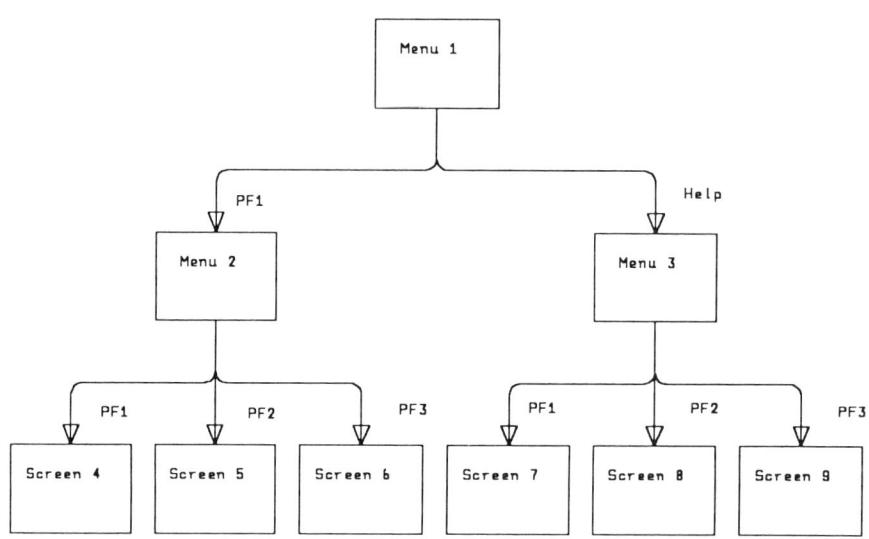

FIGURE 3.20 Screen hierarchy diagram

3.6 JACKSON CHARTS

3.6.1 Description

Michael Jackson, in his book *Principles of Program Design* (1975), introduced a charting technique consisting primarily of boxes and arrows that depicts sequence, iteration, and choice. The elements of Jackson charts are shown in Figure 3.21. Jackson builds on the observation published earlier by Warnier (1974) that data on two-dimensional forms can be described in terms of sequence, iteration, and choice (as with code – see 'Structured Programming' in Section 3.2). Warnier observed that it is then possible to specify the structure of the code from the description of the data that is processed by a program. For example, consider the report in Figure 3.22, which consists of a *sequence* of the following:

1. A page header.
2. A number of detail lines (i.e. *iteration*).
3. A summary line.
4. An optional error line (i.e. *choice*).
5. A page footing.

The Jackson chart in Figure 3.23 depicts the organization of the report form in Figure 3.22. Figure 3.24 shows code with the same sequence, iteration, and choice structure as the Jackson chart in Figure 3.23. The code processes the data in the correct order, because it is one-to-one with the layout of the data. In both the data and the processing of the code, the heading comes first, followed by several detail lines, then a summary, a possible error line, and the footing.

3.6.2 Comments on Jackson design

The preceding would seem an easy and productive way to produce code once the data is specified. However, there are advantages and disadvantages that are important to understand in order to apply the Jackson approach productively. The big advantage of Jackson's approach is the ability to create the branching logic from data definitions. Unfortunately, even small integrands have both input *and* output data. Thus, there may be more than one data structure from which to create the code, and the various structures may not be compatible. Jackson explains ways to merge different structures, including looking for similar subsets between the two structures. However, the larger the amount of code to be designed, the more data structures there are, and consequently the harder it is to merge them – especially if the merge is done manually. Jackson charts become less valuable as the amount of code to be designed gets bigger, more complex, the logic is based on conditions unrelated to data layout, or where the layout of the data is simple, likely to change, or not an important part of the requirements. For some software the arrangement of data is unimportant – the function performed by the software is the critical part, rather than how the input and output data are arranged. For example,

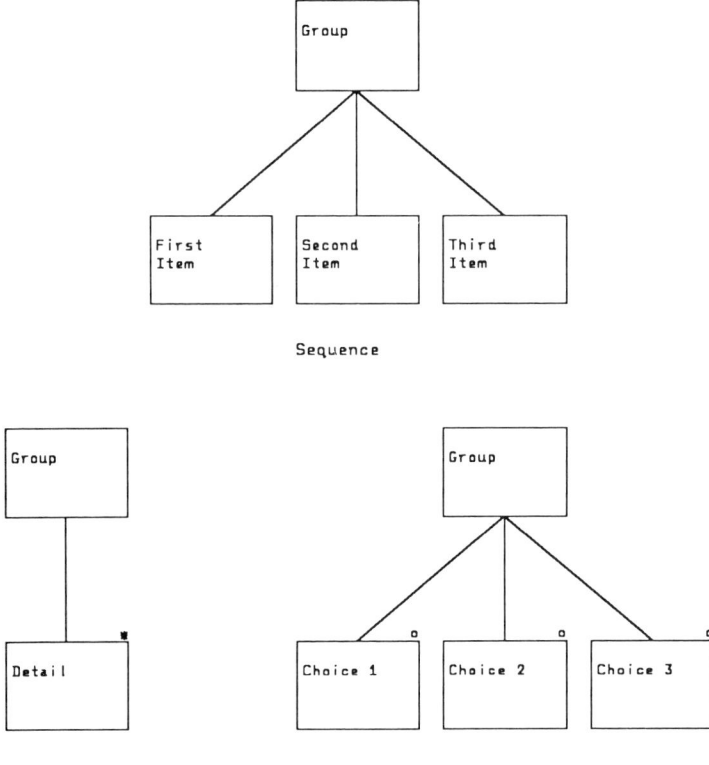

FIGURE 3.21 Jackson chart constructs

Page heading
Detail line
Detail line
.
.
.
Summary line
Error line (or confirm no errors)
Page footing

FIGURE 3.22 A sample report

control and audit output data must be accurate, but the format of the reports is not too important. Other examples where the logic of such software has little to do with the layout of data include software for making scientific calculations (e.g. determining the trajectory of a satellite around the earth), controlling machine tools, displaying graphics, or analyzing video images.

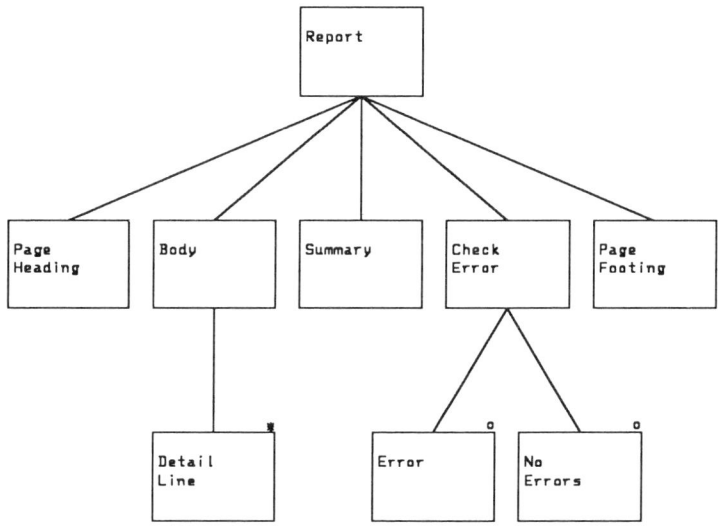

FIGURE 3.23 Jackson chart for report

```
PROCESS Page heading
    DO UNTIL end of details
        PROCESS Detail line
    ENDDO
    PROCESS Summary line
    IF error THEN
        PROCESS Error line
    ELSE
        PROCESS NO errors
    ENDIF
PROCESS Page footing
```

FIGURE 3.24 Process Report program

The Jackson approach is more useful when the integrands are small (e.g. one-page) and where the logic is primarily determined from the visual arrangement of data. The Jackson approach works better to the extent that each piece of data is processed independently, as opposed to cross-field edits that will not be reflected in the data layout. For small integrands that map data between different layouts, Jackson's approach works so well that it should be possible to generate the code automatically. It is also possible to use Jackson charts as formal descriptions of data formats and input and output forms (see Lundberg *et al.* 1981). However, even if the Jackson approach produces code from a data layout, this does not mean that the code is necessarily correct or easy to change. One reason is that the Jackson approach does not create *all* the code – only the *branching* logic associated with the data format. The Jackson approach does not specify how to write the calculation statements or the branching statements necessary to process the data (though it does indicate *where* these statements should be placed).

Much of Jackson (1975), and his book *System Development* (1983), is devoted to developing systems. However, the Jackson approach is not particularly appropriate for decomposing a system into integrands. In *System Development*, Jackson agrees that data structures do not play a central role in system design (1983, page 365). Instead, the book recommends the use of a data flow approach much like that explained in Appendix A (see also 'Code reuse', Section 5.3). There are a number of valuable criteria for decomposition, as covered by the methods given in Chapter 2. During architectural design, the designer is interested in what data and control are shared, rather than the sequence, iteration, and choice characteristics of input and output data that the Jackson chart shows. Sequence, iteration, and choice concepts are more suited to specifying the internals of an integrand than to architectural design. Basing logic on the format of data is more valuable for producing one-page integrands where the data format is determined independently and the logic is based primarily on the layout of the data. It is then possible to create much of the code directly from the Jackson chart (or data format).

Another important consideration relative to using Jackson's approach is the developer's ability to make changes to the code rapidly and accurately. Even if the code is entirely without errors, maintenance is still required in order to accommodate changes in the users' needs, company policies, laws, and the environment. However, if the same field shows up several times in the output data, the Jackson approach will tend to result in duplicate functions to process that data. Duplicate functions make maintenance harder (since each implementation of the function has to be changed, instead of only one implementation). In addition, since the Jackson approach groups function by how data are arranged on input and output forms, function groupings may display sequential binding, if they share data, or even as low as coincidental binding, if the data are unrelated (see 'Structured Design', Section 2.5). As a result, functional decompositions produced by the Jackson approach tend to be harder to change than code decomposed into functional integrands.

3.7 DECISION TABLES

3.7.1 Description

Decision tables (called 'truth tables' by Warnier 1974) are a more natural way to specify some logic than computer languages (see also Kowal 1988). Because decision tables have only a few defined tokens in their syntax, they are language-independent. An example of a decision table is shown in Figure 3.25. The tested conditions are shown at the top of the left column, with possible actions below them in the lower section of the column. The conditions are generally assumed to be binary. Each column to the right of the conditions

Alarm ringing?	NYYY
Saturday?	-NYN
Sunday?	-NNY
Get up	111
Turn off alarm	222
Get dressed	3 4
Eat breakfast	4 3
Go to work	5
Go back to bed	3
Go to church	5
Sleep	1

FIGURE 3.25 Decision table

is marked with a Y (Yes), N (No), or '-' (do not care) and represents a specific combination of conditions. The columns to the right of the possible actions indicate whether to take that action for the conditions above and can be marked with an 'X' (and executed in order from top to bottom), or numbered by order of execution – see Figure 3.25.

In Figure 3.25, if the alarm is not ringing, I continue to sleep. If the alarm is ringing and it is not Saturday or Sunday, then I get up, get dressed, eat, and go to work. If the alarm is ringing and it is Saturday, I get up, turn off the alarm, and go back to bed. If the alarm is ringing and it is Sunday, I get up, eat breakfast, get dressed, and go to church.

Decision tables can specify the logic for an integrand. However, there are four major capabilities missing from the traditional form of decision tables which are necessary to make the decision tables more generally useful (in addition to their natural sequence and choice): hierarchies, loops, initializations, and terminations. *Hierarchies* are needed because a decision table with a column for each unique combination of conditions will have 2^N columns, where N is the number of conditions. Thus even a relatively simple decision table with ten conditions could need over 1000 columns. If the '-' (do-not-care) condition applies because the same actions apply to multiple conditions, the number of columns may be significantly reduced, but there is no guarantee that the do-not-care can be applied. Hierarchies can be made by allowing an action to link to another table. The link can be a transfer without return (usually as the last action in a column) or a transfer with return (similar to a 'call'). The ability to call another table with a return requires the ability for the called table to 'return', either implicitly at the bottom of the column that is executed, or as a specific action. Figure 3.26 shows an example of two linked decision tables.

A facility to connect decision tables allows the ability to *loop*. One way is to link tables in a loop (table A connects to B, . . ., which connects to table A). Another is to allow table A to link to itself. However, these are rather limiting (and confusing) ways to implement a loop. An alternative, and more natural and direct, way to implement a loop is recommended by Larson in his doctoral dissertation (1979). Larson proposes that evaluation of conditions be repeated automatically. Normally the conditions in a decision

148 INTEGRAND SPECIFICATIONS

Alarm ringing?	NYYY
Saturday?	-NYN
Sunday?	-NNY
Get up	111
Turn off alarm	222
Get dressed	3 4
Eat breakfast	4 3
Go to work	5
Go back to bed	
Go to church	5
Sleep	1
Go to table B	3

Table B

Summer?	Y--
Raining?	NY-
Car working?	YYN
Get dressed	111
Eat breakfast	222
Mow lawn	3
Do odd jobs	434
Fix car	3

FIGURE 3.26 Linked decision tables

table are evaluated from left to right (evaluation order is relevant whenever conditions are not mutually exclusive). Thus Larson's recommendation is that after evaluation of the rightmost column, the evaluation and execution of conditions resumes at the leftmost column again – thus looping indefinitely. There are two possibilities for ending the looping execution of each table. One is to invoke another table; a second is to allow the actions to modify the conditions, including an 'END' action to stop execution. Ultimately, the actual exit from the table is still by the 'END' condition or transfer to another table, but the modification of conditions tested by the decision table becomes the control on the termination of the loop. The ability to modify the conditions tested by the decision table raises the question of when the conditions are evaluated – at the beginning of the table, or after evaluation (and possible execution) of the preceding column. Flexibility and simplicity in understanding a table lead to the latter choice – i.e. conditions for each column are evaluated as the column is reached.

Larson also recommends adding sections to the decision table – an *initialize* section, which gets executed prior to evaluation of the conditions, and a *terminate* section, which is executed as the table is exited (see Figure 3.27).

Another variation is a 'triangular' decision table. In this approach, the conditions are restricted to be in the form of a triangle as in Figure 3.28, with 'Yes' entries down a diagonal from left to right. The conditions below the diagonal are 'No' and the conditions above the diagonal are 'do not care' (i.e. the condition can be true or false), signified by the symbol '-'. Alternatively (and equivalently) the entries on the diagonal can all be 'No', with 'Yes' entries below and 'do-not-care' above. The triangular shape can be achieved by having all conditions mutually exclusive. However, other combinations of conditions can also result in the triangular shape. In order to cover every condition, there is one more column in a triangular decision table than there are number of conditions, with the extra column for the situation where none of the conditions is true. Because of the pattern of the condition section, a triangular decision table can be implemented as a CASE structure (see Figure 3.5).

DECISION TABLES 149

Alarm	000 123	Table name and column numbers
Go to bed		Initialize section
Alarm ringing? Saturday? Sunday?	NYYY -NYN -NNY	Conditions
Get up Turn off alarm Get dressed Eat breakfast Go to work Go back to bed Go to church Sleep	111 222 3 4 4 3 5 3 5 1	Actions
Exit	XXX	Exit (i.e. stop iterating)
Kiss my wife		Terminate section

FIGURE 3.27 Decision table with all sections

Alarm on? Alarm on & Sat.? Alarm on & Sun.?	Y--N NY-N NNYN
Get up Turn off alarm Get dressed Eat breakfast Go to work Go back to bed Go to church Sleep longer	111 222 3 4 4 3 5 3 5 1

FIGURE 3.28 Triangular decision table

3.7.2 Decision trees

Decision trees are another way to describe the logic of an integrand. The decision tree shown in Figure 3.29 is from section 1.33 above. The information shown by a decision tree is basically the same as that in a decision table. Although usually used with binary conditions, decision trees can now show conditions with multiple values.

3.7.3 Comments on decision tables and trees

Decision tables are a useful way to specify logic for integrands containing relatively few actions and whose execution is dependent on multiple conditions. They can depict

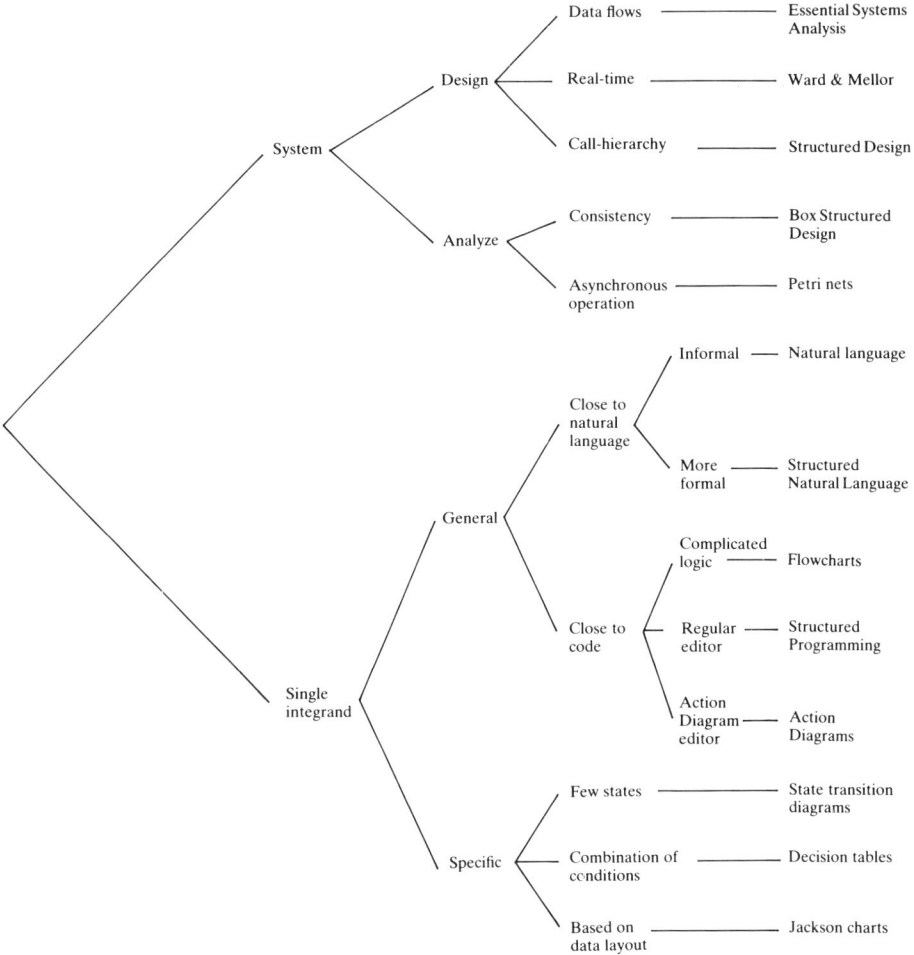

FIGURE 3.29 Decision tree

specifications in a way that people without formal computer training can understand more easily than they can understand flowcharts. The decision table can be translated into code, but the actions will have to be specified in the target execution language syntax either in the decision table or after it is translated. A disadvantage of decision tables is that they can have a large number of columns to cover all possible conditions, even for a relatively small number of conditions (ten conditions results in 1024 columns unless some can be combined using the do-not-care condition). However, if do-not-care conditions are used, it is especially difficult to check manually for completeness. Assuring that every possible condition is covered can be a formidable task – at least without automated help. Warnier (1974) deals with graphical and mathematical ways to reduce the number of columns in decision tables. As with other things, the approximate limit for the number of

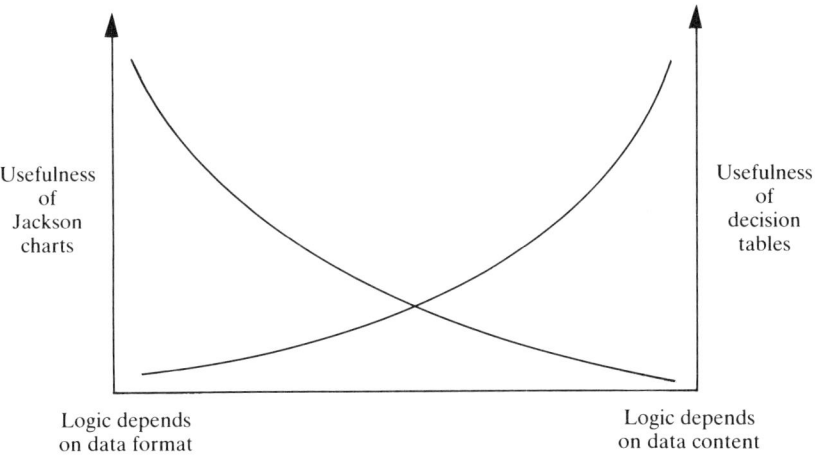

FIGURE 3.30 Jackson charts vs. decision tables

columns of conditions that people can deal with easily is 'seven plus or minus two' (Miller 1956).

One advantage of triangular decision tables is reduction of the number of columns that occur in regular decision tables. As a result, the table stays in the shape of a page rather than extending far to the right. Thus the tables tend to be smaller, which makes them easier to specify, understand, test, and change. Also, a triangular decision table covers every possible condition automatically, since this is inherent in its format. A disadvantage with triangular decision tables is that they lead to artificial and compound conditions in order to meet the requirement of the triangular shape. Also, the most significant question often has to go last (after testing the exceptions). Triangular decision tables also blunt the greatest advantage of decision tables – the ability to specify actions to be taken based on arbitrary combinations of several conditions.

It is not clear that decision trees have any advantage over decision tables except possibly for informal depiction of small problems to people not familiar with decision table syntax. Decision trees become unwieldy unless they can be contained on a page or two and there is a single action for each combination of conditions. Hierarchies of decision trees can be made by having the end of each branch refer to another decision tree. However, a decision tree is much clearer if it does not have to be extended horizontally across more than one page, since each path from the beginning to end of a branch represents a related compound condition that can be difficult to grasp when spread across many pages.

It is possible to contrast the usefulness of Jackson charts versus decision tables, as shown in Figure 3.30. At the left (Jackson) end of the scale are integrands whose branching logic is primarily determined by the *layout* of data. An integrand to check an input for valid data would be at this end of the scale. At the other (decision table) end of the scale is an integrand whose decisions are based on the *values* of data or other conditions unrelated to the data format. An integrand that processes a tax return – where the input fields are basically sequential and conditions tend to be related to the *values* within multiple fields – is at this end of the scale.

Since neither Jackson charts nor decision tables help to produce the *actions* to be executed, there is a dimension other than those shown in Figure 3.30 where both of these techniques become less valuable; that is, when the branching logic of an integrand is simple, or mostly due to the processing of the data. Examples of simple logic include moving a large existing data structure to a formatted report definition – which requires many move statements, but little or no logic. Another example is a single large CASE structure (see Figure 3.5), such as code which decides which of many algorithms to use for a particular set of data.

CHAPTER FOUR
DATA BASE DESIGN CONCEPTS

> The first step in data base design is to document and validate an *enterprise schema*, which consists of the definitions of entities, attributes, relationships, and constraints (described below). A common way to depict relationships among data is with an *entity–relationship (ER)* diagram. The enterprise schema is transformed to third normal form – a standard form for the design of related data, whether stored in data bases or flat files. The result is used to create a data base description, which depends on the type of data base management system to be used. The data base administrators, who both design and administer the data bases, create a physical data base design. Despite available methods, however, the major problems in data base design are the difficulty of gathering information from people and promoting the changes that result from introducing a computerized data base.

The topic of data base design is large enough to warrant volumes to explain it. However, when designing software that will access or create the stored data, it is important to at least understand the basic concepts of data base design. Readers interested in an in-depth presentation of data base concepts are referred to *An Introduction to Data Base Systems*, Volumes I and II by Chris Date (1983 and 1987). The steps involved in data base design are shown in Figure 4.1. It is best if the data base is designed in parallel with the software design so that insights gained through each activity can be incorporated into the other design (as shown in Figure 1.3). The information and quotes in this chapter and Figures 4.2–4.13 are based on, or reproduced with permission from Tsichritzis and Lochovsky (1982).

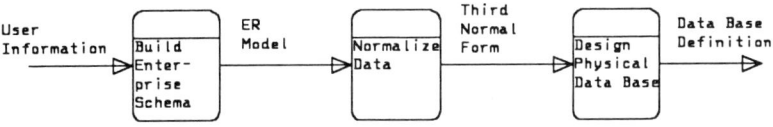

FIGURE 4.1 Data base design steps

4.1 ENTITY–RELATIONSHIP DATA MODEL

4.1.1 Description

For as long as human beings have been able to talk, they have described the objects and events around them; we call these descriptions 'data'. Tsichritzis and Lochovsky (1982) define data as follows:

> 'Data correspond to discrete, recorded facts about phenomena from which we gain information about the world.'

Although the Latin word 'datum' means a fact, we use the word 'data' to describe not only facts, but ideas and imprecise concepts. For the purpose of data modeling, data are anything worth recording in a somewhat precise manner. In a natural language we might say 'I am 44 years old'. This sentence combines both the datum '44' with its meaning 'years old'. However in computers, the data and their meaning are often separated. Primarily this has happened for two reasons. One is that it is expensive to store the description – especially when the interpretation of the data is implicitly contained within the programs that have to process it. The second reason is that computers are not very good at handling natural language – it is easier for a program to handle data fields by position than to try to interpret the meaning of the data from some kind of language description. As computers evolve, data bases become more massive, and the data in them becomes more critical to the enterprise. It is therefore important to capture the interpretation of the data.

Data models *describe* data much as dictionaries describe words or encyclopedias describe various entities that exist in the real world. Naturally, though an encyclopedia may contain a description and a picture of the 'Rock of Gibraltar', it does not contain the actual rock itself. In a similar sense, the dictionary contains *descriptions* of the language. Unfortunately, it must use the language in order to describe itself – there being little other choice – but no one is confused as to which is which. However, with data models, because the distinction between the model and the data is a little more blurred, some terminology can help. The data that are stored in, or depicted by, the data model are called *meta-data* to distinguish them from the data they describe, such as personnel information. The personnel information is the data, the information that *describes* that personnel information is the meta-data. (The personnel information may even describe something else: the employee.) There are some words, such as 'noun', 'adjective', and 'verb', that are used primarily to describe the types of words language contains. A noun is a type of word that represents a person, place, or thing; an adjective can be used to state a characteristic about the noun, and a verb is an action that can apply to a noun. Similarly, ER data models contain three types of objects: an *entity*, an *attribute*, and a *relationship*. An entity is similar to a noun – it represents a person, place, or thing, such as a car. An attribute is like an adjective – it describes characteristics about an entity, such as the color of the car is 'red'. A relationship is similar to a verb – at least to those verbs that connect two nouns – such as a car 'contains' an engine and a car can be 'made by' the Ford Motor

ENTITY–RELATIONSHIP DATA MODEL 155

Company. It is possible for a relationship to have attributes. For example, the relationship *married to* may have an attribute of the wedding date associated with it.

It is often convenient to talk about a collection of similar things. Thus, while a particular car may be red and made by Ford, the word 'car', itself, describes a category of objects. Similarly, in data-modeling terminology, a category of objects is referred to as an *entity type*. For example, car, person, and cities are entity types that could be included in a given data model. A particular instance of an entity type, such as my brown Toyota, is called an *entity instance*, or just an 'entity'. Thus an entity is a specific thing of a given type with all its specific attributes. For example, if the entity type *car* has attributes named *year, model, manufacturer, engine number, color, . . .* , then an entity, i.e. a particular car, may have the specific attributes of *1989, sedan, Ford, 1234567890, red, ...* A collection of specific entities, such as all Volvos registered in New York, is known as an *entity set*. For a particular application, the names of all the entity sets, relationship sets and their attributes make up a *schema*.

In addition to entities, relationships and attributes, a data model also contains *constraints*. These are restrictions on allowable objects, relationships, or values of attributes. In an employee data model, for example, constraints may include that each employee have a unique employee number, have only one manager, and not earn more than that manager.

Just as a particular person can be identified uniquely by some set of attributes (such as name, address, employee number, and birth date), an entity set may have some set of attributes that makes it possible to identify each entity within the entity set. The combined attributes that are used to identify an entity uniquely are known as the *key*. As an example, for cars a key might be a combination of the manufacturer, model, year, and engine number. Sometimes an artificial attribute, such as serial number, is added to allow unique identification of each entity instance.

A *functional dependency* is said to exist between two attributes, such as *Name* and *Home phone number* if each *Name* not only determines the *Home phone number*, but determines it uniquely (at least within the context of a given set of data). The functional dependency is from the *Name* to the *Home phone number* and is written *Name* → *Home phone number* (i.e. *Name* functionally determines *Home phone number*).

4.1.2 Entity–relationship diagrams

The ER data model was conceived to enable data base design by allowing an *enterprise schema* to be specified (Chen 1977). The enterprise schema describes the entire enterprise's view of data, which can then be implemented on some data base management system (DBMS). The ER data model has gained wide acceptance for its ability to specify an enterprise schema in a way that is adequate for data base design and in a form that can also be communicated to the users. The *entity–relationship diagram (ERD)* is used to depict the entity types and the relationship types that connect them. Figure 4.2 shows an ERD for a medical data base.

In an ERD, entity types are shown as rectangular boxes labeled with the name of the

156   DATA BASE DESIGN CONCEPTS

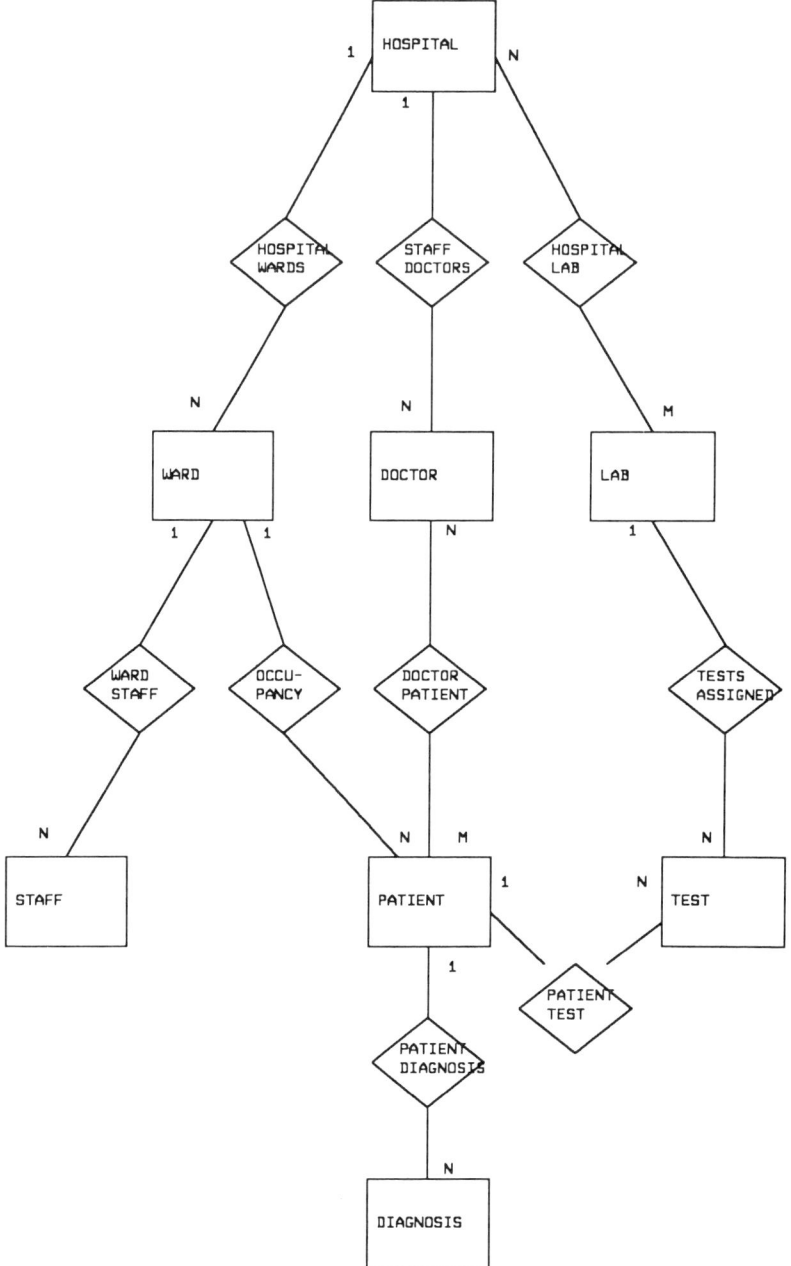

FIGURE 4.5 Entity–relationship diagram for medical data base

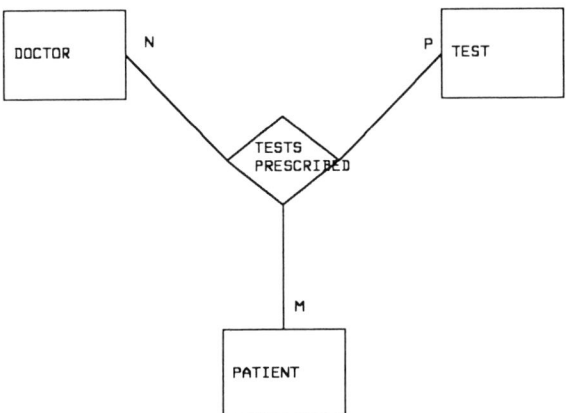

FIGURE 4.3 Ternary relationship set

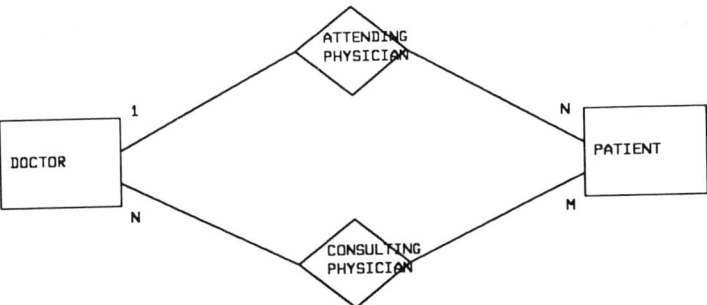

FIGURE 4.4 Two relationship sets between the same entity sets

entity type, e.g. HOSPITAL, DOCTOR, and PATIENT are entity types in Figure 4.2. It is possible to identify whether an entity belongs to a particular entity set; though it is possible for entities to belong to several entity sets simultaneously – for example, a doctor can also be a patient. A diamond represents a relationship type, such as PATIENT TEST, PATIENT DIAGNOSIS, and HOSPITAL WARDS. Annotations on the links indicate whether the relationships are one-to-one, functional (one-to-many), or many-to-many with a '1' indicating one and any letter (usually 'N') indicating many. In this enterprise schema, a hospital can have many staff doctors, but each of those doctors is staff to only one hospital, i.e. there is a functional mapping from doctors to hospitals because each doctor is only on staff to one hospital.

The ER data model allows a relationship type to connect more than two entity types, as in Figure 4.3, which indicates that a patient can have several tests prescribed by several doctors; a test can be prescribed by several doctors for several patients; and a doctor can prescribe several tests for several patients. The ER model also allows two (or more) entity types to be connected by more than one relationship type, such as in Figure 4.4.

158   DATA BASE DESIGN CONCEPTS

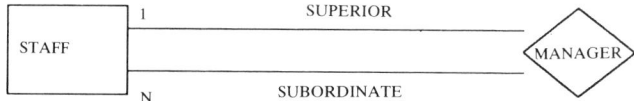

FIGURE 4.5 Recursive relationship set

This diagram indicates that a patient may have several consulting physicians but only one attending physician. A doctor can be the attending physician for more than one patient and may consult on several patients. Recursive relationships are also allowed, as shown in Figure 4.5.

4.2 THE ENTERPRISE SCHEMA

There are many different ways of looking at data. Each group looking at data may view them differently. For example, the color of a car may be an attribute of the car to the automobile manufacturer, but may be an entity to the company that makes the paint. Similarly, within an enterprise, various groups usually look at data different ways. Tsichritzis and Lochovsky (1982) state: 'It is very difficult to argue persuasively that one data model is best uniformly. Each data model has advantages, depending on who is doing the schema design and the realm in which one is working.' It is perhaps realistic to have two data models, one for the user's viewpoint and one for the computer system's viewpoint.

4.2.1 Describing the enterprise

The first step in creating an enterprise schema is to create a view of the schema for each area in the organization. This is done by gathering the entity types, relationship types, and constraints of interest to each area (Chen and Yao 1977). The second step is to integrate the various individual views to form an entire schema that describes the enterprise (Navanthe and Schkolnick 1978; Baldissera et al. 1979; Ceri et al. 1981). The resulting ER data model should be sufficiently informal to allow good communication with the users and need not have the same model as the intended DBMS.

In order to define the various individual views, data classes are identified during the requirements analysis efforts. One way to identify data classes is to look at the data going into and out of various functions in the organization. For example, data classes may include sales, customer, and production information. Entity types can be identified for each of the data classes, along with meanings and appropriate names for each of the entity types; entity types identified for an insurance company example are shown in Figure 4.6. Attributes of interest are identified for each entity type with their meanings and appropriate names. Typically, defining entity types and attributes is an iterative process

Underwriting and issue

POLICY	– Policy number, Last activity, Last activity date, Next activity, Next activity date, Social security number
COVERAGE	– Coverage type, Coverage amount, Premium rate, Issue date
CLIENT	– Social security number, Name, Address, Birthdate
PRIOR COVERAGE	– Policy number, Type, Amount, Rating
BENEFICIARY	– Social security number, Name, Address
TERMINATION	– Termination date, Reinstatement date, Termination reason

Agency

AGENT	– Agent number, Name, Address, Area
POLICY	– Policy number, Coverage type, Coverage amount, Issue date
CLIENT	– Social security number, Name, Address, Birthdate
COMMISSION	– Type, Rate

Insurance administration

POLICY	– Policy number, Last activity, Last activity date, Next activity, Next activity date
CLIENT	– Social security number, Name, Address, Birthdate
BILLING	– Mode, Amount, Next premium date, Name, Address
LOANS	– Principal, Balance, Interest rate, Interest due date
COMMISSION	– Type, Rate

FIGURE 4.6 Entity types and attributes for insurance company example

during which it may be necessary to gather some new information from the users. The description of an entity type may have to be changed many times before everyone agrees that it is correct.

A description is created for each entity type, which includes the name of the type, its attributes, what is represents, its synonyms and its acronyms, and is entered into the data dictionary (see 'Software design tools', Section 5.1). The importance of the data dictionary should not be underestimated; it is a crucial tool that allows common access to the data model as it is being gathered and refined. Otherwise those attempting to define the data model could end by having different copies of the evolving definitions. This would *contribute* to the situation that the data model is attempting to eliminate – that there are many different local meanings for the same words – rather than working towards a single common definition for the objects in the data model.

Relationship types are determined by looking at the entity types and the functions that use them. The relationship types for the insurance company example are shown in Figure 4.7. Some questions that can help to identify relationship types follow:

1. What kinds of relationships exist between entity types associated with each function?
2. Can the relationship type be expressed as a formula using attributes of the entity types? For example, the policyholder attribute is true if the social security number in the client attribute equals the social security number in the policy attribute.
3. Are there any possible meaningful relationships that are not used?
4. Are there combinations of relationship types, such as client's beneficiaries, that make sense as separate identifiable relationship types?

Underwriting and issue
POLICY COVERAGE — between *POLICY* and *COVERAGE*
PRIOR POLICY COVERAGE — between *POLICY* and *PRIOR COVERAGE*
POLICY BENEFICIARY — between *POLICY* and *BENEFICIARY*
POLICY TERMINATION — between *POLICY* and *TERMINATION*
POLICYHOLDER — between *CLIENT* and *POLICY*

Agency
POLICYHOLDER — between *CLIENT* and *POLICY*
POLICY COMMISSION — between *POLICY* and *COMMISSION*
AGENT COMMISSION — between *AGENT* and *COMMISSION*
CLIENT AGENT — between *CLIENT* and *AGENT*

Insurance administration
POLICYHOLDER — between *CLIENT* and *POLICY*
POLICY BILLING — between *POLICY* and *BILLING*
POLICY LOANS — between *POLICY* and *LOANS*
POLICY COMMISSION — between *POLICY* and *COMMISSION*

FIGURE 4.7 Relationship types for insurance company example

Relationship types are given appropriate names and their meanings are described either informally, or formally, in text. As with entity types, it usually takes a number of approval cycles with the users before agreement on the relationship types chosen is reached. A description is created for each relationship type, which includes its name, meaning, any synonyms, acronyms and related entity types.

The constraints on the entity types, relationship types and attributes are identified. Some of the constraints for the insurance company example are shown in Figure 4.8. By stating the constraints explicitly, the users can help to validate their accuracy. Constraints are easier to validate if a list is built a few constraints at a time, making sure that as it is built the constraints in the list are correct. At least four types of constraints can be identified as follows:

1. Range of valid values for each attribute.
2. Functional dependencies among attributes and on relationship types.
3. General dependencies among entity types and among attributes.
4. Other general constraints.

Questions that can help identify constraints include:

1. What is the valid range of values for each attribute? For example, birth year must be between 1850 and the current year.
2. What functional dependencies exist between attributes? Location code may determine the risk class.
3. Can keys, such as policy number, be identified for each entity type?
4. For each relationship type, it is one-to-one, one-to-many, or many-to-many?
5. What constraints must be placed on the data?

It can be very difficult to define for an application a satisfactory set of constraints that are consistent with each other. The form of some of the constraints may be difficult to

Keys
Policy number in *POLICY*
Social security number in *CLIENT*
Policy number in *PRIOR COVERAGE*
Social security number in *BENEFICIARY*
Agent number in *AGENT*

Functional dependencies
Coverage type, Coverage amount → Premium rate
Type → Rate

Mappings
(a) One-to-one
POLICY COVERAGE
POLICY BILLING

(b) Functional
PRIOR POLICY COVERAGE	*POLICY → PRIOR COVERAGE*
POLICY BENEFICIARY	*POLICY → BENEFICIARY*
POLICY LOANS	*POLICY → LOANS*
POLICY TERMINATION	*POLICY → TERMINATION*
POLICYHOLDER	*CLIENT → POLICY*

(c) Many-to-many
POLICY COMMISSION
AGENT COMMISSION
CLIENT AGENT

FIGURE 4.8 Some constraints for insurance company example

understand and even more difficult to communicate clearly to the users, which results in misunderstandings and errors. Demonstrating consistency among a given set of constraints is itself a problem with no easy answers. Even after specifying what seems to be a proper set of constraints, existing databases – which already contain some or all of the data – may be unable to satisfy those constraints. As particular as the data base designers are about the definitions of the data for the data base, the users may produce special cases or values that do not meet the constraints. For example, it may be quite clear that employees may not earn more than their managers, but further investigation may uncover a special case where someone does earn more than the manager. In fact, it is not unusual to discover that many of the existing data do not abide by the constraints derived from the requirements analysis. This situation is not a fault of the data base, nor of the requirements process; sometimes the world is just not as orderly as we would like it to be. In order to get the real task accomplished, some of these data must be allowed in the data base.

The results at this point are a view of the schema for each area of the organization. These views contain a list and description of the entity types, relationship types, attributes, and constraints. The next phase is to integrate these views into one schema. This necessarily involves resolving name conflicts, redundancies, and ambiguities. For example, POLICY in Figure 4.6 has several definitions. During this resolution process, the information received from the various areas is summarized and presented in usable

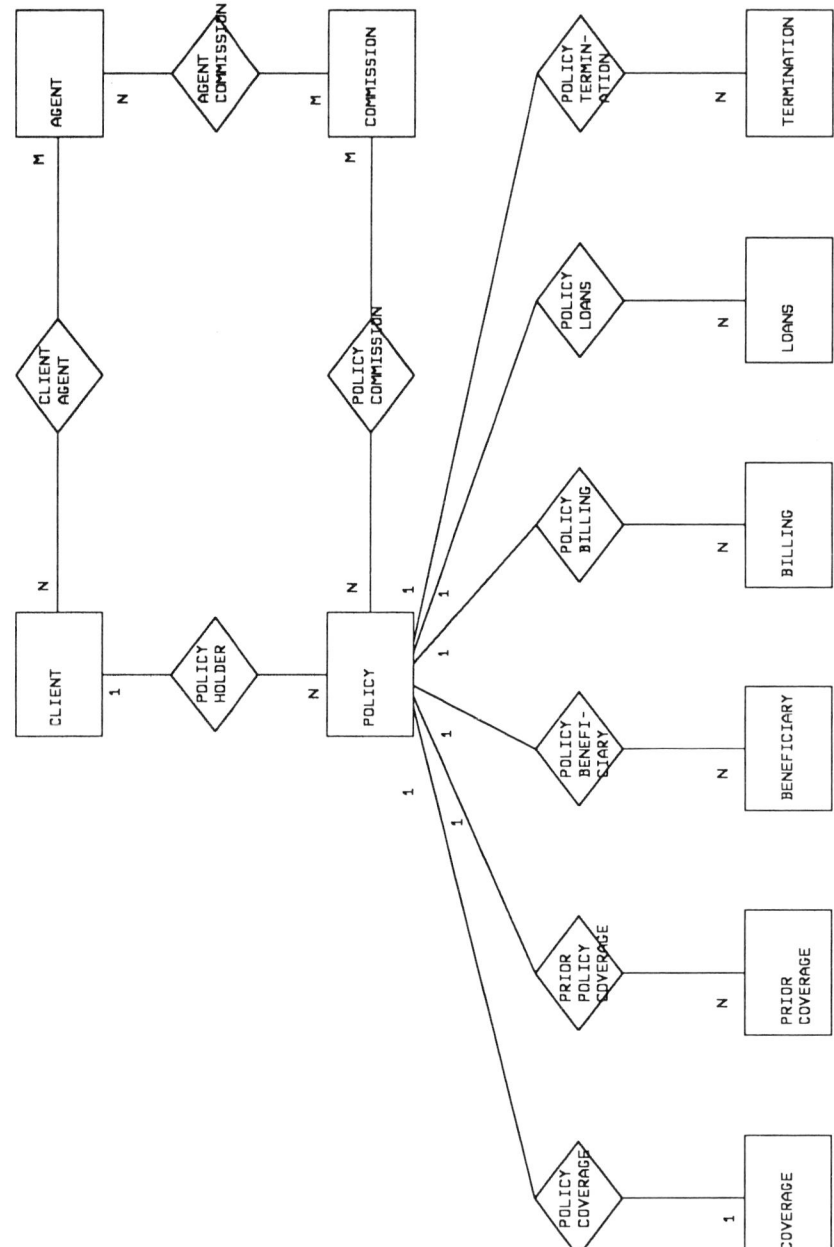

FIGURE 4.9 Enterprise description for insurance company example

TRANSACTION: List the policies held by a client.
  Entity types: *CLIENT, POLICY.*
  Relationship types: *POLICYHOLDER.*
  1. Retrieve the *CLIENT* entity.
  2. Retrieve a *POLICY* entity related to the *CLIENT* entity via a *POLICYHOLDER* relationship.

TRANSACTION: Perform today's policy-processing activities.
  Entity types: *POLICY, BILLING, LOANS.*
  Relationship types: *POLICY BILLING, POLICY LOANS.*
  Description
  1. For each *POLICY* entity where *Next activity date* is today, do the activity indicated by *Next activity*.
  2. Update *Last activity* and *Last activity date* in *POLICY*.
  3. Determine the *Next activity* by finding the minimum of *Next premium date* in *BILLING* or *Interest due date* in *LOANS*.
  4. Update *Next activity* and *Next activity date* in *POLICY*.

TRANSACTION: List a client's beneficiaries by policy.
  Entity types: *CLIENT, POLICY, BENEFICIARY.*
  Relationship types: *POLICYHOLDER, POLICY BENEFICIARY.*
  Description
  1. Retrieve the *CLIENT* entity.
  2. Retrieve all *POLICY* entities related to the *CLIENT* entity via a *POLICYHOLDER* relationship.
  3. For each *POLICY* entity retrieved, retrieve all *BENEFICIARY* entities related to the *POLICY* entity via a *POLICY, BENEFICIARY* relationship.

FIGURE 4.10 Some simple transactions for the insurance company

form. Data flow diagrams (see 'Structured Analysis', Section 2.2) can be used to describe information flows. Information about which areas use each entity type and relationship type are kept for later use. The information is then shown to each organizational area for its approval. It is usually an iterative process to negotiate with each organizational area until all agree that the enterprise description accurately reflects its view and needs. The result of this process for the insurance company example is shown in Figure 4.9.

The last phase of describing the enterprise is to identify the current and future transactions required by each organizational area – Figure 4.10 shows some of the transactions for the insurance company example. Transactions can be described in text or in a problem specification language, and should be expressed in terms of the enterprise description. For each transaction that is identified, information is needed about the following:

1. Who uses it.
2. How often it will be used (times per day, month, or year).
3. What entity types, attributes, and relationship types it uses.
4. How it accesses the data (read or update, and access order).
5. Security requirements.
6. Processing priority.
7. Possible need for concurrent update activity.

8. Type of transaction (e.g. batch, on-line).
9. Response time requirements.
10. Criticality of data.

In addition, specifications are gathered for reports that are needed, including the format and time frame for producing each report; and those parts of the data base essential for the operation of the organization are identified. The various transactions are analyzed to determine patterns of data base usage that can be expected. Languages that describe the data, such as the data definition language of SQL, are much better for defining the transactions than are languages that describe the navigation of data in a data base. Once the transactions have been defined, the concurrence of each affected organizational area is obtained so that they represent their uses and needs for data correctly. At this point, the users' priorities for implementation of the transactions can be gathered.

Note that the above was achieved without reference to existing automated files. While there is, of course, information in those files, they were often implemented in an unorganized way that reflected only the needs of individual applications. Thus they usually contain redundant and improperly defined data elements. Tsichritzis and Lochovsky (1982) point out: 'Merely converting existing files to a DBMS without any analysis of current needs . . . can result in even more costly and less effective operation that prior to conversion.' Moreover, it is important to identify what the users *need* rather than what they *have*.

4.3 NORMALIZATION

There are many ways to group attributes and associate them with keys. The keys provide unique access to the groups of attributes and may, themselves, be a set of attributes, such as manufacturer, model, and serial number for a refrigerator. Depending on the intended semantics of the schema, some undesirable conditions may result from certain groupings of attributes. These undesirable conditions are known as *anomalies*, which can be illustrated using the following relation scheme from Codd (1972):

COMPANY (Employee#, Department#, Manager, Contract type)

Anomalies that may arise when manipulating this relation are as follows:

1. *Update* anomaly. If the manager of a department changes, the information has to be changed in many records in order to keep the data base consistent and correct.
2. *Redundancy*. Both the contract type and the manager are repeated many times in the data base. The problem is not the waste of storage (the DBMS may avoid physically repeating the information anyway), but, rather, the difficulty of maintaining the consistency of those redundant data.
3. *Insertion* anomaly. When an employee is hired for a department, there may be no associated contract type, or possibly no manager. The ability to store information

about an employee should not be affected by unrelated decisions regarding contracts and manager assignments.
4. *Deletion* anomaly. If the last employee in a department leaves the company, deletion of the record for the employee may also delete valuable information about the department.

With the particular grouping of attributes in the relation example above, undesirable side effects occur when there is a change in the data. Those side effects can be avoided by dividing the relation scheme into two relation schemes:

EMPLOYEE (Employee#, Department#)
DEPARTMENT (Department#, Manager, contract type)

This choice of relations is not arbitrary but, rather, is based on the following two functional dependencies (assuming there is only one contract type per department):

Department# → Manager, contract type
Employee# → Department#

By separating these two dependencies into separate relation schemes, the above anomalies are eliminated.

Anomalies can be avoided by enforcing restrictions on allowable structures. Relation schemes that abide by these restrictions are said to be in *normal form*. The method for turning a relation scheme into normal form can be found in Codd (1971, 1972); Armstrong and Delobel (1980); and Zaniolo and Melkanoff (1981). Descriptions of first, second and third normal forms are summarized below. The idea of the normal forms is to ensure that all attributes stored together depend on the key, the entire key, and on no attributes except those that are part of the key. If the key is a single attribute, such as employee number in the EMPLOYEE relation below, then every attribute of that employee, such as the employee name, must be functionally dependent on that key. However, a key may consist of more than one attribute, such as a supplier number and part number, in order to identify shipments uniquely. Then it is possible to have an attribute, such as supplier address, that is dependent on the supplier number but not on the part number, i.e. the address depends only on part of the key. If so, the address data should not be stored with the entity for which supplier number and part number is the composite key.

EMPLOYEE (employee#, employee name, . . .)
SHIPMENT (supplier#, part#, supplier address, . . .)

A relation is in *first normal form* if every attribute is a simple attribute, i.e. none of the attributes are structures, composites, or repeating fields.

For example, consider the relation scheme:

CLASS SESSION (Course#, Session#, Course name, Professor#, Professor name, Time, Location(Day, Room#), Room size)

This relation is not in first normal form because it has a composite attribute of *Location*. A relation that is not in first normal form can be put into first normal form by expanding the composite attributes into their parts. Putting the example above into first normal form means expanding *Location* into its parts, i.e.

CLASS SESSION (Course#, Session#, Course name, Professor#, Professor name, Time, Day, Room#, Room size)

A relation in first normal form is in *second normal form* if no subset of the key can determine uniquely any attribute that is not in the key.

In the example of the CLASS SESSION relation above, the key consists of Course# and Session# (as underlined), because both are necessary to identify a session uniquely. However, Course#, which is a subset of the key, uniquely determines the Course name, Professor#, and Professor name. A relation in first normal form can be put in second normal form by decomposing it into relations so that all attributes (other than ones in the key) require the full key to be determined uniquely. The CLASS SESSION relation can be put into second normal form by decomposing it into two relations. Those attributes that can be determined uniquely by the Course# are in a relation that has only Course# as its key.

CLASS SESSION (Course#, Session#, Time, Day, Room#, Room size)
CLASS (Course#, Course name, Professor#, Professor name)

A relation is in *third normal form* if all attributes outside the key are determined uniquely only by the full key. Thus no attribute can be determined uniquely by some attribute, or set of attributes, other than the full key. In the CLASS SESSION example, Room# determines a unique Room size and Professor# uniquely determines Professor name. In order to eliminate these dependencies, the relation is again decomposed, which results in:

CLASS SESSION (Course#, Session#, Time, Day, Room#)
ROOM (Room#, Room Size)
CLASS (Course#, Course name, Professor#)
PROFESSOR (Professor#, Professor name)

(Note that in a complete schema, each of the relations in this final example would undoubtedly have additional attributes.) The requirement of third normal form is sufficient to assure second normal form as well because it does not allow attributes to be determined uniquely by subsets of the full key. Achieving third normal form is sufficient for most business situations, although there are higher normal forms that can achieve an anomaly-free design. To summarize, dependencies among data elements other than functional dependencies involving the key can cause anomalies.

4.4 DATA BASE DESCRIPTION

Once the enterprise description is complete and approved, it is transformed into a *data base description*. It might seem that the data base management system should be chosen at this point, based on the characteristics of the enterprise model. However, in practice the DBMS is usually chosen before the enterprise model is constructed. Often, the users choose a DBMS rather than a data model, and this determines the data model. Furthermore, the choice of a DBMS is usually a long-term commitment and usually the form of the data base description is determined by the chosen DBMS. It is therefore difficult to change to another DBMS or another data model. Most existing commercial data base management systems implement one of the three major approaches as follows:

1. Hierarchical.
2. Network.
3. Relational.

The insurance company example is converted into each of the three types of data base descriptions below.

For a *hierarchical* DBMS the mappings between the enterprise description, entity types, and relationship types are as follows (as depicted by Figure 4.11 for the insurance company example):

1. enterprise description → set of spanning trees
2. entity types → record types
3. relationship types → parent–child relationships

Each transaction is expressed in terms of this hierarchical schema. The types and frequencies of transactions affect the choices for the hierarchy for a particular DBMS. In some systems, access to root record types (those in the beginning segment of the hierarchical tree) is faster and more efficient than access to other record types, so it is an advantage to place more frequently accessed record types physically at or near the root record type of the hierarchy.

For a *network* DBMS, the mappings for the enterprise schema are (see Figure 4.12):

1. enterprise description → data structure diagram
2. entity types → record types
3. relationship types → DBTG-set types

'DBTG' refers to the Data Base Task Group specification of a network data model by the Conference on Data Systems Languages (CODASYL), and is discussed in Chapter 6 of Tsichritzis and Lochovsky (1982). Each transaction is mapped into a navigation through the data structure diagram. DBTG-set type-restrictions have to be observed and may require changes to be made to the enterprise description before relationship types are mapped. For example, many-to-many relationship types must be transformed into one-to-many relationship types, which can be accomplished through either duplication or introducing intermediate record types. In Figure 4.12, COMMISSION records are duplicated so that the many-to-many relationship types of POLICY COMMISSION and AGENT COMMISSION (in Figures 4.8 and 4.9) can be made one-to-many relationship types. Introducing an intermediate CLIENT AGENT record type transforms the many-to-many relationship type CLIENT AGENT into two one-to-many relationship types.

168   DATA BASE DESIGN CONCEPTS

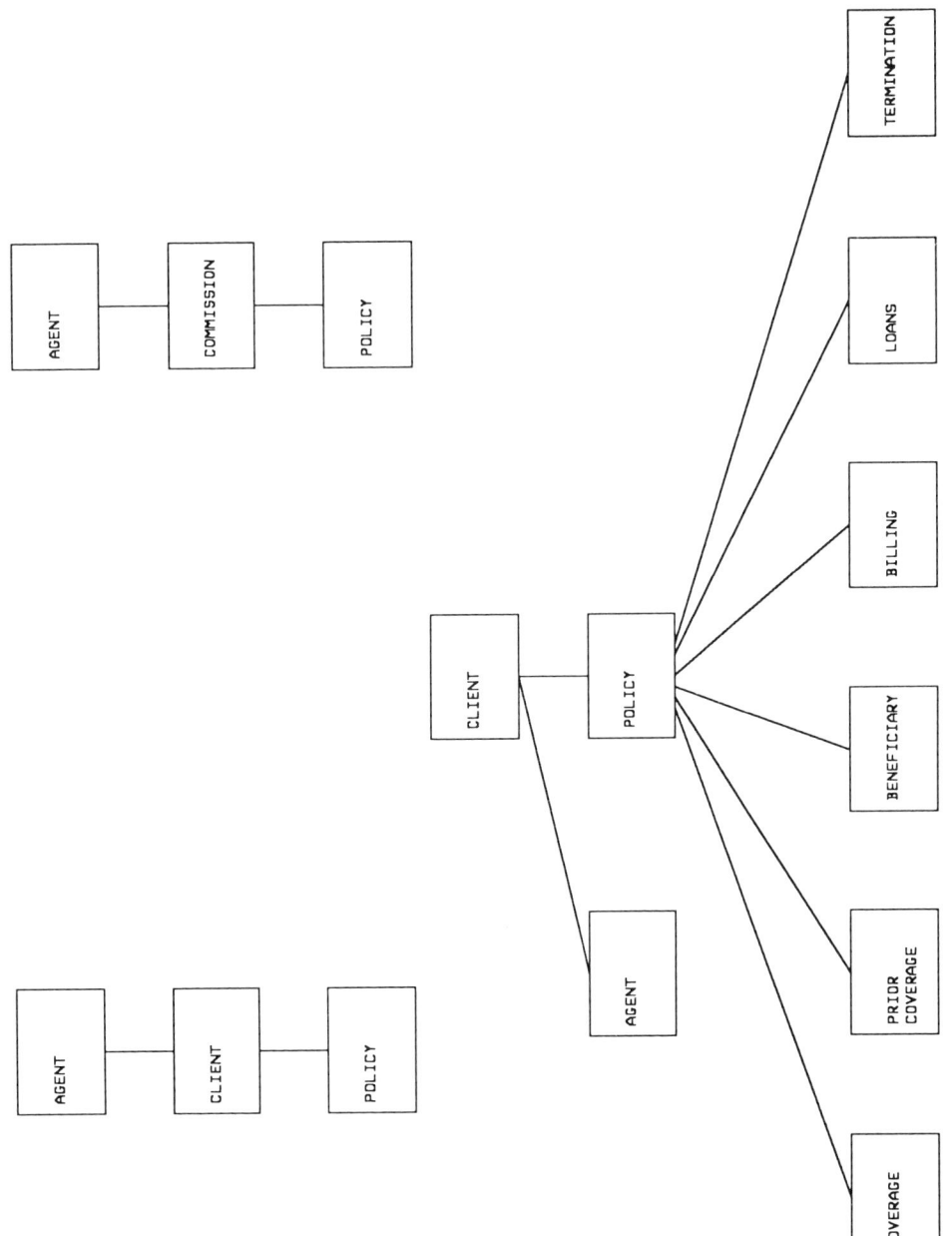

FIGURE 4.11 Hierarchical schema for insurance company example

DATA BASE DESCRIPTION 169

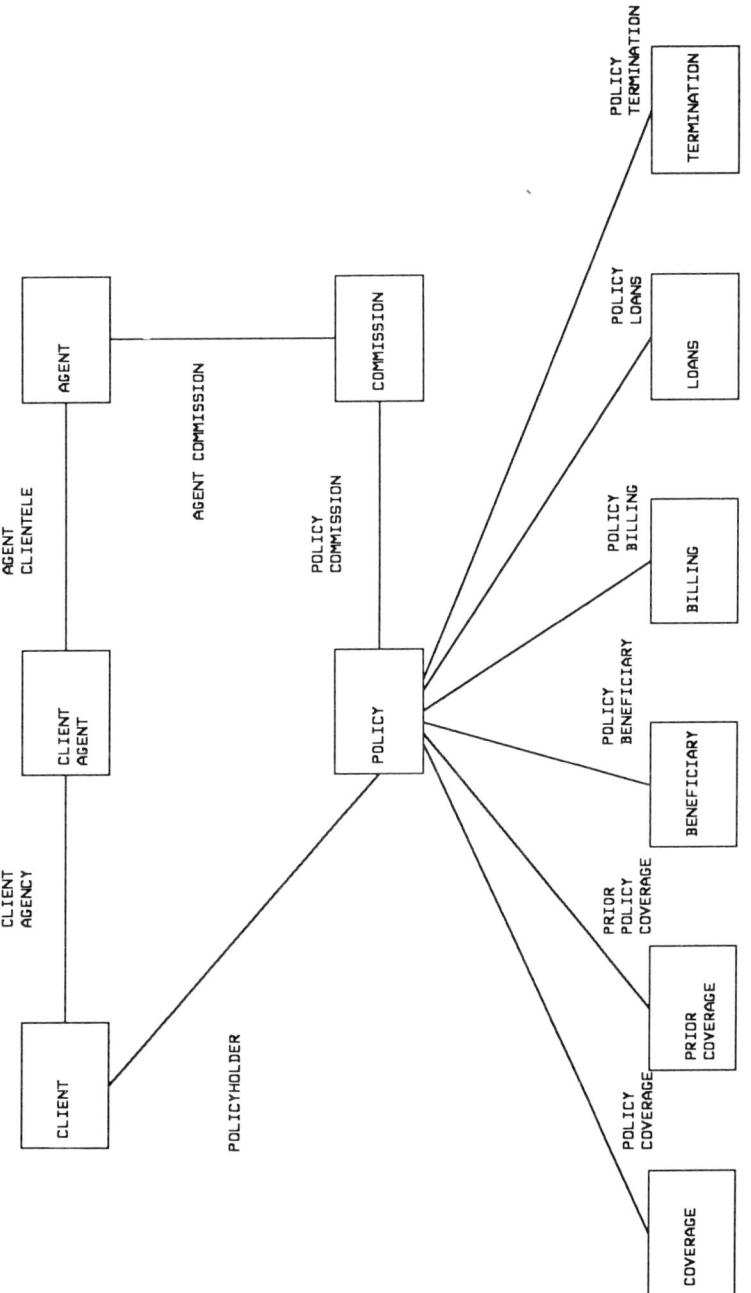

FIGURE 4.12 DBTG-network schema for insurance company example

POLICY(Policy number, Last activity, Last activity date, Next activity,
   Next activity date)
COVERAGE(Policy number, Coverage type, Coverage amount, Premium rate,
   Issue date)
CLIENT(Social security number, Name, Address, Birthdate)
POLICYHOLDER(Social security number, Agent number)
BENEFICIARY(Policy number, Social security number, Name, Address)
PRIOR COVERAGE(Social security number, Current policy number,
   Prior policy number, Type, Amount, Rating)
BILLING(Policy number, Mode, Amount, Next premium date, Name, Address)
LOANS(Policy number, Principal, Balance, Interest rate, Interest due date)
TERMINATION(Policy number, Termination date, Reinstatement date,
   Termination reason)
AGENT(Agent number, Name, Address, Area)
CLIENT AGENT(Social security number, Agent number)
COMMISSION(Policy number, Agent number, Type, Rate)

FIGURE 4.13 Relational schema for insurance company example

For a *relational* DBMS, the mappings for the enterprise schema are (as illustrated in Figure 4.13 for the insurance company example):

1. enterprise description → relational schema
2. entity types   → base relations (those stored in the data base)
3. relationship types   → joins (if derivable from other stored data)
                        → base relations (otherwise)

(Tsichritzis and Lochovsky (1982) discuss 'joins' in Chapter 4 and relational data models in Chapter 5). Each transaction is mapped into relational operations on the base relations. Joins expected to be used frequently may be mapped into permanent joins (if the DBMS allows it).

4.5 PHYSICAL DATA BASE DESIGN

There is a large degree of flexibility in how a particular schema is implemented. Since the DBMS supports the ability of each user to view the data organized in various ways, the implementation of the schema is free to be different from all of those views. Thus the data base designer can choose alternatives that optimize the *performance* of accesses to the data base for the most frequent and most crucial transactions. Tsichritzis and Lochovsky state: 'Data base performance is an extremely complicated issue. The choices in the data base parameters are many. . . . There is a need for a unified framework for data base performance estimations.' Because data base management systems provide a freedom in how the data are organized, which can be used to make substantial performance improvements in data access times, performance is likely to remain a high-priority design criterion for physical data base design.

The basic objective is to implement a schema that accurately supports the data accesses required by the users. The best design is the one that provides the required data with the best possible performance given: the various ways the users need to see data grouped, the sequences which users need to access the data, whether data will be updated or just retrieved, and the frequencies for these various types of accesses to data. Unfortunately, the need for data is not totally predictable because users may not accurately describe or predict their use of data; and their needs change over time. There is also an increasing use of *ad hoc* queries into the data. Thus the schema must be implemented considering likely future needs and changes. The inevitable existence of these uncertainties makes prototyping the schema a valuable step at this stage. Some parts of the schema can be implemented and made available to the users. For example, for the entity and attributes in Figure 4.6, a prototype could implement the CLIENT and BENEFICIARY entity types for people with names starting with the letter A. Through use of the prototype, two categories of information can be discovered, as follows:

1. Information that was incorrect, inaccurate, or misunderstood.
2. New ideas and insights gained through using the prototype.

It is important to discover both these types of information as early as possible to reduce the cost of making the changes later. The users may find out, for example, that they need additional information about beneficiaries for certain policies because of a new state law (passed since they were interviewed and since they approved the attributes for the BENEFICIARY entity type). Whatever part of the schema is implemented by the prototype should be in its expected final form on the production DBMS; it should be a prototype only in that it implements a *subset* of the schema. Note that performance of the prototype will decrease as more of the schema is implemented and additional data loaded. Since 'good' performance is often perceived by people as 'better than yesterday', users should be warned that the prototype will be faster than the final implementation. The new ideas and insights gained by using the prototype can lead to significant improvements over what users and developers saw, or predicted, during the requirements efforts. The users may discover, for example, that it would be very convenient to be able to link from the BENEFICIARY back to the CLIENT information – something they have never been able to do before. In fact, it may be difficult to decide when to move from iterative improvements into implementing more of the schema.

Ultimately, the schema implementation should be validated with the users. In theory, the validation would seem to be straightforward, especially since the schema itself has already been approved by the users. However, in practice the actual implementation usually has to confront the problems of 'dirty' data (annoying exceptions to the rules), which can be so conveniently ignored during the processes of gathering requirements and designing the schema. Ultimately, some of the real-world data is usually 'bent' to conform to a realistic, implemented schema.

4.6 DATA ADMINISTRATION

The creation and maintenance of data bases requires the services of people who are responsible for certain ongoing activities that are not directly the responsibility of any of the software development projects. These include:

1. Enterprise administrator.
2. Data base administrator.
3. Application administrator.

The *enterprise administrator* is responsible for the logical data base design and the resulting enterprise schema that describes the enterprise. The *data base administrator* creates the physical data base design and is responsible for the data base descriptions that comprise the internal schema. The *application administrator* provides the external schema – the views of the data that the various software systems require. In each case, the administrators are responsible for creating, describing, and maintaining their respective view of the data; relationships among the data, rules, and controls; and for the mappings to other views. While each of the above administrative roles are required, they may be assigned to different people or to the same person (who is often then called the 'data base administrator').

There is currently no complete method for data design. Methods are easy to outline in concept; 'and very difficult to apply in practice. In order to be successful, the operation of the DBMS should be completely integrated into the operation of the organization. However, introducing a DBMS will cause some changes in the way people work – and possibly even in the organization. Tsichritzis and Lochovsky (1982) state: 'The world needs better DBMSs. It may even need better data models. But what it really needs is better ways to use what is at hand.' The biggest difficulties with data base design are understanding what the organization does and trying to influence it to change the way it operates.

4.7 COMMENTS ON DATA BASE DESIGN

In their book *Data Models*, Dionysios Tsichritzis and Frederick Lochovsky (1982) give a thorough explanation of data models and a comparison of the various types of data models commonly used. For readers interested in pursuing more in-depth knowledge of data design, Tsichritzis and Lochovsky (1982) is a good reference for both the terminology and the concepts, and it has an extensive bibliography. However, neither the presentation here, nor the book by Tsichritzis and Lochovsky, is sufficient to teach someone how to design data bases. None the less, software designers can better share appropriate information with the data base designers if they understand the general concepts of ER data modeling, constraints (and enforcing them with software), normalizing data, and the need to design the physical data base for performance. For example, if the software designer discovers that a frequently used transaction must access data in a different order than previously thought, the data base designer should be notified of that fact as soon as possible.

The flexibility of data base management systems allows various users to have their own view of the data, even though some of the data is shared with other users who have different views. This flexibility provides both a significant advantage and a substantial challenge. The advantage is having a system that accommodates various users who will not agree on how they view data – and who should not be forced to do so by the system. The challenge is for the data base designer to deal with the complexity of the diverse – and sometimes conflicting – views and to extract some consistent model that adequately addresses each user's needs. The capability to store the data physically in a way that is independent of the users' views allows the data base designer to choose a physical storage arrangement that provides the best overall system performance for the most users, based on their priority. Physical data base design is one of the few areas of computer system design where performance is one of the highest priority considerations. (Teleprocessing network configuration is another such area.) The performance gained by good physical design directly affects users' productivity. Conversely, the possible impact on users of bad performance when accessing data can be much more severe than that caused by inefficient code. The flexibility for performance optimization provides yet another major area of complexity for the data base designer.

CHAPTER FIVE
OTHER DESIGN TOPICS

Tools can help designers to improve the speed and accuracy of the software design process. Graphical design tools can capture, display, and modify the architectural and integrand specification diagrams (e.g. data flow diagrams and Jackson charts). Special tools, such as Action Diagrammers, can help create textual forms of integrand specifications. Data base design has several activities that can be aided by tools, including drawing data model diagrams and checking for third normal form. There are several ways in which tools can be integrated, but the most valuable way is that which allows different tools to be used to design the same software; then the designer can use the best tool for each activity. A data dictionary can help communication and consistency within the development team by keeping current definitions of designed objects available for reference.

Understanding the general principles that control systems can improve the ability to design systems that work. Design reviews are an aid to producing high-quality designs if they are conducted in a helpful environment where everyone, including the designer, helps to identify possible errors and omissions.

Items can be reused when they meet a need, when the user knows they exist and can acquire them, when they can be used without having to be modified internally, or when there is someone who can repair them. It is possible for code to satisfy these criteria, and many examples of code that is reused do satisfy these criteria. *Abstract Data Types* surround data with code to create, change, access, and delete the data so that other integrands do not access the data directly. They can improve functional decompositions because they reduce dependencies of multiple integrands on common structured data. There is not yet general agreement on what *Object-Oriented*, is, but many definitions include the concepts of sending messages to objects, explictly declaring the type of data and functions, and associating all valid functions with the data to make an object. Designing systems as combinations of independent objects that communicate by sending messages is a valuable improvement over other ways of developing software. However, objects should be built to minimize the number of functions having direct access to structured data.

In order to design software that is *portable*, one must minimize the use of unique facilities, design software as a combination of independent functional integrands, and separate input and output from logic. *Time-dependent systems* raise issues of designing asynchronous processes, synchronizing use of global data and resources, and deadlock. Diagrams that naturally depict asynchronous processes, such as data flow diagrams, can help design, but asynchrony still makes design more complex. Although there are approaches and solutions to synchronizing resource use and avoiding deadlock for specific situations, there is no general solution to these problems as yet.

50 percent of the performance load on most computers results from about 1 percent of the programs. Thus performance optimization is less important than building simple programs for most software; and optimization efforts, even on that 1 percent of the software, will be more efficient if the software is simple.

5.1 SOFTWARE DESIGN TOOLS

Software design involves a number of activities, some of which can be automated or aided by computer tools. The graphical design tools that have been implemented using the graphical user interfaces on personal computers have made it more practical to use design methods. These tools have also made it more practical to use more than one type of diagram and method for various parts of the same design (e.g. ER diagrams linked to data flow diagrams and structure charts – see Chapters 2 and 3). However, it is the person rather than the tool who discovers, invents, or otherwise creates the design alternatives. Software design tools generally *document*, rather than create, the design. Design tools can help the designer to document and change designs more rapidly and accurately than can be done on paper. Tools can guide designers in the use of a notation or method and can help evaluate whether designs meet specified criteria. However, the tools do not teach the methods – books and classes do. To be useful during design creation, computer tools should be at least as fast at creating and changing diagrams as are pencil and paper. Since diagrams are used to communicate designs to others, tools should print, plot, and allow electronic transmission of diagrams. There are advantages if a tool will evaluate designs at the request of the developer and indicate possible errors with warnings, rather than inhibit actions it considers as invalid. Warnings allow designers the freedom to extend the use of a method in ways that may not be considered valid by a pre-determined set of validation rules. Also, warnings allow the designer to modify designs in the most efficient manner (such as duplicating a part of the diagram and then modifying each part), even if the intermediate results are technically invalid. In the future, tools may support three-dimensional diagrams since people *can* work in three dimensions. Three-dimensional diagrams could show more aspects of the design problem; time-dependent designs already need more dimensions to help depict, for example, the changing states of various components or the change in relationships among components over time.

Special tools can help with the definition of integrand specifications, such as those described in Chapter 3. For example, special editors can help to create and modify the brackets in action diagrams as the developer writes the code. Data base design requires a number of activities that can be assisted by automated tools. The ER diagrams can be drawn by graphic design tools; normalization can be aided and checked by automated tools; the DBMS may be able to prototype part of the schema; and performance evaluation tools can help to determine the possible effects of various choices for the physical data storage options.

When comparing tools, all other aspects being equal, a tool that accepts input in a form more natural to the designer is preferable. What is more natural depends on the activity and the designer. The activity may be drawing architectural diagrams or specifying integrands; the designer could be an engineer working with mathematical equations or a developer of more traditional business applications working with screen and report layouts. In any case, the designer can be more productive and make fewer mistakes if computer tools understand the types of objects and descriptions that are natural to that designer (i.e. require less special training to understand). Some have suggested that the development process could be improved by developing (yet) another specification language that can be translated automatically into code. Figure 5.1 illustrates the development process as two major steps: specifying the design for the system and turning that specification into code. Naturally, each step can include activities other than just 'Specify' or 'Convert'. Some suggested specification or design languages optimize step 2 in Figure 4.1 at the expense of step 1. It is possible to create a variety of specification syntaxes that can be turned into code in a more automated fashion, thus reducing errors in step 2. However, if the suggested specification syntax is unnatural, then the people who have to specify it may make more mistakes, so that the overall process of getting from specifications to code may end up worse than with a more natural syntax. Thus the value of a tool is not measured solely by how well it can produce its output once its input is specified, but also by how successful and productive a person using that tool can be.

The ability of a tool to translate some portions of a design is no guarantee that its particular approach can ever be fully automated. For example, consider the translation of a call hierarchy chart (see 'Structured Design', Section 2.5). A call hierarchy chart only shows which integrands call which other integrands and the parameters that are passed. Thus all that can be translated (or generated) from that chart is the entry, call, and exit statements for each integrand, plus data definition statements for the parameters. The developer has to add the rest by hand. Even if the rest of the code could be produced automatically, it would still have to be merged manually; the call hierarchy chart does not show where the call instruction is placed within the integrand's code. If a change is made to the call hierarchy chart, that change cannot be propagated forward automatically. Statements created from the changed call hierarchy chart have to be merged by hand again. Thus the call hierarchy chart is not an effective base for automating the process. Even though part of the call hierarchy chart can be translated, it can never be completely translated and requires manual intervention whenever a change is made. If instead, a data flow diagram is used for the software architecture, then the connection information in the data flow diagram *can* be used independently of the technique used to create the code (see Appendix A). While the use of data flow diagrams for software architecture does not automate the whole process, it does provide a base where techniques can create part of or all the integrands. The techniques can also be used on individual integrands, as applicable, without having to create all integrands in one program the same way.

Tools could help design even more by suggesting, formatting, and creating part or all of

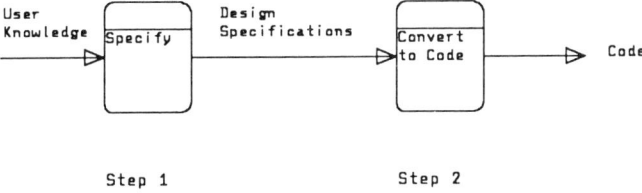

FIGURE 5.1 Design specifications

the input that designers currently provide manually. Such input could come from models tailored by the designer or possibly inferred from previous activities and choices by that designer. For example, after the designer defines two or three screens, the tool may be able to infer the screen standards and propose the next screen based on the definitions of data to be displayed. This ability to propose screen designs might be enhanced by asking the designer questions, such as whether to use a horizontal or vertical format for the screen. Tools could also help designers by suggesting and evaluating alternatives. People can make choices much more rapidly than they can create design alternatives. With pointing devices, such an approach may be limited primarily by the speed of the computer in creating and presenting design alternatives.

There are several ways in which tools can be integrated, as follows:

1. They can produce results which can be combined with results from other tools for the same software.
2. They can be accessed from the same workstation.
3. They can share data that they gather and create.
4. They have similar user interfaces.

The ability to work with other tools on the same design may be the most valuable type of integration for tools. Then the best tool for each activity can be used on each component. Too often, a tool chosen for part of the software effort determines the tools for other activities – for example, an application generator may contain tools to define the objects it needs and may not accept data from tools other than its own.

It is no longer necessary to have tools run in the same environment as long as they can be *accessed* from the same keyboard and screen. Many workstations can emulate mainframe terminals, thus giving the designer access to tools on several mainframe computers as well as access to work station tools. The ability to access tools that run in various environments from the same work station makes design convenient and helps the designer to avoid having to justify, or work with, multiple terminals.

It is valuable if design tools can share their data. This would be easier if every tool made its output data available in a machine-readable and *published* form. Publishing the form and meaning of the data would also allow other tools to evaluate the design. In order for tools to be able to accept input from other tools, each tool should also accept the inputs it expects to receive from a person in a published machine-readable form. A standard form for the input and output data would allow tools to be integrated more easily. However, since data-sharing standards are still evolving, it is more important for tools to share data in *some* published form than to keep their data private until an acceptable standard appears.

While there is some value in having tools use the same user interface style, it is not really desirable or practical for tools to look exactly alike. Different tools accomplish different functions and thus need different interfaces. For example, the 'user interface' to a shovel and to a car are quite different, for obvious reasons. However, the interface to a stove and a television are also different, even if they have flat panels where the user keys in numbers. Each interface is designed by its manufacturer based on appropriate objectives, which are different for a stove and a television. Theoretically, a single company that made both stoves and televisions could make its two appliances with the same interface. However, the company would probably still define different interfaces for the stove and the television in order to meet the evolving industry standards more closely for each type of appliance. Similarly, a text-editor and a spell-checker have different objectives. It would be less productive for the user if the same function key definitions were used for each because the most commonly used functions in each are different. It is convenient to have tools invoked using a similar style and using the same approach (e.g. same function keys) to access common functions such as help and exit. However, it is not crucially important for interfaces of each tool to be similar; people find few problems using the wide variety of interfaces to various tools and machines.

A data dictionary is a facility which can store definitions and descriptions of objects being developed. By keeping the active definitions in the data dictionary, members of a team can access the most current information. Such access is especially helpful for keeping the various parts of a software system consistent. A data dictionary is especially useful with larger projects where communication between team members becomes even more crucial. Many data dictionaries use entity–relationship (ER) data models (see 'Entity–relationship diagrams', Section 4.1.2). Entity–relationship data dictionaries store entries for objects, called 'entities', that contain the name of the object and its description. Entities also contain various attributes of the entity. The assigned names for the relationships among entities can also be stored. Thus, for example, it is possible to record in the dictionary that:

1. Program_A *reads* Screen_B
2. Program_C *calls* Program_D
3. Program_E *accesses* File_G

along with definitions for each of the objects named. Storing such descriptive information is particularly useful for tracking objects during design and development. The data dictionary can contain descriptions of objects that are designed, such as definitions of data, the enterprise schema (see 'The enterprise schema', Section 4.2), screen and report layouts, and integrand definitions. The data dictionary can then be used to access the latest information about the software objects, thus improving consistency and communication among the members of the development team. The data dictionary is also a place where information from many tools can be gathered to enable global checking and analysis to be performed (e.g. asking which objects are related to a given object).

5.2 DESIGN REVIEWS

The quality of designs can be improved by having people other than the designer review them. Design reviews should be a standard part of any design process no matter how large or small the project. The process of explaining how the design meets the objectives in sufficient detail for someone else to understand it provides an opportunity for both the reviewer *and the designer* to discover possible errors and omissions. These are the same benefits found in the 1970s for reviewing code with walkthroughs and inspections. These advantages apply to the review of any development work product. Designs can be reviewed with the same approach as is used for code. The design materials to be reviewed are distributed a few days before the review to give the reviewers a chance to study them. Reviews are limited to not more than two or three hours, including a break. The duration is specified beforehand and time spent is not allowed to exceed the allotted amount. If additional work is needed, another review is scheduled. Someone is responsible for recording errors and omissions that are found. In order to be most productive, it is important that the atmosphere of a review be one of helpfulness and an effort to discover errors; the review must not be used to evaluate the designer. If designers feel the results of the review will be used to evaluate or compare them with others, they will cover up errors and defend those errors that are exposed. This would be tragic since the designer can usually discover the most errors. The reviewers' objective is to determine whether the given design meets its objectives and *not* to debate whether they would have used the same design (since they undoubtedly would not). The subject of reviews of work products is covered more fully in Volume 1 of this series (Macro 1990) and readers who desire a more in-depth coverage are referred to that volume.

5.3 CODE REUSE

5.3.1 Reuse

Code is reused when someone uses code written previously and thus avoids having to write new code. Reuse of code that we or others have created can be difficult; some have even said that code reuse is impossible and may never be accomplished. However, more recently, especially with the advent of Object-Oriented languages (see 'Object-Oriented', Section 5.6), there has been a growing interest in reuse and a belief that it is possible. Some insights can be gained into how to reuse code by considering endeavors other than software development where reuse is the norm (i.e. find an existing system that works, as per 'General systems principles', Section 5.4).

Reuse is quite prevalent in manufacturing industries other than software development. In fact, virtually everything made is either a standard reusable item, or is built from standard reusable parts – or both. Examples of standard reusable items are abundant: tables, chairs, televisions, rugs, windows, airplanes, lawn mowers, light bulbs, houses, ties, tie tacks, belts, cars, tires, telephones, door knobs, doors, etc. In a real sense, 'manufacturing' *means* to make many copies of a standard item. These items are reusable in several senses (using a door knob, for example), as follows:

1. Once an item exists, it can perform its function again and again – each door knob can be used to open a specific door over and over again.
2. Many copies of that item can be built so that many people can use it – many door knobs can be sold to people who each use the knob they bought.
3. A specific item can be used again after one use is finished – a knob used initially on one door can be removed and used again on another door.
4. An item can be used with various designs – a door knob can be combined with a number of types of doors in many different houses.

Relative to computer software, the first type of reuse listed above is not a problem – programs are usually written to be executed again and again. For example, once an on-line transaction or scientific calculation is built, it can be executed again and again whenever its function is needed. The second type of reuse is also easy: a software product is built so that many people can buy a copy and use it. A good text-editor or spread-sheet program may be sold to millions of users, each of whom uses that copy. The third type of reuse – moving a 'specific' instance of an item to a new use – has little meaning for code since even *moving* code requires that a copy be made of it. The question of interest with respect to the third type of reuse is whether there is another use for the code, which is covered by the fourth type of reuse. Thus the important question with respect to code reuse is: how can we reuse existing integrands in software that we are designing and constructing? People's ability to produce reusable code and to reuse it does not change depending on whether the component is a program or an integrand: it is the characteristics of the integrands that inhibit their reuse.

Considering manufacturing industries other than software manufacturing can yield insights into how to reuse existing components in new designs. It is unusual for a manufactured product to consist mostly of newly designed and created parts; most products consist of about 60–80 percent standard parts. Consider a particular lawn mower, for example. The motor was not created just for that model of lawn mower (it is a standard motor) – neither were the wheels, blade, wires, cables, or bolts and nuts. What *is* new is the case, the handle, and that particular combination of parts. Consider a jetliner: while it might seem initially that the airplane manufacturer created the entire plane, it did not create the navigational radios – or the engines, windows, tires, sheet metal, brakes, seats, rugs, wires, or light bulbs. What *is* new is the body of the plane and the particular combination of parts that make up that plane. If we were to consider all the design effort that has gone into the construction of rubber, glass, metal, radios, engines, etc., building the plane may be only a small percentage of the total design effort for a plane. However, considering only the parts, again only about 20–40 percent are new.

5.3.2 Requirements for reuse

How do manufacturing industries manage to reuse components, and how can we apply that to software? There are five characteristics, as follows, that items which are reused to any great extent always seem to have (using a tie tack as a specific example):

1. The item serves a useful purpose (not some random combination of unrelated things) – it holds a tie to the shirt in a way that is decorative.
2. The user knows the item exists and can acquire it – tie tacks can be bought at jewelry and department stores.
3. The user knows how to use it – often from accompanying instructions.
4. The item can be used in combination with various other items *without* having to modify it internally – the tie tack can be used with different ties, shirts, and various outfits without having to modify it. If the users had to use the same skill as its manufacturer to re-solder the tie tack in order to move it to each new tie, people would not even use, much less reuse, that tie tack.
5. There is someone who will fix the item – the ability to get repairs done is important if the tie tack is expensive, although inexpensive items may be replaced rather than fixed. However, if there were no one who could maintain a more expensive item, such as a specific make of car, people would be unlikely to buy that car.

The five conditions above are true of almost everything we reuse. Consider, for example, a nut that screws on to a bolt to hold something tightly (a useful function). People know that there are stores were nuts can be bought and they know how to use them once obtained. The nut can be combined with bolts of various lengths without having to modify it first (though it is limited to bolts of the same width and thread – nothing is good for *everything*). Plus, the nut can be replaced (nuts are seldom 'fixed' because they do not cost very much). Consider a car: it transports people and things; it can be bought through a car dealer; it can be used with any house, road, and most garages; and there are places that will repair the car.

5.3.3 Reusable Code

We reuse code as well when the five conditions above are true – and the conditions are true much more often than not. The conditions are true for software products we use (they perform a desired function; the user knows they exist and acquires them; they are used with other programs; and the manufacturer fixes errors and produces new releases). The conditions also hold for the software *systems* we produce – if no one maintained it, the users would not be likely to use it, at least not for long. What about the *integrands* we produce – how can we reuse those? Interestingly enough, there are many instances where

182   OTHER DESIGN TOPICS

software integrands are reused, and in each case they satisfy the above conditions for reuse. Examples of software *integrands* that are reused include:

1. Commands in any on-line system.
2. Commands within any text-editor (which are integrands – few include physical input or output, they just change the data in memory).
3. Various functions within a graphical editor.
4. 'Filters' with Unix® and PC/DOS pipes (e.g. DIR | SORT > PRN sends the normal directory listing through the SORT filter and redirects the output from the screen to the printer).

Each of these is an example of an integrand within a bigger system and each satisfies the five reuse characteristics. In fact, in each of these cases, they are so reusable that end-users can use and combine them with other components in any ways they choose. Software developers also reuse integrands, including the following:

1. System services, such as the time of day.
2. Data base management systems for storing data.
3. Terminal subsystems to read and write screens for user interaction.
4. Teleprocessing subsystems to communicate with other systems.
5. Services to read and write to various devices.
6. Standard subroutine packages, such as financial calculations and scientific subroutines.
7. Callable subroutines.
8. And even the individual instructions in a high level language (each instruction is code written by someone else, which the developer uses and thus does not have to write).

Though these are integrands for which one has to write code in order to use them, they still satisfy the above five conditions for reuse.

Why is it that all these examples of items and integrands are so easy to reuse but reuse is so elusive for the integrands we write? Unfortunately, two of the five characteristics for reuse are usually absent in the integrands we build:

1. They cannot be combined with other things without modifying them internally.
2. There is nobody responsible for fixing the item.

The most independent way to construct integrands in many systems is to have them called, as illustrated in Figure 5.2. Unfortunately, the call instruction imbeds the name of the called integrand in the caller's code. Thus, in order to reuse integrand B in Figure 5.2, for example, where it calls D, it is necessary to modify the insides of B. Linking integrands with calls is like using a rivet instead of a bolt and a nut to link components – one of the pieces has to be modified to separate the pieces. While the modification to a software integrand may seem to be minor, it requires the user to have the source code (which can be difficult or impossible, depending on its origin), understand the code well enough to modify it correctly, and be able to recompile it. In addition, the user ends up with a *different* integrand – it is not B anymore – and thus there are two integrands to

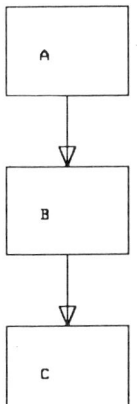

FIGURE 5.2 Calls rivet integrands

maintain. Consider how far a developer of navigational radios, for example, might get with an airplane manufacturer if the sales pitch went like this: 'I have a navigational radio that you can use in your next airplane. All that is necessary, once the weight of the airplane is known, is to open up the radio and replace the resistor on the third circuit board at the location shown in diagram A with the one listed in table B.' Assuming that the sales representative had not already been thrown out of the door, the response might go something like this: 'Not only are we *not* going to open up your radio, nor modify the insides – which would surely void your warranty anyway – but we do not even want to know that there *is* an inside to the radio.'

A key factor to making integrands easy to reuse is whether their links to other integrands are specified in the code within the integrands or whether the user can specify the sequence without having to change the integrands internally. It is possible to have integrands meet these conditions for reuse, but not if they call each other. The connections among integrands must be specified *outside* the integrands in order to combine integrands without having to modify them. Having connections specified outside the integrands is true of each example of reusable code given above: batch job steps, on-line transactions, editor commands, and DOS filters. Another example of technology that accomplishes this can be found in Morrison (1978), and Stevens (1982), and is discussed in Appendix A. Conversely, it can be quite difficult to reuse *existing* code that does not have the required characteristics. Knowing the conditions for reuse may help to make the code we design and build easier to reuse, but it is of little help for existing code that does not satisfy the conditions.

A second important factor in why the integrands we produce are not reused is the lack of someone responsible for maintaining them. While developers may be responsible for maintaining code within the software they create, they usually have no responsibility for maintaining integrands reused in other projects. Project A cannot depend on potentially reusable components from project B because project B might fail, be phased out, or have other priorities when maintenance is needed. If companies want to be able to take software components off the shelf, they need a 'shelf', which requires someone with the responsibility to find, acquire, publicize, explain, and *maintain* the reusable components.

A third factor necessary to promote reuse is to give developers an incentive to reuse code. IBM has discovered that their measurements have implicitly given developers an incentive to refrain from reusing code. There is no way for project A to gain credit for taking time to share and explain potentially reusable code with project B, and such activity may cause project A to miss its delivery date. However, project B cannot afford to reuse project A's components anyway, because there is no assurance that the second project will still exist or apply the same priority on fixing the problems. Note also that, essentially, measurements often reward developers for how many lines of code they write. With reuse, developers should perhaps be paid for how many lines of code they do *not* write.

Something significant missing from the list of conditions for reuse is a computerized catalog for finding reusable parts. Such a catalog may be useful, but it is not a prerequisite. Even with a computerized catalog, more than 99 percent of reuse will still come from the user's memory. People work naturally and productively in a world of thousands, even millions, of reusable parts. People can remember an almost unlimited number of standard parts if they are grouped into categories. Consider how many cars people can remember and how many song titles, sports, states, flowers, TV shows, movies, plays, actors, etc. Consider specifically your hobby – how many standard parts that go with your hobby can you remember? Probably 99 percent of the things and parts we use we select from memory. When we do use a catalog, it is often to find the location of something we already know exists rather than to find out what exists. We seldom look up bolts or nuts, screws, tools, washers, pots, pans, cars, bicycles, shoes, socks, shirts, records, movies, etc. Consider how many editor commands a programmer remembers, how many system commands, how many commands of a second editor, of a screen painter, a debug tool, the system executive language, language verbs (for several languages), etc. We may look up unfamiliar ones, but we probably use at least 100 commands for each one we look up. If we change environments, there is an orientation period when we are not really very productive. We are becoming acquainted with the available reusable elements so that we can use them from memory and do not have to look everything up. Once we learn the standard things needed for the job, then we can be productive – using them mostly from memory.

Catalogs are one way to find out what exists, but far from the only way, and maybe not even the most common way. Often, we find new things by asking a person who specializes in that category of thing. For example, there is usually someone who knows the editor or the print subsystem better than other people. For many objects we go to a store that specializes in them, such as a tire store. The specialists who work there know about many more tires than we do and can help us choose – and if they do not know the answer themselves, they know who to call.

5.3.4 Designing for reuse

The ability to reuse code varies with the strength of connections between that code and the other code around it. Below is a list of various ways in which integrands can be connected, varying from easiest to reuse (at the top) to hardest:

1. Completely unconnected (but this is not very interesting because in order to build systems the parts have to be connected somehow).
2. Passing only data from one part to the next.
3. Calling separate integrands.
4. Including macros (which generate source statements).
5. Including segments of source code with one control path into the top and one path out from the bottom of the segment.
6. Having a function implemented in physically contiguous lines (e.g. a COBOL paragraph).
7. Sharing a common data area.
8. Intermixing code with code of another function (i.e. physically scattered code).

These characteristics apply to the *ease* of reuse, not the *likelihood* of doing so. The latter is more determined by what the segment of code does. Even a segment that is trivial to reuse may not be reused unless it provides a defined, separate, useful function that someone needs.

There are several principles that can be applied during design to improve the ability to reuse the resulting integrands. These include the following:

1. Design each integrand to have high functional binding (see 'Structured Design', Section 2.5).
2. Give each integrand a name that implies its function clearly.
3. Make each integrand as independent of other integrands as possible (i.e. low coupling – see 'Structured Design', Section 2.5).
4. Avoid adding extra functions that are presently unnecessary in an effort to generalize the integrand.
5. Separate input and output into different integrands from the processing logic.
6. Avoid accessing global data.

Design integrands with high binding and low coupling and separating input and output into different integrands helps to ensure that the integrand contains a single function, which increases the chance of its being reused. Giving the integrand a good name encourages the user to select it in order to reuse it. Making the integrand independent of neighboring integrands increases the ability of the user to combine it with other things without having to modify it. Data flow connections make integrands more reusable than calls (see above). Too often, efforts to generalize pieces for reuse result in unnecessary parameters, multiple functions in one integrand, and more complicated code. As a result, the integrands end up being *less* reusable. Good reusable parts are usually evolved rather than designed correctly for widest reuse the first time. A productive way to create reusable parts is to create a specific one the first time, changing it to make it more general when and as it is needed a second time, and making it even more general as needed for subsequent reuses. When a part evolves to where it is generally usable, then it can be made more widely available.

Often hardware and software systems differ in their use of input and output. Thus integrands that combine logic that interfaces to input and output with logic that processes the data are less likely to be reused than integrands which contain only input and output or only logic for processing data. Even if all of the above measures are used to improve the likelihood of reuse, it will be difficult to reuse integrands if they access global data. The disadvantage of accessing global data areas is that a global data area requires the other integrands that create the data to be in the new system as well (which tends to bring all the old integrands into the new system – i.e. the integrands are not independently reusable).

5.3.5 Executing architecture specifications

Given data flow diagrams and reusable integrands, it is possible to execute data flow diagrams (as explained in Appendix A). This can enable designers to work in the context of the design diagram, make changes and enhancements in order to understand, test, debug, and enhance the design. For small simple diagrams it is even more productive to execute from a language. Appendix A illustrates a language that represents the connection information in data flow diagrams (similar to the syntax for pipes in PC/DOS). In this language, each element in a diagram becomes a verb, and connections between the nodes are indicated putting '&' between the verbs. Thus the diagram shown in Figure 5.3 becomes 'Read & Edit & Select & Sort & Print'. (Conversely, putting a box around each of the preceding verbs and replacing each '&' by an arrow yields the data flow diagram.) The language can be executed if there is an integrand available for each node. Thus this language is a very high level language that can be expanded and tailored to any field of interest by specifying new verbs (as combinations of existing verbs or new integrands).

Given the ability to execute architectural specifications as described above, rapid assembly of software becomes much easier. Integrands do not need to be modified internally in order to be reused in various combinations. This rapid assembly makes implementation and testing much easier (see Stevens 1982) and, in addition, allows iterative prototyping, which can substantially improve designs.

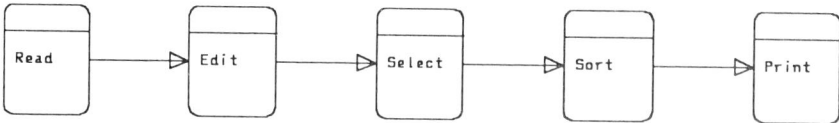

FIGURE 5.3 Read & Edit & Select & Sort & Print

5.4 GENERAL SYSTEMS PRINCIPLES

Systems that people built – both manual and automated – are controlled by general principles that are independent of the function which designers put in them. One principle is that expanding the dimensions of a system does *not* yield the same system. For example, the procedure for counting the number of people in a room, if expanded, is not a successful way to take the census of a country. Another example is that the Space Vehicle Preparation Shed at Cape Kennedy, designed to protect space vehicles from the elements, generates its own weather including clouds and rain. This and other system principles are explained in a delightful and amusing book by John Gall (1986) entitled *Systematics: The underground text of systems lore; how systems really work and how they fail*, and is recommended for anyone who designs systems. One can choose to ignore the principles by which systems operate and continue to be puzzled as to why they do not seem to act as we intend, or recognize the principles and thus improve the ability to design systems that work. Another systems principle is that large systems have components that have internal objectives (e.g. departments of a company which have departmental objectives); and internal objectives take priority over external objectives. Gall (1986) cites an example:

> The United States Coast Guard and the Canadian Environmental Protection Service have richly earned recognition for their *Operation Preparedness*, a proposal to study the effects of an oil spill upon the ecology of Lake Saint Clair (above Lake Erie) by actually dumping jet fuel into the lake . . . .

Other principles explained by Gall include:
1. Systems display antics. They act up.
2. Under precisely controlled experimental conditions, a test animal will behave as it damn well pleases. . . . Not just animal behavior, but the behavior of complex systems generally, whether living or non-living, is unpredictable.
3. The function performed by a system is not operationally identical to the function of the same name performed by a person. (For example, compare picking a tomato from your garden with acquiring one at a local fruit stand or from a large supermarket – the latter is ripened entirely differently from the one picked from your garden.)
4. Designers of systems tend to design ways for themselves to bypass the system.
5. When a fail-safe system fails, it fails by failing to fail safe, e.g. the fail-safe component concludes that the main system has failed, when it has not, and wrests control from it – thus causing a failure itself.
6. Adding numbers to a bad study doesn't clarify it.
7. Bad design can rarely be overcome by more design, whether good or bad.

Gall also includes good recommendations for designing better systems, including:

1. A complex system designed from scratch never works and cannot be made to work. You have to start over, beginning with a working simple system.
2. A complex system that works is invariably found to have evolved from a simple system that worked.

3. Plan to scrap the first system. . . . You will anyway (Brooks 1975).
4. Systems run best when designed to run downhill. Go with the flow.

That is, the best systems are those that *help people do things they want to do*, and the way they want to do them. Thus, it can be very helpful to *look to natural human endeavors* – those without computer involvement for rules for systems that already work.

If the above principles seem incorrect or inappropriate to 'real' systems design, Gall (1986) has much fuller explanations and a myriad of examples of how real systems do indeed exhibit these behaviors. Suffice it to repeat one example: because of their size, supertankers cannot go through most canals and have to navigate the capes, with some of the worst weather in the world. However, they were designed with only one boiler and screw – and the radio, lights, and radar are powered from that one boiler. Twenty minutes after they lose power, they cannot communicate. While *Systeantics* is written in a very humorous style, the recommendation to read it to improve the ability to design systems that work is quite serious.

5.5. ABSTRACT DATA TYPES

The idea of Abstract Data Types started primarily with Parnas (1972) who wrote about information hiding. Parnas recommended having the format of structured data known to as few integrands as possible, thus 'hiding' that structure from the rest of the code. This hiding can be accomplished by surrounding data structures with functions that create, access, and change the data upon request of other integrands (see Figure 5.4). A data base management system is an example of an abstract data type. It supplies functions that perform the necessary operations on the data – create, retrieve, change, and delete – and may even format it for the requester.

Abstract Data Types are a valuable concept that can be added to the concepts in Structured Analysis and Structured Design (see Sections 2.2 and 2.5). In particular, paying attention to Structured Design only could yield functions being implemented separately, but each accessing passed data structures. This access results in implicit coupling among the functions, even if they do access the data one at a time; if the format of the data is changed, each of the functions will have to be changed as well. This implicit coupling could be reduced by passing an Abstract Data Type rather than the structured data. Abstract Data Types can be helpful in reducing complexity, but can also actually increase complexity. Examples of helpful uses of Abstract Data Types include data base management systems and encapsulating a control block into an Abstract Data Type. Hiding the format of a control block from the myriad of places that may need to access its data can significantly reduce the complexity of understanding and debugging the system. Abstract Data types are especially helpful when the data have structure and will be used by more functions than it takes to isolate them (usually four – create, access, change, and delete). Abstract Data Types are also more attractive to the extent that data may be accessed by several users – especially if the data organization is complex, likely to change, or access is concurrent.

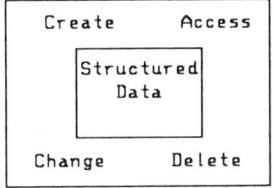

FIGURE 5.4 Abstract Data Type

However, Abstract Data Types are not useful for all data, e.g. they are less helpful for a temporary data area used only by a single integrand. The data may have a structure, but if the data is acessed only by the code within that one integrand, then making that data area an Abstract Data Type would increase complexity. The data area would still have one user, who would have to explicitly create, initialize, and use the data (just as before), but who now has to use an interface to do so – which increases complexity. It is less helpful to encapsulate data in an Abstract Data Type if the data are used by few integrands, are not organized in a complex fashion, or have little likelihood of needing modifications in the future.

5.6 OBJECT-ORIENTED

5.6.1 Object-Oriented programming

Another evolution to software development, similar to those which Structured Programming (see Section 3.2) and Structured Analysis and Design (see Sections 2.2 and 2.5) made in the 1970s, is presently happening due to the Object-Oriented paradigm. Similarly, Object-Oriented has taken on the aura of 'goodness', as 'Structured' did in the 1970s: i.e. 'if it is Object-Oriented, then it must be good', and 'if it is good, then it must be Object-Oriented'. There are people talking and writing about Object-Oriented programming, Object-Oriented design, Object-Oriented languages, and Object-Oriented data bases. The concepts of Object-Oriented are rapidly evolving and being defined and re-defined: a very necessary and valuable process. During this process, there are three kinds of presentations and publications on the subject of Object-Oriented: what it *was*, what the speaker thinks it *ought to be* to be good, and what the speaker *thinks is good* and thus wants to label 'Object-Oriented'. The latter, whether including good ideas or not, does not help to define Object-Oriented. The first is useful as background.

Object-Oriented concepts originated in part from research of the Software Concepts Group at Xerox and were implemented by them in a system called Smalltalk (see Cox 1986). Smalltalk pioneered the concepts of icon-oriented and widowing systems. One problem that Smalltalk faced was the inability to foretell which object the user might point to, since the user was allowed to point to anything on the screen using the mouse and ask the system to move it, change its size, rotate it, etc. Thus, it was rather difficult to be in a hierarchy of functions at the right place to execute the next function, because the user, not the program, was controlling the actions. To address this problem, Smalltalk modeled the software more closely to what was happening on the screen. 'Objects' were set up in the software to represent the objects on the screen. These objects could move 'themselves' (i.e. move the image on the screen), rotate themselves, copy themselves, create copies, and do anything else that would be valid for that type of object. The software object was passed messages by the system indicating what action had been requested. Programming with these concepts is called 'Object-Oriented programming' (OOP). A good reference book on Object-Oriented programming is *Object-Oriented Programming – An Evolutionary Approach*, by Brad Cox (1986). Although closely associated with icon-oriented user interfaces, Object-Oriented Programming is neither defined by, nor dependent on, such an interface. Object-Oriented programming can be useful regardless of the user interface, and icon-oriented user interfaces could be supported by other ways of writing code. Similarly, the success of icon-oriented user interfaces does not mean that everything called 'Object-Oriented' is necessarily good.

5.6.2 Object-Oriented design

Of more relevance to this volume is Object-Oriented design (OOD). Ever since Object-Oriented programming became popular, there has been intense pressure to answer the question: 'How does one design software that is to be implemented with Object-Oriented programming concepts?' Unfortunately, at the time of writing, the various books describing what will undoubtedly be alternative proposals for Object-Oriented design have not yet been released, and are thus not available for evaluation. However, discussing the various concepts that have been associated with Object-Oriented can help with the evaluation of various proposals for Object-Oriented design. Concepts often associated with Object-Oriented include:

1. Sending messages to 'objects'.
2. Declaring the type of data and functions.
3. Associating all valid functions with data to make an object.
4. Inheritance.

To get the maximum benefit from the Object-Oriented paradigm, we need to separate and enhance the concepts that improve software development, and avoid those that do not.

Sending messages to objects is a substantial advantage in allowing for flexibility and reuse (as with the concepts discussed in 'Code reuse', Section 5.3). The coupling concepts of Structured Design (see Section 2.5) show that systems are more independent, simpler, more flexible, and easier to *reuse* if their integrands are connected by flows of data than by calls.

Declaring the type of functions means specifying the types of data with which the functions can work. For data, typing can indicate what type of data it is (e.g. numeric, character, floating point) and its format. Declaring the type of data and functions is an improvement over approaches that leave data and functions undeclared because it helps to validate that data and functions are correctly matched. The ability to type data and functions dynamically can also allow the developer more flexibility than languages that have only a static or default typing since the latter are usually much more limited in the range of definition types allowed.

Associating all valid functions with data to make an object is a commonly accepted Object-Oriented concept. For example, the valid functions for a numeric data object include add, subtract, multiply, divide, square, cube, power of N, invert, absolute value, round, truncate fractional part, etc. The operations on a date may be subtract, add increment, convert to month–day–year format, convert to day–month–year format, etc. The question is: 'Is it valuable to group all the valid functions with the data?' If each of the valid functions is given direct access to the structured data encapsulated in the object, maintenance can be very difficult. The difficulty of changing a flat file record layout or global common data area that is accessible by many programs illustrates the complexity of maintaining such a design. Giving *all* functions direct access to the data results in more dependencies, more complexity, and thus, as shown by Structured Design (see Section 2.5), less flexibility, and *less* reuse. A way to avoid these problems is to *minimize* the number of functions that have access to each set of data. Abstract Data Types (see the preceding section) reduce those interdependences by limiting access to the data object to the create, retrieve, change, and delete functions. All other functions that operate on the data are then independent of how the data are stored. These four are the only types of functions that need to be bound with an object – other functions can access the data via messages (or calls) to the object with those four functions. Then a diagram should be drawn that shows how the other functions are related. If all connections are via message flows, the diagram would be a normal data flow diagram. This diagram would represent the structure of the object and is more useful than just a list of the functions in an object.

There are other possible reasons for grouping all valid functions with the data, but none justify the increased complexity of trying to develop and maintain such a definition. One problem is that it is not even possible to group *all* the valid functions with data anyway. The list of all possible valid functions even for a single numeric field is virtually endless, as are the potential uses of a payroll record. What is usually in such a list are only those functions implemented *in this system*, rather than all valid functions. However, other objects that receive data from a given object can also operate on that data. Thus, the list of functions *in* an object is not necessarily all the valid functions in that system either. Even if a list of all possible valid functions were possible, it is not that useful. What is more valuable, in order to more easily design, understand, debug and change systems is not the long list of all possibilities, but, rather, the short list of those chosen to be used. That is, designers and developers need to be able to identify easily and quickly those functions that are *used* by which other objects – the list of the possible ones is much less helpful.

Another proposal is that the list of all valid functions enhances reuse. Brad Cox, in his book (1986) states that reuse is enhanced if the *supplier* of functions and data explicitly declares which combinations are valid (see Cox (1986), page 25). However, it is how the functions are written that enables their reuse (or not). The purpose of specifying which functions are valid is to allow the system to check for *improper* use – it cannot *increase* the possibility for reuse beyond that of the implemented functions. Observation of other manufacturing industries shows that the myriad of reusable items they produce do *not* derive their abilities to be reused by enforcing predetermined sets of uses. For example, the consumer can use a hammer to hit anything that the consumer chooses – even though the hammer may have been *designed* for hitting nails. Producing a hammer in such a way that it could *only* hit nails would *reduce* its reuse, not increase it. If the hammer came with some mechanism which would restrict it to only hitting 'valid' things, then that mechanism would add some bulkiness and restriction. This would not only restrict reuse, it would even complicate its use for the things that were intended. (While it might be necessary for safety or other reasons, such restrictive devices would decrease, not increase, ease of reuse). Even if the hammer were somehow allowed to hit everything its producer could think of, specifying any finite list of valid objects would still reduce reuse because the hammer could not then be used for any objects created after the hammer was made. Similarly, consumers choose how to use tables, chairs, plates, cars, radios, skate boards, and pencils. It is the *consumer* who decides what to use and how to use it and consumers find uses for things that were never conceived by their developers. (A stewardess on an airplane once used a hearing set to tie back the curtains for landing – surely not a use intended by the developer of the hearing set, but it worked.) Naturally, the consumer may use a tool in a way that does not work, but that is the consumer's choice.

Another problem with specifying all possible valid functions with each object is that such lists are long and difficult to specify. Since this list is so large for many types of data, concepts of *inheritance* are adapted from classification schemes (such as biology) in an effort to reduce the difficulty. The idea of inheritance is to group objects into classes, and hierarchies of classes, so that common characteristics (e.g. valid functions) can be inherited from the class rather than having to be specified for each object individually. For example, if a 'number' class is defined with common operations for numbers, then each number identified as being in the 'number' class can inherit the valid functions for all numbers. Ideally this should reduce the specification effort. However, in practice there are usually many exceptions to the inherited definitions. For example, positive numbers will have functions that have to be excluded. Personnel numbers may have particular values which are invalid or reserved. Even if classes and inheritance worked well for numbers, if the data in an object are a structured collection of alphabetic fields such as 'address' and 'zip code', it is less obvious what functions are valid or what classes make sense. Although arbitrary classes, such as 'customer', can always be defined, the class name may do little to communicate what its valid functions are. It may then also be difficult to find another member for that class. More sophisticated schemes for 'multiple inheritance' (an object inheriting characteristics from more than one class) and overriding class functions within a specific object add more flexibility – and more complexity – but are still not sufficient to resolve the general diversity of specifying all valid functions. Inheritance is very useful for classifying *existing* things (such as plants and animals) and conveying those fixed sets of characteristics to others. However, it is much more difficult to define classes at the same time that the characteristics of the objects for those classes are also being defined and changed. Moreover, the resulting classes are basically arbitrary and may be of little help in communicating which characteristics are grouped. The irony is that the whole effort of defining all those classes is unnecessary because maintenance is simpler if only create, retrieve, change, and delete access the data. Specifying inheritance classes is also extra work because it only specifies the limits on available functions. The actual choices to be used still all have to be designed and specified (and are sufficient for the system, once specified). In fact, much of the complexity of designing Object-Oriented systems comes directly from this complex task of defining the classes and trying to define all valid functions. Thus, inheritance turns out not to be a simple solution to a complex problem, it is instead a complex, unsatisfactory solution to a complex, unnecessary problem.

Inheritance is being used to effect reuse in Object-Oriented systems – and with good results. However, were the functions in an object shown by a diagram, the lists of functions created by inheritance would be superfluous. Furthermore, the reuse claimed for inheritance would be achieved by copying the diagram and changing the functions necessary to make the new object.

5.6.3 Valuable characteristics for Object-Oriented design methods

Object-Oriented is going through a transition typical of many new technologies or capabilities. If one considers the first car: one has tremendous flexibility in being able to drive around a field in any direction one wants. However, consider 1000 cars in the field and there is rapidly an important need to identify roads, rules for driving on them, and precisely defined intersections among those roads. The basic purpose of such rules is to limit the number of interactions among those cars so they can all accomplish their objectives, hopefully without errors. The same thing happens with programming. At first one can show amazing things that can be achieved using techniques such as self-modifying code and common data areas. Such techniques can be made to work when the entire system under consideration can be created and understood by one person. However, as programs become larger than is practical for any one person to develop or understand (in its entirety), understanding and maintenance become much more difficult unless the number of interactions among components is reduced. The more the interactions are reduced, the simpler the system is to design and develop (relative to an implementation with many more interactions).

One of the values of an architectural design phase is to identify the components and the interactions among them. The fewer the interactions, the easier it is to understand the architecture and to build each component. Thus, one objective for Object-Oriented design is to have an architectural design diagram showing the interaction of the components. Here again, as above in this section, the concept of defining hierarchies of classes with inheritance causes unnecessary complexity. Inheritance indicates the superset of all possible functions rather than the ones actually used, which is what the designers and developers need most. In fact, the whole class hierarchy adds extra relationships to the connections that must exist in order to perform the work – the messages passed among components. An architectural diagram for Object-Oriented should show at least the objects and to which other objects each passes messages. Such a diagram would be sufficient to describe accurately the execution time relationship among objects. Thus a class hierarchy would add unnecessary connections and complication to such an architectural diagram. Note that an architectural diagram that shows objects and message passing is a data flow diagram. Thus, data flow diagrams, and the techniques used to create them (see 'Essential Systems Analysis', Section 2.3) can accomplish the architectural part of Object-Oriented design.

One apparent problem with using data flow diagrams to show the architecture of Object-Oriented systems is the perception that, in Object-Oriented, messages are sent dynamically at execution time. However, in practice, most connections are decided during design and hard coded into the objects. Object-Oriented approaches do not avoid the need to determine the subset of connections among objects that is needed to meet the requirements. However, those design choices are buried in the code of the objects and the connections then occur invisibly at execution time. Anyone who desires to understand the system must understand the internals of all the objects. While this may not be a problem for a small system, it may be almost impossible for 100, or 1000, objects. However, it would be very unusual if, in a system of many objects, each object would, in fact, send messages to every other possible object under the right conditions. The designer will more likely have decided which objects would send messages to which others. It would be very helpful if this information were recorded in an architectural diagram. If there are a few objects that can actually send messages to any other object, then that information could be added with a note to the diagram. If Object-Oriented follows other systems paths as it evolves, we will eventually even want the system to flag as errors interactions that were not specified during design.

Conversely, explicit links, as with a data flow diagram (see 'Structured Analysis', Section 2.2) allow a program to be designed, developed, understood, debugged, and changed more easily than with unconstrained relationships. Fixed links are easier because the possible relationships among components can be determined easily from the architecture diagrams rather than having to inspect the *inside* of all components (objects). In addition, explicit links provide the same advantage of increased reuse as dynamic links.

5.6.4 Object-Oriented and reuse

The concepts of Object-Oriented techniques have been proposed as a way of achieving reuse (including Cox 1986; Booch 1983). Reuse is possible in any language when the conditions are right (see 'Code reuse', Section 5.3); and is hardly the sole domain of Object-Oriented or Ada®. Object-Oriented includes the concept of sending messages between independent objects, which enhances reuse. However, the objects usually specify the targets of their messages themselves (by specifying the name, e.g. 'Move', of a set of objects with the data type inferring the actual 'Move' object to receive the message), which means they may have to be changed internally in order to work in a different system with different objects. Thus they fail the fourth condition for easy reuse: usable without having to be modified internally (see 'Code re-use', Section 5.3).

DOS and UNIX® deliver integrands ('filters') in a way that allows *end-users* to reuse them trivially. The filters do not restrict how they can be connected or what data they receive. The users can choose combinations of functions and data that the producers could never have envisioned (since files created by the user can be sent through the filters). Cox (1986, pages 18–21) agrees that the UNIX® pipes lead to easier reuse (but still opts for Object-Oriented on the claim of better performance). However, the performance of data flow connected integrands can be as good or better than Object-Oriented approaches. DFDM (described in Appendix A) does not transfer byte streams like UNIX® and DOS pipes, but passes typed blocks of storage (optionally via pointers), which results in a level of performance equal to or better than passing data to subroutines or messages to objects.

Object-Oriented languages provide a capability to pass messages among integrands (their 'objects'), a capability that many other high level languages do not have. Normally, however, objects send messages by indicating the name of the object to which the message is to be sent, thus limiting the ease with which objects can be reused (the objects they send messages to have to be in every system they are used in, as do the objects that those objects send messages to, etc.). For example, consider a system where object A sends a message to object B and B sends a message to C. If one tries to reuse A in another system, B has to come with it; but if B comes, then C has to come, i.e. the whole system comes along too. This is not the idea of reuse. True, A could be modified internally so that it sends its message to a new object, but it is then no longer A – rather, it is another object that must be maintained separately. The inhibitor to reuse is the same as with integrands in a call hierarchy – objects contain the names of adjacent objects and thus cannot be reused in another system without being modified internally. However, having objects contain names of adjacent objects can be circumvented by defining a message manager object (see Figure 5.5). Objects could send all messages to the message manager object, identifying which stream of data they are sending (similar to the output 'port' identifier in Appendix A). The message manager, which would have access to the data flow network specification, would identify what object is connected to that flow and forward the message. Forwarded messages would indicate the intended input port of the receiving object. (Object-Oriented objects often have only one logical input stream, but this approach would allow the flexibility of multiple logical input and output streams.) Such an approach could allow interfaces among objects in a system to be reconfigured without having to change the code of the objects. The message manager could even enforce message passing based on defined interfaces, or allow dynamic connections, if desired. Such a message manager would be similar to that described in Appendix A, but would be much simpler to create because it could rely on the Object-Oriented system for invoking objects and passing messages.

Object-Oriented, however, has something to add to data flow systems in helping to eliminate coupling among integrands in a data flow network. Normally, nodes pass messages that may contain structured data. Thus, many objects may access the same structured data, which makes changing the format of that structured data difficult. If,

196   OTHER DESIGN TOPICS

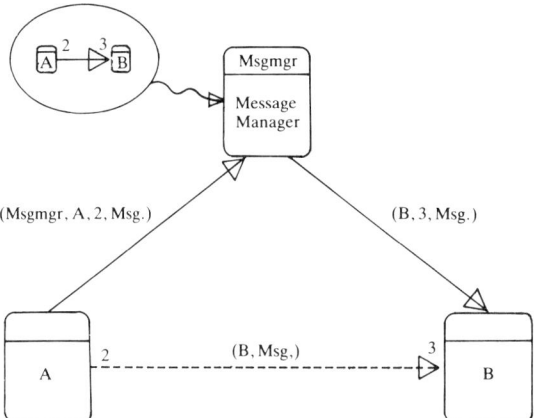

FIGURE 5.5 Reusable objects

however, the 'messages' that are passed are actual objects (i.e. structured data encapsulated as an Abstract Data Type), then the integrands in the data flow network would not access the structured data directly, but, rather, through the objects' functions. The result is a system where 'objects pass objects', or, rather, 'function objects' (mostly functions with some internal state data) pass 'data objects' (mostly data with some access functions).

5.6.5 Recommendations regarding Object-Oriented

Object-Oriented has focused the software industry on sending messages and reuse, both of which can be of substantial benefit (even though neither of these were initially unique to Object-Oriented). However, there are some concepts that have been associated with Object-Oriented that can detract from, rather than help, increase reuse and reduce complexity (see the discussion directly above). The following are observations on using Object-Oriented concepts:

1. The fewer functions that have access to data in an object, the simpler maintenance will be. Abstract Data Types are a good model for defining objects.
2. Defining a list of *all* possible valid functions as part of an object is difficult or impossible and unlikely to yield benefits that justify the effort.
3. An architectural diagram that shows the designed possible routes for messages among objects can be of significant help to those who have to understand, debug, and enhance the system. If some message routes have to be allocated dynamically, a verbal description of the intended conditions of that dynamic allocation would be helpful.
4. A diagram drawn to depict which objects send messages to which other objects is a data flow diagram.

5. Essential Systems Analysis is a method for designing systems with independent integrands that pass messages – and thus should be helpful in designing Object-Oriented systems. Methods based on data organization, such as Jackson (see 'Jackson charts' in Section 3.6), may be helpful for designing the structured data but are probably less helpful for designing the interactions among objects.
6. Not all objects have to contain data. Implementing some objects to be like functional subroutines in high level languages may make useful objects (in addition to those that contain structured data).
7. The message passing capability of Object-Oriented languages means that they are architecturally structured to allow integrands to be distributed (since the objects which receive messages have no knowledge of whether the sender is on the same computer). However, if objects access global data areas directly, that will restrict the ability to distribute the objects. If data must be accessed in a global data area, having one object access the data and then send them in messages to other objects can help to avoid the restriction.
8. In order to enhance the ability to reuse objects, avoid having objects contain names of other objects.

5.7 PORTABILITY

5.7.1 Description

Portability is not a characteristic that programs have or do not have. The easier it is to move a program to another execution environment, the more portable the program is. A program is portable to the extent that it can be moved between environments that are somehow *different* (if the environments were the same, the issue is not one of portability). If the environments are different, then there is something in one that, if used by the program, will prevent it from working in the other environment. Ways to make programs execute in another environment can be divided into the three following categories:

1. Using only features common to all intended execution environments.
2. Supplying versions of any functions or interface syntaxes missing in one or more of the execution environments.
3. Writing a different version for each execution environment of integrands that use unique features.

Usually a combination of the above ways is the most useful. Another consideration affecting portability is the language for the program. Naturally, if a compiler for the language is not available in the other execution environment, the program has to be re-written completely in order to run in the other environment. Even if a compiler is available, there are frequently differences between various compilers of the same language. Unless the code is limited to a common subset of language statements available across the environments of interest, it will have to be changed.

198 OTHER DESIGN TOPICS

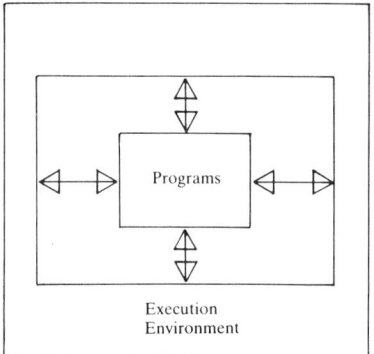

FIGURE 5.6 Environment interfaces

Figure 5.6 illustrates the interfaces between a program and its execution environment. In order to have the program execute automatically in another environment, the interfaces that the program uses must be available. Thus the *only* way for a program to be *automatically* portable is for it to use a subset of interfaces that are available in both execution environments. Portability can be straightforward when the target execution environments are known in advance – use only common features. Conversely, it is impossible to assure portability of the characteristics if the target environments are not known; there is no way to guarantee that everything the program uses will be available in an unknown environment. If functions needed by the program are available – but require different syntaxes – then conversion routines can be written that translate one syntax into the other. Naturally, it is possible to enhance the minimum common available subset by writing additional functions missing in one environment.

Portability is a type of conversion, and the same techniques that help make programs changeable also make them easier to move to another execution environment. To the extent that a program uses unique features that are not in another execution environment, it will have to be changed to work in the other environment. There are several design principles that can help make programs easier to move to another execution environment. A good way to make a program easier to change is to make it *modular*. This reduces the amount of code that has to be considered in order to make necessary changes. Portability for business applications has more to do with input and output; the type of logic used in these applications generally works on any computer that has a compiler for that language. Conversely, portability for many scientific and engineering programs has more to do with the calculation statements than with the input and output. Thus, it is helpful in both business and scientific programs to place input and output statements in different integrands than those containing the logic for processing the data. Input and output statements are also easier to modify if they are not intermixed with statements that perform computational functions, and vice-versa. Separating input and output helps make integrands functionally bound and is thus a good way to reduce complexity anyway. In addition, isolate the use of unique system features to separate simple integrands so that they can be re-implemented easily for the other target environments.

5.7.2 Virtual machine interfaces

Some companies have tried to assure total automatic portability by building a cocoon between the programs and every interface in the execution environment. The idea is to implement the cocoon in each execution environment instead of having to re-write the code. Unfortunately, building a cocoon to make programs totally and *automatically* portable results in several characteristics that work against its success, including the following:

1. The cocoon must be between the programs and every external interface, such as systems services, disk services, data base interface, terminal interface, and communications interface. (Any interface used directly by a program might prevent portability.)
2. The cocoon limits programs to the minimum common subset of functions available in all target execution environments (possibly as enhanced a little by the cocoon). Thus, functions such as queueing on a serial resource may not be supported by the cocoon unless it is available in each target execution environment. (Subsets are acceptable if one controls the subset. The larger the number of clients for any subset of functions, the greater the chance that one or more clients will need something not in the subset.)
3. Every I/O interface syntax has to be re-designed to eliminate direct use and prevent programs from reaching any function that is not common. If a program were to access the DBMS directly, for example, then there would be no way that the cocoon could assure it was not using, say, a 'get previous', that is not available in another DBMS.
4. A program that uses the cocoon cannot use any new facilities until a new interface is designed and implemented for it. For example, if a relational DBMS adds support for dynamic SQL, programs cannot use it until the cocoon interface is also upgraded to support it.
5. Since the cocoon limits function, there will be some programs that require functions the cocoon does not support, and thus cannot use the cocoon. Similarly, the code written before the cocoon existed will use the native interfaces for services. As a result, the cocoon does not eliminate use of the native interfaces to services; it just adds a new set of interfaces for which skills have to be maintained in the organization.
6. The resources for the cocoon's support will probably be taxed by trying to keep up with new features that become available in the environments first supported: new subsystems services, new communications support, new languages, and new functions added by each of the existing subsystems. Often, no resource is left for moving the cocoon to the rest of the intended execution environments. Thus, the proposed advantage of automatic portability does not materialize.
7. Automatic portability cannot be guaranteed unless the portability cocoon implements its own unique *language* (since few widely used languages are totally portable).

Implementing a new language requires implementing language tools to support it, which alone can absorb all the resources of the cocoon's development team.

The fundamental problem is that most, if not all, of the work on the cocoon changes syntax only, without adding function. In fact, the cocoon accomplishes its goal of automatic portability by *subtracting* function. As a result, the funding for the cocoon is ultimately questioned – usually even prior to completion of the cocoon in its first environment, but frequently before support of the second environment. By that time, there are often programs that depend on the cocoon, making it difficult for management to stop the support. Ultimately, however, management will not be able to continue justifying the expenditure – especially as the cocoon deviates farther and farther from new attractive common interfaces and programming environments.

Since portability cocoons can also add function, it can sometimes be difficult to identify whether a given system is a portability cocoon or a useful functional subsystem. One way to distinguish the two is to focus on the objectives. Functional subsystems add useful functions without having to limit access to lower level detail functions. For example, a DBMS adds useful capabilities for managing and storing data beyond that available from the basic disk access routines in a given execution environment. However, the advantage of the DBMS does not depend on preventing programs from also using the basic disk access routines for other data storage needs. However, if the primary objective of a software subsystem is automatic portability – and especially if its success depends on programs *not* using other interfaces – then it is probably a portability cocoon with the difficulties indicated above. Also, if interfaces with new syntaxes are created that do not exhibit new or higher level functions, then the interface is probably just for portability. For example, a subsystem may be proposed for isolating programs from future changes in telecommunications methods. However, to obtain the advantages, programs must not use any telecommunications method directly, but, rather, only through this new subsystem. The proposed system will probably contain either no, or few, new functions – just a redefinition of the syntax of the current telecommunications method. Such a subsystem has the characteristics of a portability cocoon or layer, not those of a functional subsystem.

5.7.3 Isolating from change

Programs are made easier to change by techniques such as modularity, functional binding, and low coupling which are contained in Structured Design (see 'Structured Design', Section 2.5). Sometimes, however, people make choices that are implicitly aimed at trying to avoid the *need* to change programs. Unfortunately, efforts to do so are usually self-defeating – resulting in programs that are harder to change rather than easier. One erroneous way to attempt to avoid change is to add extra function today, anticipating future requirements. Some expected future requirements take so little time, and seem so useful, that the developer decides to add them. However, the effort required to make the programs more general by trying to add the future functions today may well add extra complexity and subtract time and effort from better satisfying the specified requirements. At best, extra function or generalization is what is needed in the future. However, even if it is correct, the extra effort is still charged to the wrong project (today's) and makes today's project more complicated, and thus harder to develop. More often, the enhancement misses the mark, assuming a need that does not materialize as anticipated. Then the enhancement not only wastes time and makes the project harder to develop, but may even have to be removed. The correct new functions then have to be added to a program that is more complex than it needed to be. The need to change programs cannot be eliminated by adding more function, but adding function that is currently unnecessary makes the programs more complex, harder to develop, and *harder* to change.

Another way to try to avoid the need for change is to attempt to isolate programs from changes, often in the form of a generalized layer of code. The idea is that programs must use the layer for services, so external changes can (presumably) be accommodated by changing the layer. This idea of a generalized layer is both surprisingly attractive and unexpectedly deadly. The logic for building such a layer *seems* good since much of the need for changing programs can come from changes to system facilities. The data base management system (DBMS) may change, the teleprocessing interface may change, the video capabilities may change, the operating system may change, and in general any facility of the system with which the program interfaces is subject to change outside the developer's control.

As an example, consider the rationale for putting a layer between programs and the current data base management system (DBMS): if the DBMS changes, only the layer will have to be changed rather than all the programs. Assume the company decides to change to a new DBMS that has desirable capabilities that the old one did not have (otherwise there would have been no reason to buy the new DBMS.) In order to access these new functions, the layer has to be changed. Unfortunately, the programs that use the layer *have to be changed too* in order to access the new function that the layer did not have before. The program changes have to wait for the portability layer to be updated with the new function.

The basic problem is trying to isolate programs from change from which they cannot be isolated. Consider the original objective: to isolate programs from change when the DBMS changes. Unfortunately, this objective must, by its very nature, also isolate programs from *new* capabilities in the new (and old) DBMS. Had the users of the original programs been asked if they would like their programs to be unable to use new DBMS capabilities, they would surely have said 'no' – especially since the reason for buying a new DBMS is to obtain its new functions. Using those new functions in the DBMS often require changes to the programs anyway.

Well-structured programs should have integrands that isolate the rest of that program from changes to input and output services (see 'Structured Design', Section 2.5). However, to the extent that an interface layer tries to be the only source of function for *others*, it cannot succeed – because its very nature is to offer a smaller set of choices (under the control of *its* developer). The wider the audience or the longer it is used, the more likely it is that users will want to access some facility beyond the chosen set, and the less likely it is that the layer will provide the new function (due to the growing complexity and the inertia of programs that are already using the layer).

5.8 ISSUES WITH TIME-DEPENDENCIES

A set of potential problems that can arise in systems for real-time applications is:

1. Mutual exclusion ('deadlock').
2. Unproductive looping.
3. Inaccessible topology, such as when parts of a network of asynchronous, potentially concurrent processes cannot, by any combination of real circumstances, be reached.
4. Asynchronous, concurrent access to data.

These problems can arise from faulty design, or implementation, or both. Designs can be investigated for potential problems of types 1–3 listed above via adequate Petri net simulation (see 'Petri nets', Section 2.7); mutual exclusion can be diagnosed at the implementation stage by the use of Dijkstra's semaphores (Weitzman 1980). Asynchronous, concurrent access to resources may be tackled at design and implementation stages by Ullman's 'two phase commit strategy' (Ullman 1982), for all accesses to common data and global variables. When a 'lock out' system is implemented for data accesses – for example to prevent a file that is being read from being updated at the same time – the mutual exclusion problem may arise. It must be understood, however, that deadlock in general is a wider area of concern than just this special case of it, arising from a solution to problem 4 above, and that the problems of 4 itself are different to this 'deadlock' problem arising from one of their possible remedies.

Since flowcharts are the first view of a computer program that many see, many tend to relate other computer concepts (consciously or unconsciously) back to flowcharts. Unfortunately, flowcharts are synchronous by their very meaning and nature. Call hierarchies (see 'Structured Design', Section 2.5) are also synchronous: the code that follows a call statement must be considered by the system to be *invalid* until the called integrand returns. Thus, calls cannot be used to link asynchronous integrands.

Fortunately, there are natural analogies for integrands that operate asynchronously. Many things around us operate asynchronously: machines (relative to each other), jobs within a single multiprocessing system, other people with whom we work, and groups of organizations operate asynchronously relative to each other. Data flow diagrams document interactions among asynchronous components and thus can *help* design efforts. Much of the asynchrony can happen automatically if messages are passed and each integrand does its job. For example, a line of people passing pails of water does not have to concern itself with asynchrony: if each person does his job and passes the pails properly, the asynchrony basically takes care of itself. Thus our problem of dealing with asynchrony and concurrency may be caused more by trying to map asynchrony onto *synchronous* diagrams than because it is somehow 'unnatural' to work with asynchronous objects. However, there is more to real-time design than just depicting the interactions and not all asynchrony will yield to what can be done with data flow diagrams alone.

Real-time design can be a three or multidimensional problem as things such as asynchronous signals and states of the system add additional dimensions.

Systems with time-dependencies bring up difficult problems of *synchronizing* tasks. For example, the possibility of simultaneous update of data by asynchronous tasks requires some mechanism to synchronize such updates. Were there no synchronization, two users could retrieve the same data, both change it, and the first one to store it back would have that update erased as the second user's changed record is written back. The standard way to avoid this difficulty is to declare an intent to update a record when reading it. The system then allows other users to read the data, but inhibits any other request to read it for update until the first record has been returned (or its lock released). Thus the second (and subsequent) users who wish to update the record are locked out, pending return of the first record. Similar locking facilities are available to control any resource that must be used serially, such as many input and output devices.

Deadlock can occur, among other reasons, because of these mechanisms that serialize the use of resources such as shared data. If programs use several such files or resources, a deadlock is possible if the two programs each need some of the same resources. Assume two programs each want to update tables X and Y, and need to update both together. If Program_A locks table X and tries to get table Y, while Program_B has already locked table Y and is trying to get table X, then there is a deadlock. Naturally, in this simple example an easy solution is for both programs to get the locks in the same order – a standard approach for preventing deadlocks. However, in asynchronous systems with different programs acquiring multiple resources in orders determined by their input data, such strategies may not apply and the possibility of deadlock still exists. (Many data base management systems can detect and recover from deadlocks once they occur, however.)

It would be desirable if one could determine if a specific design has the possibility of producing any of the four types of potential problems listed above. Petri net simulation can only demonstrate the presence of conditions that might lead to deadlock, deadly embrace, and inaccessible topology, and even then the permutation of possible conditions to be investigated represents an effectively infinite behavior space, and therefore an infinite number of simulations. So, in fact, there is no general case solution to the problem of determining whether a given design can fall into deadlock or deadly embrace, or whether its topology has parts that may, in some real circumstances, be unreachable. There are specific solutions to specific cases, but many of the problems solved are in the theoretical realm and not easily applied by the practitioner of software design. A complete explanation of these is beyond the scope of this book. Readers who are interested are referred to Ben-Ari (1982). One of the more promising theoretical approaches, however, is the development of a 'language' for expressing the asynchrony of events. Given such a language, which includes verbs such as 'shuffle' (which represents all possible arrangements of its operands), it is possible to *express* formulas that represent all possible sequences of relevant occurrences. It is then possible to prove theorems about whether certain operations will maintain a deadlock-free situation if one existed before the operation. This approach can already handle specific cases of determining potential deadlocks and may be expanded to broader cases in the future. Readers who are interested are referred to Avrunin *et al.* (1986).

204   OTHER DESIGN TOPICS

5.9 PERFORMANCE

The distribution of resource-usage by programs is typically very skewed, with a small percentage of the programs accounting for most of the computer cycles, memory usage, and input and output operations. The curve that describes this skewed distribution is shown in Figure 5.7 and was discovered by Doherty and Kelisky (1979) based on extensive research including many computer installations and systems from various vendors. Figure 5.7 depicts the accumulating percentage of cycles used by on-line transactions during a given period – with the transactions ordered from low use of cycles to high. The period is long enough to cover one or more complete executions of most programs (e.g. several days or weeks). The computer cycles measured for any particular program is the total for all its executions during the time period. Some significant points on the curve are:

1. 50 percent of the programs account for only 1 percent of the computer cycles.
2. 1 percent of the programs account for 50 percent of the computer cycles.

The same curve results if programs are plotted relative to the input and output resources used, or to the computer memory seconds consumed. Not only does the same curve result, but the programs are in the same order (with minor switching of adjacent programs). This does not contradict the concepts of some programs being limited by input and output while others are limited by cycles. The programs are in the same order because those that consume the most cycles execute often or for a long time. Thus they use large amounts of input, output, and memory as well as cycles. The ones that execute infrequently do not have time to use a significant amount of any of the resources.

The same results as shown in Figure 5.7 were also discovered independently by Bob Kendall of IBM (Kendall 1977) in studying batch programs in various installations. (The original paper reported slightly different numbers but an analysis shows that Kendall's data agree exactly with Doherty's.) Kendall also discovered that half of the programs – those that consumed the least execution resources – cost from 62 to 10,000 times as much to *develop* as they will consume in computer resources during their entire lifetime. The next 40 percent of the programs cost between 2 and 62 times as much to develop as to run. Only with the top 5 percent of the programs – those that used the most resources – did the hardware cost to run the programs exceed the development cost (and this was in 1977 when developers were less expensive and hardware more costly than today). However, even those larger and more frequently used programs – which tend to be large on-line systems – often cost more to maintain *each year* than they cost to run.

Based on the above, if an installation wishes to improve the performance of its computer system, optimization efforts should be concentrated where they are most beneficial – on the top 1–2 percent of the programs. If additional optimization is needed, it is still most profitable to optimize the same top 1–2 percent. The code *within* a given program probably also has the same distribution. Thus, to provide the greatest benefit, optimization efforts should be concentrated on the 1 percent of the code that causes half the performance problems. Even if performance optimization could completely eliminate the cycles of that half of the programs that use the fewest cycles, the installation could

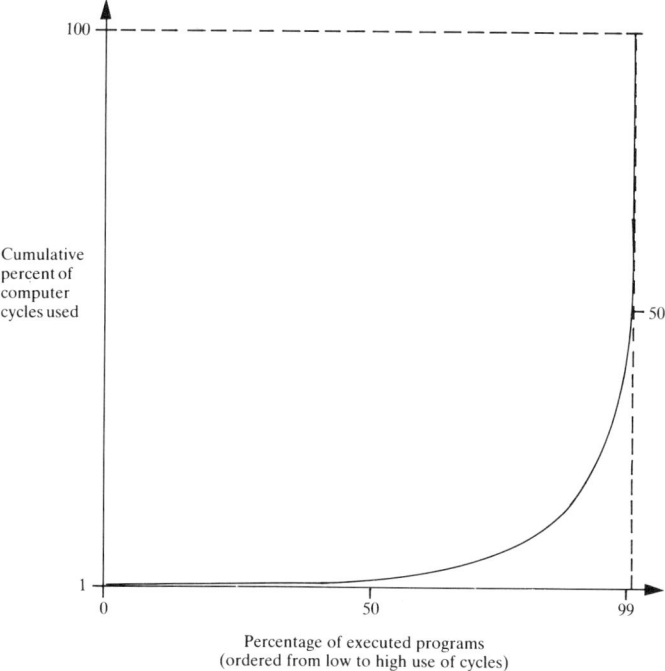

FIGURE 5.7 Cumulative computer cycles

not detect the difference (only 1 per cent more cycles would be available). Thus any time spent optimizing most of the programs developed is a waste of resources and results in software that is harder to maintain. (Either the simplest design is also the fastest, or performance optimization will make it more complex to develop and maintain.) Even for on-line software – where performance is extremely important – having software available early, reliable, and able to be changed quickly is even more important, outranking performance for all but the worst offenders.

A useful approach, then, is to design the simplest solution first (see 'Structured Design', Section 2.5). Then, if performance optimization is warranted, optimization efforts can be applied where they produce the greatest benefit for the least increase in complexity. Also, the simpler solution is easier to optimize than one that has been complicated by optimizing every part throughout the design. Given the equivalent development time, optimizing a system that has been designed to be simple should always produce a faster running solution than spending time optimizing all of a system that is more complex and harder to change (much of the optimization would be wasted, but all of it complicates the code). Finally, some of the development time that will be saved by designing the simplest system can be used for optimizing.

CHAPTER SIX
CONCLUDING REMARKS

The topic of software design is much broader than can be contained in one book, or even in the set of books recommended herein. The area of Petri nets alone spans volumes and many conferences and papers; so does data base design and Object-Oriented. There are many methods that have been made 'standard' by various companies or governmental departments; tens of methods with documentation and a history of prior use (see Teledyne 1989) and many more that are being developed or used by individuals or groups. The modern software designer, manager, or student faces a virtually impossible task of sifting through the wide array of available material on software design in an effort to identify, evaluate, and learn those methods that could be useful on the next, or even the current, design effort.

It is unfortunate that the area of Object-Oriented design is just now emerging because so little that is definitive can thus be said about it yet, and anything that is said is highly controversial. It is hoped that the concepts discussed under Object-Oriented in Chapter 5 can help the reader to evaluate the inevitable competing proposals for an Object-Oriented design method. I firmly believe that Object-Oriented is more a new way of viewing the problem than it is a combination of totally new ways to design or write code.

Next to Object-Oriented, code reuse has received the most alternative views, not the least of which from the series editor, Allen Macro. I have grown more and more convinced that reuse is quite possible and am continually amazed at how many examples there are of code that is already being reused. The characteristics needed for reuse are an important new contribution of this book. The technology illustrated in Appendix A allows components to be reused at the level that batch programs and on-line transactions and commands are today. This technology is a key to enabling much higher productivity, rapid prototyping, and reduced complexity.

General Systems Principles (Section 5.4), although done in a humorous style, is highly recommended for any serious system designer (software or not). It contains important insights into designing systems which every designer should know.

Performance was made much too high a priority for many software designs during the 1960s and 1970s (and probably still is). However, to ignore it completely during software design would also be an error. The very skewed nature of performance effects discovered by Doherty and Kelisky (1979) are important insights for any software designer.

However, as illustrated by the position of the performance topic in this book (Section 5.9), performance optimization should be left until last, and only after the system has been assured to work using appropriate methods and after it has been identified that performance will be a problem.

Validation of designs remains a thorny problem. Formal methods purport to prove equivalence based on various proposals for requirements specifications. However, formal methods can do nothing about inevitable discrepancies between captured specifications and the users' 'real' needs, which they may or may not understand themselves, much less communicate in an error-free and unambiguous manner. Moreover, the more formal the specification syntax, the more likely that the non-trained user cannot specify it or check its accuracy. Communication in general is fraught with peril and is an inherent part of capturing specifications. Details of formal methods today do not seem to be something with which all software designers need be familiar. However, as more progress is made, formal methods are likely to become increasingly significant, since most other engineering disciplines include them. Prototyping has the advantages of letting users see if the designer understood the requirements correctly and if the users like what they asked for, now that they see it. Since users can still be incorrect in what they need and there are almost always changes needed as the environment changes in the future, it is important to build systems so they are easy to change (see 'Structured Design', Section 2.5).

The methods recommended in this volume turned out to be not so much alternative as complementary. Many of the concepts of Structured Analysis (as expressed by Essential Systems Analysis), the Ward–Mellor method, Structured Design, and general systems principles (Gall 1986) can be used simultaneously. Box Structured Design and Petri nets can be used to analyze the systems designed by those methods. Then the various components in any one design can each be defined with the most appropriate integrand definition technique – such as those given in Chapter 3. Once the descriptions of the methods in this book have been absorbed, software designers are encouraged to read the reference books for each method in whatever order is most appropriate. If additional information is required on the latest in each method, read the periodicals dealing with software design and attend conferences on the various subjects. In this manner, it is hoped that we can all improve our knowledge of good, available design methods. I know I have in writing this book.

APPENDIX A
DATA FLOW DEVELOPMENT MANAGER

It is possible to connect integrands with flows of data only (as indicated above in Chapters 2, 3, and 5). Data flow yields the lowest coupling of any connection technique (see 'Structured Design', Section 2.5). Data flow connections also allow the five criteria for reuse to be satisfied (see 'Code reuse', Section 5.3), thus making reuse quite practical and easy. In order to take advantage of data flow, some mechanism is needed to pass data among the integrands as specified in a data flow diagram (or equivalent connection specification) at execution time. That way, separately compiled integrands can pass data without using the call statement. Because the call instruction names the called integrand, the call hierarchy ends up imbedded in the integrands that implement it. Thus the integrands cannot be reused without modifying them internally (except for the bottom level integrands, and even these require the user to write code to call them).

An architecture for passing data among separately compiled integrands as specified in a data-flow diagram is described here. It allows normal subroutines and mainlines to be used as nodes in the diagram. Integrands written for this architecture have additional capabilities available to them, but are basically written in the same style as normal subroutines or mainline programs. There are two parts to this architecture: one part defines the data flow connections among integrands; the other part defines the execution time interfaces to the executable nodes. Each node may be created by any technique the developer finds advantageous. It is also easier to develop the integrands than it is for call hierarchies since integrands connected by data flow do not have to include integral connection information internally.

This appendix explains an architecture for executing a data flow network (the interconnections among a set of nodes) that can be depicted by a hierarchy of data flow diagrams, once each of the nodes exists as either another data flow diagram or an executable integrand with proper interfaces. The detailed definition of the architecture has been published by IBM and is reprinted here (with permission).

1 DEFINING THE CONNECTIONS

The language for expressing the data flow connections is patterned visually after the data flow diagram itself (and has similarities to DOS and UNIX® pipes). The definition

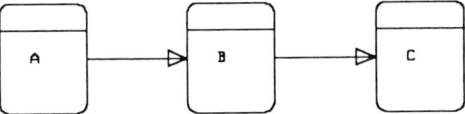

FIGURE A.1 Data flow diagram for A → B → C

language can be derived from the diagram by simply removing the boxes around the integrands. For example, for the simple data flow diagram in Figure A.1, the result is: 'A → B → C'. A synonym for '→' is '&', so an equivalent form of the same definition is 'A & B & C', or 'A&B&C'. This also can be pronounced 'A and B and C', or, with more descriptive integrand names: 'Read and Sort and Print'. No distinction is made between integrands that contain input and output versus those that do not (as with DOS and UNIX® pipes). The name of the program or set of connections may be specified by putting it in front of the connections and separating by a colon, e.g. 'Program_A: A & B & C.' A period terminates the scope of the program definition. Individual connections may be separated by commas, e.g. 'A & B, B & C'. When the connections are each specified separately (e.g. 'A & B, B & C'), the connection specifications are non-procedural with respect to each other and can be specified or sorted in any order and still describe the same connections. Thus, the program in Figure A.1 can also be specified as 'B & C, A & B'. Parameters may be specified for any integrand by including them within parentheses after the integrand's name. For example, 'A & B(1,File_W) & C' passes the character strings '1' and 'File_W' to integrand B as it starts its execution. Parameters need only be assigned once (e.g. 'A & B(parms), B & C'), but if specified several times for the same instance of B, the last one specified prevails.

Each integrand may have multiple inputs and outputs, as with the integrands 'Edit' and 'Merge' in Figure A.2. Each of the input ports of an integrand has a unique input port number, and each of the output ports has a unique output port number. The default port number is 1 (for both input and output) if not otherwise specified. It is possible to make multiple connections to the same input port – in which case the data from each connection may arrive randomly. If multiple streams are connected from an output port, duplication of the output data is implied. The format for specifying port numbers is derived again visually from the data flow diagram by eliminating the boxes around the integrands. Thus, the connection between output port 2 of 'Edit' and the input port 1 (by default) of 'Fix' is specified as: 'Edit 2 → 1 Fix', or 'Edit 2 → Fix', or 'Edit 2&Fix'. Similarly, the connection from output port 1 of 'Fix' and input port 2 of 'Merge' is specified as: 'Fix & 2 Merge'. Thus, the entire program in Figure A.2 can be specified as: 'ReadA & Edit & Merge, Edit 2 & Fix & 2 Merge'.

The same integrand may show up more than once in a data flow diagram, as in Figure A.3. The various instances of the same integrand can be distinguished from each other by appending a period and any string that produces a unique name within this diagram, e.g. 'Increment.2'. Thus, the diagram in Figure A.3 may be specified as: ReadA & Increment & Increment.2 & WriteB'. The reason for the '.2' suffix on the integrand 'Increment' is that although each instance could be distinguished by sight to be unique in the data flow

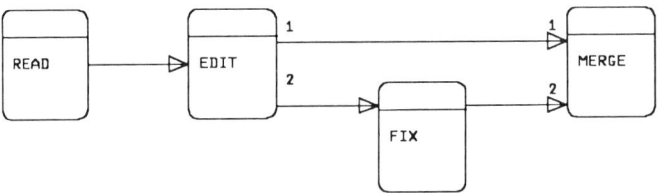

FIGURE A.2 Multiple inputs and outputs

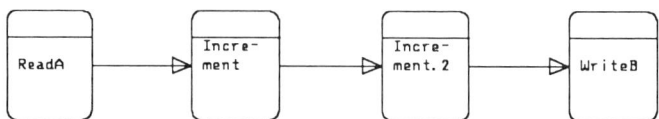

FIGURE A.3 ReadA & Increment & Increment.2 & WriteB

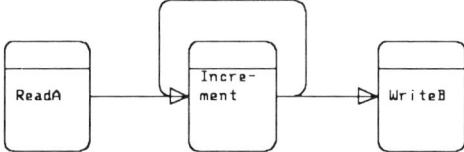

FIGURE A.4 ReadA & Increment & Increment & WriteB

diagram, synonyms would result without suffixes for the verbal form. The problem with specifying 'Read & Increment & Increment & WriteB', is that this string describes the diagram in Figure A.4, not the one in Figure A.3 (because 'Increment & Increment' means to connect the output port 1 of 'Increment' to the input port 1 of 'Increment', i.e. to its own input port). Another example of the need for unique suffixes is an integrand that has multiple input or output ports used more than once in a diagram as in Figure A.5. Without the suffixes, it would not be possible to determine the verbal form to which node 'WriteB' and 'WriteC' were connected.

A node in a data flow diagram may be a single executable unit or another data flow diagram. Thus the architecture supports hierarchies of data flow diagrams (or of equivalent connection language). For an example, see Figure A.6. (The symbols '&' and '→' are synonyms and are shown in Figure A.6 only to aid the clarity.) Each connected port for the integrand in the higher level diagram is shown in the lower level diagram (and language) as an arrow unconnected at one end. However, the port number for connection to the integrand at the higher level diagram may or may not be the same as the port defined within the integrands that make up the lower level diagram. The visual form of the diagram again is the model for the verbal syntax, as illustrated in Figure A.7. Integrands within one data flow diagram are considered different instances from

DATA FLOW DEVELOPMENT MANAGER 211

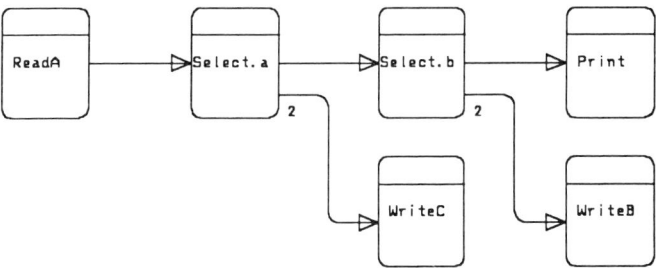

FIGURE A.5 ReadA & Select.A & Select.B & Print,Select.B 2 & WriteB

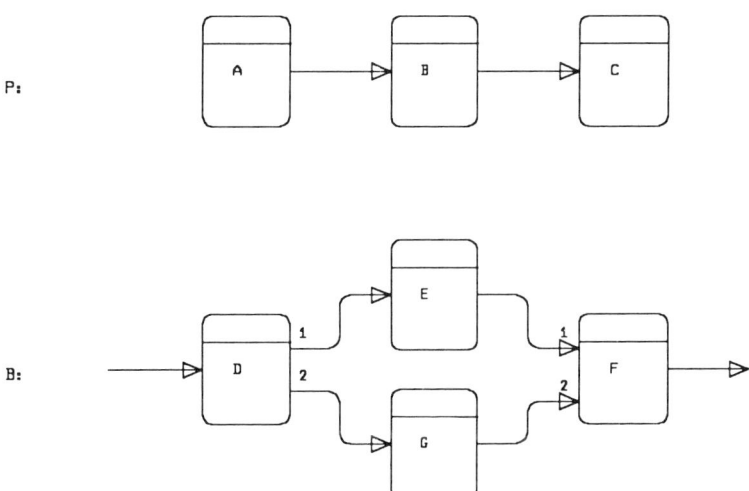

FIGURE A.6 P: A & B & C,B: → D & E & F D.2 & G & 2F →.

integrands in another diagram with the same name. However, the same code can still be used at execution time for all instances of an integrand (if the code is re-entrant as required by the execution environment). Parameters specified for a node are available to nodes in its lower level diagram by specifying a parameter of '*' in the lower level diagram. For example, if the node B is defined as 'B: → E → F → G →', then 'A → B(File1) → C, B: → E(*) → F → G(*) →' results in both E and G receiving the parameter 'File1'.

It is possible to connect integrands to the data flow mechanism itself to obtain trace or error messages. Trace information is available by defining the connection 'DDM 1→ integrand', and error messages are available by similarly connecting to output port 2 of 'DDM'.

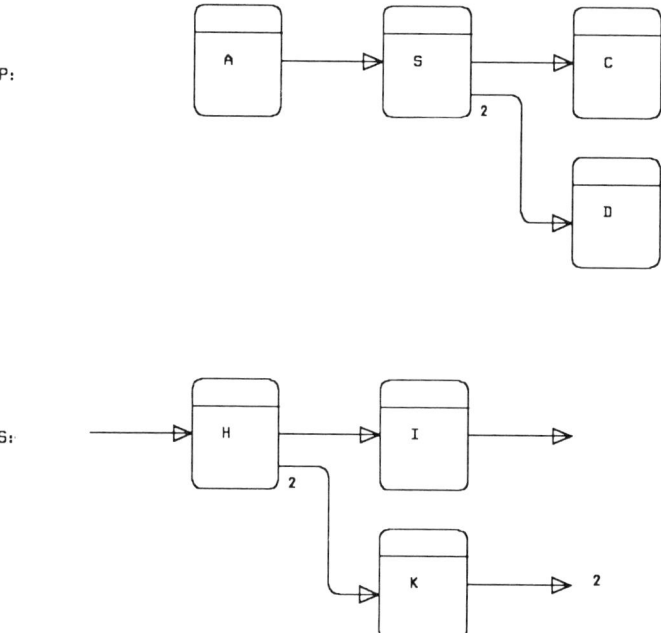

FIGURE A.7 P: A & S & C, S 2 & D. S: & H & I &, H 2 & K & 2.

The result of the above is the ability of DFDM to execute a hierarchy of data flow diagrams if executable integrands exist for each node without a further diagram definition. (Technically, a node needs to be present only if some data are sent to it at execution time. However, this is more valuable as a prototyping option than as a feature for production software because of the general inability to recover if some data is sent to a missing integrand.) Unlike Petri nets (see 'Petri nets', Section 2.7), DFDM invokes a node if data shows up for *any* input port. This is specifically because the internal coding of a node determines how it handles input ports (except for the trivial case of nodes with only one port). Thus, to have the network also specify the required data for execution requires the one who specifies the network to understand more about the internals of each integrand than would otherwise be required, and then redundantly enter that specification (and raise the unnecessary possibility of getting it wrong as well). For the same reason, early forms of data flow diagrams that showed 'and' and 'or' conditions on data flows (as in DeMarco 1978) are *not* needed or used by DFDM.

Once a data flow connection is defined between two integrands, any data entities can flow across it. DFDM needs nothing from the data flow diagram about the data – even their names. At execution time, the integrands pass a length, type, and a pointer to a contiguous block of storage each time an entity is passed. Thus the entities can be of different lengths and types each time, e.g. a static data structure once, a trigger another time, and a self-defining data object yet another time. DFDM needs to know nothing about the content of the data area (except as told to it for the 'CHAIN' and 'UNCHN' services below). Thus, copies of the same entities can flow on multiple connections, or multiple entity types can flow on the same connection.

In the absence of a service like DFDM, a designer can usually define a simple one *if* the actions of the integrands are known and are relatively simple. For example, for the network A & B & C & D, where each integrand sends forward one entity for each one it receives, a driver like DFDM would merely have to call each one in turn, passing data from one to the next until end of file. The more general case where DFDM has no knowledge of the possible flows of data is not that much more complex (the basic algorithm is to give any data passed to it to the integrand connected to that port), but is probably more than would be undertaken for a single program.

Two types of approaches seem to have emerged for using data flow mechanisms such as the one described here. One is to send through an ordered sequence of data entities, e.g. such as the set of records in a file, or related segments from a data base. This approach is similar to how batch programs have traditionally processed sequential files or related segments, and is especially useful when the number of possible entities is unknown or large. Passing an ordered sequence of data is logically how DOS and UNIX® pipes work (though they actually pass byte streams rather than distinct entities). Another approach is to pass a single data structure, where the structure maintains the ordering desired. This approach is similar to how on-line transactions process the transaction data entered by the user, and is more useful when the set of data to be processed is known to be small. Since the time ordering of the entities in the first approach is important, queues between modules would have to maintain a FIFO (first in/first out) sequence. However, the second approach could allow priority queueing as well as allowing the parts of a given structure to be processed in parallel. That does not mean the second approach would perform better, however, because a sequence of records can be processed in parallel as well – with one module processing one record while the preceding module processes the subsequent record, just as members of a bucket brigade can all pass buckets simultaneously.

2 EXECUTION-TIME INTERFACE TO INTEGRANDS

At execution time, integrands are invoked by the data flow mechanism in the same way they would be normally in the execution environment, except that the pointer to an anchor block is added to the end of the list of any specified parameters (to allow re-entry if DFDM is called from the integrands). Parameters specified in the network specification are also parsed and presented in the same way as the environment would. In the IBM 370 implementation (see Morrison 1978), subroutines and mainlines are invoked with the same standard, so no distinction is made between mainlines and subroutines for nodes. However, subroutines of different languages must be invoked differently (notably IBM 370 PL/I subroutines require certain conditions to be set, which are normally set by the PL/I mainline). It is neither desirable to require the user of an integrand to have to know or remember the implementation language of each integrand, nor to require an execution-time dictionary from which to derive it (and each of these could in any case contain incorrect information). Thus, the 370 implementation requires a shell to be attached to integrands which contains a unique string indicating the language type and branches to the normal entry point.

For the subroutine interface, the data within the input and output data fields is presented as a *structure* to the subroutine pointed to as parameter 1. Parameter 2 is a pointer to the 'ID' control block, which consists of: 'PNTRCB, LENGTH, TAG, NAME, QUAL'. (The definition of these parameters is explained under the 'Architecture definition' topic below.) These parameters give the integrand access to the length, tag, and their qualified name (i.e. with the period and unique string if any) in this executing network. It is possible to write a subroutine to match the data flow interface and still use it in normal call hierarchies. In addition, any node in the data flow diagram can be a call hierarchy itself. Normal subroutines with multiple call parameters can also be used in a data flow network without recompilation by writing a small program that receives the entire data structure, separates out the subroutine's parameters, and calls the existing subroutine.

However, nodes in a data flow diagram can do things that subroutines cannot or cannot do easily. This includes having and controlling the flows of data into and out of multiple ports. The basic service provided to an integrand at execution time is the ability to get and put data from and to its ports. The logic within an integrand is the same as if it were a mainline and the ports were input and output files. Control signals, or 'triggers', can be sent to other integrands by setting the data 'LENGTH' to 0. By convention, and for clarity in the data flow diagram, input port 0 is used as a trigger port. However, an integrand may receive control signals through any input port (any entity with a zero length). Naturally, it is possible for an integrand to react to the arrival of any data entity as though it were pure control by simply ignoring the data.

Data are usually passed by pointer to allow integrands to be re-entrant and for better performance. However, existing subroutines and mainlines are supported by an option to move the data into (and copy from) the integrand. In this case, the integrand specifies the address and maximum length for data for a 'GET'. Data longer than this maximum are lost and the integrand is given an error return code. The options of pointer and move modes need not match for connected integrands. In fact, to facilitate reuse, it is important to be able to connect integrands that put (pointer) to integrands that get (move) and vice-versa.

Many integrands can be written as subroutines and need have *no* calls to, or dependency on, DFDM. Of those that need to manage their input or output data streams, including those with multiple input or output ports, many need only 'GET' and 'PUT' (or 'IN' and 'OUT'). There are, however, conditions under which integrands could use the other DFDM services that are explained next. Integrands which 'GET' or 'PUT' (or use any of the other services described below) may be put into a wait state while other integrands are despatched. However, this is irrelevant to the coding of the integrand (normal 'READ' and 'WRITE' verbs in high level languages may suspend the program but the developer does not have to consider that when writing the code). However, integrands that 'GET' from an input port with no available data are suspended until data becomes available. Thus, it becomes important to provide an option for integrands to query the status of a port before reading from it. This is accomplished by requesting the port number of the next higher input port that has entities waiting ('NIP'). There are services to allocate a data area ('ALLOC') and obtain the length and tag for an entity ('GLT'). Additional optional services allow an integrand to find the highest input or output port number that has connected integrands ('HIP' and 'HOP'), close input or output ports ('CLIP') and 'CLOP'), and wait for a time interval ('WTIM') or on an event ('WAIT'). Optional services include the ability to put entities on a stack ('STACK'), get them back from the stack ('UNSTK'), and inquire as to the number of entities in the stack ('STKCT'). There are additional optional services to chain pointers into a single entity that can be passed to other integrands ('CHAIN'), and to unchain those entities again ('UNCHN'). Chaining requires identifying a parent entity (pointer 'PTRP'), a child entity (pointer 'PTRC'), and a location within the parent entity (pointer 'PTRP') to store the pointer to the child. One additional service not in the previously published architecture (below) is the ability to add or delete network definitions dynamically during execution of the network. This capability is a powerful one, and especially useful for building functions that can help debug a running network. However, dynamic connections can create complexities that are difficult to debug if used within the main network itself. The syntax for the call to modify the network dynamically is:

CALL DDMS ('DEFIN', ID, PNTR)

The parameters are defined as for the calls below, and the data area pointed to by 'PNTR' contains a network connection string as specified above to define connections. A connection can be broken by substituting ¬ for the & that signifies the connection. For example, A & B would add a connection between output port 1 of A and input port 1 of B, while C 3 ¬ 4 D would disconnect a connection, if any, between output port 3 of 'C' and input port 4 of 'D'. Multiple connections can be defined and broken for the same call by separating them with commas, and the string is terminated with a period.

3 DFDM ARCHITECTURE DEFINITION

The following is reprinted with permission of International Business Machines.

> The Data Flow Development Manager (DFDM) architecture allows the execution of a data flow diagram if the nodes named within the diagram exist as object modules. The object modules can be reused easily because they do not name each other (as compared with the call or attach linkage). Thus, modules can be specified, designed, prototyped, developed, generated, tested, regression tested, used, reused, and distributed easier than with other linkage techniques. Input and output is done by the modules rather than by DFDM. DFDM passes data entities among modules per specified interconnections (and invokes the modules, since they do not invoke each other).

This technology is similar to DOS pipes, but differs in several significant ways. DFDM allows multiple input and output ports, thus supporting networks of modules. Typed entities are sent rather than continuous character streams. With DFDM, no distinction is made regarding which modules do I/O.

Nodes execute as coroutines. They can be subroutines (existing or written to DFDM specifications) mainlines (existing programs or written to handle multiple streams of entities in and/or out), hierarchies of called modules, or a subassembly network definition. They must be reentrant if they are mainlines and used multiple times in the same program. DFDM subroutine parameters are: 'DATA, PARM, PORT, LENGTH, TAG, RFLAG'. DFDM mainline parameters are: 'PARM, ID'.

Mainlines may call to get from multiple input ports, put to multiple output ports, and for other services as follows ([ ] indicates optional parameters and lowercase indicates return parameters to be set by DFDM):

```
CALL DDMGET (ID, pntr[,PORT[,length[,tag]]])          – Get entity's pointer
CALL DDMS ('GET', ID, pntr[,PORT[,length[,tag]]])     – same as DDMGET
CALL DDMPUT (ID, PNTR[,PORT])                         – Put pointer's entity
CALL DDMS ('PUT', ID, PNTR[,PORT])                    – Same as DDMPUT
CALL DDMIN (ID[,DATA[,PORT[,LENGTH[,tag]]]])          – Move data in
CALL DDMS ('IN', ID[,DATA[,PORT[,LENGTH[,tag]]]])     – Same as DDMIN
CALL DDMOUT (ID[,DATA[,PORT[,LENGTH[,TAG]]]])         – Move data out
CALL DDMS ('OUT', ID[,DATA[,PORT[,LENGTH[,TAG]]]])    – Same as DDMOUT

CALL DDMS ('NIP',    ID, PORT[,IND])                  – Next port with entities (Suspend)
CALL DDMS ('ALLOC',ID, pntr[,LENGTH[,TAG]])           – Allocate data area
CALL DDMS ('GLT',    ID, PNTR[,length[,tag]])         – Get length and tag
CALL DDMS ('HIP',    ID ,port)                        – Highest connected input port
CALL DDMS ('HOP',    ID ,port)                        – Highest connected output port
CALL DDMS ('CLIP',   ID[,PORT[,IND]])                 – Close input port (Drain)
CALL DDMS ('CLOP',   ID[,PORT])                       – Close output port
CALL DDMS ('WTIM',   ID, TIME, IND)                   – Wait for time (Interval/TOD)
CALL DDMS ('WAIT',   ID, ECB)                         – Wait for MVS ECB

CALL DDMS ('STACK',  ID, PNTR)                        – Stack entity
CALL DDMS ('UNSTK',  ID, pntr)                        – Unstack entity LIFO
CALL DDMS ('STKCT',  ID, COUNT)                       – stack's entity count
CALL DDMS ('CHAIN',  ID, PTRI, PTRC, PTRP)            – Chain entities
CALL DDMS ('UNCHN',  ID, PTRI, PTRC)                  – Unchain entities
```

Return codes are: 0-Normal. 4-entity truncated ('IN'), no entities waiting ('NIP'). 12-connected ports all closed. 16-no connected port or invalid port number, wait list full ('WAIT'), stack empty ('UNSTK'), forced timer completion ('WTIM'), 'PTRI' invalid ('CHAIN'/'UNCHN'). 20-'PNTR' invalid. 24-Invalid call.

The parameters are:

DATA A contiguous area for/of an entity (e.g. a structure).
PARM A variable length character string (like MVS execution parms).
PORT The input and output port number (32-bit binary number, default = 1, −1 discards an output entity).
LENGTH The length of the entity or data area (32-bit binary number).
TAG Optional format indicator passed with entities (32-bit binary number: 0 = undefined, 1 = break, 2 = start of file, 3 = end of file, other positive numbers reserved).
RFLAG 32-bit binary number (1 = Do not re-invoke this coroutine).
ID PNTRCB, LENGTH, TAG, NAME, QUAL (control block interface).
PNTRCB 32-bit pointer to the coroutine's DFDM control block.
NAME 32-character coroutine name.
QUAL 16-character name qualifier.
PNTR 32-bit pointer to the entity (always set on entry).
PTRP 32-bit pointer to the parent entity.
PTRC 32-bit pointer to the child entity.
PTRI 32-bit pointer to the location for PTRC within the parent.
COUNT 32-bit binary count field.
IND 1 character: (NIP: 'S' = Suspend until entity arrives, 'N' = No Suspend. CLIP: 'D' = destroy waiting entities, 'A' = entities destroyed when Application ends. WTIM: 'I' = interval, 'T' = time of day.)
TIME 8 character string: 'HHMMSSth' (t=tenths, h = hundredths).
ECB MVS Event Control Block.

DFDM connections are specified by:

[Subnetwork-name:]
name[.qual][(parm)][outport#]&[(opt)][inport#] name[.qual][(parm)], . . .
name[.qual][(parm)][outport#]&[(opt)][inport#] name[.qual][(parm)], . . .

name the name of the coroutine (network node).
qual any character string which uniquely identifies occurrences of the same coroutine within the same network. (e.g., P.1, P.2B).
parm an execution-time parameter for the coroutine.
outport# the output port number of the preceding coroutine (default = 1).
& indicates a connection (and has a synonym →).
opt a specification for connection name (or queue size if numeric).
inport# the input port number for the coroutine to its right (default = 1).

Multiple networks can be specified, separated by commas. Connections between network nodes and the boundary of lower level networks are specified in the form:

boundary-port# & name and/or name & boundary-port#

Multiple connections in a sequence can be specified without commas in the form A&B&C (optionally including ports, qualifiers and entity-ids).

Although DFDM allows sophisticated capabilities, it supports the easiest development and reuse known. The only thing subroutine nodes *must* understand is 'DATA'. Many mainlines need only 'GET' and 'PUT' (or 'IN' and 'OUT'), using 'PNTR' or 'DATA' and maybe 'PORT'. For example, A → B → C (or A 1 & 1 B,B 1 & 1 C) defines the data flow diagram in Figure A.1.

It is also easy to write the modules:

```
ENTRY A USING ID           ENTRY B USING DATA    ENTRY C USING DATA
DO UNTIL EOF                 process DATA          WRITE DATA
  READ REC                   RETURN                RETURN
  CALL DDMOUT (ID, REC)
ENDDO
```

See Stevens (1982) for a description of the power and usefulness of the DFDM architecture.

APPENDIX B
AVOIDING DEADLOCKS WITH DATA FLOW

Because data passed in data flow networks are accessible by one node at a time only, the normal potential for deadlocks due to asynchronous update of that data in asynchronous systems is not present for the data flows among the nodes. The term 'network' in the context of data flow diagrams refers to the shape of the diagram that describes the interconnections of nodes rather than to telecommunications networks. Whether one or more data flow connections are via a communication line is immaterial to the conditions of deadlock. As in any program, it is possible for nodes in data flow networks to deadlock on shared resources other than passed data. In a data flow network, each node acts like a separate program since each can run asynchronously from the others.) It is also possible for program errors to cause abends or endless loops with or without data being passed. While it is possible to construct situations that can deadlock a dat flow network due to passed data, there are only four ways that a data flow network can deadlock on flows of data. Each of the four ways is a theoretical construction, unlikely to represent the solutions to real problems since they all have nodes that demand data in ways that differ from how other nodes create them. This appendix contains a proof that these are the only four ways in which a data flow network can deadlock on flows of data. It then indicates ways to design in order to avoid those four theoretical potentials for deadlock.

Figure B.1 shows a network that deadlocks if node X only sends data out port 2 and node Y insists on receiving data only in port 1. The asterisks indicate that node Y is suspended waiting to read data and node X is suspended trying to write to a connection with a full queue. Any other mismatch between what X sends and what Y *insists* on can similarly deadlock. However, this seems to be an unrealistic case that does not solve any real problem since X and Y implement incompatible definitions of how the data should be handled. The data should be handled in one of these ways (or neither). Thus, either X or Y (or both) are implemented incorrectly. Figure B.2 shows the general case of a deadlock potential from the merging of two data streams that previously diverged. Again, the asterisks indicate that the node where the data streams merge is waiting to read from a

220 APPENDICES

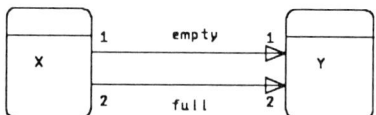

FIGURE B.1 Example: merge-deadlock

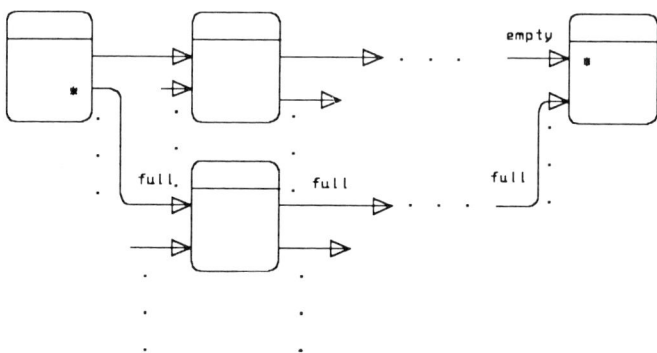

FIGURE B.2 Potential merge–deadlock

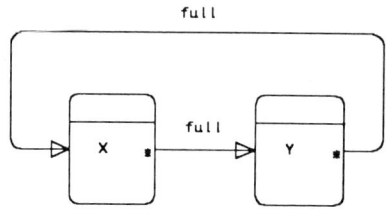

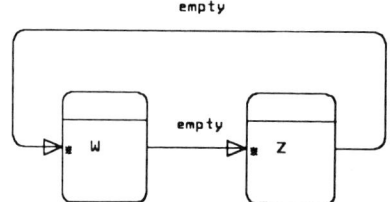

FIGURE B.3 Example: loop-deadlocks

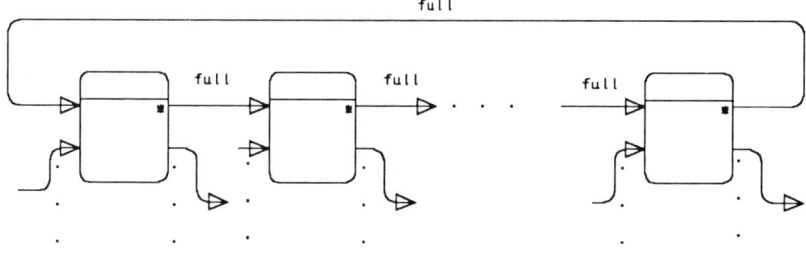

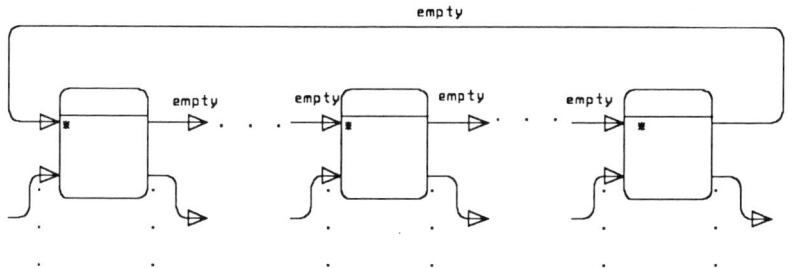

FIGURE B.4 Potential loop-deadlocks

port with no data and the node where the streams diverged is waiting to write to a port with a full queue.

There are only two other ways in which a network can deadlock on data flows. Examples of these are shown in Figure B.3. In the first network, X first creates one data entity and then outputs an entity for each entity it accepts. Y creates two output entities for each one it accepts. Eventually, for any finite queue lengths, the queues between X and Y and between Y and X will both be full. In the second network in Figure B.3, W immediately reads from its input port, and so does Z. Figure B.4 shows the general cases of deadlock potential from loops of data flow. There can be additional connections to the same and other input or output ports of any node in Figure B.4. A variation of both networks in Figure B.4 is to connect the output port of a node directly to its own input port. The top network in Figure B.4 can deadlock if any node in the loop puts out more data entities than it accepts (unless there is an elimination of entities somewhere else in the loop that exactly balances the extra creations). The bottom network in Figure B.4 deadlocks when nodes *require* data that will never arrive. Again, these both represent design errors since data are required to arrive in a different way than they are created.

1 PROOF

The following is a proof that the only ways that data flow networks can deadlock due to the flows of data among the nodes are the situations depicted in Figures B.2 and B.4. Consider a data flow network of a finite number of nodes connected only by flows of data. Replace each node that has a logical data flow decomposition by the network that describes its decomposition; then each node in the resulting diagram is an executable node (or call hierarchy of nodes). If a node in the resulting network is a hierarchy of called nodes, treat it as a single node for purposes of this deadlock analysis. Each node may have one or more input ports and one or more output ports – but must have at least one input or output port connecting it to the other nodes in the network (otherwise it is not part of the network and can be ignored). Each output port of a node can be connected to one or more input ports of other nodes or to its own input ports. Each input port can be connected from one or more output ports of other nodes or from its own output ports. Every node can be reached from any other node by following some set of connections among the nodes. Otherwise the network consists of two or more different networks, and this analysis should be applied to each of those networks.

Some assumptions are made about the way nodes are invoked as follows. These include other ways in which nodes could be suspended due to passed data, and are either handled by the dispatcher (such as that described in Appendix A above) or constitute additional ways in which networks can deadlock due to passed data:

1. Nodes with input data waiting *at any port* will be invoked so that they can process those data (like subroutines, nodes can exit between executions).
2. A node gets a bad return code if:
   (a) it writes to or reads from a port not connected to another node or connected to nodes which are permanently ended
   (b) the network has no data waiting on any connection and all nodes have excited, permanently ended, or suspended waiting to read input data.
3. Nodes are considered permanently ended and are not invoked again if they:
   (a) abend
   (b) exit and have no input ports
   (c) exit and have input ports connected only to nodes which are permanently ended
   (d) repeat an action that resulted in a bad return code.
4. The network is considered ended when every node has exited or is permanently ended (or was never started), and there is no data waiting on any connection.

Each node must be in one of six states, as follows:

1. Waiting to be invoked if input data arrives.
2. Executable (is currently executing, has not permanently ended and has input data waiting, or is waiting to continue execution after reading from a port with data or writing to a port without a full queue).
3. Suspended waiting for some other resource than passed data.
4. Suspended waiting to read from a port with no data.

5. Suspended waiting to write data to a connection with a full queue.
6. Permanently ended (due to an abend, repeated errors, exiting with no input ports connected to any nodes which are not permanently ended, or its own request).

A network is not deadlocked on data flows if it has one or more nodes in states 2 or 3 above, nor if all nodes are in states 1 and/or 6. A network is *deadlocked* on data flows if:

(a) no nodes are in states 2 (executable) or 3, and
(b) one or more nodes are in states 4 or 5 (i.e. suspended, but not on some other resource).

Thus, a network deadlocked on data flow has one or more nodes in states 4 or 5, with the rest of the nodes in states 1 or 6. If there is a node in state 5 (i.e. waiting to write to a connection with a full queue), trace forward through that node's output port with the full queue. The next node must be in states 4 or 5 (since it cannot be connected to a full queue and be in states 1 or 6). If the next node is in state 5, trace forward through the output port it has with the full queue. Since there cannot be an infinite sequence of nodes in state 5 in a finite network, there eventually either has to be a loop back to some node in state 5 previously encountered (i.e. the first situation in Figure B.4) or a node in state 4 must be reached. That is, every network deadlocked on data flow with a node in state 5 must either have a loop of nodes all in state 5 each with a full queue, or must have a node in state 4 which can be reached by following through nodes each in state 5 via their output ports with the full queues (or both).

If there is a node in state 4 in the network, trace backward from it via the port from which it is trying to read. The preceding node(s) must be in states 1, 4, 5, or 6 (since all nodes must be in only these states if the network is deadlocked on data flow). If every preceding node was in state 6 (permanently ended) then this node in state 4 would not be suspended waiting for input because it would get a return code indicating no more data. Thus, there must be some preceding node in states 1, 4, or 5. If the preceding node is in states 1 or 4, then it has at least one input port with no data. Trace backwards through nodes in states 1 or 4 all paths through ports with no data. Since there cannot be an infinite sequence of nodes in states 1 or 4 in a finite network, there eventually either has to be a loop back to some node in states 1 or 4 which was encountered earlier (i.e. the second network in Figure B.4), or a node in state 5 must be reached. That is, every network deadlocked on data flow with a node in state 4 must have a loop as in the second case in Figure B.4, or a preceding node in state 5, or both.

Except for the network loops shown in Figure B.4, for each node in state 5, there must be a following node in state 4 that can be reached by tracing through its full queue. In addition, for every node in state 4, there is a preceding node in state 5 that can be reached by tracing through the queue from which it is trying to read – and if this is a new node in state 5, then it must be suspended due to another node in state 4. If that node in state 4 has not already been encountered, then it has to be suspended due to another node in state 5. Since the network is finite, a node must eventually be reached that has been encountered before – i.e. there is at least one pair of nodes in states 4 and 5 as in Figure B.2 – i.e. a node in state 4 that is suspended due to a node in state 5 that is suspended due to that same node in state 4. That is, the only ways that networks can deadlock due to the flows of data among the nodes are as depicted in Figure B.2, B.4, or both. Naturally, once a situation shown in Figures B.2 and B.4 exists, other nodes can be suspended trying to write data to, or to obtain data from, the deadlocked nodes shown.

2 AVOIDING DEADLOCKS FROM DATA FLOWS

What remains is to show ways to avoid deadlocks from data flows and to detect and break deadlocks that do occur. These can be applied to an entire network or just to portions of a network. There are at least three ways to avoid designing networks which can deadlock on flows of data, as shown in Figure B.2:

1. A network in which all nodes have at most one input port cannot lock in this manner.
2. Have nodes with multiple input ports test for input and read only if some data is available.
3. Correctly determine how data might be produced and never have a node with multiple input ports that insists that data arrive at those ports in ways that are not guaranteed to happen.

There are at least four ways to avoid deadlocks of the type shown in Figure B.4 in networks of nodes connected by flows of data:

1. Networks where all connections can be drawn so that they flow downward or rightward cannot have a loop and thus cannot deadlock in this way.
2. For any remaining connection that goes upward or to the left, if the queue is longer than the largest number of data entities that can occur on that connection, then it cannot deadlock with full queues. (While this is impossible to guarantee in general, it can be possible for specific cases).
3. If nodes that are part of any loop absorb data in ways consistent with how it will be created or passed along, then it cannot deadlock due to full queues. This will be true, for example, if all such nodes never produce more entities than they accept (and the queue size is larger than one).
4. In order to avoid a loop with empty queues (all nodes in the loop in condition 1 or 4), make sure that integrands do not insist on receiving data that will not arrive. The 'NIP' function of DFDM (see Appendix A) can be used to determine whether there are data at an input port before reading unconditionally (with a 'GET' or 'IN') and being suspended until data arrive.

Deadlocks can be detected by the dispatcher looking for the conditions of deadlocks on data flows shown above: there are no executable nodes and every suspended node is either waiting to put data to some output port with a full queue, or waiting to receive data from an input port with no available data. Deadlocks of the type shown in Figure B.2 can be broken by giving a return code to a node in state 4 indicating that it has data waiting at another port. Then, either that node reads the data, repeats the error (which can be the condition to terminate execution of the node permanently), or the network enters another state. Deadlocks of the type in Figure B.4 can be broken by finding a node in state 4 or 5. If there is a node in state 4, give it a return code indicating that it has data waiting for another port (as above). If there are no nodes in state 4, then give a node in state 5 a return code indicating that the queue for its output port is full. If its next interaction is to try to output data to the same port again, then terminate its execution permanently. As a practical matter, it would be pertinent to give priority to dispatching nodes that have an input port with a connection with a full queue. In addition, more error conditions can be resolved gracefully if the last slot in each queue is reserved to hold the data from a node in condition 5 when it is given the return code that its output queue is full. Since it is possible for networks to repeat the deadlock conditions indefinitely, even after the deadlock detection and breaking actions above, there should be some limit on the number of deadlock condition codes that are returned to a node before it is permanently terminated.

APPENDIX C
PROBLEMS

CHAPTER 1

1.1 Define the verb 'software design'.
1.2 Define the noun 'software design'.
1.3 What makes a design a 'good' design?
1.4 What is the most important input to design?
1.5 Give several examples of design diagrams (whether software or other types of design diagrams).

CHAPTER 2

2.1 Why is reducing complexity important?
2.2 Why are hierarchies important?
2.3 What are the four possible graphical objects in data flow diagrams?
2.4 What makes a hierarchy of data flow diagrams 'balanced'?
2.5 What type of diagram is used in the method of 'Essential Systems Analysis'?
2.6 Describe the concept of 'essence' (of a system).
2.7 What is the 'incarnation' of a system?
2.8 Name three characteristics of existing systems that can make finding their essence difficult. Give an illustration of each characteristic in real-world or computer systems.
2.9 Does event-partitioning apply to an essential model or to the model of the incarnation, or both?
2.10 Describe 'event-partitioning'.
2.11 Name three graphical components included within transformation schema diagrams that are not in standard data flow diagrams.
2.12 Explain something unique about each of the graphical elements named in question 2.11.
2.13 What are the rules for expanding control transformations to a lower level diagrams? Why?

2.14 Name three graphical symbols in a call hierarchy chart.
2.15 Name four of the six kinds of binding. Order them from weak to strong. Give an example of each type.
2.16 What is the strongest type of binding? How can it be identified?
2.17 Name three things that can cause coupling to increase.
2.18 What two things can be communicated by software integrands? Which results in lower coupling and why?
2.19 What are the three levels of diagrams used in Box Structured Design and which decomposes into which?
2.20 Name the three parts of a black box.
2.21 Name three of the four types of clear boxes. Draw examples of each.
2.22 What are Petri nets useful for?
2.23 Name the two basic parts of a Petri net.
2.24 What is a Petri net *marking*?
2.25 When can a transition fire?
2.26 What happens to the distribution of tokens in a Petri net when a transition fires?
2.27 Draw a Petri net with a transition that will change the number of tokens in the net when it fires. Draw a Petri net with a transition that does not change the number of tokens when it fires (these transitions can be in the same Petri net).
2.28 If the Petri net in Figure 2.92 has the marking (1,3,1,0,4,2), is transition t_3 enabled? If so, what will the resulting marking be if transition t_3 fires?
2.29 Given an initial marking of (2,0,0,2,5,1) for the Petri net in Figure 2.92:
  (a) Can the number of tokens in p_2 ever exceed one? If so, how; and if not, why not?
  (b) Can the number of tokens in one of the places in the net ever become infinite? If so, how; and if not, why not?
  (c) Can the net ever deadlock? If so how?
  (d) Is it possible to reach marking (0,1,1,3,5,2)? If so, how?
  (e) Is the firing sequence $t_1 t_2 t_2 t_3 t_4 t_5 t_5 t_5$ possible?

CHAPTER 3

3.1 What are the conditions for the execution of the function 'J' in the left side of Figure 3.2 (Figure 3.3 may help)? Why are the conditions for executing 'J' on the right side of Figure 3.2? Are they the same?
3.2 What is a 'proper', program relative to Structured Programming?
3.3 What is an 'equivalent' program?
3.4 Given 'structured code', give a short general description of 'Action Diagrams'.
3.5 What are the parts of a state transition diagram?
3.6 What identifies a box in a state transition diagram as an 'initial state'?
3.7 When are state transition diagrams most useful?
3.8 When are Jackson charts most useful?
3.9 Name three possible parts of a decision table.
3.10 If a triangular decision table has seventeen conditions, how many columns of condition combinations will it have?

CHAPTER 4

4.1 Name two parts of an 'ER' data model. For what are ER models especially useful?
4.2 What is a functional dependency? Give an example.
4.3 What is a 'key'?
4.4 Give two examples of constraints on data.
4.5 What are the important things to know about the transactions that the users want in the system?
4.6 Describe generally what is done to 'normalize' data. Why is it important?
4.7 Name two of the three common data base models.
4.8 What is an important consideration for physical data base design?

CHAPTER 5

5.1 Name three ways in which application development tools can be integrated. Rank them in order of priority.
5.2 Are design reviews a good place for management to evaluate designers? If so, why; and if not, why not?
5.3 Name a general systems principle that can help in designing software.
5.4 Name at least three characteristics that enable reuse.
5.5 How does a call instruction inhibit reuse?
5.6 Why is the concept of an 'Abstract Data Type' useful?
5.7 Name three concepts often associated with 'Object-Oriented'.
5.8 Name two approaches for software design that can enhance its portability. Why do they help?
5.9 What should be done before optimizing software for performance?

APPENDIX D
ANSWERS TO PROBLEMS

CHAPTER 1

1.1 Sofware design is the process of inventing, improving, and selecting among alternative solutions and describing programs that meet users' requirements within the constraints of the environment and based on relevant criteria. Key concepts include inventing, selecting, meeting requirements, and relevant criteria.

1.2 A software design is a usable and understandable description of the chosen alternative for computer programs. Key concepts include usable (by the implementers and maintainers to accomplish what is required), understandable (by the reviewers, implementers, and maintainers), and description; a design does *not* contain all the detail that will end up in the implementation. It is a description – sufficiently usable and understandable to proceed accurately with implementation.

1.3 A design is a 'good' design depending on how well it meets and balances the requirements, constraints, and criteria. Design always involves trade-offs between various constraints – otherwise there is an advantage that could be gained without giving up anything (which would be a poor design). A good design is one that includes every advantage that can be included *without* compromising other advantages, and that strikes an appropriate balance among advantages that conflict.

1.4 The most important input to design is understanding – understanding of the requirements, constraints, criteria, software and hardware capabilities, costs of possible alternatives, and intended users. Some of this comes in the requirements and some by experience. The more that is known of the preceding concepts, the better the designer can make the trade-offs that are inherent in design.

1.5 Data flow diagrams, call hierarchy charts, data model diagrams, flow charts, ER diagrams, system flowcharts, circuit diagrams, blueprints (for all industries), plumbing diagrams, wiring diagrams, and architectural drawings. Allow any valid design diagrams. Organization charts and artwork are not examples since they are not used for designing something else (even though someone has to design how *they* will look).

CHAPTER 2

2.1 Making the project simpler improves the productivity and quality of every other development activity. When the project is too difficult, activities become more difficult and time-consuming and will contain more errors. And if the project is *too* difficult it may never be completed – which would make even the best (partial) design useless.

2.2 People can only deal comfortably and accurately with about as much information as can fit on a page of paper. Hierarchies allow the designer, reviewers, implementers, and maintainers to concentrate on one page of the design at a time, no matter where in the hierarchy (including the top levels).

2.3 Data flow diagrams can contain processes – rectangles or circles; external entities – squares; data stores – parallel lines (possibly closed at one end); and data flows – arrows.

2.4 A hierarchy of data flow diagrams is balanced if the flows going in and out of lower level diagrams equal the data going into and out of the node that represents it in the higher level diagram – except for trivial flows of rejected data.

2.5 Essential Systems Analysis is a method for software design that uses standard data flow diagrams.

2.6 The essence is that memory and those activities that would be required regardless of the implementation choices and without having to compensate for any errors or limitations of the system itself. Memory and activities needed to compensate for errors in manual or automated systems outside of this one *are* part of the essence of this system.

2.7 The incarnation of a system is a chosen implementation of it using real-world fallible technology. An incarnation includes the essential activities and memory plus the activities and memory needed to check and compensate for possible errors and limitations of the people, hardware, and software within the system.

2.8 Characteristics of systems that can make finding the essence difficult include:

1. Fragmentation – many companies have more than one office or location.
2. Conglomeration – many implements have equipment on them that exists primarily for safety purposes.
3. Extraneousness – conveyor belts in automobile production lines, though useful, are extraneous to the essential process of building cars and exist to compensate for the fact that the workers cannot possibly perform all work at the same exact location all the time.
4. Redundancy – the space shuttle has five computers in order to assure quality and availability (even though one could fly it alone).
5. Convolution – data encryption mechanisms are necessary in order to protect information that must be kept secret, but are not part of the essence of storing (or sending) information.
6. Vastness – software systems with millions of lines of code exist and are vast. Trying simply to catalog every function that such a system would contain can be a major undertaking.

ANSWERS TO PROBLEMS   231

2.9 As defined by McMenamin and Palmer, event-partitioning applies only to the essential model. However, a similar concept can be used to partition the incarnation processes also.

2.10 The essential model is divided such that each essential activity contains the system's entire planned response to a single event. After that activity's response is complete, the system can go idle until another event (including the occurrence of a particular time) without leaving any required system action incomplete.

2.11 Transformation schema include time-continuous flows – shown with arrows with double arrowheads; event flows – shown as dashed arrows; control transformations – processes with dotted lines for their borders; and event stores – shown as a store with a dotted border.

2.12 Time-continuous flows exist at all points in time. Event flows send control rather than data (although by passing something that can be viewed as data – but the purpose is to control the target rather than just to send it information that it can use as it chooses). Control transformations accept only event flows as inputs and produce only event flows as outputs. Note that data transformations can both accept event flows as inputs and produce event flows as outputs. However, data transformations will also accept and produce data flows. Also, event flows into control transformations can be of any meaning, but event flows into data transformations should be binary start/stop, on/off, enable/disable, or re-set types of signals. Event flows entering a diagram can be connected directly to an event store without having to go through an intervening transformation (as is required with data stores).

2.13 Control transformations may not be expanded to a lower level diagram. Doing so would necessarily cause the resulting control aspects to be in a separate diagram from the lower level diagram expansion of the adjacent data transformation to that control transformation. Instead, control aspects are grouped within data transformations until they reach a level where they can be shown as primitive components – ones that will not be expanded further.

2.14 Call hierarchy charts include modules – shown as rectangles; calls – shown as arrows from the calling module to the called module annotated by the parameters that are passed; diamonds – indicating conditional calls; loops – which are repetitive calls; and connectors – shown as small circles to connect to modules either on or off the page.

2.15 Six types of binding identified by Structured Design, from strong to weak include:

1. Functional – 'Calculate Hourly Pay'.
2. Sequential – 'Calculate Hourly Pay and Print Paycheck'.
3. Communicational – 'Print Paycheck and Store Amount in Payroll File'.
4. Temporal – 'Close Print File and Payroll File'.
5. Logical – 'Calculate Gross Hourly Pay and National Taxes'.
6. Coincidental – 'Read Time Card and Store Gross Pay in Payroll File'.

2.16 The strongest type of binding is 'functional' binding. Functional binding can be detected by writing a phrase that describes what the integrand does and checking to see if the phrase has only one clause with a single specific verb and a single specific object such as 'Edit Name Field'.

2.17 In general, coupling is increased by anything that increases the need to consider one integrand in order to design, write, understand, debug, or change another. Most coupling is caused by connections. The factors of connections that can increase coupling are: what is communicated, the type of the connection, how much data is passed across the connection, and how obvious and easy to understand the connection is.

2.18 The two types of things that can be communicated are control and data. Sharing data results in lower coupling because viewers do not have to consider the sender and the receiver of the control to determine if the control is interpreted by the receiver as intended by the sender.

2.19 Box Structured Design uses *black boxes*, which are decomposed into *state machines*, which are decomposed into *clear boxes*. The clear boxes contain multiple interconnected black boxes, each of which can then be decomposed again into state machines, etc.

2.20 A black box consists of the box itself, stimuli entering the box, and responses leaving the box.

2.21 The four types of clear boxes in Box Structured Design include: sequence, iteration, alternation, and parallel clear boxes. Figure 2.68 illustrates each type.

2.22 Petri nets are particularly useful for modeling and analyzing systems with independent asynchronous components.

2.23 A Petri net consists of *places* (or conditions) and *transitions* (or events).

2.24 A marking is a specific distribution of tokens in a Petri net. A token is a dot that indicates that the condition represented by a place is true.

2.25 A transition can fire if and only if the places that have arrows from them to that transition each contain at least one token.

2.26 A token is removed from each of the places with arrows pointing into the transition that fired and a token is added to each of the places with arrows pointing to them from the transition that fired.

2.27 The number of tokens in a Petri net will stay the same when a transition fires if and only if the number of arrows pointing into the transition equals the number of arrows from the transition to the places. (The number of input and output places do not have to be equal since multiple arrows can terminate at the same place from the same transition and a place can be both an input place and an output place for the same transition.)

2.28 Transition t_3 is enabled because places p_2 and p_3 each have at least one token. The marking that will result if t_3 fires is (1,3,0,1,4,2). One token is removed from each of p_2 and p_3 and one token is added to each of p_2 and p_4 – leaving the number of tokens in p_2 unchanged.

2.29 Given an initial marking of (2,0,0,2,5,1) for the Petri net in Figure 2.92:

1. The number of tokens in $_2$ will be two if transition t_1 fires twice (which it can do with an initial marking of 2 in place p_1).

ANSWERS TO PROBLEMS   233

2. The initial markings are finite. Transitions t_1 and t_2 each increase the number of tokens each time they fire, but transition t_1 can only fire twice since there is no way to add tokens to place p_1. Transitions t_3 and t_5 do not change the number of tokens when they fire and transition t_4 decreases the number of tokens by three every time it fires. Transition t_2 only requires a token in place P_3 in order to fire and leaves the token in p_3. Thus, once transition t_1 fires, t_2 may fire an infinite number of times resulting in an infinite number of tokens in place p_5.

3. Once transition t_1 fires twice, place p_1 is empty and will remain so. Thus transition t_1 cannot be enabled. A net that has one or more transitions that cannot be enabled is deadlocked.

4. Transition t_1 has to fire twice to remove the two initial tokens from place p_1. Firing transition t_5 puts the second token in p_6 and leaves p_2 with the desired one. Firing transition t_2 will not change the number of tokens in p_3, but firing t_3 will reduce the tokens in p_3 to one and increase the tokens in p_4 from two to three as desired.

5. No. It is impossible for t_5 to fire more than two times with place p_1 starting with 2 and place p_2 with 0 because the most p_2 can ever have in it is two.

CHAPTER 3

3.1 The conditions for the execution of 'J' on both sides of Figure 3.2 are if 'p' and 'v' are both true.

3.2 A 'proper' program is one with only one starting point, only one exit, no code that cannot be reached and no necessarily-infinite loops.

3.3 An 'equivalent' program is one that executes the same functions in the same order. It may not execute in the same time – thus 'equivalent' programs that are time-dependent can execute differently and even calculate different answers.

3.4 Action Diagrams are structured code that is indented and that has brackets connecting the parts of the standard Structured Programming figures.

3.5 State transition diagrams contain boxes that represent possible states for the system, and arrows connecting those boxes that represent possible transitions among those states.

3.6 The initial state is indicated by a box with an arrow into it from no other state. There should be only one of these boxes (and arrows) on any one state transition diagram.

3.7 State transition diagrams are most useful for a system that responds to the same input in different ways depending on the system's internal state, and the number of internal states and possible transitions among them are relatively small.

3.8 Jackson charts are useful for documenting the layout of two-dimensional forms or for describing logic whose structure is based primarily on the layout of such forms.

3.9 A decision table may contain an initialization section, a condition section, an action section, an exit section, and a termination section.

3.10 A triangular decision table has one column where each condition is true for the first time (or, alternatively, false for the first time) and then one more column where all the conditions are false (or, alternatively, true). Thus a triangular decision table with seventeen conditions will have eighteen columns of conditions.

CHAPTER 4

4.1 Entity–relationship data models have entities (similar to nouns), attributes of those entities (similar to adjectives), and relationships (similar to verbs). ER models are especially useful for *describing* data or other things.

4.2 A functional dependency exists between two attributes if one uniquely determines the other. Employee numbers is a good example. They are assigned to employees in order to uniquely identify each employee (within the context of that company).

4.3 A key is an attribute, or set of attributes, that identify an entity uniquely.

4.4 Constraints on valid data that can be entered into a system include valid ranges for numbers (e.g. employee numbers greater than zero and up to 999999 for six-digit employee numbers), valid character strings (e.g. for state or post office districts), functional dependencies among attributes (e.g. employee number uniquely determines an employee), other dependencies among entity types (e.g. only managers have employees working for them).

4.5 In order to create the best design for the data to be stored in the system, it is helpful to know who will use the transaction, how often, what data it will access, how it will use the data (create, read, update, or delete), security requirements, priority, possible concurrent update, and whether the transaction will be batch, on-line, or distributed.

4.6 Data is normalized by grouping attributes such that the attributes in each relation are dependent on the key, the whole key, and nothing but the key. Normalization prevents redundancy and prevents update, insertion, and deletion anomalies where reasonable actions on one relation would otherwise require implicit activities to other relations to prevent loss of data or inconsistent data.

4.7 The three most common data base models are: hierarchical, network, and relational.

4.8 The most important consideration is to implement a schema so that it accurately supports the data accesses required by the users. Another important consideration is to provide good performance based on how the users will access the data.

CHAPTER 5

5.1 Application development tools can be integrated because of their ability to work on the same software system, be accessed from the same workstation, share data they gather and create, and by having similar user interfaces. The suggested priority is in the order listed (with high priority first). However, discussion and specific situations may result in a consensus on a different ordering.

5.2 Reviews should *never* be used as a vehicle for evaluating the person whose work product is being reviewed. The developer of a work product can usually find the most errors if the atmosphere is conducive. Even a suspicion that the results could be used for an evaluation will cause the developer to find few, if any, errors and to waste valuable time challenging whether what others find are errors or who is responsible for them.

5.3 Two systems principles which are very helpful in designing software systems are to help people do the things they wish to do and to look to natural human endeavors for rules for systems that work.

5.4 The characteristics that items that are reused to any great extend seem to have are:
1. It serves a useful purpose.
2. The user knows the item exists and can acquire it.
3. The user knows how to use it.
4. It can be used without having to modify it internally.
5. There is a way to get it fixed (or replaced, IF inexpensive).

5.5 A call instruction imbeds the name of the called module inside the calling module. Then, in order to reuse the call in another environment where it is to send data to a different called module, the caller has to be modified internally.

5.6 The idea of an 'Abstract Data Type' is to isolate structured data from being accessed by multiple integrands directly. Isolating the data can reduce the effort necessary should there be a need to modify the structured data. Abstract Data Types allow access to the data through accessing functions – usually create, retrieve, update, and delete. Thus, Abstract Data Types reduce maintenance only for situations where more than four integrands would otherwise access the structured data directly.

5.7 Several concepts associated with 'Object-Oriented' include the following:
1. Sending messages to 'objects'.
2. Declaring the type of data and functions.
3. Associating all valid functions with data to make an object.
4. Combining functions and data to make an object.
5. Inheritance, and multiple inheritance.
6. Reuse.
7. Icon-oriented user interfaces.

Object-Oriented is a rapidly evolving area. Note that as Object-Oriented concepts evolve, items on this list may disappear and new ones may be added.

5.8 One of the most important ways to improve portability is to design the software as a combination of independent integrands. Then individual integrands can be modified or replaced in another execution environment easily and without necessarily having to consider or modify adjacent integrands. A second way to improve portability is to separate input/output and logic that processes the data into different integrands. Then each can be changed independently of the other.

5.9 Software should be implemented as simply as possible and it should be observed to contribute significantly to, or have, a performance problem before being optimized.

APPENDIX E
GLOSSARY

Action Diagrams A way of depicting code that adds brackets to the nested indented control structures of Structured Programming.
A-graph A variation of data flow diagrams that can also depict flows of material.
Algorithm Any set of defined rules for solving a problem; often, but not necessarily mathematical or logic based.
Architecture The practice of designing things made up of interdependent parts.
Attribute A characteristic of an entity or of a relationship (used in data base design).

Batch program A program that can be executed without requiring interaction with its user.
Binding The strength of relationship between pieces of code with module (a concept in Structured Design).
Black box A component (used in Box Structured Design) that is defined only by its inputs and outputs.
Bottom up design The notion or approach to program design that sees requirements in terms of details of program or integrand features in the first place, and proceeds 'upwards' by progressive aggregation to a point where the collection of detailed designs fits the requirements.

Call hierarchy A diagram (used in Structured Design) that shows the calling structure of a set of modules.
Clear box A component (used in Box Structured Design) with visible inputs, outputs, internal states, and interrelation of internal black boxes.
Component As in 'software component'; a part of a design or program. Various design methods have different names for components such as 'process', 'module', and 'transformation'.
Concurrent Happening at the same time; concurrent features are often properties of systems that are designed for real-time applications.
Control transformation A component (used in the design of real-time systems) that transforms input control signals into output control signals.
Coupling Dependencies among modules (a concept in Structured Design). Coupling is

increased by anything that increases the need to consider one module in order to design, write, understand, debug, or change another.

Data transformation A component (used in the design of real-time systems) that transforms input control or data signals into output control or data signals.

Data flow diagram A diagram (used in Structured Analysis and Essential Systems Analysis) that indicates the flow of information among (potentially) asynchronous components.

Decision table A tabular way of depicting actions that are to occur based on combinations of multiple conditions.

Decision tree A graphical way of depicting actions that are to occur based on combinations of multiple conditions.

Design (*see Software Design.*)

Design module A component of a design.

Efficiency Of programs, often expressed in terms of the computer cycles required to execute the program or the amount of main memory required by the executing program.

Entity A representation of a person, place, or thing (used in data base design).

Essence A concept (used in Essential Systems Analysis) to represent the implementation-independent parts of a system.

Essential Systems Analysis A method for designing software using data flow diagrams.

Execute The dynamic behavior of a program, translated into a working state for its defined equipment. Synonyms in this context are 'run' and 'operate'.

Flowchart A pictorial representation of the structure of code.

Functional specification (FS) The document that acts as the definition of the software system to be developed.

Incarnation A concept (used in Essential Systems Analysis) to represent the implementation-dependent parts of a system.

Information hiding A concept, due to Parnas and of use in low level design of integrands and programs in which complex data structures are accessed only through code that can manipulate that data as required rather than have the data accessed directly from many places in the program or programs.

Integrand The smallest part of a program structure directly accessible by assigned name, apart from data. An integrand may be a few statements of code, several dozen, or more.

Jackson design A software design method characterized by the use of diagrams showing sequence, iteration, and choice.

Life cycle The main activities in software development. Generally used as a management model of the process.

Method An explicit and generally accepted way of doing something. Specifically, in software design, a method will comprise a procedure to be adopted, and a notation (or language) for depicting the result. Either or both, or neither, of the procedure and notation may be elaborate, relatively simple, or even quite trivial.
Methodology A term used loosely to mean 'method', or the procedure of a method. Its proper meaning concerns the science and study of methods.
Module A named component that itself may contain subcomponents. A very imprecise term, also used in its adjectival form 'modular' to denote not monolithic, as in 'modular design' and 'modular programming'. Design modules are whatever parts of a design are being described, and may be at a high or low level of detail.

Normalization A way to group attributes to reduce or eliminate difficulties that would otherwise result as data are changed or deleted (used in data base design).

Object-Oriented An evolving set of concepts characterized by independent (potentially) asynchronous objects that contain functions and data and send messages to other objects.
On-line program A program that will or may interact with its user during execution.

Performance (of software) The use of time or computer resources by software.
Petri net A modeling technique especially useful for analyzing to execution of interrelated asynchronous processes.
Place A component of a Petri net often used to represent a real-world condition.
Portability (of software) The ease with which software can be moved to another execution environment.
Program A set of statements in a computer language that, when translated into executable form, will cause a computer to perform specified tasks in a required way. A program may be a small number of such statements, or a larger aggregation up to any size.
Prototype An original pattern or model built to increase knowledge.

Real-time The property of applications that requires software to behave in a manner corresponding to events in the external world and, to some degree, synchronized with them. An instance would be critical response to stimuli. Consequently, the execution time of programs becomes a critical feature and software systems for real-time applications may contain highly elaborate devices to achieve a required response-time. *Also*: a type of system characterized by the need to focus on timing issues in order to create a properly working system of interaction asynchronous components.
Relationship A named connection between two entities (used in data base design).
Reuse (of code) The use of code written previously to make a computer do something that is needed.

Quality Of software in general; the properties of compliance and modifiability.

Software design (verb)   The process of inventing and selecting among alternative solutions to the requirements for computer software.

Software design (noun)   A usable and understandable description of a chosen software solution.

Software development   The set of activities in specification, design, implementation, and validation required to produce programs to satisfy their requirements when executed as software.

Software engineer   A person versed in software engineering and skilled in its enactment.

Software engineering   The corpus of knowledge, from computer science and empirical practice, whereby software development may be done best.

Software system   The dynamic behavior of programs, in their lowest order translated state on the computer for which they were developed.

State transition diagram   A graphical representation of various conditions a system can remember and the actions which will cause it to change its remembered condition.

State box   A component (used in Box Structured Design) with visible inputs, outputs, and internal states.

Structured Analysis   A software design method characterised by the use of data flow diagrams.

Structured Design   A software design method for functional decomposition illustrated by the use of call-hierarchies.

Structured English   (*see Structured Natural Language*).

Structured Natural Language   The application of rules of Structured Programming to natural language text.

Structured Programming   An approach for writing code that uses only simple nestings of one-in/one-out branching structures divided into one-page segments.

Synchrony   The quality of being co-incidental in time.

Target machine   The computer configuration of hardware and software and ancillary equipment on which programs are designed to execute as software, as distinct from any other configuration on which they were developed.

Token   A component of a Petri net often used to indicate which conditions currently exist.

Top down   An approach to detailed definition, e.g. in the design of programs, in which the independent parts (usually at a higher level in the designed structure) are defined before defining parts that are dependent on them (such as lower level components).

Transition   A component of a Petri net, often used to indicate a real-world event.

Transformation   A component (used in the design of real-time systems) that transforms inputs into outputs.

Walkthrough   Alternatively, 'Structured Walkthrough', a purposive review for one of two distinct reasons, i.e. technical considerations of design, implementation, or testing; or management planning resource allocation and control.

APPENDIX F
RECOMMENDED READING

DeMarco, Tom (1978) *Structured Analysis and System Specification*, Yourdon Press.
Gall, John (1986) *Systemantics, The Underground Text of Systems Lore, How Systems Really Work and How They Fail*, Systemantics Press.
Hughes, Joan K., Michtom, Glen C. and Michtom, Jay I. (1987) *A Structured Approach to Programming*, Prentice-Hall, Inc.
Macro, Allen (1990) *Software Engineering: Concepts and Management*, Prentice-Hall International.
Macro, Allen (1991) *Software Specification and Feasibility*, Prentice-Hall International.
Macro, Allen (1992) *Software Estimating and Technical Quality*, Prentice-Hall International.
Marcotty, Michael (1991) *Software Implementation*, Prentice-Hall International.
McMenamin, Stephen M. and Palmer, John F. (1984) *Essential Systems Analysis*, Yourdon Press.
Mills, Harlan D., Linger, Richard C. and Hevner, Alan R. (1986) *Principles of Information Systems Analysis and Design*, Academic Press, Inc.
Peterson, James L. (1981) *Petri Net Theory and the Modeling of Systems*, Prentice-Hall, Inc.
Stevens, Wayne P. (1981) *Using Structured Design*, John Wiley and Sons.
Tsichritzis, D. C. and Lochovsky, F. H. (1982) *Data Models*, Prentice-Hall, Inc.
Ward, Paul T. and Mellor, Stephen J. (1985) *Structured Development for Real-Time Systems*, Volumes 1–3, Yourdon Press.
Yourdon, Edward and Constantine, Larry L. (1979) *Structured Design*, Prentice-Hall.

APPENDIX G
REFERENCES

References marked with an asterisk are also contained in *Classics in Software Engineering* (Yourdon 1979).

Aktas, A. Ziya (1987) *Structured Analysis & Design of Information Systems*, A Reston Book, Prentice-Hall: Englewood Cliffs, NJ.
Armstrong, W. W. and Delobel, C. (1980) 'Decompositions and functional dependencies in relations', *ACM Trans. Database Syst.* Vol. 5, pp. 404–30.
Avrunin, George S., Dillon, Laura K., Wileden, Jack C. and Riddle, William E. (1986) 'Constrained expressions: Adding analysis capabilities to design methods for concurrent software systems', *IEEE Transactions of Software Engineering*, Vol. SE-12, No. 2, February.
Baldissera, C., Ceri, S., Pelagatti, G. and Bracchi, G. (1979) 'Interactive specification and formal verification of user's views in data base design', *Proceedings of the Fifth International Conference on Very Large Data Bases*, pp. 262–72.
Ben-Ari, M. (1982) *Principles of Concurrent Programming*, Prentice-Hall International: Englewood Cliffs, NJ.
Booch, Grady (1983) *Software Engineering with Ada*, Benjamin/Cummings Publishing Company, Menlo Park, CA.
British Standards Institution (1987) *Guide to Structure Diagrams for Use in Program Design and Other Logic Applications*, BS 6224.
Brooks, F. P. (1975) *The Mythical Man-Month*, Addison Wesley: Reading, MA.
Ceri, S., Pelagatti, G. and Bracchi, G. (1981) 'Structured methodology for designing static and dynamic aspects of data base applications', *Inf. Syst.*, Vol. 6, pp. 31–45.
Chen, P. P. (1977) 'The entity–relationship model: A basis for the enterprise view of data', *Proc. AFIPS NDD*, Vol. 46, pp. 77–84.
Chen, P. P. and Yao, S. B. (1977) 'Design and performance tools for data base systems', *Proc. 3rd Int. Conf. Very Large Data Bases*, pp. 3–15.
Chikofsky, Elliot (1989) *Computer-Aided Software Engineering (CASE)*, IEEE Computer Society Press; 10662 Los Vaqueros Circle, Los Alamitos, CA.
CNETDP (1987) *Computer Networks and ISDN Systems*, Volume 13, Number 2 (Special Issue on CCITT SDL).

Codd, E. F. (1971) 'Normalized data base structure: A brief tutorial', *Proc. ADM SIGFIDET Workshop on Data Description, Access and Control*, pp. 1–17.

Codd, E. F. (1972) 'Relational completeness of data base sublanguages', in *Data Base Systems*, Courant Comput. Sci. Symp. 6th (R. Rustin, ed.), pp. 65–98, Prentice-Hall: Englewood Cliffs, NJ.

Cox, Brad J. (1986) *Object Oriented Programming – An Evolutionary Approach*, Addison-Wesley: Reading, MA.

Date, C. J. (1987) *An Introduction to Database Systems*, Addison-Wesley: Reading, MA, Volume I, 4th edn, 1986, reprinted with corrections, January 1987.

Date, C. J. (1983) *An Introduction to Database Systems*, Volme II, Addison-Wesley: Reading, MA.

DeMarco, Tom (1978) *Structured Analysis and System Specification*, Yourdon Press: NY, Revised 1978.*

Dijkstra, Edsger W. (1968) 'A constructive approach to the problem of program correctness', *BIT*, Vol. 8, No. 3, pp. 174–86.

Doherty, W. J. and Kelisky, R. P. (1979) 'Managing VM/CMS systems for user effectiveness', *IBM Systems Journal*, Volume 18, Number 1.

Gall, John (1986) *Systemantics, The Underground Text of Systems Lore, How Systems Really Work and How They Fail*, Systemantics Press: 3200 West Liberty, Ann Arbor, Michigan.

Gane, Chris, and Sarson, Trish (1979) *Structured Systems Analysis: tools and techniques*, Prentice-Hall, Inc.: Englewood Cliffs, NJ.

Hughes, Joan K., Michtom, Glen C. and Michtom, Jay I. (1987) *A Structured Aproach to Programming*, 2nd edn, Prentice-Hall, Inc.: Englewood Cliffs, NJ.

IBM (1974) 'HIPO – a design aid and documentation technique', *IBM manual GC20-1851-1*.

IBM (1977) 'Improved programming technologies – management overview', *IBM manual GE19-5086-2*.

IEEE (1977) *IEEE Transactions on Software Engineering*, Vol. SE-3, No. 1, January, 1977.

IEEE (1986) *IEEE Transactions on Software Engineering*, Vol. SE-12, No. 2, February 1986.

Jackson, M. A. (1975) *Principles of Program Design*, Academic Press Inc. (London) Ltd: London, England.

Jackson, Michael (1983) *System Development*, Prentice Hall International: Englewood Cliffs, NJ.

Kendall, Robert C. (1977) 'Management perspectives on programs, programming and productivity', *IBM Report*.

Kowal, James (1988) *Analyzing Systems*, Prentice-Hall, Inc.: Englewood Cliffs, NJ.

Larson, L. E. (1979) 'Use of decision tables in multiprocessing environments', unpublished PhD thesis, State University of New York, Binghamton, NY.

Lundeberg, Mats, Goldkuhl, Göran and Nilsson, Anders (1981) *Information Systems Development* – A systematic approach, Prentice-Hall, Inc.: Englewood Cliffs, NJ.

Macro, Allen and Buxton, John (1987) *The Craft of Software Engineering*, Addison-Wesley: Wokingham, England.

Macro, Allen (1990) *Software Engineering: Concepts and Management*, Prentice-Hall International: Hemel Hempstead, England.

Macro, Allen (1991) *Software Specification and Feasibility*, Prentice-Hall International: Hemel Hempstead, England.

Macro, Allen (1992) *Software Estimating and Technical Quality*, Prentice-Hall International: Hemel Hempstead, England

Marca, David and McGowan, Clement (1988) *SADT^{TM}: Structured analysis and design technique*, McGraw-Hill, Inc.: NY.

Marcotty, Michael (1991) *Software Implementation*, Prentice-Hall International: Hemel Hempstead, England.

Martin, James and McClure, Carma (1985a) *Action Diagrams*, Prentice-Hall: Englewood Cliffs, NJ.

Martin, James and McClure, Carma (1985b) *Diagramming Techniques for Analysts and Programmers*, A Reston Book, Prentice-Hall: Englewood Cliffs, NJ.

McMenamin, Stephen M. and Palmer, John F. (1984) *Essential Systems Analysis*, Yourdon, Inc.: NY.

Miller, G. A. (1956) 'The magical number seven, plus or minus two: some limits on our capacity for processing information', *Psychological Review*, Vol. 63, pp. 81–97.

Mills, Harlan D., Linger, Richard C. and Hevner, Alan R. (1986) *Principles of Information Systems Analysis and Design*, Academic Press, Inc.: Orlando, Florida.

Mills, Harlan D. (1972) 'Mathematical foundations for structured programming', *IBM Federal Systems Division, FSC 72-6012*, Gaithersburg, MD.

Morrison, J. P. (1978) 'Data stream linkage mechanism', *IBM Systems Journal 17*, No. 4, pp. 383–408.

Navanthe, S. B. and Schkolnick, M. (1978) 'View representation in logical data base design', *Proc. ACM SIGMOD*, pp. 144–56.

Nelson, R. A., Haibt, L. M. and Sheridon, P. B. (1983) 'Casting Petri nets into programs', *IEEE (Software Engineering)*, SE-9, Number 5, pp. 590–602.

Parnas, D. L. (1972) 'On the criteria to be used in decomposing systems into modules', *Communications of Association for Computing Machinery*, Vol. 5, No. 12, December, pp. 1053–8.*

Peters, Lawrence J. (1981) *Software Design: Methods & techniques*, Yourdon Press: NY.

Peterson, James L. (1981) *Petri Net Theory and the Modeling of Systems*, Prentice-Hall: Englewood Cliffs, NJ.

Petri, C. (1962) *Kommunikation mit Automaten*, PhD dissertation, University of Bonn, West Germany, (in German); also MIT *Memorandum MAC-M-212*, Project MAC, Massachusetts Institute of Technology, Cambridge, Massachusetts; Also Clifford F. Greene, Jr (translator), 'Communication with automata', Supplement 1 to *Technical Report RADC-TR-65-377*, Volume 1, Rome Air Development Center, Griffiss Air Force Base, NY, January 1966, 89 pages.

Petri, C. (1975) 'Interpretations of net theory', *Internal Report 75-07*, Institut fur Informationssystemforschung, Gesellschaft fur Mathematik und Datenverarbeitung, Bonn, West Germany, July, 1975, 34 pages; revised December, 1976.

Stevens, W. P., Myers, G. J. and Constantine, L. L. (1974) 'Structured Design', *IBM Systems Journal*, Vol. 13, No. 2, pp. 116–39.*

Stevens, Wayne, P. (1981) *Using Structured Design*, John Wiley and Sons: NY.

Stevens, Wayne P. (1982) 'How data flow can improve application development productivity', *IBM Systems Journal*, Vol. 21, No. 2, pp. 162–78.

Teledyne Brown Engineering (1989) *Software Methodology Catalog*, 2nd edn, 788 Shrewsbury Avenue, Tinton Falls, NJ, Research and Development Technical Report C01-091JB-0001-01, prepared for CECOM Center for Software Engineering, US Army Communications – Electronics Command, Fort Monmouth, NJ, March.

Tsichritzis, D. C. and Lochovsky, F. H. (1982) *Data Models*, Prentice-Hall: Englewood Cliffs, NJ.

Ullman, J. D. (1982) *Principles of Database Systems*, 2nd edn, Computer Science Press.

Ward, Paul T. and Mellor, Stephen J. (1985) *Structured Development for Real-Time Systems*, Volumes 1–3, Yourdon Press: Englewood Cliffs, NJ.

Warnier, Jean Dominique (1974) *Logical Construction of Programs*, 3rd edn, Van Nostrand Reinhold: NY.

Weinberg, G. M. (1975) *An Introduction to General Systems Thinking*, John Wiley and Sons: NY.

Weitzman, C. (1980) *Distributed Micro–minicomputer Systems*, Prentice-Hall International: Englewood Cliffs, NJ.

Yourdon, Edward and Constantine, Larry L. (1979) *Structured Design*, Prentice-Hall International: Englewood Cliffs, NJ.

Yourdon, Edward (1979) *Classics in Software Engineering*, Yourdon Press: NY.

Yourdon, Edward (1988) *Modern Structured Analysis*, Prentice-Hall International: Englewood Cliffs, NJ.

Zaniolo, C. and Melkanoff, M. A. (1981) 'On the design of relational database schemata', *ACM Trans. Database Syst.*, Vol. 6, pp. 1–47.

INDEX

A-graphs, 44–7
Abstract Data Type, 7, 76, 82, 101, 191, 196, 228, 235
  figure, 189
  section, 188–9
ACP, 61
Action Diagram, 120, 122, 134–6, 227, 233
  definition, 236
  reference, 243
action diagrammer, 174–5
activity
  custodial, 31–3, 36, 39, 93
  fundamental, 5, 31–4, 39
Ada(R), xii, 194
  reference, 241
administrative, 35
administrator, 153, 172
analysis, definition, 3
anomaly, 164–6
  deletion, 165
  insertion, 164–5
  update, 164
architectural software design, xi, 3, 8, 12–121, 146
  Essential Systems Analysis, 30–47
  and Object-Oriented, 193
  Structured Analysis, 19–30
  Structured Design, 62–87
  Ward-Mellor, 47–61
architecture, 1–3, 11–18, 99, 120
  definition, 13, 236
  of DFDM, 208–18
  Object-Oriented and, 193–4
  specifications, executing, 176, 186
asynchronous, 44, 78, 82, 174–5, 202
  access to data, 24, 76–8, 202
  and the call statement, 78, 202
  data flow diagrams, 29, 44–7, 219, 237
  and Object-Oriented, 238
  and Petri nets, 12, 101, 115–16, 119, 232, 238
  and Ward-Mellor method, 7–8, 238
attribute, 153–5, 158–61, 163, 171, 178, 234

definition, 154, 236
in keys, 155, 234
normalization, 164–6, 234, 238

balance
  data flow diagrams, 26, 226, 230
  objectives, 1–3, 5, 43, 82, 229
binding
  coincidental, 65–8, 70, 146, 231
  communicational, 67–8, 231
    figure, 68
  functional, xv, 65, 68–70, 185, 200, 231
    figure, 69
  logical, 67–8, 70, 79, 231
  sequential, 67–8, 146, 231
    figure, 68
  temporal, 67–8, 70, 231
black box, 12, 81, 137
  in Box Structured Design, 88–90, 96–101, 227, 232
  definition, 236
  diagram, 89
  example, 94–6
bottom up, 6
boundedness, 117–18
Box Structured Design, 8, 12, 18–19, 137, 207, 227, 232, 236, 239
  section, 88–101
BS 6224, 125
  reference, 241
buffer, 36

call statement, 29, 44, 72, 76, 78–82, 127, 202, 208
capacity, 31, 43
Car Rental example, 41–3, 117
case
  Computer-Aided Software Engineering, xii
    reference, 241
  Structured Programming structure, 125, 131, 148, 152
catalog, computerized, 184

CCITT-SDL, 122–3
  reference, 241
change, isolating from, 200–2
clarity, 58, 70, 74–81
class
  and data base design, 158
  Object-Oriented inheritance, 192–4
clear box, 12, 88, 90, 99–100, 227, 232
  deducing from, 94–6
  definition, 236
  diagram, 92–3
  example, 91–6
  expanding into, 99
cocoon, execution-time, 199–200
code reuse (*see* 'reuse')
coincidental binding, 65–8, 70, 146, 231
communicational binding, 67–8, 231
  figure, 68
complexity
  and Abstract Data Types, 188–9
  for data base designers, 173
  independent pieces reduce, 5, 12–19, 34, 41, 60, 113
  and Object-Oriented, 191–3, 196
  reduce, 89, 198–202, 205–6, 226, 230
  with Structured Design, 62, 70, 73, 79, 81–2, 87
computer science, vii, ix, 101, 239
concurrency, 7, 101–202
concurrent update, 24, 44, 50, 77–9, 203
conglomeration, 34–5, 230
connection, 232, 238
  via call, 82, 87
  via data flow, 24, 82, 86–7, 176
  DFDM, 208–25
  Object-Oriented, 191, 193–5
  Petri net, 118
  and reuse, 184–6
  size of, 70, 79
  type of, 70, 76–9
connector, off-page, 25, 64, 231
conservation, in Petri nets, 109, 117
constraint
  in data base design, 153, 155, 158, 160
    figure, 161
  design, 1–2, 5, 43, 69, 100
  in Petri nets, 113, 120
context
  diagram, 25
  schema, 56
    figure, 49
control
  block, 76, 188
  DFDM, 214, 217
  flag, 73–5
  flow
    and Structured Design, 87
    and Structured Programming, 127
    and Ward-Mellor design, 8, 12, 24, 57
  flow of, 23, 24, 125

parameter, 5, 67, 74–6
structures
  Petri nets, 111
  and Structured Programming, 17, 125–6, 236
transformation, 54, 56–7, 139–40, 226, 231
  definition, 236
  figures, 49, 51, 54, 58
variable, 73, 77
  figure, 74
convolution, 34–6, 230
cost, 2, 3, 62, 129, 229
  in data base design, 164, 171
  and Essential Systems Analysis, 30–1, 43
  versus performance, 204
coupling, 5, 19, 62, 65, 70–82, 87, 227, 232
  clarity, 70, 79–82
  definition, 70, 236–7
  implicit, 188
  Object-Oriented, 190, 195
  portability, 200
  and reuse, 185
  size of connections, 70, 79
  type of connection, 70, 76–9
  what is communicated, 70, 72–6
coverability, in Petri nets, 117–18
criteria
  design, 1–3, 5–6, 18, 43, 120, 146, 175, 229
  event partitioning, 37, 44, 208
  for reuse, 181
  reference, 243
Cruise Control example, 47–50, 139
  figures, 139–41
custodial activity, 31–3, 36, 39, 93

data
  administration, 172
  classes, 158
  definition, 143, 164, 176
  design, 11, 172
  dictionary, 19, 37, 131, 154, 159, 174, 178–9, 214
  global (*see* 'variables, shared global')
  integrity, 77
  meta-data, 154
  model (*see also* 'data model diagram'), 154–9, 167–70, 172
    entity-relationship data model, 154–8, 178, 228
    reference, 244
  modeling, 41, 154, 155, 172
  self-defining data, 76, 212
  shared, 24, 76–8, 203
  shared global variables, 24, 29, 76–8, 175, 185–6, 191, 197, 202
    figure, 80
  store, 26, 33, 35, 37, 41–2, 55–6, 230–1
    figure, 21
  transformation, 5, 54, 56–8, 139, 231
    definition, 237

data base
  administrator, 153, 172
  description, 153, 166–70, 172
  design, xi, 11, 41, 153–75, 178, 206, 228, 236–8
    physical, 170–1
    references, 241, 243
    steps, 153 (figure, 153)
  management system (DBMS), 155, 158, 164, 167, 170–2, 176
    hierarchical, 167
    network, 167
    portability cocoon for, 199–201
  relational, 167, 170, 199, 234
Data Flow Development Manager (see 'DFDM')
data flow diagram
  as architecture, 12–14, 17–18
  and Box Structured Design, 100–1
  definition, 237
  and DFDM, 208–25
  and Essential Systems Analysis, 30–47
  leveling, 25–7, 56
  and Object-Oriented, 191, 194, 196
  and Petri nets, 109
  and reuse, 186
  and software design tools, 174–6
  and Structured Analysis, 19
  and Structured Design, 62, 78, 82–7
  and Ward-Mellor, 47–61
  see also 'A-graphs', xi, 2, 6–8, 163, 202, 226, 229–31, 236–7, 239
data model diagram, 2, 14, 155–8, 174, 229
DBMS (see 'data base management system')
DBTG, 167
dead code, 126–7
deadlock, 175, 202–3
  analyzing with Petri nets, 101, 117, 227, 232–3
  avoiding for data flow networks, 44, 219–25
deadly embrace, 202–3
decision table, 120, 146–52, 227, 233
  definition, 237
  linked, 147
    figure, 148
  reference, 242
  triangular, 148, 227, 234
    figure, 149
decision tree, 118, 149–51
  definition, 237
  figure, 150
decomposition, xi, 5, 7, 12, 16–19, 41, 174
  and Box Structured Design, 99, 100
  and data flow diagrams, 139, 222
  and flowcharts, 121
  and Jackson, 146
  reference, 241
  and Structured Design, 74, 82, 87, 239
deferral, 16
deletion anomaly, 165
derivation, 90
  figure, 94

design
  architectural (see 'architectural software design')
  criteria, 1–3, 5–6, 18, 43, 120, 146, 175, 229
  definition (noun, verb), 1–3, 239
  diagram (see 'diagrams')
  for reuse, 185–6
  method (see 'method')
  module, 5, 62, 238
    definition, 237
  notation, 6, 8, 17, 99
  objectives, 5
  order, 6–7
  review, 174, 179, 228, 235
  specifications, 23, 100, 177
  tools, 6, 174–9
DFDM (Data Flow Development Manager), 195, 224
  architecture definition, 208–18
diagrams (see 'Action Diagram', 'black box diagram', 'clear box diagram', 'context diagram', 'data flow diagram', 'data model diagram', 'entity-relationship diagram', 'IDEF0', 'Jackson charts', 'organization chart', 'parent diagram', 'screen hierarchy', 'state box diagram', 'state transition diagram', and 'systems flowchart')
distributed, 7–8, 29, 34, 36, 61, 79, 197, 215
  reference, 244
dividing
  programs, 16, 62–87, 239
  a system, 16, 120
dominant factor, 10–11
duplicate functions, 30, 146

encyclopedia, 154
enterprise, 154
  administrator, 172
  description, 158, 163–70
  model, 166–7
  reference, 241
  schema, 153, 155–64, 170, 178
entity
  definition, 237
  DFDM, 212–18, 221
  instance, 155, 165, 171, 178, 234. 236
  reference, 241
  set, 155, 157–8
  type, 155–63, 167–70, 234
entity relationship data model, 154, 158, 178, 234
entity-relationship diagram, 6, 37, 155
  figure, 156
equivalent
  Petri net, 115, 117–18
  program, 125–7, 129, 227, 233
ER data model, 154, 158, 178, 234
essence, 12, 30–1, 38–44, 59, 226, 230
  definition, 30, 237

essence—*contd.*
  finding the, 34–6
  modeling the, 36–7
essential
  activity, 31–2
  memory, 31–7, 39
    definition, 30
    figure, 40
  reference, 243
  and Ward-Mellor design, 59–61
Essential Systems Analysis, 5–7, 12, 17–19, 29, 55, 61, 83, 87, 100, 194, 197, 207, 226, 230–1, 237
  section, 30–47
event
  asynchronous, 203
  in BS 6224, 125
  in DFDM, 215, 217
  driven, 47
  and essential activities, 31–2, 36
  in Essential Systems Analysis, 18, 19–44
  flow, 54, 55–7
    figure, 54
  nonprimitive, 113–15
    figures, 114–15
  event partitioning, 30, 37–41, 44, 55, 226, 231
    figure, 40
  in Petri nets, 102, 105–6, 111, 232
    figure, 114
  primitive, 113
    figure, 114
  in real-time systems, 7–8, 19, 47, 54, 238–9
  store, 55–6
    figure, 55
  trigger, 54
  examples (*see* 'Car Rental', 'Cruise Control', 'Fill Tank', 'Garage Door Opener', 'Insurance Company', 'Inventory Control', 'Machine Shop', 'Master-File Update', 'Medical Data Base', 'Payroll System', 'People-Mover System', 'Reorder Policy for Navy', and 'Update Orders')
expansion, 18
  in Box Structured Design, 88, 95, 99–101
    figure, 94
  in data flow diagrams, 26, 50, 56, 231
external
  control flows, 57
  entities, 56
    figure, 21
  stimuli, 36, 41
  variable, 76, 230
extraneousness, 34–5, 230

factor, dominant, 10–11
fallibility, 43
Fill Tank example, 59
filter, 182, 184, 195

firing, 106–11, 113, 117–18, 227, 232–3
flexibility, 5, 74, 125, 148, 173, 190–2
flow of control, 23, 24, 125
flowchart, 2, 14, 82, 116, 120, 229
  and CCITT-SDL, 122
  converting to a Petri net, 111–12
  and decision tables/trees, 150
  definition, 237
  section, 121–4
  and Structured Programming, 126–7
  and Structured Natural Language, 130
  systems flowchart, 2, 14, 21, 23–4, 82, 229
  and time dependencies, 202
formal method, 207
Fortran common, 76
fragmentation, 34, 230
functional
  binding, (*see* 'binding, functional')
  decomposition, xi, 5, 7, 19, 87, 121, 146, 174, 239
  dependency, 155, 160, 165–6, 228, 234, 241
  module, 69
  specification, 2–3, 6, 8, 237
functions, duplicate, 30, 146
fundamental activity, 5, 31–4, 39

Garage Door Opener example, 138–9
General net theory, 119
general systems principles, 187–8
graphical
  design tool, 174–6
  notation, xii, 8, 12, 17, 120, 123, 125

hierarchical
  DBMS, 167
  decomposition, 17, 100
  schema, 167
    figure, 168
hierarchy of diagrams, 16–17, 226, 230
  Box Structured Design, 87, 90, 101
  data flow, 17, 25–7, 55–7
  decision trees, 151
  and DFDM, 208, 210, 212
  in Petri nets, 113–15
  and Structured Design, 16–17, 62–4

icon-oriented user interfaces, 189–90, 235
IDEF0, 61
implementation model, 37, 59
  figure, 60
inaccessible topology, 202
incarnation, 30, 36–7, 43–4, 226, 230–1
  definition, 237
  description, 31
  as 'implementation' model, 59–61
indentation
  in Action Diagrams, 134–6
  in Structured Programming, 120, 122, 125, 130–3
indented list, 14

INDEX 249

figure, 14
independent pieces, 5, 12, 16, 62, 113
Information Engineering, xii
information hiding, 188
  definition, 237
inheritance, 190, 192–3, 235
initialize, 67, 70, 73, 89, 148, 189
input function, 115
input place, 102, 108–9, 115, 117, 232
insertion anomaly, 164–5
inspection, 179
Insurance Company example, 158–64, 167–70
integrand
  definition, 3
  specification, 120–52
integrate tools, 177–8, 228, 234
Inventory Control example, 90–6

Jackson
  charts, 120, 143–6, 174, 197, 227, 233
    versus decision tables, 151–2
  design, 18, 82, 143–6
    definition, 237
  references, 242
job control language, 7, 31

key
  composite, 165
  in normalization, 164–6, 234
  as unique identification, 65, 85, 155, 160, 228, 234

language, job control, 7, 31
leveling (data flow diagrams), 25–7, 56
list, indented, 14
liveness, in Petri nets, 117
locking, 44, 77, 87, 202–3
logical
  binding, 67–8, 70, 79, 231
  data flow diagrams, 43–4
looping, unproductive, 202

Machine Shop example, 102–6, 109, 118
macro, 62, 70, 82, 185
mainline, 208, 213–14, 216, 218
maintenance, 2–3, 43–4, 62, 69, 72, 88, 121, 127, 146, 172, 184, 191, 193, 195–6, 204–5, 235
many-to-many, 157, 160, 167
marking (*see* 'Petri net marking')
Mascot-ACP, 61
Master-File Update example, 90
matrix equations, in Petri nets, 118–19
Medical Data Base example, 155–6
meta-data, 154
method (*see* 'Abstract Data Type', 'Action Diagram', 'Ada(R)', 'Box Structured Design', 'BS 6224', 'CCITT-SDL', 'data base design', 'data modeling', 'decision table', 'decision tree', 'Essential Systems Analysis', 'flowchart', 'formal method', 'Jackson design', 'Mascot-ACP', 'Object-Oriented', 'Petri net', 'SADT^{TM}', 'state transition diagram', 'Structured Analysis', 'Structured Design', 'Structured Natural Language', 'Structured Programming', and 'Ward-Mellor method') definition, 238
mini-specification, 19
model (*see* 'method' and 'diagrams')
module (*see* 'design module' and 'functional module')
mutual exclusion, 202

net-theory
  General, 119
  Petri, 101–2, 113
  references, 243
network DBMS, 167
normal form
  first, 165–6
  higher, 166
  second, 166
normalization of data
  definition, 238
  reference, 242
  (*see also* 'normal form'), 164–6, 172, 175, 228, 234
  third, 153, 166, 174
numeric name, 29, 81

Object-Oriented, 18, 29, 62, 82, 174, 179, 189–97, 206, 228, 235
  definition, 238
  design, 190–4
  inheritance, 190, 192–3, 235
  object, 191, 195–6
  programming, 189–90
  recommendations regarding, 196–7
  reference, 242
  and reuse, 194–6
object partitioning, 41
  figure, 42
one-in/one-out segments, 125, 127, 239
one-to-many relationships, 157, 160, 167
one-to-one relationships, 160
online programs, 19
  and data base design, 164, 234
  definition, 238
  and DFDM, 213
  and Essential Systems Analysis, 35, 44
  and performance, 204–6
  and real-time systems, 47
  and reuse, 180, 182, 184
  and Structured Design, 76–8, 87
optimization, 118, 175
  in data bases, 170, 173
  performance, 204–5, 207, 228, 235

organization chart, 14–17, 229
output function, 115
output place, 102–8, 115, 117, 232

parameter
    control, 5, 67, 74–6
    and DFDM, 209, 211, 213–17
    and reuse, 185
    and Structured Design, 5, 67, 73–9, 85, 127, 176, 231
parent diagram, 25–6
partitioning
    event partitioning, 30, 37–41, 44, 55, 226, 231
        figure, 40
    object partitioning, 41
        figure, 42
    (*see also* 'dividing')
Payroll System example, 30–2, 34, 43, 69
People-Mover System example, 100
performance
    of data base, 170–1, 173, 234
    definition, 238
    of programs, 6, 18, 31, 43, 58, 82, 175–6, 195, 204–7, 214
Petri net, 101–19
    analysis, 115–19
    executing, 106–11
    graphs, 102–15
    marking, 106, 227, 232–3
        and coverability, 117–18
        figures, 108
        and firing rules, 108–11
        and reachability, 117
    set notation, 102, 115
    simulation of a program, 111–12
    transition
        enable, 108–12, 117, 227–8, 231–3
        fire, 106–11, 113, 117–18, 227, 232–3
place
    input, 102, 108–9, 115, 117, 232
    output, 102–8, 115, 117, 232
portability, 197–205, 228, 235
    automatic, 198
    cocoon, 199–200
    definition, 238
    description, 197–9
procrastination, 16
productivity, 13, 176, 179, 184–5, 206, 230
    references, 242, 244
program
    equivalent, 125–7, 129, 227, 233
    proper, 126–7, 129

quality, vii–viii, 2, 5–6, 13, 19, 174, 179, 230
    definition, 238
    reference, 243
query, 11, 215

reachability, in Petri nets, 117–18, 203

readability, 120, 122, 127, 131–33
real-time
    definition, 238
    reference, 244
    (*see also* 'Ward-Mellor method') 7–8, 12, 32, 100, 120, 202–3, 236
recursion, 64
recursive relationship, 158
redundancy, 34–5, 230
re-entrant, 211, 214
relation scheme, 164–5
relational
    data models, 167
    DBMS, 167, 170, 199, 234
    operations, 170
    references, 242, 244
    schema, xvii
        figure, 170
relationship
    recursive, 158
    ternary, 157
    type, 155–63, 167–70
        figure, 160
Reorder Policy for Navy example, 90–6
reusable parts, 180, 192
reuse
    of code, 7, 12, 29, 68–9, 76, 79, 82, 146, 174, 206–8, 214–15, 218–35
    definition, 238
        figure, 196
    and Object-Oriented, 190–7
    requirements for, 181, 228, 235
    section, 179–86

SADT™, 61
safeness, 117
schema (*see* 'context schema', 'enterprise schema', 'hierarchical schema', 'relational schema', and 'transformation schema')
screen, xii, 7, 14, 16, 182, 189
    hierarchy, 18, 139–40
    layout, 7, 176–8
SDL, 122–3
security, 18, 43, 163, 234
    a global data area, 79
        figure, 80
    Structured Programming, 125, 127, 185, 239
semaphore, 202
sequence, iteration and choice, 17, 82
    and Box Structured Design, 88, 99, 232
    and BS 6224, 125
    and CCITT-SDL, 122
    and flowcharts, 120–1
    and Jackson, 120, 143, 146, 237
    and Structured Programming, 125–6
sequential binding, 67–8, 146, 231
    figure, 68
set-theory, 102, 115
simultaneous

execution, 44, 50, 82, 113, 213
update, 24, 44, 50, 77–9, 203
software
  definition, 2
  deliver in stages, 19
  design (*see* 'design')
  design method (*see* 'method')
  design tools, 6, 174–9
  development, vii–viii, xii, 5, 172, 180, 189–90, 237, 239
    definition, 239
  engineer, 239
  engineering, vii–ix
    definition, 239
    references, xii, 241–4, 239
  life cycle, 3, 7, 29, 237
    figure, 4
  method (*see* 'method')
  system definition, 239
SQL, 164, 199
state
  box, 12, 88–90, 93–5, 98–9, 101
    definition, 239
    diagram, 91
  information, 26
  internal, 88–90, 98, 136–7, 139, 196, 233, 236, 239
  machine, 8, 88, 232
    finite state machine, 123
  variable, 19, 89–90, 93–6, 98–9
state transition diagram, 7–8, 56, 120, 136–40, 227, 233, 239
stimulus history, 89, 96–9
store
  data, 26, 33, 35, 37, 41–2, 55–6, 230–1
    figure, 21
  event, 55–6
    figure, 55
structure
  checking algorithm, 130
    figures, 132–3
  structure charts, 17–18, 62–5, 82, 85–6, 175
    figures, 64, 66, 71, 75, 83
  theorem, 99, 127
Structured Analysis, 12, 17–18, 43, 47, 55, 61, 78, 83, 87, 99–101, 163, 188–9, 194, 207, 237, 239
  reference, 241–4
  sections, 19–30, 30–47
structured code, 125, 127, 135–6, 227, 233
  figure, 123
Structured Design, 5–6, 12, 17–19, 44, 61, 100, 121, 127, 146, 176, 185, 188, 190–1, 200–2, 205, 207, 231, 240, 243–4, 236, 239
  section, 62–87
Structured English (*see* 'Structured Natural Language')
Structured Natural Language, 37, 120, 130–4, 154, 239

definition, 239
Structured Programming, xvi, 6, 87, 99, 120–2, 130, 134–6, 143, 189, 227, 233, 236, 239
  control structures, 17, 125–6, 236
  definition, 239
  section, 125–30
systems flowchart, 2, 14, 21, 23–4, 82, 229
  figure, 20

temporal binding, 67–8, 70, 231
test, vii, 3, 5–6, 13, 79, 151, 186, 215
text versus diagrams, 14, 17, 23
time
  real-time (*see* 'real-time')
  time-continuous flows, 50, 57–9, 231
    figures, 53, 58
  time-dependency, 7, 47, 174, 233
  time-discrete flows, 50, 57–9
    figure, 58
timing, 8, 14, 18, 47, 61, 77, 238
top down, 1, 6–7
  definition, 239
topology, inaccessible, 202
transformation schema (*see also* 'real-time', and 'Ward-Mellor method') 3, 8, 17, 47–61, 100, 137–40, 226, 231, 236–7, 239
transition (*see* 'Petri net transition')
translate, 3, 150, 176, 198, 238
triangular decision table, 148, 227, 234
  figure, 149
trigger, 54, 57, 212, 214
tuple (Petri net), 115
  figure, 116

UNIX™, 182, 195, 208–9, 213
update
  anomaly, 164
  simultaneous, 24, 44, 50, 77–9, 203
Update Orders example, 64–5, 67–70, 74, 81–3, 86–7
user
  interface (*see* 'icon-oriented user interface')
  needs, 5–6, 164, 171, 207

validate, 6, 60, 191, 207, 239
  in data base design, 153, 160, 171, 175
variables, shared global, 24, 29, 76–8, 175, 185–6, 191, 197, 202
  figure, 80
vastness, 34, 36, 230
virtual machine interface, 199–200

walkthrough, 179
  definition, 239
Ward-Mellor method, 12, 17, 19, 36, 47–61, 136–40, 207
  reference, 244
  section, 47–61